LOVE,
SON JOHN

ALSO BY BRIAN McGOWAN

Thunder at Noon

Guardian Angels: Collected Stories

LOVE, SON JOHN

*Letters from Home and Back
Between a Mother and a Son
1943 - 1946*

Edited by Brian McGowan

KDP - Kindle Direct Publishing

Copyright © 2019 by Brian McGowan

ISBN: 9781075491436

All rights reserved. No part of this publication may be reproduced or transmitted in any form or by any means, electronic or mechanical, including photocopy, recording, or any information storage and retrieval system, without permission in writing from the editor.

The editor gratefully acknowledges the source of background information beyond the extent of the correspondence which forms the bulk of this work. A number of sources were consulted for this information, including: *Killing Patton,* by Bill O'Reilly and Martin Dugard; *Combat History of the 65th Infantry Division in WW II,* compiled by R. H. Cardinell, Division Historian; *Right to be Proud,* by Sgt. Bill Jordy; *Family Search,* for access to U.S. Census records for 1940; *The Dyre Avenue News,* a local Bronx publication during World War II; and numerous articles accessed in *Wikipedia,* an increasingly valuable research avenue which the editor supports financially through periodic contributions.

All characters named in this work are real. All letters are transcribed as written, with minor grammatical adjustment. No word, comment or opinion expressed by the correspondents has been in any way softened from the original. Real people such as those who walk off these pages speak in real terms. It is not an editor's job to alter, explain or excuse reality, but to record it as truthfully as possible.

*To my cousin, John Francis McGowan,
who served his country faithfully in the Second World War,
and to all who did likewise, whether abroad or at home,
in uniform or civilian garb,
in defense of good against the forces of evil.*

CONTENTS:

FOREWORD	1
PROLOGUE: STALINGRAD, JANUARY 1943	3
ONE: "SCHOOL DAYS OVER…"	5
TWO: "WHERE ALL THE GOLD IS STORED"	17
THREE: "SCHULTZ"	37
FOUR: "A WALK IN THE PARK"	71
FIVE: "DRIVING TANKS"	91
SIX: "HOSPITAL LEAVE"	111
SEVEN: "A NEW YEAR"	115
EIGHT: "INSTRUCTOR"	125
NINE: "THE VISIT"	135
TEN: "MEASLES"	151
ELEVEN: "DUKE'S GARDEN"	161
TWELVE: "WHEN THE ROSES BLOOM"	197
THIRTEEN: "WINDS OF CHANGE"	215
FOURTEEN: "A DROWNING"	223
FIFTEEN - "NINE WEEKS TRAINING"	231
SIXTEEN - "SOLVING PROBLEMS"	241
SEVENTEEN - "FOURTH TERM"	253
EIGHTEEN - "THE BULGE"	259
NINETEEN - "OVER THERE"	267
TWENTY - "CAMP LUCKY STRIKE"	271
TWENTY-ONE - "IN THE FRONT LINES"	277
TWENTY-TWO - "GERMANY"	291
TWENTY-THREE - "THE REICH FALLS"	305
TWENTY-FOUR - "WHERE TO NEXT?"	315
TWENTY-FIVE - "OCCUPATION ARMY"	319
TWENTY-SIX - "NO MORE PACIFIC PLANS"	325
TWENTY-SEVEN - "WISHING FOR HOME"	331
TWENTY-EIGHT - "CHRISTMAS ABROAD"	341
TWENTY-NINE - "HOMEWARD BOUND"	345

LOVE,
SON JOHN

FOREWORD

This a story with many facets. At its most basic level, it is the story of a young man's transition from youth to manhood, moved along by the rigors and risks of uniformed service to his country; and the love of a mother for that son, slowly recognizing the boy has become a man.

It is the story of a family, Irish and proud, with warts and beauty intermingled, ambition and accomplishment and unrealized hopes and dreams existing side by side, whether hidden or showcased in the light of day. As it unfolds we see some struggle with the crutch of alcohol, while others embrace sobriety. There is jealousy, pride, opinion and mockery of those loved or loathed, all of it both fairly and unfairly dispensed. I haven't changed a word, even where some raised a definite eyebrow.

It is a story of wit, and wisdom, both casually dispensed, and charming in their application.

It is the story of a classic Bronx neighborhood, carved from the vestiges of former country estates in what once was Westchester County, slowly absorbed by the metropolis of New York City to the south. An oasis of peace and security, it seems in memory a place that could scarcely have been thought possible to exist in the urban environment of New York City. But it did exist, as close-knit and peaceful as any New England village, with a heyday between the wars and for some time after, until progress wiped out the vacant lots and open spaces, and time moved on to lend less and less of a sheen to its streets and byways.

It is the story of a war fought for good, and against evil, and the young men and women who fought it, who suffered in it, who sacrificed their blood and sweat and tears and in some cases their lives to that struggle. It is a story that brings out the ultimate humor and pathos of life, and all manner of emotions in that range of experiences we call living.

And it is a story largely told in the words of its ultimate authors, Private John McGowan, U.S. Army, and his mother, Anna Cecelia Lynch McGowan, via letters written and responded to across distant states, wide oceans, and the din of battle. The backdrop of the larger war is there also, taking place on both a global and a regional basis, and those actions up close and personal to the individuals fighting that war, especially in the European Theater of Operations.

And it is a story of faith, and the comforting bulwark religion seemed to offer so easily years ago that it seems not to be able to lay claim to today.

It is all these things, and more. And I hope you enjoy it.

Brian McGowan
Pleasantville, New York
October 2019

PROLOGUE: STALINGRAD, JANUARY 1943

The unthinkable - to the German High Command, at least, and to Adolf Hitler - has happened. A German Army has surrendered. General Von Paulus's Sixth German Army, with 120,000 troops, hopelessly surrounded in the shattered city of Stalingrad and on the verge of absolute starvation, has given up the hope of breaking out of their encirclement, or of being rescued at the last moment by some miraculous lifting of the Russian siege, and has conceded defeat.

They have had several opportunities to rescue themselves from the debacle. A breakout had been urged by many in the German High Command, much to the Fuhrer's chagrin. In the end it does not matter, as Von Paulus's overriding concern is not to let his Fuhrer down.

And so the tide of war has changed, and the Soviets, until then on the defensive, and almost brought to their knees by successive German assaults just a year earlier, begin to go on the offensive. When the histories of this war are written, the authorities will tell us that this was the turning point. From Stalingrad there is no turning back. The Germans from this point on will fight a defensive war, and steadily lose ground. And they will lose, two and one half years later, with millions more dead along the way.

Among those Russian troops is a Major General named D. A. Drechkin, Commander of the Seventh Guard Parachute Division. On this day in January, 1943, he begins a journey that will take him two years and four months later to the little town of Erlauf, in Austria, where he will shake hands with his American counterpart, Major General Stanley Reinhart, commander of the 65th Infantry Division in General George S. Patton's Third U.S. Army, and celebrate the end of the Second World War in Europe.

A young boy from the Bronx, John Francis McGowan, will be in that Division, and in that Third Army, and part of that moment.

His journey to the Enns River, dividing line between the victorious U.S. and Soviet armies, begins just six months following General Drechkin's departure from Stalingrad.

This is his story.

ONE: "SCHOOL DAYS OVER..."

SUNDAY, JUNE 6, 1943 - THE BRONX

The invitation is crisp and still redolent of fresh printer's ink when John McGowan hands it to his mother that June afternoon. Anna McGowan beams with pride, of course, at her only child's accomplishment. She and her husband Eddie, and young John as well, have scraped and saved to pay the tuition for Mount Saint Michael Academy in the Bronx, founded just seventeen years earlier on the grounds of what had been the Bathgate family's farm, and which by the 1940 has become a solid academic institution, run by the Marist Brothers, an order with roots in France and a firm tradition in teaching young minds to strive always for excellence. The motto of the school, *Ad Astra Per Aspera*, is known by every student, and every graduate. To the Stars, Through Difficulty. It seems to some a strange motto, until one thinks of it for a while. And then the meaning becomes clear: nothing in life that is worthwhile comes easily.

And, the Mount, as it is more commonly known, has one hell of a football team, coached by a young fellow named Howie Smith. John is an avid football fan. His favorite team, aside from the Mount, are the Fighting Irish of Notre Dame.

And it has not been easy, affording the cost of that tuition. John's father, a World War I veteran, his lungs scarred by mustard gas on the fields of France, has worked long hours as an electrician at the U.S. Navy Yard in Brooklyn. John himself has worked odd jobs every afternoon, delivering papers, clerking in stores, running errands, and dutifully handing over to his mother whatever meager wages he can bring to the table. And Anna has saved every penny she can, a task at times more difficult than any, especially when Eddie decides to go off on his own, so to speak.

The graduation is flawless. For some reason the diplomas are not ready, so Father Jordan[1] makes his excuses and promises the boys they will be delivered to them as soon as possible. That is a disappointment, of course. John has looked forward to showing the plaque around to the other boys in the Edenwald neighborhood - and some of the girls as well. Like the young people of any Bronx neighborhood, the children of Edenwald are a close-knit bunch,

---

[1] Father Jordan was one of the priests of Nativity of Our Blessed Lady Parish. In August 1943 he would be assigned as Chaplain with the 86th Infantry Division Headquarters at Camp Hauze, Texas.

and that closeness extends to parents and other adults as well. And then the ceremony is over, and all there is left to do is enjoy the advent of summer.

Summer. The air smells fresh and clear. The days stretch long, one following another. There is swimming in the creek, and staying out late at night on the tree-lined streets of the neighborhood. The block the family lives on, Pratt Avenue, is packed with people of John's age, though many of his closest friends are months, or sometimes even years, younger than him. And girls. The neighborhood sports a wealth of them. It is a haven for all - insular, tree-lined, a corner of the Bronx that isn't much different than fifty years earlier, save for the progression of tree-lined streets cut through the dwindling number of farms and estates that here once had made up the southern half of the town of Eastchester, since 1898 a part of the metropolis of the City of Greater New York.

And 4030 Pratt Avenue is there to come back to at the end of each day, at the end of each long summer evening. It is a sturdy house. John's Grandfather, Dennis McGowan, had it built in the 1920's, a few years before John was born. Dennis isn't called Grandpa by John or his cousins, or Papa, Da, or Father, or any of those other titles that may have gone with his position. Both inside and out of the family, through the neighborhood and beyond, Dennis McGowan is known as "the Duke". With a long, flowing moustache, a finely chiseled face, dapper eyeglasses and a shock of flowing white hair, he resembles an English duke more so than the son of an Irish farmer and his wife who survived the *Gorta Mór*, the Great Hunger of the 1840's, just shy of a hundred years earlier, and then went on to bring over ten children into an uncertain world. Born in Lisdarush, Rossinver, County Leitrim, second son of Henry and Bridget (Gallagher) McGowan, Dennis had come to the U.S. in the 1880's and found work on the streetcar lines, along with several of his brothers. They live first in the Yorkville section of Manhattan, marry, raise children, and eventually leave for the outer boroughs of New York City, in Dennis's case to the Bronx, along with his brother Frank McGowan and his family. In fact they build their houses not far from each other in Edenwald, Frank's on Edenwald Avenue itself, at number 2132, and Dennis a few blocks away, closer to church, at 4030 Pratt Avenue, both near to the old Seton estate and mansion called Cragdon, with connections to St. Elizabeth Anne Seton.

4030 Pratt is John's birthplace. He lives there with his parents, his grandfather, the Duke, his grandmother, Bridget (Kenney) McGowan, and a family of tenants whose rent money takes care of taxes and the mortgage, and gives the Duke time to tend a beautiful garden on the side of the house, pride of his heart, where he grows all manner of vegetables, as befits a man who grew up on a farm.

June passes into July, and no one notices the few minutes shaved off each day as the month draws on. And then one day the mailman brings the notice. John is being drafted into the U.S. Army. His next destination: a processing center called Camp Upton.

⁂

Camp Upton, located in Yaphank, New York, in eastern Suffolk County on Long Island, is one of sixteen military training camps and initial processing centers for civilians entering the United States Army during World War II. It had been established in 1917, and served the same purpose during World War I. It occupies, in 1943, some 20,000 acres that are today the site of Brookhaven National Laboratory. It was completed in December 1917, and has a capacity of 55,000 troops. Its first commander was Major General James F. Bell, who formed from his draftees the U.S. 77th Infantry Division. The 77th, following training, were deployed to France, where they arrived in April 1918, one year after the United States had declared war on Germany and formally entered World War I, at that time and for the next twenty-one years to be referred to as "The Great War". The 77th played a key role in the Meuse-Argonne Offensive, where American might began to change the outcome of the war in the Allies favor, at a cost to the Division of over 10,000 casualties. Private McGowan's father Edward, who had enlisted in the U.S. Army in 1916, was part of that offensive.

Camp Upton is also the place where, during the summer of 1918, a United States Army Sergeant named Irving Berlin first writes the words to what becomes several years later the immortal song "God Bless America". Berlin, then 30 years old, had been born in Siberia, Russia, in 1888, and came to the U.S. with his family in 1893 at the age of five, passing through Ellis Island like so many other immigrants. He had just become a U.S. citizen that February, and puts his musical talents to work writing army musicals to boost morale among the troops, many of them immigrants themselves, sailing off to another land to defend their "home sweet home."

At the end of World War I the camp functions for a while as a demobilization center, processing troops as they come back from Europe and returning them to the civilian fold, a task completed in 1919, after which the camp is abandoned, with only the roads remaining. During the Great Depression of the 1930's it is the site of a reforestation project by the Civilian Conservation Corps, one of the New Deal initiatives of President Franklin D. Roosevelt. The land remains unused until 1940, when storm clouds are once again upon the horizon, and America's entry into World War II seems almost unavoidable, given time and the right spark. A peacetime draft has begun, and Camp Upton is reactivated to serve a dual purpose as both an induction center and training camp. It also serves for a spell following America's entry into the war as an internment camp for Japanese-American citizens on the East Coast, as well as Japanese nationals stranded in New York in the wake of the Japanese attack on Pearl Harbor on December 7, 1941.

Following the war the camp will be converted into a facility that ultimately becomes Brookhaven National Laboratory, which remains there to this day.[2]

୨

Camp Upton is where citizen and recent high school graduate John McGowan is headed to on this First Friday of August 1943, to begin his journey to becoming a soldier in the United States Army. He is eighteen years old. A few nights earlier his family threw him a going away party that is to define for the neighborhood for years to come the proper sendoff of young men going to serve their country and put themselves in harm's way. But on this morning John has a clear head, and knows the mission before him.

It is not much past five in the morning, but the August sun has already started to cast a golden light on the red and brown shingles of his home. The day ahead promises to be a warm one. His father, Edward McGowan, working nights at the Brooklyn Navy Yard, cannot be present. He has said his farewells the evening before. His mother, Anna McGowan, is practically speechless as she quickly prepares a breakfast for her only son, afraid she will break down and cry. And finally, as John says goodbye, she does just that, and bids him leave quickly, or he will be late. John hides the knot in his throat as ably as he can, and kisses his mother farewell.

His dog, Muggsie, watches him leave the house, wondering what the satchel her master carries is for and why she is not at his side for an early morning walk. The family has always had dogs, a favored animal of the Duke, each one a vaunted memory when gone. John leaves out the back door, and heads down the hill behind their house on Pratt Avenue through vacant lots brimming with new growth trees and brush, a far cry from the farmers' fields that lay there not that many years before, prior to the neighborhood starting to grow with families fleeing the tenements of Manhattan for the fresher air and relatively open spaces of the Northeast Bronx. The first leg of his journey is short, hoofing it to the Dyre Avenue station, and the shuttle train affectionately called "the Dinky" which will take him a few stops to the Gun Hill Road Station, where he and his fellow recruits will be herded on board buses for the trip downtown to West 34th Street and Pennsylvania Station, and then a long

---

[2] Brookhaven National Laboratory (BNL) is a United States Department of Energy national laboratory located in Upton, New York, on Long Island, and was formally established in 1947 at the site of Camp Upton, a former U.S. Army base. Its name stems from its location within the Town of Brookhaven, approximately 60 miles east of New York City. Research at BNL specializes in nuclear and high energy physics, energy science and technology, environmental and bioscience, nanoscience and national security.

ride on the Long Island Railroad to Yaphank, New York, and Camp Upton, where he will get off the train at ten o'clock in the morning. He carries with him a pad of writing paper, a pen, some pencils, envelopes, and a handful of stamps, all of which his mother Anna McGowan has given him with the sternest of instructions to write home often - every day, if he possibly can. And thus begins the written record of a young man going off to war, and the home front experience of his family, friends and neighborhood.

Here is the first letter, written the evening of the day he arrived at Camp Upton. In the days that follow he makes an effort to write a letter every day, keeping, he hopes, his mother's worries at a minimum.

"Pvt. John F. McGowan
A.S.N. 32 985 511
Barracks 1-L, 1st R.C.
Camp Upton, Long Island, New York

Aug. 6, 1943 [Friday]

Dear Mom,
    This is a short letter to let you know that everything is okay. The army isn't as bad as they say. I arrived at Camp Upton at 10 o'clock and when we got off the train we had to take a physical. We then went to mess where we had a short lunch. After mess we received a toilet set containing a comb and toothbrush. The officer told us that we may be here from 3 to 5 days. I went to supper where I had a big meal with cream potatoes and hamburger. At 5 o'clock we took an I.Q. test and mechanical tests. The tests weren't hard but most of the fellows were all upset over everything. We saw movies on sex relations and diseases. Mom do you remember the Rabbi that played ball against us one day at Seton Park?[3] Well, he is the head chaplain out here. Tomorrow I will get my uniform and also the needles. How is Pop behaving himself? Don't let him get too much beer. Muggsie[4] cried after me as I went out the back way. Pop and you ought to give her a bath. Mom if I was you I would not write to me out here because I may be here only for a few days and may not receive your letter. Will close now as it is getting late.
                                                  Love,

---

[3] Seton Falls Park, in the Northeast Bronx, is the remnant of the country estate of the Seton Family, called Cragdon, which was carved up into lots and sold off at the turn of the century by the Edenwald Land Company, giving rise to the succeeding neighborhood's name, Edenwald.
[4] Muggsie, the family dog, evidently a lovable mutt.

Son John

P.S. *Don't worry about me because I am okay. I will write soon."*

ତ

"Camp Upton, New York

Aug. 7, 1943 [Saturday]

Dear Mom,
    I am going to the movies tonight. I got my needles and uniform today. The weather out here is swell. This morning I got up at 5 o'clock. I had to mop the floor. I also made my bed. The fellows out here are swell and help you if you need aid. I will close now, so be good.

Love,
Son John"

ତ

"Camp Upton, N.Y.

Aug. 8, 1943 [Sunday]

Dear Mother,
    I just got Sunday afternoon off so I thought I would drop you a line. This morning we slept to 5:30 instead of getting up at 5. We go to mess at 6:30 and finish eating about 7. At 8 o'clock we had church call and it seemed as if all the fellows were Catholics because there were only a few Jewish and Protestants standing around. When we got to the church about 500 of us could not go in to hear Mass. But the commander of our squad said that we might be able to go to the 5:30 mass in the afternoon. The Masses out here are at 6 - 8:30 and 5:30 in the afternoon. I hope I can make the 5:30 mass but if I can't I will just have to say some more prayers before going to bed. For lunch today we had pork chops, mash potatoes, peas, and a big piece of watermelon for desert.
    Many of the fellows think that we will be shipped on Monday but they aren't certain. You may write to me out here because the squad commander told that letters would be forward to us no matter where we are. This getting up in the morning is all right too. It is better than staying in bed. I took out $10,000 dollars' worth of insurance and I am taking out for an $18.75 bond each if I have enough money. I will send home as much money as I can. Last

night I went to see "Hell's a Poppin'"[5] At the open air theater. It was very good and gave many of us some laughs.

 How is Dad feeling? I guess he is still taking his daily glass of beer. Tell him that we get beer out here at the Post Exchange. Muggsie would have a good time out here with all the dogs that run around. Today in the mess hall a dog just like Mugs was having a feast on what the soldiers gave her. Mom we are not allowed to have visitors out here so if you see Robert Mahon[6] tell him that I could not call him up this morning because I had a special detail. There are many telephones out here but they all are crowded. Tonight I am going to see a WAC[7] show and a concert by the camp band.

 You will have to excuse the writing because I am writing this letter on the floor of our barracks. Incidentally I have to make my own bed and I do a good job. How is Duke making out with the garden? Tell him to take good care of it. Out here we get special detail to go cut the grass or planting some trees. Well I will close now. Remember me to Mom and all the boys and tell them I will write soon.

Love to all,
Son John"

℘

But his mother writes anyway, and the letter makes its way to her son.

"4030 Pratt Avenue
Bronx, N.Y.

Aug. 9, 1943 [Monday]

---

[5] "Hellzapoppin" was a 1941 Universal Pictures adaptation of the popular musical of the same name, directed by H. C. Potter. The cast included Ole Olsen, Chic Johnson, Martha Raye, Mischa Auer, Shemp Howard, Whitey's Lindy Hoppers and the Six Hits.

[6] Robert ("Bobby") Mahon was a close friend of John's. The Mahons lived at 3937 Harper Avenue. In 1940 the family consisted of William, 56, his wife Frances, 54, who was born in Germany, and children Mary, 26, William, 23, Josephine, 22, Richard, 20, Francis, 16, Robert, 14, and Rosemarie, 11. Mr. Mahon was a dispatcher in the communications field.

[7] The Women's Army Corps (WAC) was the women's branch of the United States Army. It was created as an auxiliary unit, the Women's Army Auxiliary Corps (WAAC) on May 15, 1942 by Public Law 554 and converted to an active duty status in the Army of the United States as the WAC on July 1, 1943. Its first director was Oveta Culp Hobby, a prominent woman in Texas society. The WAC was disbanded in 1978, and all units were integrated with male units.

Dear John,

    Your letters and card arrived this morning. I was so anxious to hear from you that I think I must have run out when the mailman arrived and I was delighted with the letters you sent. They contained so much information about your activities and were cheerful along with it. Hope your eats are good and that your appetite returned. We were all so anxious to hear from you that Mom[8], Duke[9], Ed[10] and I got together and I read them out loud. In fact I have read them several times. We all had to laugh about your mopping the floor and making the bed.

    Needless to say John we all miss you very much, especially Mugs. Every time she hears a whistle she listens as if she waited for you to arrive. Duke and she are getting to be fast friends. He takes her out walking and carries a stick big enough as Mom said to drive home a herd of cattle. We expect to have some pictures taken of Duke and her and I will forward them to you. The Windells[11] went to Rockaway[12] today so Mugs has her freedom.

    The Friday morning you went away John, Mrs. Windell told me later how she watched you leaving and how Mugs stood at the gate whining. About nine o'clock that morning Dad came rushing in. The boss told him to take the day off and he almost flew home in hopes he would see you. Friday evening Mr. Lang and Mr. Walsh came over looking for you. They said they wanted to see you before you went. Walter and Andy's brother[13] were here the other night. Andy they say was so disappointed he didn't go away with you. His brother said he counted on you and him going together. I think I understood them to say that Richard Simmons[14] was to go for his physical. Perhaps I will see them tonight after the Novena.

    Your father wanted to visit you yesterday Sunday but I refused to go. He was talking with Father Broderick[15] after mass and Father said if you are

---

[8] "Mom", John's grandmother, Bridget (Kenney) McGowan.

[9] "Duke", his grandfather, Dennis McGowan.

[10] "Ed", his father, Dennis and Bridget's eldest son, Edward Joseph McGowan.

[11] The Windells were good friends of the McGowans. No 1940 Census record found.

[12] Rockaway Beach, a favorite getaway place for the Irish.

[13] Walter Cubita and Victor Garbarini, Andy Garbarini's brother.

[14] Richard Simmons was a very good friend of John's. His family lived at 3714 Secor Avenue, two blocks away from John's house. They had moved there not long after the 1940 census was taken, at which time they lived at 1904 Vyse Avenue in the Bronx. The family consisted of Richard, the father, 43; Josephine, the mother, 43; May, 17; Richard, 14; and Joan, 10. Mr. Simmons was employed as a salesman for a tour agency.

[15] Father Edwin Bernard Broderick was born in the Bronx, New York, in 1917, to Patrick S. and Margaret M. (née O'Donnell) Broderick. His father was a member of the New York City Fire Department who later died during a Mass celebrated by his

at Camp Upton next Sunday he will be over to visit you but from what you tell me I doubt whether you will be there.

I was surprised when I read about the rabbi. It is a small world after all. Were you talking to him or did he remember you?

Your father met Roemer's (the aviator) father and mother last night[16]. They almost fainted when they heard you were in the army. The mother told Ed that her son - the orchestra leader[17] - the fellow who was in "This Is the Army" is stationed at Camp Upton for the present. If you are there when you get this letter look around. Maybe you would see him. He is with the fellows who were in the show.

I had a lovely letter from Margaret[18], telling me what a grand, brave boy you are and all the nuns are praying for you. Well John I always thought you were a boy who was liked by many but I never knew how popular you were for there is no one in Edenwald[19] don't stop me to ask about you. Everybody seems to have a great opinion of you, telling me you are a boy who will succeed and take care of himself. So John I am hoping and praying you will continue to be as good a boy in the army as you were at home. Don't worry about little troubles at home. You are a soldier now so put your best into everything you do. It will take courage and perseverance and plenty of prayers. But stick to your guns John and keep away from temptation. Pick your company and I know you will come out on top.

Just a few more lines before I close. If you want anything - money or clothing - let me know. I thought it would be nice John if after every day you would write a few lines home. I could keep the letters and they would be like

---

son in 1948. Broderick received his early education at the parochial school of St. Anselm Church in the Bronx, graduating in 1930. He attended Regis High School in New York City from 1930 to 1934, and then began his studies for the priesthood at Cathedral College, where he remained for two years. He continued his studies at St. Joseph's Seminary in Yonkers. On May 30, 1942, Broderick was ordained a priest by Cardinal Francis Spellman at St. Patrick's Cathedral. His first assignment was as a curate at Nativity of Our Blessed Lady Church in the Bronx. He then taught history at Cardinal Hayes High School from 1943 until 1947, when he was assigned to the staff of St. Patrick's Cathedral. He ultimately became the Bishop of Albany, NY, where he served from 1969 to 1976. He died in 2006, aged 89.

[16] Henry and Helen Roemer lived on Hollers Avenue. Their son was a famous aviator.

[17] Another Roemer, an orchestra leader, was stationed at Camp Upton.

[18] Margaret, a cousin, was Sister Mary Albert, a nun in the Sisters of Mercy.

[19] Edenwald is the neighborhood in the Bronx where the McGowans lived.

a diary with your experiences during the day. By the way I met Mr. Savage[20] and he was telling me not to worry about you and of course related all about his son's experiences and how they kept him over at Camp Upton for so many weeks they couldn't get a pair of shoes to fit his big feet.

Dad is behaving wonderfully. I think your going away reformed him in many ways. I still tell him I might join the Wac's, he has to treat me good.

Did you get to the 5:30 Mass Sunday afternoon? Every time your father comes in he will say, "Guess who was asking for John."

Duke said to tell you not to forget he wants a big price for minding Mugs. Well John I will have to close. Best of luck. Keep your chin up. Love and regards from all.

Mother, Dad, Duke and Mom

P.S. John, if you phone call Butlers[21]. Mooneys[22] are away."

ଡ

AUGUST 10, 1943 - SANTO STEFANO, SICILY

The war might have seemed remote at the time, but in Europe it has definitely begun to heat up at this point. U.S. General George S. Patton has racked up a string of successes against the brilliant German tank commander, Erwin Rommel, in North Africa, where U.S. troops landed in 1942 as part of Operation Torch. From there they sprang across the Mediterranean to Sicily, where in August of 1943 a bitter struggle to wrest the island from the Germans rages on, with many causalities. And General Patton's reputation, despite his brilliance as a tactical commander, is about to get besmirched as a result of his seeming inability to restrain his temper.

---

[20] Harry and Mary Savage lived at 3917 Dyre Avenue. In 1940 he was 51, she 47. He was a laborer with the Bureau of Highways. The 1940 Census lists one child, William, aged 17.

[21] The Butlers lived around the corner from the McGowans, at 2236 Strang Avenue. In 1940 the family consisted of Vincent Butler, 41, the father, who was an Assistant Engineer in Oil Distribution; Helen, the mother, 36; three children, Katharine, 15, Vincent, 11, Ellen, 4; and a niece, Roberta McIntyre, 12, living with them at the time. At this point the McGowans did not have a phone. Calls for the family would normally be made to the Mooney's, but they seem at this time to have been away on vacation.

[22] The Mooneys were very good friends of the McGowans. They lived at 4050 Pratt Avenue. In 1940 the family consisted of Michael Mooney, the father, aged 49; Rose Mooney, the mother, 47; two daughters, Mary and Anna, 20 and 18 respectively; a son Robert, 17, and a son Richard, 15.

In the 93rd Evacuation Hospital, a field hospital, General Patton slaps a soldier who complains of "nerves". It is the second such incident involving this brash General in the last seven days, and he is almost cashiered for it by Eisenhower. But Patton is a tactical genius, and essential to continuing the dislodgement of German troops in Sicily, necessary to allow the invasion of the Italian mainland, and put Allied troops finally on the ground in mainland Europe. Patton's hide is saved, but his reputation is sullied, and it will cost him in the end as men of lesser talent end up getting rewarded with the choicer gems of military leadership. For now, the story of the slapping incident will be kept under wraps, with the public none the wiser.

General Patton is important to this story. Private John McGowan, at this moment just a few days in the service, will one day be one of Patton's soldiers, as they push forward to an ultimate Allied victory in Germany. But that is a ways down the road.

℘

"Camp Upton, New York

Aug. 10, 1943 [Tuesday]

Dear Mom,

Well I am still in Camp Upton. This is my fifth day here and I am getting to like the army life better and better. The only thing that I have a little trouble with is getting up in the morning. Do you remember how I used to sleep until 11 and 12 o'clock? By the way Mom I got to church Sunday at the 5:30 afternoon Mass. The church was very crowded and I was lucky in getting a seat. There were two priests, one saying the Mass and the other giving the sermon. After church the priest was at the door and gave every soldier a new testament and the Sunday Visitor. I also got scapulars and he told us to say three Hail Marys and we would be enrolled in it. The priest seemed to be very nice. He said his name was Fitzgerald.

Army life isn't as bad as you might think. I like it, but the only thing I don't like so much is the getting up at 5:30. Do you remember how late I use to sleep until? I am writing this letter on the floor of the barracks because the rest of the older fellows are playing cards. How are Dad and Mugs? Don't forget to give him the pep talk on Thursday morning.[23] I sent Robbie Mahon a card Monday but I didn't have a chance to write anybody else. I am kept pretty busy out here with details like cleaning up or cutting grass. Tell the fellows I was asking for them and that I will write soon.

Love,

---

[23] The "pep talk", I think, may have had something to do with pay day at the Navy Yard.

                                                    Son John

P.S. Write if you have a chance to do so."

TWO: "WHERE ALL THE GOLD IS STORED"

By the 13th of August John finds himself stationed at Fort Knox, Kentucky. Fort Knox, near by the Ohio River and south of Louisville, is at this time in its military life the home of the U.S. Army Armor Center. It sprawls over almost 170 square miles of rich Ohio River soil, encompassing parts of three Kentucky counties - Bullitt, Hardin and Meade. To its south is Elizabethtown, Kentucky. Fort Knox has an interesting neighbor, the United States Bullion depository, where the lion's share of the nation's gold reserves are stored. Indeed, more people associate Fort Knox with the nation's gold than do with the Fort's principal purpose in the military hierarchy. It is named for General Henry Knox, of Revolutionary War fame, who became Washington's chief officer of artillery, and subsequently served as the first U.S. Secretary of War. Today a museum named in honor of General George S. Patton graces its grounds, and portrays the history of the U.S. Army's Cavalry and Armored forces, as well as the military career of General Patton, tank commander supreme.

In his posting to Fort Knox, John is now a recruit in Company A, 5th Battalion, Armored Replacement Training Center (A.R.T.C.). Nick Kenny's column in *The New York Sunday Mirror*[24] on November 28, 1943 pays homage to "the men of the armored command" with a ditty written by a recent recruit.

"Home sweet home is a battle torn tank
For the men of the Armored Command.
There's a spirit in those walls of steel
That strong men understand.

Castles on tracks complete the attacks
With blasts from 75s.
For the men who sweat are the men who set
The scene for Victory drives.

'We forge the thunderbolt,' they roar.
'We've got the foe in hand.'

---

[24] *The New York Sunday Mirror* was the Sunday edition of *The New York Daily Mirror,* launched by the William Randolph Hearst publishing empire in 1924, probably to compete for readers with the still-extant *New York Daily News.* The *Mirror* ceased publication in 1963. Nick Kenny was a popular columnist of the era.

Yes, Victory lies with the battle born guys,
The men of the Armored Command."

            Private Sherwin S. Cloth
            Armored   Replacement
            Training Center

  Private Sherwin ("Sherry") Cloth, the author, is a former Broadway Press Agent who has been drafted and finds himself in Fort Knox with the A.R.T.C. He writes, "Here at the Armored Replacement Center each man is what you might call a 'military stand-in', trained to take over the job of an unknown comrade wounded in action. Our training in tanks, jeeps, peeps and other mechanized vehicles is thorough and sure, provided to guarantee victory."

  For the immediate future, Private McGowan will be training to be a "tank man". He does well, and becomes so adept at the intricacies of the equipment that he will be asked at some point down the road to remain at the Center as an Instructor, quite an achievement for an 18 year old.

            ℘

  The next few letters, though addressed to Camp Upton, have Private McGowan's new locale penciled in: "Armored RTC, Ft. Knox, Ky."

"R. Simmons
3714 Secor Ave.
Bronx 66, N.Y.

August 11, 1943 [Wednesday]

Hi John,
  Or should I say Private McGowan? How is the Army treating you kid? You know Lee Hart.[25] *Well he was drafted into the Navy and he is on his one week furlough now. He was disappointed though because he wanted to go into the army. He wanted the Air Corps. And who else do you think is going into the Navy? As a matter of fact he too is on his furlough. Only he enlisted. Well if you can't guess it's Bobby Witacker. He enlisted the other day and he now has a week to himself before he leaves. Kind of surprising, isn't it? So our gang is getting smaller and smaller. Well John believe it or not the Nativity of Our Blessed Lady indoor team is in first place. We have won two games and we haven't lost any. You see we were supposed to play*

---

[25] Edwin and Dorcas Hart lived at 3718 Rombouts Avenue. Their son, Edwin Lee Hart, was 17 in 1940.

three games so far but we have only played one. And that ended in a tie score. But the reason we have two victories is because two games have been forfeited to us. So far we were supposed to play two games at the Mount and one at Macomb's Dam.[26] Well, at both times at the Mount they never showed up. And the game at Macomb's was a tie 9 - 9. So we have to play that game over again. So that's that.

My sister Maye got engaged to Jimmy Supple.[27] He is a Sergeant now.

I saw Red Gibbons for the first time in a week last night. He was up my house last night. We ae supposed to have a blackout sometime this week. I'm going to the movies tonight. I'm going to ask Diemer to come with me. We will go to Loew's Post Road.[28] "Cabin in the Sky"[29] is playing. I don't know what the other picture is.

We was supposed to have a meeting[30] last night but because of the ball game we couldn't have one. And we can't have one next week because we play Wednesday night. There goes the damned air raid siren now. But getting back to the meeting we might hold it this coming Monday night after novena. I'm still dying to get my hands on Dorothy Kuntz.

---

[26] Macomb's Dam gave birth to the name of the Macomb's Dam Bridge and the surrounding neighborhood in the Bronx, located near Yankee Stadium. The bridge connects 155th Street in Manhattan with 161st Street in the Bronx.

[27] Jimmy Supple will come up again several times throughout this memoir. He ends up fighting in Europe, where he will be reported "Missing in Action." The Supple family lived at 3824 Pratt Avenue. In 1940 the family consisted of Daniel, 58, Bertha, 48, Charlotte, 28, James, 18, and Florence, 6. Mr. Supple was a Collector for Consolidated Edison.

[28] Loew's Post Road was a movie theater at 3475 Boston Post Road.

[29] "Cabin in the Sky" was a musical film produced in 1943 based on the 1940 Broadway musical of the same name. Directed by Vincente Minnelli, the film stars Ethel Waters, Eddie 'Rochester' Anderson and Lena Horne. Waters and Rex Ingram reprise their roles from the Broadway production. The film was Horne's first and only leading role in an MGM musical. Louis Armstrong is also featured in the film as one of Lucifer Junior's minions, and Duke Ellington and his Orchestra have a showcase musical number in the film.

[30] This probably refers to a meeting of the Air Raid Wardens, of which many of these young men were members of before being drafted into the service.

I had a swell time down Rockaway last weekend. Boy there must be about fifteen girls to every fellow. What girls! Wow! Boy if you ever get a furlough while I am still around that's where I am going to take you. I swear to Christ, I never seen so many girls in all my life in one place. You almost go nuts. Everywhere you look you see nice looking meat. Well, so long.

Your pal,
Dick Simmons

PS - Write and tell me about you."

"Aug. 13, 1943 [Friday]

Dear John,
 I think the mailman must suspect I am falling in love with him as I am running out every morning to meet him. I am so anxious to receive mail from you.
 We received your letter and card Thursday morning. Mom and Duke were delighted with your card and had a good laugh over the picture on it. I sent a letter to you Monday evening. Did you receive it? Mom sent one yesterday.
 Walter Cubita[31] was here Tuesday night. He took your address and said he was going to write. I don't know how Richie Simmons made out with his physical exam, but if I was you I would send a card to those boys as soon as possible. They were all so kind and generous toward you. While I think of it send a card to Martin Moynihan[32]. I think he has been having trouble with that pain he was complaining about.
 John I couldn't begin to tell you all the people who ask about you and want to be remembered. Mr. and Mrs. Wiedy, Henry's mother and father enquired about you and want to send their regards.

---

[31] Walter Cubita was a very good friend of John's. His family lived on Mill Lane off Boston Post Road, also called Reeds Mill Lane after a 17th century tidal grist mill that once stood at the end of the lane in the salt marshes off of Eastchester Bay. In 1940 the family consisted on the father, Lewis, 51, born in Austria; his wife Cecelia, 50; and Walter, 14.

[32] Martin Moynihan was a first cousin of John's, the son of his Aunt Rosemary (McGowan) Moynihan and Uncle Timothy Moynihan. They lived at 4268 Barnes Avenue in the Wakefield section of the Bronx, the next neighborhood going west from Edenwald. In 1940 the family consisted of Timothy, 45, born in Ireland; Rosemary, 45; Helen, 17; Martin, 13; and Dorothy, 10. Tim Moynihan's occupation is listed as "Clerk", working for "City Gov't".

This evening I received a letter from Tom Lucas[33]. He tells me the Navy life is wonderful, that he works hard and is kept busy but they get leisure time too and get plenty of entertainment. He will finish Boot Training first week in September and will then get a seven day's furlough. He wanted to know all about you and your address so you will probably hear from him.

Muggsie is having a great time. Duke takes her out like clockwork every few hours. The other day I left your suit on the bed. I was going to take it to the tailor's. Mugs happened to pass by the suit and you should see her smelling it and wagging her tail. Just let her hear a whistle and she is running from one window to the other.

Duke tells us he is kept so busy now taking care of dogs, garden and kids that if he was getting paid for it all he could be a rich man. The other day he sold a big load of newspapers so he has got money in all his vest pockets. He said, "Tell John I expect a monthly check for taking such good care of his dog."

The Windells are away so their mother Mrs. Carroll[34] and Cookie are staying here. We have lots of fun with Duke saying what a gay little woman she is. Lo and behold the other day she brought him out a glass of beer. He was spell-bound. Said he, "I think the widow is getting fond of me."

Don't worry about Dad, he is O.K. I am keeping him down to brass tacks. He takes his one glass of Eichler's[35] but he falls asleep and that is the end of it. When you send a letter he reads it himself and then he makes me sit down and read it all over again to him. You represent the whole army to him now. He couldn't wait until we hung a service flag in the window so I bought a beautiful one yesterday and it is hanging proudly by itself and when I gaze on it, it makes me feel proud too for I know that the star represents a boy who will be a fine and honorable soldier.

I was glad to know you got to Mass Sunday John, and I hope you said the three "Hail Marys". This Sunday will be August 15th, the Assumption. Maybe you could get to Holy Communion. You don't always have to go to Confession before. Say a good Act of Contrition and above all no matter what comes or goes say your prayers and get to Mass and receive Communion as often as you can. Because as you know yourself John, faith moves mountains and when you get in difficulties and little crosses are hard to bear, it is your prayers that will carry you through.

I was hoping you might be left at Camp Upton for a while. It might help you to get more experience about the army before you are moved for basic training.

---

[33] Tom Lucas was John's first cousin, son of Anna's sister, "Aunt Kitty".

[34] Mrs. Carroll was Mrs. Windell's mother.

[35] Eichlers was a brand of beer popular in the 1930's.

Your letters John are a source of consolation to me. They are so cheerful and no complaints and I am thanking God you are adjusting yourself to army life as you tell me you like it better and better. But I knew you would get along O.K. So be a good, obedient boy and respect your superiors. That is what counts in all walks of life.

I notice too John you don't ask for anything. Are you sure you have everything you need. Take care of your body and especially your feet. Change your socks often. If you need more I can send them to you. Did you have any milk to drink?

We would all love to see you mopping the floor and making the bed. You will be a good help to me when you come home again. Your pants and blouse came back Tuesday. Will close. Write. Tell us all about yourself.

Love from all.
Mother

P.S.   Thomas Lucas (A.S.)
U. S. Navy
Newport, R.I.
Co. 803, 8th Bat."

"Fort Knox, Kentucky

Aug. 14, 1943 [Saturday]

Dear Mom,
   I received your letter Wednesday just before I was shipped to Fort Knox, Kentucky. Wednesday night we left Camp Upton at 6 o'clock and arrived in Penn Station where a Pullman sleeper was waiting.[36] *We left Penn Station and went through the towns of Newark, Pittsburgh, Columbus Ohio, and Indianapolis Indiana. It was a swell trip and we ate in a dining car. We arrived in Louisville, Kentucky which is just 30 miles from Fort Knox on Thursday night. Down here at Fort Knox we have tanks and armored cars. The Fort is swell and the eats are 100% better than Camp Upton, but it is pretty warm. I did not have time to see Romer's brother at Camp Upton because of the little time I had. This is a very big fort down here and the officer said I will train for 22 weeks instead of the regular 18 for other parts of the army. Tell Duke to take good care of Muggsie because if he is good I will*

---

[36] New York City's Pennsylvania Station, finished in 1910, was one of the most magnificent train terminals ever built. It's "headhouse", or superstructure, was demolished in 1963, an irrevocable loss to the architecture of New York City. A Pullman Sleeper promised comfortable accommodations for the 24 hour train ride to Louisville, Kentucky.

reward him by giving him a baby tank someday. Boy Mom, the tanks are beauties, big ones and small ones. The officer also told us we are not allowed to have visitors. Excuse the pencil because I ran out of ink, and mistakes. Mom would you send me some coat hangers and soap and a wash rag? Love to all and write. I will be expecting some.

Love,
Son John"

℘

AUGUST 16, 1943 - CAMP SHELBY, MISSISSIPPI

Almost 600 miles south of Fort Knox, in the humid heat of Mississippi, an event is taking place that will prove to be of tremendous importance to Private McGowan, though he is completely unaware of it at the time. In a brief ceremony, the 65th Infantry Division is created, command of it being given to Major General Stanley Eric Reinhart, Jr.

Camp Shelby was established in 1917. The post was named in honor of Isaac Shelby, Indian fighter, Revolutionary War hero and first governor of Kentucky, by the first troops to train here, the 38th Division. It then was closed as a federal installation, and was used in the 1920's and 1930's as a Kentucky National Guard camp. Because of Camp Shelby's natural advantages of climate, terrain and location, it was reopened in 1940 as a federal military training installation, for preparation in case the U.S. was drawn into World War II. A number of divisions then trained here, including the 31st, 37th, 38th, 43rd, 63rd, 65th, 69th, 85th, 94th, and the 99th Divisions. The famous Japanese-American 442nd Regimental Combat Team and the 100th Battalion trained here as well. In addition, Women's Army Corps (WAC) units also trained here. The post contained a large convalescent hospital and had a prisoner of war camp which housed soldiers of the famous German Afrika Corps, and a large number of Italian POWs, who will cause some controversy later during the war, following Italy's surrender, when they are given the choice of serving as U.S. soldiers, or continuing as POWs.

But all that is in the future, at this point in Private McGowan's service experience, and he is happy to be part of the Armored Branch, where he will dig in with his keen mind to the intricate workings of the modern miracle weapon - the tank.

℘

"Aug. 17, 1943 [Tuesday]

Dear Son John,

It was with a great sigh of relief that I read you were sent to Fort Knox as I had a great fear you might land in one of those far off places in the woods. Dad tells me Fort Knox is one of the finest military places in the country. Judging from the picture souvenir you sent us, it must be a great place as Duke told us, "That is just the right spot to be in, where all the gold is stored!"

Well John are you satisfied with your assignment to the armored division? Was that your choice or did they just pick you out for that special work? Dad wants to know if you are attending that school down there for armored forces or just what are you training for, the tanks or other knowledge of all kinds of armored trucks? Also if it isn't a military secret let us know the meaning of A.R.T.C. and is it 5 Br or 5 Bn? Dad is kind of anxious to learn more about your branch of service and if you are happy about it all. When you write again explain more about it. However John we all feel proud about you and as your father tells me you had what it takes or you would never have got that assignment. It will take a whole lot of skill and study no doubt on your part but I think if you keep on your toes and put your best effort into what you do everything will turn out O.K.

Last night I met Father Broderick when I was going to the Novena and right away he asked me if I had any news from you. I told him about your new assignment to Ft. Knox and he said, "That is fine, now he can get all gold fillings in his teeth." Well we were just going to have a nice conversation when who calls him over but Mrs. Springer[37] and I went on my way. You should write to him John, he is so nice and kind. Mom tells me Father Foley[38] also enquires about you. He told her today you would be some tough man when you finish up with the armored forces. Drop a card someday to him. I think he would appreciate it. I also met Walter and Bobbie Mahon. They are all going to write to you. They all agreed you landed just in the right place where all the money is stored. Richard Simmons went down for his physical last night, so his mother told me with tears in her eyes. Peter[39] came in one night to take his music box and told me his mother felt very bad because you didn't visit her before you went. So I made a hundred excuses and said you couldn't get there. Drop them a card. Don't forget. Dick Mooney was asking for you. He is anxious to see you in uniform.

---

[37] Mrs. Springer, obviously not a favorite of Anna's.

[38] Father Foley was the Monsignor of Nativity Parish. He was born in New York in 1890. In 1940, he was assisted in his efforts by two other priests, Father Joseph S. Smith, 42, and Father Joseph M. Jordan, 27. The staff at the Rectory on East 233rd Street included Mary O'Connor, 60, and Margaret Dooley, 42, both of whom were born in Ireland.

[39] I am not sure who this "Peter" refers to, but obviously his family was saddened by John's departure.

Well John if I was to try to tell you about everybody who asks for you I would be writing until next year. We received an invitation to Louie Romano's[40] wedding which is to take place next Sunday. By the way I saw Romano's brother here the other day driving his car. I wanted to tell you about the sermon Father Broderick gave the Monday night after you went. It was on obedience and for example he told about a very young boy in the parish who is called away by the Draft Board and how he obeys, just accepted it as his duty and goes without a word of objection. Well the way he told it I thought he was going to say John McGowan. He said if we accept things as the will of God, how much easier it is rather than fight against it. That kind of consoled me.

We have Mary Ann and Rose Mary[41] staying with us for a few days. Believe me we will be glad when the vacation is over. The Jordans from Staten Island[42] are coming tomorrow. Helen[43] was over and took some pictures. I will forward them to you later.

Well John I would love to see you more than anyone else in the world, especially with that haircut you got. I do hope you didn't spoil your hair. I am so glad you get plenty to eat and especially milk only don't overdo it. If possible get a picture taken and send it to us. I am sending you all the things you asked for and more than that. Keep writing to us John. We all love to hear from you.

Mother, Dad, Mom, Duke, Muggsie

P.S. Did you receive a letter from Mom? She and Walter sent to Camp Upton, L.I."

"Wed. Evening, Aug. 18, 1943

Dear John,

---

[40] The Romanos lived at 4025 Pratt Avenue, across the street from the McGowans. In 1940 the family consisted of the mother, Rose Romano, 70, born in Italy, listed as "Head" and "Widowed"; Frances, 39; Louis, 34; Lucy, 30; Jesse Miele, 50, "Widowed"; and Edith Miele, 18, Jessie's daughter. Louis, apparently, is engaged to be married. Another son apparently lives elsewhere.
[41] Mary Ann and Rose Mary McGowan were first cousins of John's, daughters of his Uncle Frank and Aunt Anna (Kenesky) McGowan.
[42] The Jordans were from Staten Island, and possibly connected to the Gallaghers, cousins of the Duke through his mother, Bridget (Gallagher) McGowan.
[43] Helen may refer to John's first cousin, Helen Moynihan, Martin's sister.

Your requests are on their way. It is taking the whole family to pack the box - Dad, Mary Ann, Rose Mary, myself and even Muggsie. She is so excited that she is barking at us. Duke is upstairs with the Irish music.

Enclosed you will find the following - towels, wash cloths, hangers, soap, candy, sewing kit, handkerchiefs and socks and also newspaper and by the way Dad is going to try to have the newspapers sent to you.

Do you want a shaving kit, hair brush or shoe shine or money? I have your brown shoes here, if you can use them, or want a pair of rest slippers. Tell me and I will send them in another package.

Enclosed is the paper from Hickey[44]. He wants your address so send him a card and he will have the paper mailed to you.

Received your letter today. Do not take too much [illegible], it isn't so good for the kidneys. Eat the best and take care of your body. If you want socks let me know. Bobby Mahon enlisted for the Navy today. That is all for now John. Answer soon. I sent a letter to you yesterday. Remember to say your prayers and receive Holy Communion if you can. Love from all.

Mother"

"Fort Knox, Kentucky

Aug. 20, 1943 [Friday]

Dear Mother,

I received your letter today and was very glad to receive it. I just got off of K.P. so I thought I would write the answers to some of your questions. Well first, they pick out the best men to go in the Armored Force and I can't tell you everything I do while I am training because it is a military secret. I can tell you that I will learn all about tanks and armored cars. I had to put food on the table and peel potatoes in K.P. today. I did not have a chance to

---

[44] Bill Hickey's *Dyre Avenue News* was a hometown newsletter organized by a band of patrons of Hickey's Bar on the corner of Dyre Avenue and East 233rd Street in the Edenwald section of the Bronx. It was designed to spread news of the neighborhood to all serving in the armed forces, and keep everyone updated on just where those servicemen and women were, and what they were up against. The Hickeys lived at 4024 Pratt Avenue, just down the block from the McGowans at 4030 Pratt. The family in 1940 consisted of the father, William ("Bill"), aged 30; his wife, Catherine, 37; and a 6 year old daughter, Joan. Also in the family were two stepchildren, presumably from an earlier marriage of Catherine's: Eileen Hamill, 12, and Thomas Hamill, 11. A brother of Bill's, Jack Hickey, 32, lived there also. He ran a one-truck egg and butter company. There was also a Hickey family on nearby Amundson Avenue.

go anyplace. By the way Mom, I ran into Johnny Murray that lives on the corner of Light Street and Secor. I met him in the Service Club. He was very surprised to see me. While at the Service Club I wrote a letter to Richard Simmons. Well Mother, A.R.T.C. means Armored Replacement Training Center, and it is Company A, 5th Battalion. Tell Duke that the gold down here is protected day and night by armed guards. I received a $5 payment from the Army. Boy, did it come in handy. I am pretty sure that I am going into Louisville, Kentucky for the weekend. How is Dad making out? Is he still talking about the Navy Yard and his friendly Jews? I think I will close now as I am getting tired. Love to all,*

*Love,
Son John"*

This next letter, postmarked Aug. 21, 1943, from Louisville, Kentucky, is on letterhead of the "Soldiers' Club Rooms of Warren Memorial Presbyterian Church, Fourth and Broadway, Louisville, Ky." John also encloses a postcard from the local U.S.O. Club, which is operated by the "National Catholic Community Service, 525 South 5th Street, Louisville, Kentucky"; no doubt to assuage any fears his mother may harbor lest he is being swayed by the Presbyterians!

"Louisville, Kentucky

Aug. 21, 1943 [Saturday]

Dear Mother,
This is another letter to tell you that I had a free supper at this Presbyterian Church. The people were very nice to us. They gave us all we could eat. They have the whole cellar of their church made into a dining room and they will feed anyone, Catholic or Jew. Love to all.
Son John"

This next letter is from John's first cousin, Morgan Lucas. The Lucas's lived in Bernardsville, New Jersey. Morgan, John says, was "the smartest one in the family." He died tragically in a car accident while his brother David was at the wheel.

"30 Alcott Square
Bernardsville, N.J.

August 21, 1943 [Saturday]

Hello John,

    We received your card this morning and we were quite surprised to find you in Kentucky. You will soon miss "Little Ole New York." Don't get in the way of any tanks. What exactly is your job? All the feminine attractions of this town are still on the loose, so come up and visit us on your first furlough. Do you hear from Tom, John or David? Dave is now in the Air Corps, unattached. Write and give me full particulars. Do you ever see any of those Army nurses that are supposed to be training at Fort Knox? If so how are they? Don't answer any nurses or WACs back or else, the Brig. Tom wants to smoke a pipe now that he is in the Navy. Write soon, and forgive penmanship as I am in a hurry.

Lots of luck,
Morgan Lucas

P.S. How's about insignias?"

"Aug. 23, 1943 [Monday]

Dear Son John,

    Today Monday I received four letters from you which made me very happy to receive so much news of your activities. Two letters that you wrote at the fort arrived this morning and the two from Louisville[45] arrived this afternoon. Duke usually gets the mail, and when he yells, "Word from John," everybody gathers to hear what you have to say. I imagine you must have had an enjoyable time in Louisville. I wondered if you didn't have reactions from the injections. Did you go alone to town or did your pals go with you? Are they Catholics? When I read to Duke about you having supper in the church, "By George," he said, "He must be changing his religion." Judging from the Post Card the Catholic Club must be a very fine place. I suppose those southern belles are all beauties but can't compare with our northern girls.

    I was surprised when I read how you met J. Murray. It was only yesterday the Farrell girl was telling me how she would write and tell Jimmy about you being at the Fort. Is he in officer's training school? While I think of it the Savages are always asking for you so send them a card with your address as Mrs. Savage said Billy[46] wanted it. Last week they announced his engagement. I am enclosing the clipping. I am writing these things John as they come to my mind so don't mind if I go from one subject to another. By the way, Dick Mooney came down last evening with a big pan of tomatoes.

---

[45] Louisville was a favored place to unwind for the soldiers at Fort Knox.
[46] William ("Billy") Savage.

They are swell. In fact we could sell them now we have such a supply. Write a card to Dick. He would like to hear from you. He thinks Buddy is in Africa.

We have Mary Ann and Chubby staying with us. Last week we had Rose Mary. Yesterday Sunday we had the whole family. Poor Duke gave up in desperation trying to watch everything so he told Mom, "I am a son of a gun but tomorrow I will go down and enlist." Send Mom and Duke another card. They got a big kick out of the last one you sent.

I wanted to tell you that I sent those things you wanted Thursday morning from White Plains Post Office. Did you receive them yet? You asked for a watch and camera. Well the watch I intend to send but Dad wants to know if you are sure you can use one down there. Let us know. I didn't quite understand about the money situation, that is, did you get $5 from your pay or how? I am enclosing a money order for $5. It will help carry you over until later.

I am afraid John you are getting a tremendous appetite. Don't overdo it. Glad to know you can get milk. Ice cream is good too.

Well John you are in for a little criticism now by your mother in regard to your letter writing. Your handwriting has improved and you compose the letters O.K., but the spelling is bad. One word in particular when you close (correct now) meaning time. (Know) is to know something. Read your letters over after you write them sometimes and see all your mistakes. Take your time when you write. Of course with me it is all right. I wouldn't care if you wrote in Chinese, so long as I heard from you. But with others it may be different. Write a card to Peter[47]. The Farrell girl was asking for you. She told me they are going to have another outing to Rye Beach[48]. The boys are supposed to have ball games but it seems the other side never shows up to play. When I go down to Dyre Avenue I need to take the day off to answer all the people who inquire for you. Dad is doing fine. Reads your letters over about a dozen times. Frank[49] is going to have a sport sheet mailed to you. George[50] was home again for a few days. He thinks Walter[51] is in the Pacific. I am glad to know you are taking good care of yourself. Keep polished up. Watch your

---

[47] Possibly refers to Peter Hickey.
[48] Rye Beach was a very popular outing place for people from Northeast Bronx neighborhoods like Edenwald and Wakefield.
[49] John's Uncle Frank, his father Eddy's younger brother. He had moved recently to Yonkers, New York. At the 1940 Census, aged 39, he lived at 3931 Secor Avenue, with his wife Anna, 33, and daughters Mary Anne, 3, and Rosemary, 9 months old. His occupation is listed as a "claims adjustor" in "bus transportation".
[50] Probably refers to George Stanley. He and his brothers were orphaned at an early age, and George, the youngest, was taken in by Frank and Mary McGowan, and raised like a son.
[51] Probably refers to Walter McGowan, John's first cousin.

shoes. *You know how Mother is on the shoe polish. Don't forget to say extra prayers for yourself especially now for success at training that God may guide you to do what is right. Well John I will close now. Love and regards from all. Take it easy and don't worry. Keep on writing.*

Love,
Mother

P.S. *Enclosed are pictures. Duke said he looks like Uncle Joe, the colored man.*"[52]

The next letter is from John's friend, Richard "Dick" Simmons.

"Aug. 23, 1943 [Monday]

Dear John,

    I received your letter this morning and was glad to hear from you. John, are you trying to persuade me to go into the Army? Now you know better than that. I still think I'm the man for the Navy. You know Edenwald section fell apart after you left. Bobby Whitaker left this morning for the Navy. Lee Hart leaves this week for Seabees. He was drafted right into it. Buddy Porch, whom you know I think, leaves this Tuesday for the Army. Matthew Maxwell leaves this week for the Army. He enlisted. George Teidermann from Duryea Avenue is on his three week furlough prior to going into the Army. He wanted the Navy but he flunked the color blindness test. Dick Mooney is home every week. He is in the Navy going to Columbia College. So far, I have mailed in my questionnaire which was over two weeks ago but I haven't heard since but only to take some silly old pledge. And that didn't make any sense. Billy Savage got another stripe which makes him a Tech Sergeant. Pretty good. By the way he is engaged to be married. So is my sister Maye. Gerard Deimer still chasing Gussie for you know what reason.

    You know, John, the Junior Holy Name Society is going on another bus ride to Rye Beach this Saturday night. I am going stag this time. And I'm going to have a hell of a good time. Red (the goon), Gerard, Red's cousin Bobby and myself are going stag. The four of us, so you can imagine. We are going by way of Fordham Bus Company again. They want that bus. I'm chairman of it again and I received via mail this morning a check to cover the reduction money on bus ride.

    As you can see you're in for a hell of a long letter. I've only started.

---

[52] It's a mystery who was "Uncle Joe, the colored man." Perhaps it was a radio show the Duke listened to.

Father Broderick took the money from the treasury and mailed me a check for the same amount. He mailed it Saturday night as he is away on his three week vacation. He then comes back and will be with us for one year and then he is off to Cardinal Hayes as a teacher. We are sure going to miss him.

Well, tomorrow night is a great event in the history of the Junior Holy Name Society of Nativity. If we win the softball game tomorrow night, Tuesday we become Bronx Champions. We will receive medals and also play Manhattan for the trophy if we win tomorrow night. Right now we are in first place. We have won four games and haven't lost any. Ain't that swell? And as can be expected, I'm happy as a lark. Oh, if we can win tomorrow night. And we are at a disadvantage too, because Paul Porchen has quit his job and has gone on a two week vacation upstate in New York prior to going back to school. And you know how much he means to the ball team. Just cross your fingers and hope for the best.

Yesterday I made some money for myself. In other words, I was playing poker. Yes, we was playing poker. Bobby Whitaker, Red's cousin Bobby and myself. Well, for some reason I was the only winner and those poor, poor boys lost. I won a measly ninety cents. But it's lunch and carfare.

You know I was elected the new secretary when you left. Well, at our last meeting Father said our next meeting would be late in September, so I didn't know if I would be around at that time so we elected a new secretary. Guess who? Well, it's Walter Cubita. Yes, sir, windbag got it. You know, the secretary is furnished with an index file with a card for every member. Also on that card is the branch of service he is in if he is in the armed forces, and the activity he is in.

Well, so long for now. Please write soon John.

Your pal,
Dick

P.S. Stay away from the girls!"

℘

"Thomas Lucas
(A.S.) Co. 803 Bat. 5th
Newport, R.I.

Aug. 25, 1943 [Wednesday]

Dear John,
 I hope you like Army life. How is everything? I am doing very well. I go home the 7th of September. What is that you are in? Are you gaining weight? Do you think you will like it? Write soon.

Love,
Tom"

"Aug. 27, 1943 [Friday]

Dear John,
    This is Friday morning, an ideal day for letter writing, like a fall day. Mary Ann is still here on her vacation. You know she is my bedfellow sometimes. You would think she is swimming from the way she moves from the top of the bed to the foot. Helen Butler has been taking her to the beach every day to bathe so maybe that accounts for it. She has a new wind-blown haircut and never stops looking in the mirror at herself.
    Well last night the boys paid us a visit. Ritchie Simmons and Red Gibbons met Walter here by surprise. You should hear them what they had to say to Walter. I had to come to his defense. They said he was the gossip sheet and they hope he would bring a better looking girl on the bus ride Saturday night to Rye than the last time. Red told me she had such a face that everybody gave up drinking when they looked at her. Richard said that you were the smartest boy there, didn't bother taking any girl on the ride. Red said, "Oh, yeah, but he cut me out with my girl!" We really enjoyed their company listening to them. Red heard Duke's Irish music and he put on Mary Ann's little white hat and started jigging. He had us all screaming. When he was leaving he told me he wants me to learn how to jig because he wants to dance with me and to tell you he wants a letter with good understandable English so he won't have to call in the neighbors to read it for him. When you learn how to drive a tank he is going down to get a ride in it.
    Richard told me Walter is going to take your place in the club but he knows it won't last long. He doesn't seem to care a great deal about Walter. Of course he is a sensible type of a boy. He should have been the secretary. Father Broderick is gone away on his vacation for three weeks. They tell me Bobby Mahon is leaving September 8th. He was here one evening. I think you will receive a letter from him soon. Martin Moynihan had a good laugh over that picture you sent him on the card. He couldn't make out what your address was on account of the stamp put on it. So if possible John send him one of those souvenir picture albums that you sent to me. I thought it would be nice for you to do so. They were so generous toward you.
    You told me you received a letter from Morgan.[53] What is it he wanted you to send? I wouldn't send them. Are they insignias? Maybe he shouldn't have them things.
    Well John I hope you are not dancing too much as you know that tires you out for the next day. So take it easy. From what you tell me I think you are eating plenty but take less coffee and more milk. I am glad John they give

---

[53] Morgan Lucas.

you little lectures as it will enlighten the boys to ward off temptation. Value your body John and your health and be proud of yourself and the uniform you wear. Stand for what is right and just no matter what the price. Don't let anybody induce you to do what you know is wrong. There is where our faith and the beautiful teachings of our religion come in. Hold fast to them John. Remember always to pray and try to get to confession and communion. They are what help to make us strong. Is there a Catholic chaplain at the Fort? If you do what is right when you are young you will have nothing to regret when you are old.

Did you receive the letter I sent with the money? You know Seigal gave up the Post Office business. All you can get now is stamps so I couldn't send it registered, unless I went over to White Plains Avenue.[54]

I was talking with Mr. Trainor[55] the other night. He was telling me Romeo[56] is a navigator and bombardier. He was grounded for thirty days. It seems he went in swimming and got an ear infection from it. So that is why he was home on leave.

The other day I read in the paper that Mr. Janisch[57] had a new little daughter. Write a card to him, also one to Mr. Bernabe.[58] I will write their addresses. Mrs. Bernabe's father died and left a big estate. So poor Ralph is all upset but he takes his nightly trips just the same. Duke is keeping up his morale by giving Ralph tomatoes to eat.

Well John I am going in to Mt. Vernon to shop so I will close now. Would you like one of those shoe polish sets? Later on I will pack another box for you with things I think you need. How were the bath towels? Be a good boy. Love from all.

Mother

P.S. A kiss or lick from Muggsie."

---

[54] More properly named as White Plains Road, "The Avenue" was a major shopping artery for the Edenwald and Wakefield neighborhoods. The "El" shadowed its pavement, and the streetcars wound their way beneath it, bustling north and south.
[55] The Trainors lived at 4010 Pratt Avenue. In 1940 the family numbered Joseph, 46, a pharmacist in wholesale drugs; his wife Claire, 46, born in Canada; a daughter, Claire, 19, a private secretary in the stock market; and a daughter Dorothy, 15 years old.
[56] Not sure who Romeo refers to, unless it is a son of Mr. Trainor's who was on his own in 1940.
[57] No Paul Janisch could be found in the 1940 Census, but Anna includes his address at the bottom of the letter: 707 So. 6th Ave., Mt. Vernon, N.Y.
[58] The Bernabes lived at 4038 Pratt Avenue, just up the block from the McGowans at 4030 Pratt. In 1940 the family consisted of Ralph, the father, 39; Frances, the mother, 33; a son, Ralph, Jr., 6; and a daughter, Anne, 4.

John's father cannot resist the urge to travel and pay a surprise visit to his son. This is not an event that will be looked upon very favorably by his wife, Anna. John will put the best spin he can on it, the dutiful son navigating a tricky path between two parents sometimes at odds with one another.

"Fort Knox, Kentucky

Aug. 29, 1943 [Sunday]

Dear Mother,

Kindly excuse me for not writing because I did not have a chance to do so. Dad came down and visited me Saturday. I think he was on one of his travels but he said no. He was swell to me. He got supper for me and a piece of pie and a quart of milk. We also went into the Post Grill and had a couple of beers. We talked over everything and he told me all the news from home. I think he came here right from New York because it said that on his ticket. He is traveling home by bus and it will take him about 30 hours to get home. It was good to see him. I told him when he was going to go right home. I guess he will. He also gave me two dollars and asked me if I wanted any more. Last night I went around the Post with some friends of mine. I got to bed about 11 o'clock and got up today at 7:30. We ate breakfast at 8:00 and then I went to 9:30 mass in the movie house. This week I expect to go out on the firing range for some practice on the rifle so if I do not write every day please excuse me because I may not have a chance to. Love to all.

Love,
Son John"

"Harry F. Gibbons
2204 Light Street
Bronx, N.Y.

August 31, 1943 [Tuesday]

Dear John,
I am indeed glad to hear you are in the Armored Division. Your Mother told me you liked it very much. I go up with Richy quite often to visit your Mom and we spend a quiet evening talking about all kinds of things. Your Mom is trying to talk me into being a priest. Yes, I said me.

By the way, don't worry about the girls for I've got them all taken care of. I hated to take your place with them but fortunately for me I had no alternative.

I am truly sorry that I didn't write sooner but I was so busy I just couldn't find time. We're having a party for your pal up here for his going into the Navy. When you write tell me all about it down there. I am interested in that branch of the service myself. You will write soon I hope. Well don't forget now that you're in, make the best of it and come out on top. I miss you since you've been away. Even on our short acquaintance we were still Irish you know. Keep that good name too.

Some of the boys went to Rye last week but I missed as I arrived home too late. I'm still working and waiting for my chance to get away. This Saturday Richy, I and Gerard are going to Rockaway to visit Jackie. We expect to have a good time. "Plenty of women, you know." The neighborhood is still as busy as always. Plenty of life, you know. There's always Richy and myself together. I don't know where Gerard keeps himself, with Gussie I suppose. Richy went in a few minutes ago with the hound (flea catcher). He just finished seeing John the Bishop all evening.

I don't know where I get all the ambition to write so much but nevertheless it seems I have. I was out with my pet Doris late last week and lately I'm going after a new one whose name is Dot and what a tomato, a real young heifer. She is solid all there and stuff. I seem to be making out okay with her too. What a necking party we had Saturday night till 2 A.M. Well Rummy I guess I'll sign off here. Hope you enjoy this letter and the next one will be better. Providing you write to me. Okay. Your Mom is looking swell and your old man's doing fine.

Your pal,
Red"

THREE: "SCHULTZ"

"Dick Simmons
3714 Secor Avenue
Bronx 66, New York

Sept. 2, 1943 [Thursday]

Hi John,
    I received your letter yesterday morning and was glad to hear from you. I was up to your house last night and your mother also got a letter from you. Your mother loves to receive mail from you.
    We was supposed to have practice for the softball team last night but only two or three fellows showed up, including myself. So from there I went to your house. You know your mother and father are swell people. Your father is funny as hell. After I left your house last night I was with Red.[59] He can't go with us Saturday because he can't get off. So I told him to come down right from work. But he says that he can't because he is broke this week and that he will be very tired after he gets finished working. You know we are going down to Rockaway this Saturday, Jack, Gerard and myself. Red was supposed to come. We are leaving Saturday morning and will get home about 4:00 A.M. Sunday morning. We are sure to have a good time. Jack is going to sleep over at my house Friday night. We are going to Bobbie's party, Jack, Red, Red's cousin Bob and myself. Other fellows are going but us four are going together. I think we are going to have a ¼ keg of beer. We invited your father down. There is going to be no girls.
    You know who Red has been going out with lately? Dorothy. You know, the girl that lives right across from me. He says that she is some musher or commonly known as necker. Tonight I think I am going up to see Mrs. Curtin. I have been promising her for the longest while that I would come up. And I hear that she has Wednesdays off. I mean Thursdays off.[60]
    Father Broderick is still away on his three week furlough from church. Gerard Deimer is working nights now. But he must still have Saturdays off because he says he is coming with us this Saturday. I got a letter from Bobby Whitaker the other day, that is, yesterday. He says that he is having a pretty tough time with his boot training. He says that it either kills you or makes a man out of you. It must be killing him. Well, he was underweight anyway. He

---

[59] "Red" Gibbons.
[60] Who "Mrs. Curtin" is, is a mystery.

expects a furlough, or liberty if you want to call it that, in six weeks. He says that us guys won't stand a chance with the girls when he comes home. That is a laugh. But I hear you have nice looking chicken down there. Don't do anything I wouldn't do.

  Your father brought back from camp a newspaper, and the newspaper was swell. Boy you guys can't get bored with all the things going on down there. Dances, and everything. But I would like to play with those softball teams. They must be pretty good according to that newspaper. But I will still be only too glad to get in the Navy. I still wouldn't take the Army. Well, I will be saying so long for now.

Your pal,
Dick"

"Sept. 3, 1943 [Friday]

Dear Son John,
  This being First Friday morning I have just returned from early Mass and Communion. Everything happens to be so quiet, I thought it would be a good time to write a few lines. In fact John if things keep up I will need a private secretary to take care of my correspondence.[61] I owe everybody I know a letter and they are all writing asking me why I don't write but it seems to take me all my time getting mail off to you. By the way John do you find that you receive my letters quicker by air mail? Let me know. I would like to be sure about it. Well at last we obtain the watch we wanted through Richard Simmons's efforts and it is on its way. If it proves itself as good as it is recommended, I am sure you have a dandy watch. Don't wind it. Just set the hands for the correct time. The bracelet I bought extra. Richard tells me you can wear it from one end of your arm to the other because it expands. It is made for military purposes. They couldn't engrave your name on it on account of the material or steel used in it. So try not to lose it. Take note of the little shoebox it is enclosed in. I had to take it out of the hope-chest where it held your first pair of baby white shoes given to you by Mrs. Hull. Keep the box if you can and John I would like you when you write to Richard to thank him for his kindness in obtaining the watch. He certainly was very kind about it and nothing was too much for him to do. In order to show my appreciation I hope to remember him when he is called into service. Perhaps you could send him a little souvenir from there. Just to thank him. His father and mother bought one just like yours for him. So now you are [illegible].

---

[61] Indeed, Anna seemed to keep up a voluminous correspondence with a large number of the neighborhood boys who had ended up in uniform, as well as relatives, neighbors, friends and parents as well.

Well John I wondered how you made out getting up at 4 o'clock. It must be a great experiment in the rifle range. Tell us more about it if possible, what your reaction was. Hope you hit the target. Last night I was down to confession (Thursday night) when a big storm broke out and I had to wait there. After a while Mr. Goeth[62] told me Ed was waiting for me so out I went and home with him, umbrellas and rain coats he brought. So everything is working fine again. He tells me he may go on night work.[63] You know he has all the boys charmed telling them about you and Fort Knox. Walter and Richard [64]was here last night. Your father can give everybody hot air but Schultz, as he calls me. I am too wise to him. It cost $54 for the round trip, so he tells me, but I told him it is the last round the world trip he will make.

Duke and Mom certainly appreciated that letter you sent. If you have an extra dollar someday enclose it for Duke. I am sure he will be tickled with it. He is the news reporter for your activities. He has everybody talk about you. I have to read your letters to him when they come.

Tonight the boys are having a surprise party for Bobbie.[65] Your father and I are invited. I gave them a contribution toward it in your name. They didn't ask for it but I felt I wanted to help. Bobbie was very thoughtful toward you.

I was glad to know you received a letter from Kitty[66] and Martin[67]. Try to send him (Martin) that souvenir folder if you can. I met Gerard Diemer, he was asking about you. Said he would like to hear from you too. Well, Duke just brought me in a letter from you telling me about your infantry experience. Good for you John. I know you would hit the bull's eye. Glad to know Fr. Broderick wrote. Bet you were tired out after your long hike. Get plenty of sleep. I think they feed you well from what you tell us you got on the range. Take good care of yourself. I will write more later. Mary Ann[68] sends her love. We are going to have breakfast now. She and I celebrate a birthday September 7th. Suppose to have ice cream and cake. Muggsie didn't get her annual bath yet but it will take place soon I am hoping. Did you receive a letter from Red?[69] I heard he wrote to you.

We just had intermission. The kettle was boiling and as usual I had to run out and use the water before it all boiled away. Mary Ann has been a

---

[62] Possibly Mr. Gueth.
[63] Night work at the Brooklyn Navy Yard, where Ed McGowan worked as an electrician.
[64] Walter and Richard probably refers to Walter Cubita and Richard Simmons.
[65] Bobbie is Robert Mahon, about to go into the service.
[66] Kitty is John's Aunt Kitty Lucas.
[67] Martin Moynihan.
[68] Mary Ann refers to John's first cousin, Mary Anne McGowan.
[69] "Red" probably refers to Henry ("Red") Gibbons.

great deal of fun for us. She is here now three weeks. You would be surprised how fond Muggsie is of her. She got a new pair of slippers with heels and it is pound-pound. Duke calls her Eleanor Roosevelt, ready to travel all the time. Send her a funny card. Had a card from Betty. She is in Connecticut with John.[70] Did you write to them? Well John I could keep writing until tomorrow but will give you more news in the next letter. I am writing with your pen from Frank.[71] Writes swell. Do you want it? Love from all.

Mother

P.S. Enclosed find a clipping. Read about Fort Knox and heat."

This next letter is from Bridget (Kenney) McGowan, John's grandmother, the Duke's wife.

"D. McGowan
4030 Pratt Ave.
Bronx, N.Y.

Sept. 4, 1943 [Saturday]

Dear John,
    I received your letter. Glad to hear you are well. I suppose you got a great surprise when your dad called on you. He got back home O.K. and is still talking of the nice place it is. Well John, Robert Mahon is leaving us tomorrow. Just one month after you. This is the First Friday and you left on the last First Friday. They will have a party tonight for him.
    Mary Ann is down for the last 3 weeks. She is going to start in St. Barnabas School next week. We will miss her when she goes home. She has been great company to us. Rose Mary was down for a week and Margaret was down for 4 days so they all had a vacation.[72] Muggsie and the Duke got to be great friends. She comes to the foot of the stairs and barks up at him to come down to take her out. The garden is getting along good. We had a lot of tomatoes. Pop pulled your string beans last Sunday. They were very good.
    Mother went to the Post Office today to send you your watch but they would not take it. It had to be packed in a certain kind of a box. So she will have to get Ritchie[73] to take it back to the store until they pack it. It is a very nice watch. You will be some dude when you wear it. Is there any nice girls

---

[70] Who "Betty" and "John" were is not clear. Perhaps a family relative?
[71] A present from John's Uncle Frank McGowan.
[72] Rose Mary and Margaret were younger sisters of Mary Ann McGowan.
[73] No doubt Richie Simmons.

down there? Keep a good distance away from them. There is very nice girls in Edenwald when you come back. Louie Romano was married last Sunday. Frank was down to see them.

John I think I have told you everything I know. The summer is over and kids are all going back to school next week. Paddy is gone on his vacation for 2 weeks. I do not know who is looking after the church. I guess F. Gueth will have to do the work. The Duke was sound asleep while I was writing this letter. It is very nasty and cold like rain. Good bye John, best wishes from Duke and Mom also Pop and Mother. Be a good boy till you come home.
Mom"

On letterhead of the "City of Louisville, Kentucky Service Club, 824 South Fourth Street: For Men in the Armed Forces of the U.S." John and a couple of "fellows" are enjoying a weekend pass. Not enough time to get back home to New York, but certainly enough to enjoy a night or two on the town, which Louisville must have offered plenty of attractions to while away the hours until return to barracks beckoned.

"Louisville, Kentucky

Sept. 5, 1943 [Sunday]

Dear Mother,

I just got up out of bed so I thought I would write you. I came to Louisville all right. I got here about 9 o'clock last night. Two other fellows came with me. They are both Catholics. Boy did we have a good time. I didn't get to bed till 2 o'clock. This late hour reminded me how at home I used to come home. I am sorry I did not write yesterday but I did not have a chance to do so. I received a letter from Walter Cubita and he told me all about the boys giving Robbie Mahon a party. Guess who I received a letter from? Well it was from Red Gibbons. The nut, he gave me all the neighborhood news and what the girls were doing. He ended his letter by saying, "Your Mom looks swell and your old man is doing fine." You can see what kind of letter he sent me. How is Dad behaving? Tell him to be good. Love to all.
*Love,
Son John"*

This next letter is from John's father.

"Sept. 5, 1943 [Sunday]

Dear John,

I am writing you this letter to let you know that we are all well. How are you getting along with Army life? Mary Anne did not go home yet. She is going to write a letter to you that will be some note. Robbie Mahon had a party last night. We all went to it. There was only his sisters were there. It was not like the party you had. We got home about 11:00 PM. He is going into the Navy. They was all asking for you John. Red wrote you a letter and you did not send him a letter. R. Simmons is going to have a blood test Saturday morning so I guess he will be in the Army soon. I got home Monday night about 7:00 PM. That was some trip. So I will be closing, hoping to hear from you. Love from all,

Dad"

The postscript is added by John's mother, very tongue-in-cheek.

P.S. Muggsie is going to get her grooming. I am supposed to be the censor on this letter but your father wouldn't dare let me correct the spelling. Hope you can make it out. This is Saturday morning, Sept. 5. We received your beautiful pillow case and the very nice verse on it. It will be one of my dearest possessions. Dad is off today. We are going into Mount Vernon to shop and see the movies. Helen Butler just called over and told us Robbie is returning until Tuesday. They are crowded and have no room.

*Love,
Mother*

Passed under the board of censorship. Anna Cecelia McGowan."

ⓢ

"Fort Knox, Kentucky

Sept. 7, 1943 [Tuesday]

Dear Mother,

Well it is raining down here now and I thought it would be a good time to drop you a few lines. I went out to the rifle range today and had to get up at 3 in the morning and we started out at 4:30. Boy was I tired. We had a very hard day. How are things at home? Did the kids go to school and do they still play ball out in the street? Send some cake if you get a chance and send me anything I might need. You can send me slippers. Well I will close now. Love to all.

                                                          Love,
                                                          Son John

P.S. *Write. Tell Dad to take it easy. I might get a three day furlough in the future."*

                                   ℘

"Mr. W. A. Cubita
32 Mill Lane
Bronx 66, N.Y.

September 8, 1943 [Wednesday]

Dear John,
 In the first place I wrote you a letter last Wednesday and did not hear from you since I wrote that letter. I wrote that in response to a letter I had received from you on the previous day. Well now I will let you know what is going on around here. Mother and dad are all right and hope that you are making out all right, but I told them not to worry for you have the luck of the Irish with you and you always will.
 Bobbie Mahon did not feel too bad about leaving. If he did he didn't show it outwardly. You asked me in your letter what girl I go out with at the present time. Well to tell you the truth I do not go out with any girl in particular right now because I calculate that if I do I might fall too hard and that will be the end of me, it would just put me out of circulation for good and I do not want that to happen at this present moment.
 Dick Simmons went for his blood test last night, and on encountering him today he stated that he passed. He expects to be placed in 1-A at any moment now. It will, in all probability, be only a short while before he is gone also.
 I intend to return to school this Monday. I am going to request to be put into the class that is going to double up in English and American History that will take the Regents exams in January. I am asking for this because I want to enlist in January. If I am not able to do this I will quit and enlist this month no matter what anyone says as I am getting damn sick of seeing all the fellows go one by one and my having to remain home.
 Bill Savage is engaged to be married as you must already be aware of. He finally appears to have settled down at last. A new issue of the "Dyre Avenue News" will be coming out in about a week and a half so be expecting to see one in the very near future.

Pete Thomas is after Barbara again.[74] *I saw him tonight and there he was hanging around her. I told her what I thought of her (which I was glad to get off my chest) and went home feeling quite happy about the whole thing.*

The Junior Holy Name won the Bronx C.Y.O. title.[75] *We expect to compete for the City title in the near future. I will write again, probably Saturday, and will do my upmost to correspond with you frequently. Until then I remain,*

Your pal,
Walter"

෨

"Sept. 8, 1943 [Wednesday]

Dear Son John,

This morning (Wednesday 8th) I mailed to you from White Plains Avenue Post Office a large package containing coat hangers, shoe polish set, papers, books and etc. that I thought you would like to have. Also at last the watch went on its way. You know I wanted to send it last Friday but they wouldn't accept it. They wanted it wrapped a certain way on account of the insurance risk. They are very particular when the value of the article is high. So Ritchie Simmons had the jeweler to wrap it for shipment. I am sure you will like it very much when you see it. Don't forget to thank Richard when you write to him. He went down for his blood test last night. His mother told me his father went with him. I told them how you went down for your test like a little soldier, nobody to bolster you up but yourself. And when you came back Muggsie and I sitting in a corner praying during the blackout.[76] When I asked you how you made out you informed me how you answered the Jewish doctor, "It takes the Irish every time".

We are having a triduum[77] down at church, started Monday and ends tonight Wednesday. Given by a Father Sheehan - teacher at Cardinal Hayes

---

[74] Peter ("Pete") Thomas was one of the "gang of five" that comprised John and his best friends. I'm not sure who Barbara was, but it sounds like she must have broken poor Walter Cubita's heart at some point.

[75] The Junior Holy Name Society was comprised of youths of the Parish. C.Y.O. stands for Catholic Youth Organization. Apparently the Parish had a damned good softball team.

[76] Blackouts were not an uncommon event in New York during the war. The expectation of a German attack was continuously on the mind s of New Yorkers, though it never materialized.

[77] A *triduum* is a three day sequence of religious observances preceding a major feast, such as the Christian devotions from Holy Thursday, through Good Friday and Holy Saturday, preceding the feast of Easter.

high school. He is a fine speaker. Does you good to hear him. It is for peace and the boys in service. And the church is crowded every night.

Well John we attended Robert Mahon's party but it was more like a wake than a party. What I mean is there were no girls. I believe the boys were told not to bring them and that little Joe was worrying about them leaving early. No refreshments, only beer and soda. Ritchie was hurt about it. He said the best party they ever had was McGowans. We treated them so good. Your father said, "Oh! There's a bunch of old maids down there!"

We might all faint at your sudden appearance. Poor Muggsie I am afraid would be tearing your clothes off with welcome. In regard to the test you speak of Dad never mentioned a word to me about it and refuses to do so. I only hope he doesn't reveal it to anyone else. Well John whatever it is all about I only hope you will be successful if it is for your welfare. And while I am on the subject John it would make me feel happy if you would tell me in one of your future letters that you got to confession and offer it up that God may give the wisdom and courage that you need in your activities and for your spiritual and temporal welfare. If it means a little sacrifice or inconvenience for you to do so offer it up as a penance and remember to pray to the Blessed Mother. Did you ever meet the Catholic chaplain there? Remember John all the boys there are not Catholics but you can be an example of what it means to be a Catholic. Don't think I am preaching a sermon to you John but if it wasn't for our faith and prayer many of us wouldn't pull through any trials or troubles.

Tuesday morning I received a lot of mail. By the way a card was among it from St. Michael's School to call for your diploma. Martin Moynihan told Mom the brother said he heard from you and that we shouldn't worry, that you John could very well take care of yourself. You would get along any place because you never worried. Mom said that brother didn't know John very well or he wouldn't say that he never worried. Of course he was referring to killing yourself over books. Another letter arrived too in a large envelope from the chaplain at Fort Knox containing a letter to tell me how you were now a soldier stationed down there and all about how you were taken care of and how to contact you if need be and if he could be of any help to us at any time we should get in touch with him. Altogether it was a very nice form of a letter and a very good idea. It was signed "W. V. Goldie". Is he a rabbi? That is a Jewish name?

Your father and I are invited to attend ceremonies tomorrow night at Grace Baptist Church[78] The air wardens[79] are having your name put on a special honor roll with others who are in service. Mr. Weber[80] sent us a letter. I will tell you more later. Robbie Mahon is at Great Lakes Naval station. Do you remember your lady school teacher friend from Edling's? She told your father her son is an officer down with you and she was going to have him look you up. So get ready to salute.

How is your money holding out? Did they ever ask you about dependents? I will close now John. Keep writing every day. Did you receive Mom's letter? Came by airmail.

Love,
Mother

P.S. *Duke is still in the paper business and is gone out with a big pack today. He said to tell you the tomatoes are only beginning to open in your garden but he had quite a few from his plants and he also had more string beans. Send Duke a dollar when you can afford it. Dick Mooney is going to write to you. Frank is going to write too and half a dozen more. So you should get mail. Answer Sonny's[81] letter. Did you receive letters from Mom and I mailed last Friday 3rd by airmail. It takes exactly two days for your letter to come here. If you mail it on Sunday 5th, I received one today Wednesday 8th.*
Write a card to Mrs. Mary McGowan, 2132 Edenwald Avenue, Bronx, N.Y. John did you do anything for your sore lips. Did you write to Margaret? Mr. Gold was asking for you and your friend Mrs. Ray."

∽

"Fort Knox, Kentucky

Sept. 10, 1943 [Friday]

Dear Mother and Dad,

  I received the letter you both wrote and I was very glad to hear from Dad. I am sorry I did not write yesterday but I did not have a chance. I am lucky I have a minute to write tonight because we are scrubbing and fixing up for Saturday inspection. I made Marksman on the rifle and I will get a rifle

---

[78] Grace Baptist Church was a neighborhood church on Dyre Avenue on the way to the City Line and neighboring Mount Vernon, New York.

[79] Air wardens were civilians tasked with coordinating neighborhood responses to blackouts and air raids. Prior to joining the service, John was one of them for Edenwald.

[80] Mr. Weber was apparently the head of the local group of air raid wardens.

[81] Sonny Lucas, John's first cousin.

medal for it. I am glad you liked the pillow case that I sent home. Tell Dad that as soon as I get payed I will send him and Duke something. Boy am I going down on money. It seems that I spend more than I get. I am expecting to get payed soon, I hope. Yesterday I learned all about booby traps and how they worked. The team I was on was the best because the other teams couldn't find our trap but blew it up and if there was power in it they would have been killed. But we found the other team's trap and disconnected it. Well I am fine. I have K.P. tomorrow and I don't think I will go to Louisville this weekend. We saw English war films today. They were very interesting. I think I have told you everything. Mother, when did you mail that watch? I did not receive it as yet. I also want to know about those hangers I asked you to send me. Love to all.

Love,
Son John

P.S. Write soon. Tell Dad to write too, and be good."

"Sept. 10, 1943 [Friday]

Dear John,

This is Friday night. Dad and Muggsie are tucked away in bed, both snoring out loud. I have just finished reading all the newspapers. The "Thanks to the Yanks"[82] *program is on the radio so I thought while I was listening I would write a few lines to you.*

We have had a very busy week rushing to church every night making the triduum. Last night we attended a very nice affair, dedicated to all the air wardens, you included. Mr. Weber sent us a letter inviting us to attend. So we went down to be present. When we arrived Mr. Weber had us ushered up to the front seats. There were eight names called and as each was mentioned their relatives present had to go on the platform and take a bow and stand there while a song was sung by all. When you name was called Dad told me to go up but he was also told to take a bow and there was great applause when they mentioned your name. I am enclosing the write-up in the paper so you can read it.

Jackie Walsh and Ritchie Simmons were up here the other night and had tea with us. Ritchie had his blood test last Tuesday. He thinks he may be inducted soon. Jackie Walsh let me read a letter his cousin sent him. You know he is training for a paratrooper. Well from what he writes believe me I think he is going through some training. Robert Mahon is stationed at Great

---

[82] "Thanks to the Yanks" was a popular comedy quiz show on CBS radio hosted by Bob Hawk. It ran from 1943 to 1945.

Lakes.[83] His mother seems to feel very bad about his going. Don't mention this news if you should write to them. Willie[84] was supposed to be married last Saturday the 4th, had all arrangements made to come home and suddenly his leave was cancelled. So I imagine his mother was against him getting married during wartimes and with all I guess she is all upset. It was she who told me about Willie when I was down at the party.

Helen Butler told me they expect George home in October. Jackie Walsh invited your father and me down Saturday, tomorrow night to his house. They are giving a surprise party for his parents 25th wedding anniversary. That means silver, so I bought a nice silver salad fork for them.

Well John the letter you wrote on Monday 6th arrived yesterday Thursday and Tuesday 7th arrived today, Friday, so you see there are just two days in between. In regard to that test you mentioned John, Dad explained to me what he understood about it. I don't like to ask you any secrets but it won't harm your body or health, after all they are responsible for any reaction. Did you have to sign to undergo all this? If it proves successful and is going to help our boys in any way I have no objection at all. I only admire your courage for doing it and pray it proves harmless to you. Let me know, if it is possible, how you are progressing and if it proves successful.

Did you get to Mammoth Caves? You didn't tell us how you made out on the rifle range. Dad was interested in that part. But from what you said I guess you were mighty tired. John I am going to send a pair of slippers to you as soon as possible as I want you to take care of your feet. Change your socks. If you need more let me know. Cut your toenails too. Put a little talcum powder on them. It is very refreshing. I won't forget the cake, either. If there is anything else you want badly, let me know. I do hope you get the wrist watch and the package. I sent them September 8th.

John you speak of a 3 day furlough. Would you be able to travel home and back again in that length of time? You would spend all your time traveling and have no time for home. Of course don't think I am not anxious to have you if it was only to say, "Welcome home John." It thrills me to think of you coming home. Do whatever you think is best. Mrs. Springer sends her

---

[83] Great Lakes Naval Station in Illinois is the largest naval training station in the United States, a task it has performed since its opening in 1910. On December 7, 1941, Pearl Harbor was attacked by Japan, and around 6,000 sailors were training at Great Lakes. This grew to 68,000 in six months; by September 1942, over 100,000 sailors were training at Great Lakes. The base grew to 1,600 acres in the next 10 months. By mid-1943, there were over 700 instructors at the Class A service schools. Four million served on active duty in the Navy during World War II. Over one million sailors were trained at Great Lakes.

[84] Not sure who "Willie" was, but the war certainly got in the way of his wedding plans.

regards. Her son is studying to be a pharmacist's mate. It is almost 11 o'clock. Time for tea. Write John. We all wait to hear your news. Remembrance and love from all.

Mother"

৸

"Fort Knox, Kentucky

Sept. 12, 1943 [Sunday]

Dear Mother,
 I received Communion this morning at the seven o'clock Mass. This morning I sat down and wrote letters to Father Broderick, Dick Simmons, Walter Cubita and Peter Thomas.[85] We had a good meal for dinner today. There isn't much to do today so I'll go to the movies. The watch keeps time very good. How is Dad behaving? Tell him to stay on the ball as they say down here. There is not much to write to you about because everything is nice and quiet down here. I am writing this letter while I am laying on my bed. Most of the fellows are writing letters or reading the papers. Well that's about all for today. Love to all.

Love,
Son John"

৸

Another letter from John's father, Ed. It is clear how much he misses his only son and child.

"Sept. 12, 1943 [Sunday]

Dear John,
 I am writing you this letter to let you know we are all well. Did you receive your box and watch yet? We went to Jack Walsh's house Saturday night and we did not get home until about 3:00 o'clock in the morning. They were married 25 years. How are you getting along? I was off today, Sunday. Mary Anne was down today and all the children. Rose Mary was to stay a week but when she saw her father go home she had to go home. All the fellows was asking for you John. When you get your leave ask if you can get home on Saturday so we will have a party for you. You can let us know. So I will be closing my letter hoping to hear from you.

---

[85] Richard Simmons, Walter Cubita and Peter Thomas were all boyhood friends of John's. Their names come up again and again throughout these letters, charting their progress and eventual lives in the military.

Love from Dad and Anna"

The postscript is Anna's addition.

"P.S. John, did your money hold out? Dad insisted on me writing a few lines. Well, Muggsie is lying on the divan watching Dad writing. Do you remember how she kept guard over him? It is very cool here now, you could almost wear a winter coat. We went to Walsh's party last night and had a very good time. Tonight we were playing cards when the bell rang and who came to call but a young fellow who was on the retreat with. He is from Mount Vernon. His name is Avallone. He is going to write to you. Tells me he would like to go on another retreat. Said it was the most pleasant experience he ever had. Well John, I will close now. Dad is doing fine again. The kettle is boiling for tea (10:30 PM). Will write more.

Love,
Mother"

⁂

"Sept. 15, 1943 [Wednesday]

Dear Son John,

This is Wednesday evening. Dad and I decided we would both write to you. So I am getting my lines written first while Dad is reading the papers.

I am very glad that you received the watch and that you like it so much, and I am very well pleased that you get to confession and communion because that is what counts and will strengthen you in many ways. Receive Communion as often as you can and remember Dad and me in your prayers.

We received your letters written Saturday 11th on Tuesday and the letters written Sunday 12th on Wednesday 15th which is today. Dad liked that letter especially that you sent to him. You know John your letters coming home every day got to mean as much to us as eating our breakfast. What I mean is Duke, Mom and I all watch for the mailman and the first thing your father looks for at night is your letter. I can be pouring water in his tea and he don't even notice. So keep writing. It is good for home morale and Dad too.

Tuesday night I was down to a church meeting the purpose of which is to get together and arrange to send a Christmas package to each boy of the parish who is in service. So I am in the committee to help and believe me John they will be as nice a Christmas surprise as any boy would like to receive. That makes me think to tell you Father Broderick is teaching and will only be here on weekends. When you get a chance write a card to Father Foley and O'Hara. They both ask for you all the time. I understand Father O'Hara knows all about Ft. Knox. He was stationed down there somewhere. Mrs. Savage took your address. She is going to send it to her son. She told me he is ready to go overseas. Johnny Conniff is gone over. I think Richard Simmons is going into service soon. Peter was here tonight, told me he received a letter from you. He is going to hold his job until he is called.

I was surprised to hear Walter Cubita wanted to enlist. We feel very proud of you getting the medal John. When Duke heard it he said, "Indeed when this war is over and that fellow comes home with all his medals and meets all the big shots up the hill, the gas will fly so strong Edenwald will blow up!" Frankie said, "Duke, I bet John's medal is for dancing instead of shooting." Duke's reply was, "By George, I wouldn't be surprised."

Mom and I were down to Mrs. McGovern's for lunch today. We were treated royal. Father McGovern was there. He was asking for you. I saw the card you sent to them. That was some picture on it. Next time send or look for a nicer one. Not that they didn't appreciate it. Mrs. McGovern said the bull meant an Englishman. You are going to hear from them. Jo's husband seems to be a very nice fellow from his picture. He is now on some ship at sea.

All the children are back to school again. I think Tommy Hickey is attending St. Michael's. Martin Moynihan expects to graduate in January and enter Manhattan College to take up mechanical engineering. I didn't know he was interested in that subject. Mom gave me this information. Helen's boyfriend passed his exams for meteorologist. His people bought a house on North 7th Street in Mt. Vernon.

Well John I hope you have received your hangers. That box I mailed last Wednesday 8th with the watch. Did you laugh when you saw the little dictionary? I thought it might come in handy.

John, I don't want to ask questions about military secrets but I would like to know how you are getting on with the test you told me about. Give me a little information if you can. I am anxious to know about your reaction. Did you go to Mammoth Caves? I hope you received your pay by this time. Do you have to pay for a bond every month? People have asked me if you put in for the allowance for another. The reason I ask you these questions are you did not explain anything about it. As far as I am concerned John, the little money you get is yours to do with what you think best. I know you have good judgment. So be a good boy and write often. Love and regards from all.

Mother

P.S. It is now 12 midnight. Time for bed. Dad is snoring."

And the letter from his father, tucked in alongside.

"Sept, 15, 1943 [Wednesday]

Dear John,

I received your letter and was glad to hear from you John. Did you receive the box we sent you? I was drawn to the Holy Name meeting Monday night and I got in a card game with the fellows. I won $1.00 off of them. They were all asking for you. Sgt. Schultz is still buying water for the tea. I still keep my eye on her on the tea pot. Muggsie is still getting her 1 pound of meat every night. I owe Mr. Edbling so many Red Stamps he is going to get the OPA after me. We will send you another box soon so if there is anything you want us to send, let us know. Write soon. Love from all.

Dad"

℘

John heard from neighborhood friends also. This letter is from his friend Richard Simmons, written on letterhead from Saks Fifth Avenue, where he holds a position in retail.

"Richard Simmons
3714 Secor Avenue
Bronx 66
New York, N.Y.

Sept. 15, 1943 [Wednesday]

Hi John,

I received your letter this morning and I suppose you are wondering why I haven't wrote to you sooner. Well I'm sorry but the other day I cut my finger right down by the nail and it was a pretty deep cut. So for the last couple of days I haven't been able to write. It is the finger next to my thumb on my right hand.

How do you like the watch? It is a beauty, isn't it? I have one just like yours. Mine keeps perfect time. I bet yours does too. I wear it to bed and wash with it on.

Last Saturday was Mr. and Mrs. Walsh's twenty-fifth wedding anniversary and Jack and his sisters threw them a surprise party Saturday night. Gerard[86] and I were the only ones, and Red,[87] I forgot him, invited. But Red had a date that night. Well we had a swell time. I got home five minutes to four the following morning. They had a whole half of a keg of beer and a couple bottles of whiskey. When I first went in Mr. Walsh handed me a stiff highball. Boy was it a baby! After that I had five beers all night long. After the fourth I felt kind of sick. I had another one anyway. And I wasn't supposed

---

[86] Gerard Diemer.
[87] Harry ("Red") Gibbons.

to eat or drink after one o'clock because I was supposed to receive with the Holy Name Society Sunday morning. But all the Walshes and myself went to 11:30 Mass.

Well we played Manhattan Sunday afternoon and boy did we get beat. The final score was twenty five to nothing. We got one hit. And Murphy got that hit. You know Daniel Murphy.[88] But I think we will get credit for the game. We will get credit for the victory. You see, they have a semi-pro center fielder. And so the game went under protest. Mr. Ford says that he is almost sure that we will get credit for the game and we will then get the trophy. But I hope the protest is granted to us.

Well Father Broderick left us. But he is coming back every weekend. The reason for that is because they can't get any priest to take his place. But he will be with us every weekend. I helped him move from Nativity Parish house to Cardinal Hayes.[89] Boy what junk he had. We put it all in Father Foley's car and took it down to Cardinal Hayes. Boy was it nice in Father's new room down there. His own telephone, his own bath, elevator right down the corridor. He is going to teach ancient history. That is one subject that I hate.

The Junior Holy Name Society is breaking up because we haven't a priest to take over. I think, as a matter of fact I'm almost sure, that with the money in the treasury, we are going to buy him a traveling bag. I think I am going to get it down my place. I got a thirty percent discount.

We, that is, Jack Walsh and I, went to the Senior Holy Name Society meeting last Monday night. We played cards. Your father was playing with us. I won a nickel. Jack lost a quarter. I don't know how your father made out. I think he won. The Holy Name Society is going to hold another outing. It is going to be held the second week in October. Our softball team is going to play the Senior Holy Name Society team. We will make up for the last time. Well so long for now. Write soon.

Your pal,
Dick"

℘

"Fort Knox, Kentucky

---

[88] Daniel Murphy was obviously quite an athlete. Not sure if Manhattan is the college, or a high school. The sport is baseball, with talk of a semi-pro center fielder.

[89] Cardinal Hayes High School was, and still is, at 650 Grand Concourse in the Bronx. Dedicated in 1941, it quickly became an arch rival to Mt. St. Michael Academy, from which John graduated. An intense football rivalry continues to this day, with the annual Mount-Hayes Game played every Thanksgiving.

Sept. 17, 1943 [Friday]

Dear Mother,
    Sorry I did not write last night but I did not have a chance. Tonight I am going over to our company dance. I ought to have a good time. Today I led a patrol in scouting and reconnaissance. I was the leader. I think I will go to Louisville Saturday and come back and go down to the Mammoth Caves Sunday. Please excuse writing because I am doing this in a rush. I received the letter that you and Dad wrote Wednesday. There is not much more to tell you. Love to all.

Love,
Son John

P.S. Tell Dad I like to hear from him and tell him to keep on writing because I know he is all right."

∽

"*Sept. 19, 1943 [Sunday]*

Dear John,
    This is Sunday night and as usual we are reading and listening to the radio. Muggsie is lying on the floor, giving herself a lick here and there. All we have to do is call your name and she picks up her ears.
    Today I had a talk with Father Broderick. He told me how he had received your letter and that you told him all kinds of things. You know how he kids everybody. He said you will be able to drive all kinds of vehicles when you get back and I will be coming to church on a tank. He looks fine. He really is a very wonderful priest. Everybody is very fond of him.
    Did you get a letter from Sr. Mary Albert? She told Frank she wrote. I had a card from Uncle George. He was on vacation with John in Connecticut. Did you hear from Uncle John in Newark?[90] Mrs. Dixon came to visit the other day. She is working in an airplane factory in Connecticut. Wanted to know if I wanted a good job she could get me in up there. It is too far away. Have to keep my eye on Dad. Mrs. Dixon expects to sell her house. I met Andy's[91] brother today. Did you hear that Andy was in the army stationed at Fort McClellan?[92] He is going to give me Andy's address for you

---

[90] Uncle John in Newark probably refers to one of Anna McGowan's brothers, John Lynch. Uncle George may refer to another brother.
[91] Andy may be Andrew Garbarini. If so, the reference to his brother is Victor Garbarini.
[92] Fort McClellan, originally Camp McClellan, was a United States Army post located adjacent to the city of Anniston, Alabama, established as Camp Shipp in 1898.

so you can get in touch with him. Ritchie Simmons is in IQ waiting for his call. Walter Cubita is working in the Safeway but from what I can see he is entertaining the customers instead of working. Buddy Mooney wrote home the other day and complained he never received one letter since he went out. They (his family) claim that a letter is sent to him every day. The Company said he couldn't be located. You know he is on an Army Transport now. Walter McGowan wrote home. He is somewhere off California. Getting along O.K. I had a card from Tom Lucas. He was home on a furlough. Said David and John were doing fine. He has been transferred to the Signalman's Service School. I must get a letter off to him. He asked for you and wants your address. Did you write a card to Catherine and Roberta? Roberta said she was going to write to you. They expect George home on furlough in October. You know, this is his first leave since he went away. Helen Butler tells me she is going to give him a big party, so as soon as we see the cleaning started, that will be our cue George is arriving. Remember Helen sweeping the walks? She is a good-hearted person. She sent me over a nice picture of you that was taken in the spring - Robbie Mahon, Catherine, Roberta and you. It is a dandy picture of you all. Mr. Lang wants to be remembered to you.

  Well John I think I have given you all the outside news I can think of now so we will get down to our own family circle. Your letters arrived Saturday morning. Dad was off so we all gathered in the kitchen to read them. What a surprise I got when that new ten dollar bill flew out. It was very fine of you John to send that. I am going to save it and will invest it as you request. But I was thinking you had $13 left and then as you said you were going to remember everybody. I am afraid you will be running short of funds. Do they take $18.75 out of your pay every month? It's really a good idea because that is saving. You know you won't get paid for another month so you will have to hold tight to your money but in the meantime I will send you a few dollars if possible because I wouldn't want to feel that you are without any funds.

  Did you go to Mammoth Caves? I suppose if you did go that it was some experience and you must have seen interesting sights there. Your tomatoes John are just ripening. They are rather late but I must say they are really fine specimens. Duke takes great pride in showing them off. He is now upstairs listening to the Good Will Court[93] as usual. Mom and he painted the bathroom. Mary Ann was here today. She doesn't like school very much because she said, "You can't talk with the old teacher." She fell in love with your St. Michael's hat. Wants to wear it all the time. Rose Mary tells me she is going to school after one more birthday. They are all waiting to see you

---

During World War II, it was one of the largest U.S. Army installations, training an estimated half-million troops. It closed in 1999.

[93] The Good Will Court was a popular radio program that provided legal advice to lay people over the air, much to the chagrin of the legal community.

dressed up as a soldier. I am afraid you are going to be on exhibition. Dad is trying to get the phone. We are getting a box packed to send off to you. Let us know if there is anything special you want. Write.

Love from all.
Mother

P.S. You could wear an overcoat here for the past two days."

֍

This note, half-written, is from John's father Ed.

"Sept. 19, 1943 [Sunday]

Dear John,
    We received the 2 letters and was glad to hear from you and the 10 dollars. George Kelly that friend in Edling house was asking for you. I had to work this Sunday. We are going to send you a box. All the fellows was asking for you."

The second half is finished by Anna.

    "Your father wrote this John with one eye open and the other shut. So I have to put the finishing touches to it. I have to pour the tea John. Do you get any oranges down there? Remember us in your prayers. Love from Mother and Dad."

֍

"Sept. 20, 1943 [Monday]

Dear John,
    Your box arrived Saturday afternoon. Frank's family happened to be here at the time. Mary Ann and I had just gotten into the house from shopping on Dyre Avenue when the bell rang. Before I could reach the door Mary Ann was taking the box from the mailman and yelling, "A box from John!" Well finally I managed to get it opened with all the children trying to help me. I hardly had a glance at the picture when Mary Ann had it rushing upstairs to Mom. Duke and Dad were both delighted with the gifts. Don't forget to remember Mom as soon as possible. The Duke has the pictures you sent out to everybody that stops at the gate.
    The pictures were very nice John, but you held such a serious look on your face. Next time put your winning smile on. I would like that better. Did I tell you that they are going to erect a new honor roll at Seton Avenue for all the Edenwald boys in service? So your name will be inscribed on another roll.

Last night Andy's brother stopped here and gave me his address at Fort McClellan. I am enclosing it. Write him a few lines. He also took your address. Tells me that Andy told him in a letter, all he does all day is put a gun together and take it apart. Mt. St. Michael had their first football game today against St. Agnes. Later I will send you the write up and results.

I met Joey Roda's mother and she told me Joey is gone away down to Georgetown to start his study for the priest hood.[94] She is rather shaky about it all. Told me she tried to discourage him at first because he needed so much money and clothes to go with but somehow out of a clear blue sky the money came into them out of unexpected sources. So you see as she said, God is good. Many people told her she was foolish to let him go but he was so anxious she couldn't do anything with him. Then when the money came, she thought maybe it is God's will that he should go. I heard they are giving him medicine for his glands to see if it helps his growth. Poor little fellow. I hope he succeeds. His mother took your address down to send Joey so you will be hearing from him.

After Mass today Mrs. Faurenback from Rombouts Avenue called me over to meet her son Robert. You know him. He is a pilot now, a Lieutenant. He is a fine looking soldier John, and such a nice boy. He is ferrying planes now, I think. They were asking for you. By the way the oldest Gleason fellow is going to be married next Saturday morning over at St. Francis of Rome.

I meet so many people John who ask me about you that I forget the half of them. What I want to tell you is I went to 10:30 Mass. Dad tells me I go with the Society people now. When I got back home Mr. Janisch was here talking with Duke. Of course he wanted to hear all about you. From what he tells me he was with the French forces during the World War and he seems to know a lot about tanks and as usual Duke brought out your pictures. He thought you looked fine. Was giving you great praise, said he thought you were a boy with character and that you would succeed. He would like to hear from you so write a few lines to him. By the way John did you know that you returned the pictures and some addresses I sent to you in those letters?

I read Sister Mary Albert's letter. It was very nice. Write to her once in a while. Send a card to her mother. Dad thinks George is on one of the new invasion boats. They didn't hear from him in some time.

Buddy Butler is painting his house instead of playing ball. Tommy Hickey and Charlie Yost are both attending St. Michael's Academy, so I am told. John would you want me to get your diploma or would you rather get it yourself? No doubt you will want to pay them a visit when you get home.

---

[94] The Roda family were well known. As reported in the *Dyre Avenue News,* in its August 1943 issue, "Joe Roda, Sr. put up at the Veteran's Hospital...for treatment to his back. They tell us that Joe ran the place during his stay. He is back home and on the job again." *DAN,* Vol. 1, No. 3, August 1943.

I have my stamp book filled so I am ready to "Back the Attack" with another bond. We got Hickey's news report. Your name is mentioned in it. Told Dad he would send it to you. We have so many tomatoes now John we could sell them. Duke is busy taking the screens down and painting the windows. Mrs. Windell's mother gave Duke a big bottle of beer. So tonight he had Dad open it. It almost exploded when the cap was taken off and Mom said, "Mrs. Carroll must have put coaxloram[95] in it," whatever that is. Duke looked at it and said, "By George, there must be dynamite in that bottle!" It struck us all so funny I am laughing yet about it. It is very cool here, in fact yesterday Duke put the heat on and believe me it felt good. Mom said, "That is the reason the tenants are giving Duke a bottle, they want him to put it up to 250!"

I haven't heard from Aunt Kitty in some time. Of course I owe her a letter. If I can get away for a few days maybe I will pay her a visit, get all the news. Next week I intend treating myself to new shoes and etc. I keep saying this every week but mean it this time. John do you need a sweater and if so what kind?

It is getting rather late so I will close John. Take good care of yourself. Hope you got to Mass today. What did you do with your time over the weekend? Try to get to Confession and Communion as often as you can. It will strengthen you a great deal. Remember Dad and me in your prayers. I think John from what your friends tell me that you kind of influence them for good behavior. So maybe your example of being a good Catholic down where you are may be the means of helping some other boy and yourself too. Actions speak louder than words.

Well John I will say good night and God bless you. Muggsie is scratching like a good fellow. She will have to get that annual bath soon. Love and regards from all.

Mother"

℘

"Sept. 21, 1943 [Tuesday]

Dear John,

As I write this letter Dad is packing a box for you and if you were here I am sure you would have a good laugh watching Mugs. She is about in the box, smelling everything. I told her that is for John and the way she looks at us and wags her tail, as if she knew what we say and she herself would tell you if it were possible for her to do so that she didn't get that annual bath yet although Dad gave her some sort of a massage with powder and a brush and she never stopped scratching herself since. Duke has the front gates down

---

[95] Some sort of ingredient a home brewer would have put in their product.

painting them and he is having a terrible time between watching the children getting at the paint and keeping Mugs home.

Do you remember Mom complaining all the time about her hearing? Well, she visited the doctor last week and the trouble was she had an ear full of hard wax that came out. The doctor was asking about you. Mom said to tell you to write him a card. She imagines he would appreciate hearing from you. I will send you his address. By the way, you should hear Duke's comments on Mom's hearing. He said, "Indeed she could hear well enough without getting her ears cleaned." I told him the doctor gave Mom medicine so she could sleep. He said, "By George, when I see the doctor I will tell him it is me that should get the medicine so that woman won't keep me awake all night with her snoring." Do you remember John all the good laughs we had together with Mom and Duke? He still visits up the hill to see if Johnnie is still settling the cases. Don't forget to send him a little remembrance.

Last Friday night 17th Dad had a card party here - Frankie and the men from his office. It was a very nice party. Dad won a little money. They were all asking for you. Yesterday (Monday 20th) we received a letter from you which was written on Friday 17th. How was the Company dance? I hope you didn't overdo it. I take it you were in a great rush. Dad said he bet there was some excitement, everybody getting dolled up. How about the scouting party? Did you make a satisfactory leader? Dad said you must be picked out for that. Your armored news arrived today. Of course we both read it. There was an article in it telling about boys being picked out for lance corporals and sergeants. We thought maybe you had a chance for that leadership. Your father was very much interested in the story of the 15 year old boy. He must have been a clever kid. Mrs. Windell's brother was home on furlough from Camp Campbell, Kentucky. He is a technician (college graduate). He told them if he gets a chance to visit Fort Knox, he would look you up. His name is Carroll.

Martin Moynihan insists on buying a second-hand car some fellow wants to sell and Mom tells me he threatens to enlist if his mother doesn't consent. Helen's boyfriend John Allen was studying to be a meteorologist if you recall. Well, after all his studying and passing the tests he and the other fellows are all put into some other service for overseas duty. Told they were needed there, and that was all there was to it. I guess he is very much disappointed. Mrs. Mooney tells me that is liable to happen in any college where Dick is too. She said from what Dick tells her the exercises they go through for combat that it is a wonder all their bones aren't broken. They are rushing them through their course.

The Bernabe's have not returned yet. Did you send them a card? Are you falling down on your mail? Edenwald people are erecting a roll of honor up on Seton Avenue so your name will be inscribed on it. Did you meet Johnnie

Murray again? How were the mammoth caves? Tell us something about that visit. Is your test still on? I received the encyclopedia you ordered. It is a very fine book. They sent a letter along saying there are nineteen volumes costing 89 cents and 11 cents for mailing which means $1.00 for each volume. Considering John that these volumes may be closed on a book shelf most of the time, perhaps I won't take them all. Unless you want me to. Write a few lines to Sonny Lucas and tell him I want him to write to me and give me his address and rank. I have some pictures to send to him. Did you hear from Sgt. J. Lynch? Enclosing article for you to read. Maybe you know officer. Do you want a sweater? Be good and say your prayers. Love from everybody.
Mother and Dad"

"Sept. 23, 1943 [Thursday]

Dear Mother,
    Today we went to the machine gun range. It was pretty muddy out there. Tonight I am on my first guard duty. It isn't bad because after we come off we get sandwiches to eat. I was surprised to hear that Andy[96] is in Texas. Do you know what branch of the army he is in? I just received a letter from you and I did not read it yet because I thought I would write you before the lights went out. That's about all for now.
Love,
Son John"

"Sept. 24, 1943 [Friday]

Dear Son John,
    This is Friday night. Dad said, "Let us write to John," but before he got started he was asleep. So he will have to do his writing later. Somehow or other I think that visit he made down with you did him good. He has been doing fine since (Thank God) home on Thursday night right on time and no drink. Just say a prayer for him once in a while John and I don't think there will be anything to worry about.
    Well John I suppose your visit to the Mammoth Caves was very interesting. I am glad you got a chance to visit there as sightseeing like that adds to your education in a great way. I was sorry you didn't get to Mass but couldn't arrangement have been made beforehand? The next time anything comes up like that, you and the other Catholic boys should get in touch with the Chaplain and explain to him. Perhaps he could arrange to have you attend

---

[96] Perhaps Andy Garbarini.

Mass either earlier in morning or late in the afternoon. I hope you won't have to miss Mass again. Say a few extra prayers.

From what you tell me I think you boys are having a mighty good time over the weekends, high class nightclubs and everything. Enjoy yourself John but don't overdo it because your training requires a clear alert mind and body. Get plenty of rest and sleep, eat nourishing food, [and] take care of your body, especially your feet. That is important. Change your socks every day. If you need more socks let me know. How is your underwear? Would you like me to send any, now that the weather is getting cooler? Dress warmer. Do you think you need a sweater? If so I want you to write a list and let me know. I hope you got the box we sent O.K. and that you like the slippers. They are supposed to be the regular rest shoe for the boys in service. Did you laugh when you saw all the boxes of crackers? You can feed all the army. Dad put them all in along with his funny sheets.

From what you tell me about all the medals you are going to receive, I will expect to see John J. Pershing coming home to me. You should hear Duke when he heard you were going to get another medal. "That's the McGowans all right. Smart people."

Dad said you are supposed to get more money when you are an expert marksman, but I doubt that. I never heard of anybody getting it. By the way John it will be dandy if you get paid 1st of October. I am thinking you will need some money by that time. You were always good about handling money so I guess you won't need any advice. Hold on to it as tight as you can. It was nice of you to remember Dad and Duke. Don't forget Mom when you can get a little remembrance. And John while I think of it send one of those souvenir folders to the Moynihans. I would like you to remember them they were so thoughtful toward you. Bernabe's didn't come back yet. I guess they are settling the estate. Did you receive a letter from Sister Mary Albert? She said she wrote to you. Let me know. Mrs. Savage told me she wrote to you. Don't forget to answer if she did.

I received a card from Sonny today. I take it he is in the Air Corps, down at Miami Beach, Florida. He said he would write again. Had a letter from you which he expects to answer.

Had a card from Uncle George. He was spending a few days with John in Connecticut. I had a letter from Betty the other day, telling me all about Connecticut and how busy John is kept. They may visit us here later on, perhaps when you are on your furlough.

Walter Cubita didn't go back to school because they refused to let him graduate in January and he is enlisting in the Navy. Did he tell you about it? We have now 275 on the honor list. All the boys will soon be gone. In fact, most of them are gone already.

John you should see Mugs with your father in bed. They are both snoring on the one pillow. I had to laugh about the washing machine. Don't worry John, I am taking it easy, washing very little and sleeping until 10 o'clock in the morning. I am going to take vitamin pills and get fat. Well John it is getting late so I will close. I will write more later. Be good. Love from all.

Mother and Dad"

∽

"Fort Knox, Kentucky

Sept. 25, 1943 [Saturday]

Dear Mother,
    Today is Saturday and is really the first chance I had to write you a good letter. Well Thursday night I had guard duty from 6 to 8 and 12 to 2 in the morning. Friday I went on a 15 mile hike. It took us about 6 hours. Today I had a needle and saw a war film this morning. Last night we were really busy scrubbing and washing up for Saturday's inspection. I received a letter from David Lucas and he told me that he is in Miami Beach Florida and he said that if he passes some tests he will probably go to college for specialized training. I also received a letter from Martin Moynihan in which he told me of his buying a car. I think it is a good idea because if he gets in the army it will help him. Just who wrote me, no one but Mrs. Savage from Dyre Avenue. She said that she was going to give Bill my address so that he might write. She also gave me her address. Well Mother how are things at home? Is it still quiet as before I left? By the way Mother did you get my diploma from the Mount? You wrote and said that they said to pick it up and you did not mention any more about it. I would like you to send my sweater because we have pretty cold days down here. I am still taking the test and it won't be over till November. I won't be able to get a furlough until the test is over. I think they will let us go home over Thanksgiving or Christmas. Mother they were telling us that the Armored Force is the best part of the army and that they get the best men and that the training we get is more than equal to that of the Marines or any other service. How are you and Dad making out? Do you have your little scraps now and then like you used to have? How are Duke and Mom making out? Do they still listen to Mr. Antony's court and the Irish music? This afternoon I think that I will take a good sleep because when I was on guard duty I did not get much. Do the people in the back still go through the yard like they used to do? On October 4 we will begin to wear our winter uniform. It's very nice and very warm. If I do not write every day please excuse me because I do not have the time to write to anybody. The only time I have is on the weekends. By the way Mother do you know that we work 12

hours a day in the army from 5:30 in the morning until 5:30 retreat at night? Tell everybody I was asking for them. Love to all.

*Love,
Son John"*

There was also the occasional "man to man" letter from his father, Edward McGowan, himself a World War I veteran of the fields and trenches of France, and a victim of mustard gas, the effects of which would ultimately claim his life.[97]

"Sept. 26, 1943 [Sunday]

Dear John,
I am writing you this letter to let you know that I am off today, Sunday, so I had time to write you a letter as when I come home at night I have supper and to bed so you know 4:00 AM comes early. We received your box. Your mother did not get out of bed this morning. I went to 7:00 o'clock Mass. I had to make the coffee. I ask her did she like eggs and bacon and she said no. But when she got up goodbye eggs and bacon. Muggsie was in bed and have to have her coffee. All the fellows was asking for you. Did you receive the box we sent you? When your mother make the tea she paid for the water. The tea pot is full up, you only get 1 cup, so I am going to buy a good big pot. So I will be closing this letter hoping to hear from you. So be a good boy.
Dad"

Not to be outdone, though, Anna adds her own postscript:

"P.S. Don't believe everything your father tells you John. It is true though that he cooked the eggs and bacon. Remember how you and I would say we didn't want any until it was on Dad's plate. The family egg. He went to Communion this morning so he was out to seven o'clock Mass. Father Broderick is teaching but he comes back to our church over the weekends.

---

[97] Edward McGowan, as a Private in the U.S. Army from 1916 to 1919, participated in a number of crucial World War I battles following U.S. entry into the war in April 1917, including the Meuse-Argonne. A *New York Times* article on Nov. 10, 2018, commemorating the 100th anniversary of the November 11, 1918 armistice ending the war tells us: "At the Meuse-Argonne American Cemetery in northeastern France, the largest American military graveyard in Europe, 14,246 white headstones mark the burial places of United States First Army soldiers who perished in the final, 47-day campaign that ended with the armistice." Ultimately his son John would be involved in a similar campaign in the final months of World War II.

Your father tells me he had a conversation with him in the confessional last night all about you and Ft. Knox."

⸸

"Fort Knox, Kentucky

Sept. 26, 1943 [Sunday]

Dear Mother,
    I forgot to tell you that these pictures that you sent me were in the envelopes in my package so don't rip them. I went to 9 o'clock mass this Sunday. We have a new chaplain. I think he is a Franciscan because he wears that hat over his head. He was telling us how much they need priests here. He seems to be very nice. This afternoon I went to the movies and saw "Frontier Bad Men." It was a good Wild West picture. Today we had chicken for lunch. It was very good. We call the mess hall Murphy's Bean House. I think it is a good name for it. Tomorrow night I will be unable to write you because I am going on bivouac, or camping out, for the night. I guess it will be cold out there so I am going to wear two suits of winter underwear. We are supposed to get payed Friday of this week. I hope so. Well that's all for now. Love to all.

                                            Love
                                            Son John"

⸸

The next letter is from Father Broderick, who has accepted a position teaching at Cardinal Hayes High School.

"Cardinal Hayes High School
650 Grand Concourse
New York, N.Y.

Sept. 27, 1943 [Monday]

Dear John,
    I received your letter last week. It is good news to learn that you really like the Army. I think your Mother is worried that you will not want to come home, even on furlough.

Perhaps you know I have been transferred to Hayes High. I teach Ancient History to about 210 second year boys. No one from the parish[98] is in my class. Jimmy Juliano[99] now goes to Hayes.

We finally won the City Softball Championship. Our pictures were in The Catholic News last Sunday. We hope to get medals and trophies.

I still go to Nativity on weekends until they get a new priest. I believe Fr. O'Hara will take over the Junior Holy Name. Fr. Foley has the Senior Branch. I hear Cue Ball[100] is about to enter the Navy. You should be glad you are in the Army.

Mike Gleeson[101] is getting married on Saturday. "Veritas"[102] was at the game. I think she misses you.

When you get a chance, drop a line.
Best of luck.

Sincerely,
Fr. Broderick"

"Dick Simmons
3714 Secor Avenue
Bronx 66 N.Y.

---

[98] "The parish" being Nativity of Our Blessed Lady Parish, in the Edenwald section of the Bronx.
[99] Juliano was a well-known Edenwald name. The family owned a store, and did quite well by it.
[100] A nickname that can only refer to Walter Cubita.
[101] The Gleesons were a large clan, and lived at 4021 Duryea Avenue. In 1940 they number Michael Gleeson, 63, his wife Kathleen Gleeson, 52, and their children Michael 31, James, 26, Anthony, 23, William, 20, Daniel, 18, Desmond, 16, and Marianne, 10 years old. All of them, save the two youngest (Desmond and Marianne) were born in Ireland. They must have immigrated sometime between 1922 and 1924, when Ireland was being rocked by a bitter Civil War between the Irish Republican Army and the forces of the Irish Free State. It is interesting to note the different ways in which Ireland is listed as a birthplace throughout these census records. Many people refer to Ireland as "Eire", much preferred by the Republicans, while others use "Irish Free State", perhaps signifying support of those who accepted the partition of Ireland as a necessary evil on the pathway to independence from England. The sympathies of John's grandparents Dennis and Bridget McGowan are left in no doubt. They proudly proclaim Eire as their birthplace, and comment repeatedly throughout these pages on the poor treatment their native land has received from the British.
Mike Gleeson, the oldest, is tying the knot in this reference, at the age of 34.
[102] Who "Veritas" was, though obviously a female, is a mystery.

Sept. 28, 1943 [Tuesday]

Hi John,
    I received your letter this morning and was glad to hear from you. I guess you haven't heard the big news. Walter Cubita has enlisted in the Navy. He leaves in a couple of weeks. Can you imagine Cubita in the Navy? He claims to be tired of hanging around doing nothing. He quit high school too. And he was in his senior year too. What a jerk. Boy, the Navy is sure getting a prize package.
    I'm still waiting for my induction papers. It is almost two weeks ago that I got my card telling me that I was put in 1A. I wonder if I will be gone before Cubita. If they put me in the Army, he will go before me. My father has given me permission to ask for the Coast Guard if I don't get in the Navy.
    Red Gibbons is moving tomorrow. They are going to live out in City Island. What a place to move to. Can you imagine what time he will have to get up in the morning to start for work? His sister is coming back for to live with them. Red is still going strong with Dot. I can't for the life of me see what he sees in her. You know Dot who lives across from me.
    Earl Haug is going into the paratroopers in a couple of weeks. They had a party for him Friday night and it stunk. The only good part was at the end when they played wink. You know how to play wink. Jack W. and myself went stag. We had a pretty good time at the end of the party. It was the only kissing game they played and it lasted for about a half hour. Saturday night a bunch of us went bowling. No, wait, that was Sunday night. Diemer, Ray Ritter and Jackie Walsh and Red was bowling. Freddie Muller, Red's cousin Bob and myself were watching. I still got the bandaid on my finger, so I couldn't bowl. I kept score. After that we went and had ar beets. I don't know how to spell that last word of last sentence. Red was low bowler with 95 and Jack W. was high man with 155. Saturday night Jack and I went to Loews and saw "Best Foot Forward". Didn't like it very much. Jack is taking driving lessons for $15. He is going to take his driving test pretty soon.
    So long,
    Dick Simmons"

℘

This letter, signed "Mom", isn't from John's mother, but rather from his grandmother Bridget (Kenney) McGowan[103], the Duke's wife and Edward McGowan's mother, Anna McGowan's mother-in-law. Her spelling is in

---

[103] Bridget Kenney McGowan, John's grandmother, was born in Ireland. She was one of the multitude of Irish immigrant women who found employment as maids in their adopted country.

some cases classically phonetic, as in use of the word "masarge" for "massage".

"Sept. 29*th*, 1943 [Wednesday]

Dear John,
    I received your letter and was glad to hear from you. Well John the summer is over and it is getting cold. Mary Ann[104] is gone home and back to school at St. Barnabas. She is a terrible chatter box. The teacher had to put her in the corner last week. Did I ever tell you what she done when she was down hear on her vacation? Well her and Ellen Butler[105] got Bobby Walsh on the steps of our front door and started to give him a masarge (sic). One was putting water on his head and the other was rubbing him with a towel. Your mother told me to see what they were doing. I near had a fit for if Mrs. Walsh ever seen him so wet you know what would happen. But he pulled his cap over his hair so it got dried before he went in. They wanted Billy to sit down for to be the next customer and they had little Maryanne for the next day but Frank came that night and took Mary Anne home so there was no more hair dressing done. Pop[106] is painting all the window sills before the storm windows goes up. Your Dad will be off Saturday so your mother has planned to have him clean all the windows. He will have some job. You remember you cleaned them last year. Buddy Butler[107] is painting there house. He is almost through and it looks good. George is to be home Saturday. Some big time. Martin Moynihan is going to graduate in February 1944 and then going to Manhattan College. He is getting a car but has not got it yet. His father went out with him to Long Island to look at the car. There is some delay in getting the Bill of Sale from the owner. Well John we are all well at home and everything is going fine. I have told you all the news that I can think of. Muggsie is just the same. Her and the Duke got to be good pals. Good night John. Be always a good boy.
                                                  Mom"

---

[104] Mary Ann McGowan, her son Frank's eldest child.
[105] Ellen Butler was the 7 year old daughter of Vincent and Helen Butler.
[106] "Pop" is how she refers to her husband, Dennis, when she isn't referring to him as the Duke.
[107] "Buddy" was possibly a nickname for Vincent Butler, Ellen's father. Or maybe an older son, who isn't living with the family at the time of the 1940 census. Or maybe from another Butler family entirely!

"Fort Knox, Kentucky

Sept. 29, 1943 [Wednesday]

Dear Mother,
    I am glad that Dad and Duke liked the things I sent. I will send you and Mom something as soon as I get payed (sic). Mother I am going to get a big color photo of myself taken as soon as I get to Louisville. Mother please explain to everybody who writes to wait a while till I get caught up with my mail. I am lucky I can write to you nevertheless anybody else.
    Today we learned all about street fighting and how to take villages. Mother guess what I am going to the dentist to have some pinpoint cavities filled. I got them after I got into the army. I guess it's from eating too much candy.
    I was reading the Dyre Avenue News and I see that Dr. Cahill[108] has another child. I wonder when he is going to stop. I also see where they put about Walter McGowan getting married.[109] Mother I hope you take those pills to build you up. Boy Mother it sounds good to hear that you got bacon and eggs. Save some till I get home.
    Tomorrow we go out to the machine gun range. I also received letters today from Bill Savage. He told me that he is getting ready to move over the pond.[110] Don't tell his mother. Tom Lucas wrote me too. He wants me to write to him. That's all for today. Good night. Love to all.
                              Love,
                              Son John"

℘

This letter is from John's close friend, Walter Cubita, who also is mentioned many times throughout. He lived at "32 Mill Lane, Bronx 66, New York", according to the return address on the envelope. This is no doubt Reed's Mill Lane, an old colonial route from the village of Eastchester through the salt

---

[108] Dr. Cahill, the father, created a generation of health care professionals in his wake. At least two sons, John and Kevin, followed in his footsteps. Dr. John Cahill tended to the medical needs of the entire neighborhood from his office on the corner of Strang and Seton Avenues. Dr. Kevin Cahill became an expert on tropical diseases, and served at one point as Governor Hugh Carey's personal physician.
[109] Walter McGowan, John's father's first cousin, was a sailor in the U.S. Navy. He had recently married Georgianna Claire Hamilton, from neighboring Pelham, New York.
[110] "Over the pond" refers to going overseas to England, the pond, of course, being the Atlantic Ocean.

marshes to Reed's Mill, a tidal grist mill from the 1600's that survived until the early 1900's, when it was destroyed in a hurricane.

"Wednesday, Sept. 29, 1943

Dear John,
I received your letter Monday but did not have a chance to response to it until this evening. Before I go any further I am going to tell you something that will shock you, that is if you have not already heard of it. I joined the navy last week and am awaiting my leaving notice. I will write to you when I receive it. I hope that you do not disapprove as I just wanted to get into this war and that was the only way that I could do it.
This evening we are having a Junior Holy Name meeting and I am going to resign my office as secretary-treasurer. Dick tells me that he expects his papers any day now so I calculate that we will both leave around the same time. The neighborhood is getting quieter every day. I sure will be glad when I leave also.
Joe Mansfield was home for a few days last weekend and he looks better than ever. We had a good Irish party the Sunday night before he left (a real Irish party). I cannot think of much more to write at the present time so I will close hoping to hear from you soon.

As ever your friend,
Walter"

FOUR: "A WALK IN THE PARK"

"Oct. 2, 1943 [Saturday]

Dear John,
 I have just returned from church. We are having the recitation of the rosary every night during the month of October for the boys' welfare and peace. Today the Holy Name men had their picnic over in the park. Duke and Dad and Frankie attended. They all seem to have had a good time. Beer and Frankfurters only cost $1.00. The married men and single fellows played ball. Father Broderick was there. They are having a party for Walter Cubita tonight up in Peter's house. I think it is a shame for him to leave school. If I was his mother I would have put my foot down and he would return to school to finish. Mrs. Mahon told me he was the one who found so great a fault with them for letting Bobby enlist. What surprises me greatly is that his father consented to let him do this. Well even though in my opinion he is a very foolish boy I wish him luck. I will try to remember him with a little gift later.
 Judging from your letters John and all your training I am sure you must be on the way to being a great soldier. Dad said you boys are getting a much better training than the soldiers in the First World War. Some of them hardly knew how to hold a gun. Camping must be a great experience for you. Be sure always to wrap yourself up well. Guard against dampness. I was surprised when I read about your teeth. Don't eat so much sweet stuff. Substitute something else like fruit. I am glad you all enjoyed the cookies. I am sure all the other things will come in handy. How did you like the ties? Keep them for dress. I will send you more socks. Did you read all the funny sheets? By the way I sent your old gray sweater to you. I wanted to get something to you quick. But I am going to get you a regular army sweater only I don't know the size. Could you give me any idea what to guess by? Tell me your shoulder width. Will send the nail file too. Let me know about these things when you write again. And another thing is Dad told me you lost your traveling bag. Do you want me to send one to you as you as you will need it when your furlough comes along? Perhaps you can buy one down there. Let me know about it. Don't forget.
 I will be anxious to see that swell picture you are going to have taken. Be sure to look pleasant and smile. As for the bacon and eggs John we will be stored up to give you plenty when you get home. By the way John if you get home for Thanksgiving, what about Christmas? Maybe you will get a furlough for both holidays.

You know, they have been making an appeal for people to send Christmas boxes to boys overseas who through having no relatives might be forgotten so I sent for a name and a Jewish boy's address was sent to me. His name is Goldstein. He is in the infantry. So I am going to send him a package for Christmas. Poor fellow, maybe from an orphanage or forsaken.

John, I started this letter on Saturday night and am finishing Sunday. Mom said to tell you Pratt Avenue has been swept from one end to the other. George Diemer arrived home this morning. A delegation went down to meet him, Butlers and Diemers together. He looks fine. Gained weight. Didn't get a chance to talk to him yet. Will tell you more later. The Bernabes arrived yesterday. We had plenty of noise as it was but now we have more than plenty. But the windows are shut and we don't hear them. Maurice was asking all about you and the army.

It was very nice of the Savages to write John. You should try to answer and thank them, especially Bill if he is going across. Get a few lines to him if possible. His mother told me a few weeks ago that she thought he was getting ready for overseas.

You know that little Mt. St. Michael hat you had? Well Mary Ann is in love with it, wears it when she is down here and it looks very nice on her. Neppie Bernabe spied it on her and cross examined her to find out where she got that hat and if you heard Mary Ann telling me how she just told him, "It belongs to John."

Tomorrow John I am going out to visit Aunt Kitty. Will stay a few days, so I will have a lot of news for you when I get back. Keep on writing when you can. Take care of yourself. Last Friday I realized going down to Mass you were gone just two months.

Love,
Mother"

An earlier Holy Name Society picnic was more than adequately described in the annals of the Dyre Avenue News.

"The semi-annual outing of the Holy Name Society of the Church of the Nativity was held the early part of July. Transportation facilities necessitated that it be held nearby. The main feature of the outing being food and refreshments, a spot had to be chosen permitting of beer, etc., and of course baseball. Private property didn't lend itself to baseball and the laws of the City being what they are did not permit of serving beer on park property. The committee hit upon a fair compromise that satisfied all lawful authority. The affair was staged at Pirates Field, otherwise known as Seton Falls Park. The sports, such as such as baseball, horseshoes, etc., were held in the Park area, while the allied sports of eating and drinking were held in the private area across the road. The ball game between the Married and Single men was a nip and tuck affair until the eighth inning when their (the married men) greater experience in battle was reflected by a rally that netted them three runs and the honors of the day. Too much credit cannot be assumed by the fathers in as much as the single men comprised several junior high boys and a smattering of 4Fs. When the ball game was over and the boys decided that it was time for a few hot dogs, it was found that the grammar school boys, brought along for a day's pleasure, had found the dogs very much to their liking - the committee had not planned on feeding so many - so the growing boys grew and the older boys were stumped, finding the supply exhausted. The cry that went forth from the athletes was heartrending, so the committee decided to appease them by calling into service Hickey's Butter and Egg truck and providing a second keg of beer. The extra keg seemed cooler and slightly better flavored and the boys seemed cooler and in slightly better humor (evidenced by the gurgling of this precious amber fluid) when they finished it off. It was only twilight and the usual bugs and insects of the undergrowth broke up the festivities - that is, everything but the poker game that always finished off this spring and fall event."[111]

℘

"Oct. 3, 1943 [Sunday]

Dear John,
  Did you receive the box we sent you? How did you like the apples? The next box will be cake. It is getting very cold here. I am writing you this letter so I can get to bed. So I will let your Mother carry on the letter. Hoping to hear from you so be a good boy.
                   Dad"

And Anna's postscript:

  "Muggsie got another massage with powder. Duke said she is getting so stiff now he has to invite her out to walk with him."

℘

"Pvt. A. L. Garbarini
ASN 32999604 USA
Co. A 30th Bn 1st Reg
I.R.T.C. Ft. McClellan, Alabama

---

[111] *Dyre Avenue News*, (Volume 1, No. 3, August 1943).

Oct. 4, 1943 [Monday]

Dear John,

I am stationed at Fort McClellan for 17 weeks. And I get the best chow in the whole 30th Battalion. I haven't seen anybody from our neighborhood down here at the fort. I went under machine gun fire yesterday for the first time. I had to crawl eighty yards and go under barb wire on my back with dynamite going off all around me. It felt like July 4th to me. Last week I fired the M-1 and I made a score of 160 and qualified for the marksman medal. The other day I fired the U.S. M-1 carbine and I got a score of 138. It felt like I was firing an air rifle. There wasn't any kick to it. My brother is still going to college the last time I heard from him. Yes, I do go to church on Sundays if I am not on any details. Well, that's all for now pal.

Your pal,
Andy"

"Oct. 7, 1943 [Thursday]

Dear John,

On Monday 4th I visited Aunt Kitty and came back Wednesday afternoon. They are all fine over there. Theresa is still busy with all her girlfriends and works over the weekend in the hotel. Morgan still makes his speeches. He has the walls covered with maps - moving pins here and there every day. After school he works in the A&P. Bobby is still nursing cats. He has one tiger. He calls him Big Boy. He is in a new game now, playing football. You should hear Kitty - all the trouble she had getting him to the dentist. Now he wants to get his bones broke so she will have more trouble with him. Dave is getting fatter and fatter. Kitty said he will blow up and burst when the boys all come home. While I was there a letter arrived from you and of course I was anxious to read it as they were. I read a few letters David wrote home and believe me I think he is having his own worries. According to what he tells, all they have is tests. He is attending school at night brushing up on math. No doubt you certainly have to have what it takes to make good.[112]

Well John I must confess that I certainly did miss you on my journey but I traveled the same way as usual and made very good connections. When I arrived home I found your beautiful gift, which was very thoughtful of you to

---

[112] Theresa, Morgan, Bobby and David were all children of Dave and Kitty Lucas, and lived in Bernardsville, New Jersey.

send. Mom also received her box. She was delighted with it. So thanks a lot from both of us.

I suppose there was great preparations for that major inspection you had. Was very glad to hear that you were O.K. Keeping neat, clean and polished pays dividends you know. So keep the good work up. Take it with ease and have confidence in yourself. That is what counts. Always pray for God's help and remember the Blessed Mother. I always pray for her to protect you, so you pray too, and receive communion as often as possible. It will strengthen you in many ways.

John, you speak of a furlough but I understood you to write that that other test had to be finished first. Is that all over? Let us know as soon as you get word. But don't forget to let me know about your traveling bag. If you can buy it down there, O.K. Tell me what you think because if I buy it, it will take time to send it down. Don't forget about it.

I was going down to church tonight and who did I meet but George from Mamie's.[113] He is in for a few days. Told me they brought in a lot of coffee and soldiers. Maybe prisoners, I don't know. He looked fine. I think he put on weight.

John, did you like the fruit? Frank gave up the apples for you. I hope they weren't spoiled when you receive them. If you care to have more, I will send it.

I was glad to know you received mail from Father Broderick and Roberta and the boys. I haven't seen Ritchie in some time so I don't know much about his departure. When you write, John, watch your spelling. The big words you spell correct and the little ones you miss up on - such as vice lieutenant. Look up the dictionary if you are not sure. I know you don't have much time for that business. Do the best you can about it. When you read watch how the words are spelled. You don't mind me telling you this because that is what mothers are for, to find fault and tell you about it. Remember how we used to have spelling lessons.

Martin got the car and is learning to drive. So I guess he is satisfied now. We got a letter from the Telephone Company today saying they can't install a phone for some time yet. Would you want me to get you a regular bulky sweater without sleeves? I wanted to tell you John I received the letter with the four dollars. I put them in with the ten. Use your money wisely now so you won't go broke. Isn't there two bonds due now, one from August and the other from September 30? I didn't receive any yet. They are very slow about those things. It takes time. Well John I could keep writing to you all night but it is late so I will close. Keep on writing. Love and regards from all.

---

[113] George Stanley, Mary ("Mamie") McGowan's all-but-adopted son, serving in the Navy.

Mother"

"October 10, 1943 [Sunday]

Dear John,
  I just finished writing to Aunt Kitty, informing her that I arrived home safe and sound. Saturday was her John's birthday so I sent him a card with a little remembrance. A few days ago I received a letter from him. You know the poor fellow has a hard time trying to compose a few lines as he isn't so clever with English you understand. Kitty said he has improved along those lines a great deal. She encourages him to write often because by doing so you get better and better. So you see you can gain something by writing letters, not only composing the letter but improve on spelling.
  Well John I looked out the window this morning when I raised the shade and all I could see was leaves falling in all directions. Some of the trees are almost bare now. So we really have the fall season here now. The boys are playing football again on the street and Duke is watching the wires as usual.
  George Diemer and Catherine were out having their pictures taken this afternoon. I met George last night. He looks well. I think he gained weight. He had ten day furlough home outside his traveling home. He leaves Wednesday. Did you hear from Bobby or Walter? I haven't seen Ritchie in some time. I must inquire about him.
  This morning (Sunday) I met Father Broderick - of course our conversation was all about you. He told me when he wrote to you he had twelve letters to write. I told him to keep the good work up and had to leave him so he told me as long as I got in church for the collection it would be O.K. He looks fine John. Since his vacation gained a lot of weight. Teaching must be agreeing with him.
  The Holy Name Society is going to have a barn dance this month in that hall on White Plains Avenue. October 15th is our 22nd wedding anniversary, but I am not going to remind Dad. He might want to celebrate the wrong way. He expects to go on night work soon. Well today he was off so we went to 10:30 Mass and on the way back, Banks asked him to go fishing. All he needed was an invitation so off he went. About six o'clock I looked out the window and saw your father coming and lo and behold instead of bringing fish what did he have but a dog. It seems it followed him and he couldn't get rid of it. Well I said, "A fine fisherman you are, instead of fish we get a dog." It's a little dark water spaniel, has a nice collar on it. It is down in the cellar to stay for the night only and it is going to get its walking papers. Your father said, "If John saw that dog he would keep it." "Yes," I said, "if you had your way the dogs would be sleeping in the beds and us on the floor." Poor Mugs

suspects something is wrong in the cellar. It will be just too bad if she finds out what.

That was a very nice letter Margaret wrote. I think I met Sr. Fidelis at a card party. Someday I am going to visit Margaret. We received the Armored News John. I see a list of boy's names who received a rating on the guns. I looked for your name being that you are due for medals. I thought I would see it in the list. According to what I read it looks like a great number of boys are shifted to other branches of service. How are you making out with the tests? Hope everything was successful.

Are you still having your teeth treated? I was glad you enjoyed the fruit John. Would you like more? If so I can send it and I will look for a bag for you. It looks like it will be "Home again" for you soon John. Nobody will be more excited or anxious about your furlough than Mother. We will have a great deal to talk about I am sure. Dad said he is going to start saving for a good time. I hope he means us inclusive, not just for himself.

Well John it is getting near 12 o'clock so I have to close. I am enclosing an ad about tanks, thought you would be interested. Remember to say a prayer for us. Write as usual. Regards and love from all. How is your watch working?

Mother"

℘

This next letter is from one of the often-mentioned girls in the neighborhood, Roberta McIntyre, who then lived at 4389 Matilda Avenue in the Bronx, having moved from the Butler household, where she had been listed as living in the 1940 census, aged 12, the niece of Vincent and Helen Butler. In 1943 she would have been 15.

"*Oct. 11, 1943 [Monday]*

Dear Johnny,

As long as I'm in the writing mood I thought I'd drop you a line. You know one of the boys up at Robbie's camp wrote me a letter, what a jerk. He saw a picture of me and said he fell in love with me at first sight. What baloney he throws, gosh you should read it.

I received your letter and was very glad to hear from you. You know a week ago Sunday I saw Martin[114] *at the Mount game and he was in a car. When you wrote and told me about him getting a car I thought the one I saw*

---

[114] Martin Moynihan.

was his. *But Saturday I met him on the Avenue*[115] *and he said he had a car but it was in the garage. He didn't have any gas. He said he was going to apply for a B ration card*[116] *and tell them he had to take kids to school. He said the most they could do was throw him out. I told him that's just what they'd do.*

Did you hear that George Diemer is home? He got a nine day leave. He has to leave Wednesday. He looks fine. He got stouter. By the way, Robbie gained 16 pounds. Have you lost or gained any weight? If you have a little snapshot of yourself will you send it to me? I'm anxious to see how you look. You know I just can't picture Robbie and Walter C. in a Navy suit, can you?

Did Robbie write you a letter yet? Eileen told me she was going to send you some cookies. When I make some for Robbie I'll send you some too. But it's so darn hard to get butter and I don't like cookies made with Spry or Crisco. If you get a chance drop me a line soon. Until then 'so long'.

Roberta"

§

"Oct. 14, 1943 [Thursday]

Dear John

I was very glad to know you survived that 25 mile hike. Take good care of your feet, especially after a long march.

Well I must say you are well supplied with radios but I think that it is fine that you have the opportunity to listen in on the programs. Frankie told me he was making a bet with you for the football scores. He said he knew you would pick Notre Dame.

Is that major you speak of a doctor? It looks like you are going to have plenty of leisure time. Take it easy and rest. You need it after so much activity. From what you say in your letters I take it that you boys are treated well down there. Roberta told me she got a letter from you. George Diemer went back Wednesday, Mom said. He talked with her as if he was very much dissatisfied with his place in the service. It was very nice of Eileen Hickey to remember you. Write a card or a few lines telling her how you received the cookies, thanking her for them and say how much you all enjoyed them. Dad doesn't know who the boys are from the Todd Shipyards.[117] You told us you

---

[115] White Plains Road, always referred to as "The Avenue", and the major shopping venue for residents of Wakefield and Edenwald, along with neighboring Mount Vernon, where Fourth Avenue was the center of commerce.

[116] A "B ration card" was a much-sought gasoline ration card.

[117] The Todd Shipyard started life in Brooklyn in 1869, as the Handren and Robins Shipyard. In the late 1800's it merged with the Erie Basin Dry Dock Company. In 1916 William H. Todd, an employee, bought the firm along with some associates and it became the William H. Todd Corporation, and later the Todd Shipyards

would enclose the card from them but you forgot to do so. If you have an address write and thank them anyway.

Ritchie Simmons is going away Oct. 18th, so his mother told me. Did you hear from Robbie or Walter? Send Mr. Janisch a card, just write a few lines. Mrs. Bernabe was asking all about you today. You should write to them. Get a nice card and write something like this: "Hello everybody. Army life is fine. Hope all are well. Regards, John McGowan." You could copy this on a card. Watch your spelling. Don't forget, he is a professor. Did the boys from Fordham know him? While I think of it, write to Mrs. Savage. At least tell her you received her letter. Did you answer Bill's letter? You know John I am afraid you will have to get a secretary to keep up your correspondence. By the way, you must watch your spelling - "hike" not "hick" - "wrapping paper" - "cigarets" - "tough" not "tuff" - "rumor" - "furlough" - "threw away". Take your little dictionary out.

Dad is on night work again, so Muggsie and I are companions for the night. Only we have another friend with us. We still have the little black pup and she is a great watchdog and full of pep. Your father got his old sheepskin coat down for her to lie on it and the next morning she had the whole lining tore out of it. He is a cute little dog John - a water spaniel - good breed. You wouldn't want a mascot down there, would you? If I didn't have Mugs I would keep him.

Well John Duke is taking down the screens, painting and putting up the storm windows and as usual is raving about getting the windows clean in a hurry. Now that is where I miss your help. Duke just finished painting the front door and it looks fine. Dad expects to paint the kitchen. Will close now John. Want to get this letter off with Mom. Will write more later. Love and regards.

Mother"

۞

"Oct. 17, 1943 [Sunday]

Dear John,

This is Sunday evening. I have just returned from church. Dad has been painting the kitchen but at present he and Muggsie are resting on the

---

Corporation. During World War Two construction work was carried out in the Erie Basin Yard, which eventually was closed, in 1986. Presumably Ed McGowan, as an electrician in the Brooklyn Navy Yard, would have had close friends working at Todd.

divan, listening to some operatic singer. Dad would understand it better if they were playing "Pistol Packin' Mama."[118]

Well John I suppose by this time your leisure time is gone. Did you get to Louisiana? I was sorry you didn't try to get to confession and communion. It would have been a good opportunity while you have so much time off.

In regard to your furlough I will be delighted John to have you home for Christmas and fourteen days would be wonderful. I only hope it comes true. If it should be a pick between Thanksgiving and Christmas I would rather have you pick the latter but come whenever you can. John we are all very anxious to see you. Even Muggsie will be waiting along with neighbors and friends. If you come for Christmas we will have open house for the holidays.

The little puppy is gone. Mrs. Windel's mother took it for a friend of hers. We couldn't very well keep her here John. She required a lot of care. Poor Muggsie doesn't get a grooming. So I don't know what would happen to the poor pup. Mrs. Carroll wanted to give you five dollars for it but I refused to accept it. By the way, her son is at Camp Campbell, Kentucky. He was home on furlough.

The Walsh's over at Bernabe's house[119] have a dog. A big, homely looking thing, annoys the neighborhood barking and crying. She told Duke she needed a watch dog over there.

I met Jackie Walsh and Ritchie the other night. Ritchie is going down for his induction the 18th. I thought he was leaving then. Martin got his car and is learning to drive. He was determined to get it. Maurice Bernabe was over with a chance book from the Mount. They have a $500 bond going off at the football game Thanksgiving. So I took a chance for you.

---

[118] "Pistol Packin' Mama" was written in 1943 by Al Dexter. Overwhelmed by news of bloody conflict, Americans in early 1943 just wanted to forget the war and laugh. Reprieve came in the form of this jukebox favorite about spurned love and ladies with guns. The song became the first country crossover hit of World War II, encouraging pop fans to expand their musical palettes, and paving the way for future southern superstars like Gene Autry, Bob Wills and Ray Price. The lyrics:

Drinking beer in a cabaret and was I havin' fun!
Until one night, she caught me right, and now I'm on the run!
Lay that pistol down, babe, lay that pistol down.
Pistol packin' mama, lay that pistol down!
She kicked out my windshield, she hit me over the head.
She cussed and cried, and said I'd lied, and wished I was dead.
Lay that pistol down, babe, lay that pistol down.
Pistol packin' mama, lay that pistol down!

[119] The Walshes were tenants, it seems, of the Bernabe's.

I had a letter from Aunt Kitty. She told me they were all so lonesome after I had gone. She promises to come to spend a few days with me. I would love to have her. Especially now when Dad is working night work. But she has to wait awhile. The landlord promises to paint for her. If he ever gets started. Saturday I had a letter from Sonny. He is up in Buffalo University N.Y. I hope he likes it better than Florida. He tells me he didn't care for the South. A great number of boys say that. I wonder why. Living conditions are a whole lot better up here, I guess.

This is going to be a busy week for me. Work on the altar - special meeting Wednesday for Rosarians - Friday night we are going down to the Sisters of Mercy card party in the Commodore Hotel. Saturday night the Holy Name Society are going to have a barn dance over in the ballroom on White Plains Avenue. Dad said Father Broderick had everybody laughing this morning at Mass telling the people how they would have hams and brown and black drinks for sale over at the affair and also to please the young ladies who wanted to dance, the Society had invited sixty soldiers from Fort Slocum, who were handsome and good dancers.

Mr. Bernabe was asking for you. I told him how you met the boys from Fordham and that you listen in on all the football games. He said, "Oh, yes, John was always very hot for Notre Dame. He couldn't bear to see them lose." You know John, Mr. Bernabe isn't employed at all now. It is rather a pity when you think of it, a man with his education and profession. He should get a better break.[120]

Do you remember that girl who visited Mooney's with the baby? She was married to that O'Neil fellow.[121] He was in Alaska for two years. He was sent back to the States. Had a month furlough and is now in the South - studying for officers' training school.

John would you like some more fruit? If so let me know. Dad's song just came over the wires. "Lay That Pistol Down!" Duke and Mom are listening as usual to Anthony's Court.[122] We had a heavy rain storm Friday night. Between the leaves and rain you couldn't see across the street. It is clear now but very cool. Well John I will close now. Dad wants to write a few lines to you. Take good care of yourself. How did you make out with your teeth? Keep on writing.

*Love,
Mother"*

---

[120] I wonder what the issue was with Mr. Bernabe. Was he pushed out on account of age?
[121] Haven't figured out who "That O'Neil fellow" refers to.
[122] "Anthony's Court" was a popular radio show dispensing legal advice. Apparently it sometimes bordered on the practice of law without a license.

This next note is included with the letter above. It is from John's father, Ed, with a postscript added by his wife Anna.

"Oct. 17, 1943 [Sunday]

Dear John,
    I was off today so I had to paint the kitchen. As you know I am on night work. John you will find 2 air mail stamps in the letter, in case you would like to use them. I do not know who the workers are in the Todd Ship Yards. They were telling me they send them to all the camps. I did not see Red in a long time but he is still working over there. They will have to go in the Navy. All the fellows that goes away in the service they put them in C Bee. Mugs is sitting in front of me. I will be closing. Hoping to hear from you.
                                                              Dad"

The P.S. is added by John's mother.

"P.S. John I meant to tell you that I sent a package overseas to my little Elias Goldstein. I put a carton of cigarettes in it along with different kinds of candy made up in little packages - peanut butter sandwiches - a pack of playing cards. It looks swell - tissue paper and regular Christmas seal and stickers. Hope he enjoys it. You should see the people waiting in lines at the Post Office. Some busy place.
(Extra) your bond arrived for September."

§

"Oct. 17, 1943 [Sunday]

Hello John,
    Sorry it has taken me so long to write but I have been really busy. We moved from the old neighborhood and we are now living out in City Island. Well everything is still the same with me, I'm still down at the Navy Yard working as hard as ever only now I am back on ten hours. I wish you would get a leave as I would like to see you. I hear Ricky has his induction and Cupity has joined up. There is supposed to be a barn dance up at the church this coming week. And I guess I'll be going with Dot. That is the latest and what a sweet tomato.
    It rained all day yesterday but I mean rained. I don't get to go out much being as I am working so late but I still go out Saturday nights. I haven't seen your pop in a long time. I am really supprised that I didn't hear from you. It was indeed very disappointing. Well I guess I'll sign off.
                                            As ever your pal,
                                            Red"

"Oct. 20, 1943 [Wednesday]

Dear John,
  We received your beautiful card. Dad and I were delighted with it and your cigarettes arrived too. You have been very thoughtful John. We appreciate it very much.
  When I read your letter stating how you were to have so much leisure time last week I thought to myself wouldn't it be nice if John could get to Confession, and Communion. In fact I mentioned it to you in that last letter I sent, and then when I read how you received Holy Communion I said I am convinced thoughts travel. We all thought how nice it was for you to meet that boy from the Mount. You must have had a great deal to talk about. Is he in your division? It would be fine if you could be pals. Father O'Hara was asking me how you are so I told him about your meeting the boy from the Mount. He said he bet that made you both feel good.
  Well John this has been a very busy week for me. Painting, Altar duties, Rosary meeting. Friday night we are going to the Sisters of Mercy card party at the Commodore Hotel.[123] Maybe I will win a prize. Saturday night the Holy Name is having the barn dance.
  Ritchie Simmons paid me a visit Tuesday evening. He is going away next Monday night. They are having a big party at his house Friday night. He wanted me to attend it but on account of the Card Party I can't get there but I am going to give him a gift as he was very kind toward us since you went away and tried so hard to get the watch. You say John your test will end November 19th. Does that mean you may get your furlough for Thanksgiving? If so let us know and also about the traveling bag. Do you want a bag like you had or a larger valise? Don't forget to write and let me know, as I expect to buy one soon to send it. I hear Robbie Mahon is O.K. I guess you didn't hear from him on account of him being kept busy. Wonder how Walter likes the Navy. Did you write to Eileen Hickey to thank her? John while I think of it I am going to enclose Mrs. Hull's address. Send her a card. She would like to hear from you.

---

[123] The Commodore Hotel, named for Cornelius Vanderbilt, the "Commodore." He founded the New York Central Railroad, and became one of the wealthiest men in the world. A sister of the Duke's, according to family lore, worked as a maid for the Vanderbilt family, and through this connection most of the McGowan brothers who came from Ireland in the 1880's and 1890's were able to get jobs on the railroad or on the city's streetcar lines.

Ritchie was telling me Red Gibbons moved to City Island.[124] *He is working in the Navy Yard. Ritchie doesn't see him so often now. Jackie Walsh is the only boy left now on Dyre Avenue from your old gang. The Juliano boy was asking for you, and wants to be remembered to you. His brother is an instructor in navigation. I hear the Jennings girl expects to be married soon.*

Well John I suppose all those boys who had three day passes are back at the Fort again. I bet they had a whole lot to tell when they got back again. That boy who lives on 6th Street in Mt. Vernon could have paid us a visit while he was home. Dad said it must have taken most of their time to travel, so they didn't have much time to spend at home.

Paddy Dineen[125] *was telling us today down at church that the bishop resigned. Mrs. Mooney and I said, "What bishop?" Paddy said, "Sure, don't you know who that is?" We said, "No." "Well," said Paddy, "Did you ever hear of Mr. Gueth? Well, that is the bishop." Paddy said on Sunday Gueth dressed in three different suits to parade up and down the aisle, showing them off. He had Mrs. Mooney and I screaming. He has a nickname for everybody. He calls you Jack.*

Last night John I tuned in to a program from Fort Knox A.R.T.C. It was Tuesday night. I thought maybe you attended the broadcast. Did you listen in on any of those songs from Oklahoma? They are very good, especially that one "What a Beautiful Morning, What a Beautiful Day."[126]

Dad is still on night work, from 5:30 p.m. until 4 a.m. Muggsie gets in the bed with him when he comes home and she doesn't move until he gets up. John did you hear any more news from Andy?[127] *His brother told me Andy would like to be a mechanic. I guess he isn't satisfied with the infantry. Well John I will have to close now. It is getting rather late. Write when you can. Love and regards from all.*

Mother"

℘

"Oct. 25, 1943 [Monday]

Dear John,

---

[124] City Island, in the Bronx, remains a bucolic seaport-like village most of the year, and swells in the summertime with a huge transient population drawn by its restaurants and nautical charm.

[125] Paddy Dineen was apparently quite a neighborhood character.

[126] The musical *Oklahoma*, based on the 1931 play "Green Grow the Lilacs," by Lynn Riggs, is the first musical written by the legendary team of Richard Rodgers and Oscar Hammerstein II. It opened at the St. James Theatre on March 31, 1943, and played 2,212 performances by closing night, May 28, 1948.

[127] Probably Andy Garbarini.

After a long wait your letter arrived this morning, Monday, and I must say it was more than welcome. As the last letter I received you wrote a week ago Sunday and I received it Wednesday 20th. Well at last you are in the tanks. How do you like driving? You will be able to teach Dad a few things, I am thinking, when you come home. Glad to know you are taking care of your hair but have you any hair left on with that G.I. haircut? Take good care of your body as well. Always keep clean and neat. It will help you in many ways. Appearances count.

Friday night we went to the Commodore Hotel to the card party. We went through the Grand Central Station. Believe me, I never saw so many uniforms on men and women of all kinds. It would be just interesting to sit there and watch them pass by. There is also the most beautiful scene over the balcony with an American flag. It would give you a thrill just to look at it. And speaking of your coming home, well I certainly am counting on your furlough, to tell the truth. I have told everybody you will be home soon. I do hope it will be for the holidays. Speaking of that brings up another subject. How about your traveling bag? Do you want me to send you a service bag like the boys gave you or a larger bag? John, I want you to tell me about this in your next letter. Don't forget. I was thinking maybe you could buy a bag in Louisville. Do they have large department stores there?

I started to tell you about the card party Friday night. Well, I was very lucky. I won the second prize, a box of liquor in a beautiful basket. About six or seven bottles of wine. Scotch, whiskey, Gin, all kinds. I hid the whole lot up in the attic. Dad doesn't know a word about it. I also won a wonderful plaque with Our Lord's head carved out with the Crown of Thorns on it. It is something beautiful. I also got the most points at the table for the prize but I let another lady take it. I was almost overcome with all the luck. The Barn Dance was very successful. It was almost overcrowded. Mr. Mooney won a large ham, butter and eggs. Mr. and Mrs. Hull were there also. They were at Mooney's over the weekend. Mom, Duke and I had supper with them down at Mooney's Sunday night and we really had a very good time. Mr. Hull left for home about eleven o'clock and Mrs. Hull spent the night with me and went home this afternoon.

Richard Simmons left tonight. He is hoping he will be sent to Sampson, N.Y.[128] I was invited to his party Friday night but on account of the

---

[128] The Sampson Naval Training Station facility was established by the United States Navy as a Naval Training Station (USNTS Sampson) in 1942. The station was named after Rear Admiral William T. Sampson. The Navy obtained 2,600 acres of former farmland and also vineyards for the facility on the east side of Lake Seneca, one of the Finger Lakes of New York State. Construction of the facility took 270 days to complete. Along with the training station, a 1500-bed hospital was constructed.

card party I couldn't attend. So I and Mrs. Hull visited his house today. I gave him a little remembrance. His mother feels very bad of course. She said Jackie Walsh doesn't know what he will do now with himself. All the boys are gone in the old gang. I think Robby Mahon is coming home next week for his furlough. Did you hear from Walter since? Ritchie gave me Red Gibbons' address for you. I am enclosing it. I told Ritchie I hope he will be home when you get your furlough as we are going to have open house. I am keeping that prize I won, the "Basket of Joy" - that is what they called it down there for our party. Mr. Mooney said he is going to have that prize told about in Hickey's news. So everybody will come to pay us a call.

By the way John, did you receive the gossip sheet? Dad wondered if you got any cigarettes from Hickey's. He said to tell you to write a card thanking the Todd Shipyard Boys. Tell them you received the cigarettes and you enjoyed them very much. Thanks very much - your name and address. Don't forget to thank Eileen Hickey. I realize you don't have much time but you should thank a person for their thoughtfulness toward you.

The kitchen is all shining white. The painting is done and I am busy fixing it all up. Last week I was kept so busy on the outside I didn't have time to do much in the house.

Martin Moynihan went up to Massachusetts with the team and the boys in the band over the weekend. He is learning to drive the car. They had a bazaar over at St. Francis of Rome and it was the best they ever had. Mom said they took in $9,000. Enclosed John you will find a chance book. I want you to write your name in it and the other boys too if you want to. It is all paid for so just return the book when you are ready. I sent the money over to Martin for it. Did you meet the boy from the Mount again? Do you know any fellow by the name Nolan down there? Had a card from Tom Lucas. Write soon. Love from all.

Mother"

"PFC Elias A. Goldstein 32294588
Cannon Co. - 307 Infantry
A.P.O 77
Camp Pickett, VA

Oct. 26, 1943 [Tuesday]

Dear Mrs. McGowan,

The mission of USNTS Sampson was Navy basic training for large numbers of new recruits. During the war, over 411,000 Navy recruits were trained at the station.

I want to express my deepest thanks to you for the swell package I just received. I have certainly been places since leaving Fort Jackson and my outfit is now stationed at Indiantown Gap, Pennsylvania. We just came east after a long stay in the desert and it was a most agreeable surprise to find your package awaiting me at arrival.

Again, I want to thank you most heartily and I wish you and yours a Merry Christmas and a Happy New Year.

*Yours gratefully,
PFC Elias A. Goldstein"*

℘

"Oct. 26, 1943 [Tuesday]

Dear John,
    This box as you can see is for you to celebrate Hallowe'en. I guess your pals down there will help you to do so. Dad packed the contents so we are sending it in hopes you will enjoy it. You know Hallowe'en which falls on October 31st is Dad's birthday. He tells me he is going to treat me royal that day. I hope he doesn't forget.
    Well John don't eat too much to get sick. I will write more later. Love from all. Muggsie is licking her jaws for a lollipop.

Mother and Dad"

℘

"Cardinal Hayes High School
650 Grand Concourse
New York, N.Y.

October 27, 1943 [Wednesday]

Dear John,
    I take it for granted that you are still in the sunny South. The news from this neck of the woods is rather uninteresting. We had a surprise party for Dick Simmons last Friday evening at his own house. Most of the boys and girls were there. Dick seems to be very happy about joining the Navy. I suppose you think he is crazy for not going in the Army. I believe the Junior Holy Name Society is going along very well - considering that the boys are very rapidly leaving the Edenwald section.
    I heard that Bobby Mahon was home for a few days; his mother said he gained 16 pounds. I had a letter from Walter Cubita this morning; he seems to like the Navy. The Holy Name Society ran a barn dance the other evening. It was a great financial success. In fact, they went over the top. Fifty soldiers

were invited to come from Ft. Slocum[129] but they never showed up. The girls of the parish were very disappointed - the truth is they were very sore.

Your father tells me you may be home for Thanksgiving. My oldest brother pulled in from Wales today and the young fellow came home for a few days; he is up in the Marines at the University of Rochester. Nothing new in the parish. We expect to receive our trophy one of these days. Imagine our team as the City champs, or chumps.

Hayes plays the Mount on Thanksgiving Day. I think the Mount is too strong for them; this is a frank confession. We have beaten Powers, Brooklyn Prep and All Hallows - three wins and no losses.

When you find the time drop a line. Best wishes for your health and happiness.

Sincerely,
Father Broderick"

This letter is from John's father, and on back of it his mother has added her own letter.

---

[129] Fort Slocum was a US military post on David's Island in the western end of Long Island Sound in the city of New Rochelle, New York from 1867 to 1965. The fort was named for Major General Henry W. Slocum, a Union corps commander in the American Civil War. On 16 May 1941, as war raged in Europe, Fort Slocum became part of the New York Port of Embarkation, becoming a staging area for troops moving overseas. Fort Slocum also trained cadre to set up other staging areas in Greater New York, such as Camp Kilmer and Camp Shanks in 1941 and 1942. Fort Slocum hosted the Atlantic Coast Transportation Officers' Training School, acquainting former civilians from the transportation industries with the Army. The fort was thus a key element of the Army's Transportation Corps, so named in mid-1942, whose mission was moving huge numbers of men and amounts of materiel overseas. By early 1944 the need to ship troops to Europe had lessened, and a policy of rotating troops in the US who hadn't seen action to overseas battlefields and the reverse was instituted. Battle-hardened soldiers returning from Europe were put through a "Provisional Training Center" at Fort Slocum to re-acquaint them with the stateside Army, with its surplus of proper military appearance, courtesy, and discipline, along with its deficit of actually shooting Germans. In May 1944 Private Willie Lee Duckworth of Sandersville, Georgia devised the famous "Sound off, one, two" military cadence while attending one of these classes. In November 1944, as the transportation school wound down, Fort Slocum took on a mission of rehabilitating soldiers who had been court-martialed in Europe and sent home. Following World War II, Fort Slocum was briefly considered as a nuclear research center; what became Brookhaven National Laboratory was chosen instead.

"Oct. 31, 1943 [Sunday]

Dear John,
 I am writing you this letter to let you know I went to the football game today with Duke and Frank. The Mount played Brooklyn Prep. The score was Mount 28, Brooklyn Prep 2. It was a good game. They had a great crowd. We play a good game for cards as you know. We miss you. All the fellows was asking for you. So I am sending you the score card. So John I will be closing. Hoping to hear from you. Did you receive the box we sent you? Mom and Duke and Frank was asking for you.

Love,
Dad"

And Anna's letter, on the back of this one.

"Dear John,
 I hope you will not have to ask your pals to interpret your father's letter as I told him it sounds like a Chinese puzzle.
 Frank and family were here and we celebrated a little for Dad's birthday. Had a pumpkin and apples etc. Of course we missed having you but then we were hoping you enjoyed the box of fruit we sent you for Halloween. Did they have any parties down there? Will send you the bag and gloves. Did you mean you want two pair, an old and new? Take care of yourself. We had plenty of rain here, last week every day. Will write more later. Love from all.

Mother"

FIVE: "DRIVING TANKS"

"Fort Knox, Kentucky

Nov. 1, 1943 [Monday]

Dear Mother,
I thought I would write you because today is All Saints Day and you would wonder if I got to Mass. Well I did. I went to the 6:30 mass at night. I was a little late. The priest had just unveiled the chalice and was getting ready for the first wine and water. Mother I want to tell you I really made a sacrifice to get there. I went to supper at 20 after and ate quickly and I ran down to church. I was the only Catholic fellow in our barracks that got in to go to church.
Mother I had a letter from Pete Thomas and I almost fainted when he wrote he was working as a welder. I wish him a lot of luck at his new profession. He also said Walter[130] dislikes a lot of things about the Navy but he will get used to them. He also said that you said I was coming home soon. From the way he writes you think I am coming home next week but I will be home in about six weeks. Well I am very dirty from driving tanks today so I think I will close now and take a shower. Love to all.
Love,
Son John

P.S. Dad I got the news from you and I also received one from Hickey's. Did you see that little write-up about Walter McGowan in it? Dad why don't you invite Red Gibbons up to the house some night and find out how he is with good Pop?

P.P.S. Mother I am enclosing 4 dollars to add to that 14 I already sent you. Buy a bond for yourself. 'Boy o' Boys we got payed!'"

§

"Nov. 2, 1943 [Tuesday]

Dear John,
I received your letter today telling me the good news about your furlough. It is going to be a great Christmas present for me having you home again. I hope too that you will be here over New Year's so keep your fingers

---
[130] Walter Cubita.

crossed. *Maybe you will get your wish. Getting home for Christmas is the main thing. Dad is delighted. Expects to give a party every day. Muggsie will be waiting to take a long stroll with you. I will send the bag and gloves as soon as possible and if there is something else you need perhaps we can go shopping when you get home and buy what you want.*

Bob Hope[131] happens to be on the radio at present time and I am trying to keep an ear on his program and write to you at the same time.

Well John we all got a real thrill reading about you and the tanks knocking down trees. Your father and I had to look at each other as it seems rather unbelievable that you are driving a tank. Only yesterday in our mind, Dad would have a fit if he saw you riding your bicycle down 233rd Street.[132] When Duke heard it, he said to Mom, "By George, I hope that fellow wouldn't bring a tank home. Sure he would run it through the house and knock it down." I am sure you worked very hard John to accomplish all you have. We all feel very proud of you and pray that God will bless and protect you. So take it easy. Don't overwork and don't drive your tank too fast.

The Bernabe's received your card and were very pleased to receive it. I was glad to know Martin[133] wrote. I know you would like The Tower.[134] I heard there was a lot of trouble up at the Mount over the Massachusetts trip. Did Martin tell you anything about it? Do you see that boy you met from the Mount? John did you receive that chance book I sent you? Don't forget to return the stubs.

Ritchie Simmons[135] is at Sampson, N.Y. his mother was telling me. She is hoping he will be home for Christmas too. I met the Barker boy. He expects to leave for service next month I think. You know I meet boys and girls in the

---

[131] Bob Hope at the time was one of the most popular entertainers in the world, and continued so for decades to come.

[132] East 233rd Street was the major east-west thoroughfare through the Edenwald section, continuing a path through Woodlawn and Wakefield from its starting point at Jerome Avenue and the northwest gates of Woodlawn Cemetery. There's a West 233rd Street also, but don't ever try to connect them. They never meet!

[133] Probably Martin Moynihan.

[134] The school publication of Mt. St. Michael Academy, the high school John attended and had just graduated from several months earlier. His cousin Martin Moynihan was still a student there. Five more McGowans would graduate from "the Mount" over the next few decades - Frank McGowan and Brian McGowan, sons of John J. McGowan; Timothy McGowan, Thomas McGowan, and Todd McGowan, sons of Walter McGowan. John J. and Walter were first cousins of John McGowan's father Edward, who their children all affectionately called Uncle Eddie.

[135] Richard Simmons, recently inducted into the army, and now at the same training camp where John got his first taste of military life just a few months earlier.

street and they will say, "Hello Mrs. McGowan, how is John?" I don't know who they are but I tell them you are fine.

Well we had a merry weekend here. Frankie's wife Anna went to Binghamton last Friday to attend Mary Budney's wedding and came back today Tuesday. So we had Frank and family here with us and I am telling you we had a noisy house. Mom's place upstairs looks like a whirlwind hit it. Mary Ann said she is going to tell the teacher she is quitting school tomorrow.

Robbie Mahon is expected home today so I suppose Butlers will be having a party. I suppose he will pay us a visit so I will tell you more later. I bought myself a classy pair of shoes yesterday. I may buy me a coat too. Dad said I should. So I guess I will be good to myself. How did you like the lollypops? Did you attend Mass on Monday? John if you would answer my questions there would be plenty to write about. I will write more later.

Love,
Mother and family

P. S. We have plenty of rain here too. It is pouring tonight. Am listening to election returns. Looks like Republican success."[136]

℘

"W. A. Cubita A.S.
Co 771 U. S. N. T. S.
Newport, R.I.

Wednesday, Nov. 3, 1943 [Wednesday]

Dear John,

I received your letter of October 31st. I am on mess detail again. That is the second time in three and a half weeks that our company has been assigned to mess detail. The first time we did it for six days to help out a different battalion. When we return to our own battalion, after working like hell, we are told that we must put in a week of mess detail in our own battalion. We will not get off of this until Tuesday morning. By the time that we get out of here we will all be able to be first class cooks. As of yet we do not know whether we will go to school or not. We are not told that till previous to our departure for home. Even then you are sometimes given delayed orders, which in brief means that you are subject to call at any moment wherever you may be. I got a letter from my mother today and she informed me that Richie is in Sampson, N. Y. Well, for the lack of more to say I will close.

Your pal,
Walter"

---

[136] In fact, the Democrats won.

"Nov. 4, 1943 [Thursday]

Dear John,

  I just got back from confession, tomorrow being First Friday - a very special day for me to receive Holy Communion. As you know it brings back memories of our parting and it is by that too that I keep count of how long you are gone away.
  But now Dad and I will be watching and waiting for your return. Not only us but everybody else got word of your furlough.
  Well Bobby Mahon and I met down in church. He said he was going down to Dyre Avenue, hoping he would meet somebody he knew. The street seems deserted he said. All the boys are in service. He tells me he likes the Navy so well he is going to remain in service after the war is over. I guess he didn't hit the hard spots yet. He looks well and got taller. Talks in a much quieter tone. He is a good boy. I hope things go well with him. Did you hear any more news from Walter Cubita? He is only a kid, John, so I guess he will have to learn to take the bitter with the sweet. I imagine Ritchie will get along O.K. He is of a different disposition than Walter. But I liked Walter too. He was kind of a smart kid I think.
  Butlers are tacking up classy curtains. Wonder if it means a party for Robbie? I hear you and Roberta correspond. Did you write a note of thanks to Eileen? Yesterday I was coming home from Mass. Mr. Hickey called me to say he had received a letter from you and said to tell you John Murphy is at Fort Knox - the Fire Lieutenant's son. Take a look around. You might meet him. I see my manuscript for Mr. Hickey arrived too late for you to copy.
  Today your letter came with the money. Thanks a lot, John. Dad wants to know if you are going to blow all your pay at that new night club we read about. Of course I told Dad you were too smart for that foolishness. By the way, did you see any of the big shots who visited Fort Knox?
  In a former letter John I asked you if you got to Mass Monday. Well I was more than pleased to read what effort you made to get to church. I am sure John you felt better for getting there and I am sure God will reward you. Love of God and what is good is a priceless possession John. Always hold tight to your faith and it will carry you through any difficulty. Remember - be a good Catholic and you will be a good American.
  John I am enclosing an envelope which I will try to tell you why. Mrs. Hubbard's son who is overseas now for many months was stationed at Fort Knox for a time and while there went to Louisville and had his pictures taken and paid for them. Before he got them he was moved and was unable to claim them. So his mother asked me if I would write to you and maybe if you got into Louisville you would visit this photographer whose address is on the envelope

and ask him for the pictures if he cares to send them. Give him Mrs. Hubbard's address. She had a receipt but can't find it. If he refuses to give them tell him to communicate with her. Show him the fellow's name on the envelope. You can keep them with you if he won't send them.

Duke was up to Mamie's and said Johnnie[137] got so stylish. He is putting up storm windows with kid gloves on his hands. Dad is doing good, thank God. Will write again.

Love,
Mother

P.S. Have you heard from Aunt Kitty lately?"

৶

"Fort Knox, Kentucky

Nov. 6, 1943 [Saturday]

Dear Mother,

Today is Saturday and I have just come back from tank inspection. I also received my driver's permit today. Yesterday we spent the day cleaning and servicing tanks. Mother I am enclosing the chance book. I took all the chances because I did not have enough of time to go around and ask the fellows if they wanted to take a chance. I am also enclosing the stubs so in case I win you can claim the money. Today I am going up to the main post to the shoemakers to have my civilian shoes fixed. Next week we are going to gunnery school to take up the 75 M.M. guns. Mother when I write I don't know what to write about because we don't do much to write about. Well Mother only 6 more weeks and I will be on my way home. I hope Richie Simmons gets home at Christmas too because we can have a good time together. Well Mother I think I will close now. I will write tomorrow. Love to all.

Love,
Son John"

৶

This next letter is from John's father's first cousin Margaret McGowan, who was a Sister of Mercy (Sr. Mary Albert).

"Sr. Mary Albert, R.S.M.

---

[137] John McGowan, son of Dennis (Duke) McGowan's brother Frank, and Ed's first cousin. He was one of "the McGowans on the hill", referring to the highest point on Edenwald Avenue, where it crests the hillside and levels off between Monticello and Seton Avenues.

2916 Grand Concourse
Bronx, N.Y.

Nov. 7, 1943 [Sunday]

Dear John,
    I hope you are well. Did you receive my V-Mail last week? I am writing to you again by V-Mail as it is much quicker. The only thing is that the paper isn't big enough to contain more writing as the letter paper, it means you would have to send another V-Mail. Well we can't have everything. Did you hear from your Mother yet? I suppose you did and I guess she told you how lucky she was. She certainly has got good only Irish luck. My Mother didn't win a thing. I was so sorry as she sold six tickets for me. Everyone at home is enjoying the best of health. Do you know if you will get a furlough soon? I hope you will as we are all anxious to see you in the uniform. I will close now with love and prayers.

                                      Your devoted cousin in J.C.
                                      Sr. M. Albert, R.S.M."

※

"Fort Knox, Kentucky

Nov. 9, 1943 [Tuesday]

Dear Mother,
    Well I am now going to gunnery school. It is very interesting. But the only thing is that we have very long hours, from 7 in the morning to 11:30, then from 1 - 5:30. You see, we are kept pretty busy. I am also learning about Gyro Stabilizers and boy are they something. They are a big secret of our tanks and why they have been such a success. Well Mother I read about how you want me to get the picture for Mrs. Hubbard. It will be many weeks before I get to Louisville because we guinea pigs are restricted for a couple of weeks.[138] We have to take a pill at every meal. But when I get a chance I will

---

[138] The "guinea pig" reference relates to a study of the drug *Atabrine*, administered to some 200 soldiers at the Fort Knox Armored Replacement Training Center, according to a press release of sorts that survives among the letters home and back. Atabrine was being studied as an antidote to "malaria fever, chief casualty agent in the South Pacific Theatre." Aside from turning "a yellow blue from the dying

drop in to see about it. I am glad to hear Dad is doing good. Tell him stay on the ball and be good. It is getting very cold here. It started to snow today. You know, it is a damp cold here and not a dry cold like home. Don't worry. I wear enough of clothing and I am warm. The food we've been getting lately is swell. All we have now is roast beef and chicken. Well good night. Give my love to all.

Love,
Son John"

℘

"Nov. 10, 1943 [Wednesday]

Dear Son John,
    This is Wednesday night - rather cold out doors with a feeling of snow. Mugs and I are sitting here very comfortable listening to the radio. The "Mayor of the Town"[139] is on, and it is really funny about a turkey they are raising for Thanksgiving. Dad is out working hard as usual. Frank left here about ten minutes ago. Said he wrote to you today.
    Last Sunday we were invited to Frank's house for dinner. Anna[140] had a chicken dinner prepared. She brought them from Binghamton. So Dad and I went up and really had a very nice time. In the afternoon Frank took us riding out in the country. We saw Lorder's house. It is very nice but in an outlying section. It was a beautiful day and we did enjoy it. Guess where we landed? Johnnie McGowan's[141] new apartment in White Plains and is it classy. Ack and his son were there.[142] If you should write to Margaret don't

---

properties of atabrine", no ill effects were encountered. The soldiers, it was reported, "regard the temporary coloring as a sort of service stripe."
[139] "The Mayor of the Town" was a popular radio show in the 1940's.
[140] Anna McGowan, Frank McGowan's wife, not to be confused with Anna, John's mother.
[141] Mamie's eldest son, John James McGowan.
[142] "Ack" refers to Salem Ackary, an old army friend of Johnnie's. His son was named George. "Uncle Ack" was a favorite among many members of the family. He was of Middle-Eastern heritage, a rarity in those days, and not a Catholic, though he would convert to that faith in 1947. His wife, "Aunt May", was a manager in the Operator Services division of the New York Telephone Company. Ack has the distinction of being godfather to two of Johnnie McGowan's children: his eldest son Robert, born in 1928; and his youngest son Brian (the editor), born in 1952. These two brothers would not know of each other until 2004.

mention this. I don't think we are supposed to know about this affair as Mamie never mentions it.[143]

Monday I got me a permanent wave. Getting all fixed up for your furlough. Tuesday I had to go over to White Plains Avenue so I dropped in to have a chat with Rose.[144] She is so nervous about Martin and the car. Helen's boyfriend left last night for some camp down south. Rose was telling me Jackie Walsh bought a car and it was such a bargain that his mother said the first night he brought it home she looked out and here he was with the aid of the neighborhood kids pushing it home.

Bobby Mahon was to leave today. I had a letter from Ritchie yesterday. Tells me he likes the training very much and Sampson is a swell place but very cold. Has a stiff inspection every day. He is kept very busy and said he is going to write to you. By the way, do you hear from Walter? I had a letter also from Tom Lucas. Writes a very nice letter. Told me David was an Air Corps cadet now. He is an ambitious boy. I hope he succeeds. Do you hear from him? I wrote to Kitty last night. I am going to try and pay her another visit.

---

[143] Editor's Note: This is a curious passage and warrants some mulling over. The "Johnnie" referred to is my father, John James McGowan, Mamie's son. The apartment is probably 42B Barker Avenue in White Plains, where my parents, John and Anne (McMurray) McGowan, lived when they first married, which, as far as I know, was in August 1943. It was the second marriage, possibly for both, definitely for my father, who had been divorced in 1934 from his first wife, and estranged from his first two sons, Robert and James. Given the social mores of the time, especially in clannish Irish-American families, divorce was a black mark of significant import. On my mother's part, there was also a dark secret. Pregnant and probably unwed at 21, she fled her native Canada and sought refuge in Bridgeport, Connecticut, where in 1935 she gave birth to her first child, a daughter named Patricia. Twelve days later she gave her up for adoption. Now, this passage relates to a trip "out in the country" in November 1943, but fails to mention Johnnie's new wife, Anne, at all, but alludes to some sort of affair. Was their marriage at that point being kept a secret for some reason? Given the time, social attitudes, and the backgrounds of the principals, perhaps. I learned long ago from both my parents to cast no stones. I am sure they suffered their share of that as they brought five more children into the world, the last one being me. Ironically, these secrets became known to me only long after both of my parents had died, so exact circumstances will never be known. But I challenge anyone to find two more loving people than they were.

[144] Rose Moynihan, Eddy's sister and Anna's sister-in-law.

The other day I met Walter Koch[145] from Strang Avenue. He is a First Lieutenant. Looks fine. Had about four weeks furlough. He is down at El Paso, Texas, training the boys. We had a long talk. He wants to be remembered to you. Said he couldn't believe you were in service. Still thinks of you as a kid going to school. He has to keep studying too all the time, learning the new ideas the officers bring back from overseas.

Do you remember the Supple boy[146] Ritchie talked about? He is engaged to marry his sister May. Well I happened to meet his mother the other day. She is a lovely person. Told me all about her boy, how he was in that big raid over Germany but came out safe and sound. But it would be foolish to say that the woman isn't worried. Like us all she is waiting and trusting in God for the best.

John do you recall how Dad would want a haircut and shave and I would give him a general lecture about bringing back the change from the dollar? Well try and get it now, a big sign up in Juliano's[147] window, 75 cents haircut, 35 cents for shave. Mom said, "No wonder they can throw their chest out going up the aisle, charging black market prices!" By the way John you say in your letter I never mention Duke and Mom. Why to my knowledge I am always quoting from them. They are both fine. Duke is a master painter now. Got all the storm windows up - ready for the big wind. Every time we have a cold spell, Duke is down measuring the oil, and then up to Mom and that starts the pot a' boiling. The same old tune and six pence. Where is the oil going? Duke has his Sunday night arrangement of all the court scenes - Anthony, etc. They discuss the daily news as usual, and of course the taxes are not left out. But with it all, every day they watch for your letter and when it arrives we have a general gathering and I read it aloud. It has got so bad John that everybody takes a look at the mailbox to see if a letter has arrived. So you can see how important your little letter is and what the few lines you write means to us. You mention in your writing that you don't always know what to say. Well it isn't exactly what you can tell us, the fact is we are satisfied just to hear from you. When you are going to write home, why not take out the last letter I wrote to you. Lay down and relax and read it over. Then sit down and answer some of my questions, which I notice you don't do. Of course I realize you are busy so write when you can and don't be rushing.

---

[145] The Koch's lived at 2258 Strang Avenue. In 1940 the family consisted of Theodore, 51, who was a carpenter for the railroad; his wife Madeline, 46; her mother Katherine Kest, 77, born in Germany; and Walter, 21, who was a page boy at the stock exchange.

[146] James Supple.

[147] Juliano's was one of several neighborhood barbershops, on Dyre Avenue just a few doors down from East 233rd Street.

>   By the way, Buddy Mooney arrived home today. Was away since June I think. He looks fine. Was asking for you. Mrs. Mooney got a great surprise on his arrival. She didn't hear from him since September. I guess he has seen many sights but he won't give any information.
>   Dick comes home every weekend. He had a big exam and passed it. Rose told me Martin took the V-12 exam today but didn't finish so she doesn't think he will pass.
>   I wanted to tell you John when you write again to Red Gibbons tell him to visit us. We will have him come anyway when you are on furlough. Would you like another box of fruit for Thanksgiving? If you like or want it we will send some. You said you were going to have your shoes fixed. I am going to send you a pair of your shoes I think you can use. When you get home we will go shopping and you can buy a new pair of shoes. I also saw nice shirts but wasn't sure of your size. Do you need any? Dad said you will want to get all dolled up for your homecoming. I said I hope he has some hair left on his head after getting all those funny haircuts. Ritchie told me in his letter he got a G.I. haircut.
>   Well John how are you making out with that test (guinea pig)? I suppose you are practicing on those guns you mentioned. Dad suggests we buy a car for you after the war. I said yes but I hope he won't drive it like a tank or it won't last long. Now John I realize you are working very hard and so I want you to get plenty of rest and relax. Don't worry, take it easy and answer my questions. It is 11 p.m., so I will close. Love from all.
>   Mother"

"Fort Knox, Kentucky

Nov. 11, 1943 [Thursday]

Dear Mother,
    How's everything? I thought I would drop a line as I am just sitting around doing nothing. Today we had the 50 cal. Machine gun. It is very interesting. We also saw a movie on it. By the way Mom, did you hear anything from Ritchie and did Robbie Mahon go back yet? I was also thinking that Walter Cubita will be home in a few weeks. I wonder how he is going to look in a sailor's suit. Tomorrow we are going to get up early and go on village battle training. We are supposed to put a village under attack and then take it just like in real battle. We also had inspection today. We had two Captains and three Lieutenants inspecting us. I made out okay. Just before retreat tonight I was in a parade for Armistice Day. We went and took the flag down. It was very nice. They had a band and everything was military. Well, will close now. Love to all.

> Love,
> Son John"

⁂

"Fort Knox, Kentucky

Nov. 13, 1943 [Saturday]

Dear Mother,

Today is Saturday and just got off K.P.[148] Tomorrow I will probably go to the movies and go to church as usual. Mother I was thinking could you send me $5 as I am starting to put my train fare together and I need a little change. I will thank you a lot if you send it. Mother you better not send me a package for Thanksgiving because I might be out camping[149] and anyway we will be fed good. We also take 5 pills tomorrow. You know that this is our last week as guinea pigs and they are really going to give us pills and blood tests. Frank wrote me and told me how you were up to see him. I will not tell Margaret when I write her? Mother did you send that bag yet and gloves? I will be looking for them. I did write Red to visit you when he is up in the neighborhood and I told him to come up also when I am home. Will close now, hoping you are all well. Love to all.

> Love,
> Son John

P.S. Mother the reason I am asking for the 5 dollars is because I am trying to scrape up $21.65 for my fare and 5 dollars for expensives [sic]."

⁂

This next letter is from John's father, Ed, and is not post-scripted by his mother. Also, the envelope is addressed entirely in Ed's hand, indicating he wrote it and mailed it himself, perhaps with no knowledge of it on the part of his wife, who Ed refers to in the letter by his pet nickname for her, "Schultz".

"Nov. 14, 1943 [Sunday]

Dear John,
    I went to the football game today. Mt. St. Michael won the game 45 to Haverstraw High School 0. Frankie and his family went to the game. It

---

[148] K.P. - Kitchen Patrol.
[149] "Out camping" refers to field maneuvers.

was very cold. All the boys was asking for you. We went in Fenullie's[150] for a drink on Edenwald Avenue and Mr. Bernabe served us. He is bartender there on Sunday. Good job for him.

Tonight we had a great game of cards. Duke won all the money. We all had to go downstairs so he could listen to Good Will Court.[151] Mugs and him have a great time. If Duke comes down with no hat on Muggsie starts barking at him to take her walking. The other day he said, "By George, I can't go in or out without that dog barking after me." Remember how she barked when you were getting dressed to go out? Did you read about the [illegible] going home to his dog that he had for 17 years? Now all the boys want furloughs to feed their dogs and cats.

Everything is fine at home. We are all waiting for your furlough. Schultz bought your bag and we are going to send it with a few other things you need. Would you like a box of fruit? Let us know in your next letter.

Love from all.
Write soon.

Dad

P.S. Mt. St. Michael - unbeaten so far."

☙

"Richard T. Simmons A. S.
Co. 229 Bks. D-15
U.S.N.T.S
Sampson, N.Y.

Nov. 14, 1943 [Sunday]

Hi John,

Boy, I bet you are mad at me. I have been here at Sampson for three weeks and I'm just writing to you, but the truth is I am just catching up. Today is Sunday and it is our day off so therefore I can catch up on my mail. Well, the Navy is swell John. I am having a grand time but it is cold as hell. This morning when we got up it was 18 above. We have had snow several times. Boy, is it cold. Right now it is 8:10 P.M. We have to be in bed by 9:30 P.M. But I have to get up at 3:30 A.M. tomorrow morning because I have to go on

---

[150] A popular hangout on the northeast corner of Edenwald and Murdock Avenues in the Bronx. It underwent several name changes over the years, including Fialli's during the 1950's and 60's, and Cosmo's in the 1970's and beyond, until finally closing.

[151] Good Will Court was another popular radio show.

guard duty from 4 to 8:00 A.M. We get guard duty according to alphabetical order. So far I haven't got the dog watch which is from 12 midnight to 4:00 A.M. We have inspection every day of our locker and our bunk. We have to make up our bunk the first thing in the morning. Yesterday afternoon our company won the rooster. The rooster is the name given for a marching competition. The company that wins gets ten hours liberty in the nearest town which is Geneva. Boy are we going to raise hell in those ten hours. Most of the fellows are going to try and get laid. They say it is a small town. The food up here is okay but the Navy's middle name is beans. Holy Christ, we sure see enough of them.

As long as I have been up here, I think I have seen five girls and they were all Waves. And they stunk. We have 112 men in our barracks and eighty percent of them are Catholic. So I am in with a good crowd. We have all day Sunday to ourselves. The only thing we are forced to do is go to church. Every Sunday we have chicken for dinner. And of course we get all the trimmings with it. I hear that you will be home around Christmas time. Well, Johnny, so will I, so we ought to have a good time together. Today is our last day for white hats. From now on we have to wear the black pancake hats.

The guy on the bunk up top of me is a shark at cards. In three days he has won forty three bucks. Not bad. Well, I will say so long for now. Write and let me know how you are. So long.

Your pal,
Dick"

"Fort Knox, Kentucky

Nov. 15, 1943 [Monday]

Dear Mother,
    This is just a line to let you know that I am all right. Yesterday Sunday I went to the 9 o'clock mass in the morning and went to the movies in the afternoon. I saw a good picture the name of it is "Thousands Cheer".[152] It's about the army. It is really very good. I think you would like it. Today I went to gunnery school. We did not do much but we did take a test. I am sure I passed it because it was very easy. It is raining here again. How is the weather up there? Well Mom I guess that's about all for now. Love to all.

Love,

---

[152] "Thousands Cheer" was an American musical comedy film produced in 1943. It was directed by George Sidney and released by Metro-Goldwyn-Mayer. Produced at the height of the Second World War, the film was intended as a morale booster for American troops and their families.

Son John

Dear Dad,
 How are you? Is Mom keeping her eye on you? I guess she still is. By the way Dad how is the beer in New York? Do you ever stop over at John's on Sand Street? The beer we have here is 3.2 and it is just like water. How are things over at the Navy Yard?[153] Did they build any new ships lately? Well Dad take it easy and don't work too hard.
         Love,
         Son John"

℘

The next letter is from John's Uncle Frank McGowan, his Dad's brother, a rising star in the Claims Department at the Fifth Avenue Bus Company. He was, as John recalled, a very important figure to him while growing up, and very kind to his nephew.

"605 West 132nd Street
New York City

Nov. 16, 1943 [Tuesday]

Hello John,
 The Mount won Sunday. They beat Haverstraw 35 to 0. Your father was up to the game with me. They play Cuotes [sp?] Sunday and say it will be a good game.
 What do you think of the Irish? They must have a pretty good team. Have you fellows got a team down there? If so, how are they making out? Have you won any games at all? I don't see anything in the papers. Are you too busy with instructions?
 George Stanley has been made a Chief and he is out on the West Coast. Everything up on the Hill is O.K. That was some game that the Chicago Bears

---

[153] The Brooklyn Navy Yard "played a pivotal role in World War II, building battleships and aircraft carriers, repairing over 5,000 ships, and sending troops and supplies to fronts across the globe. Not only did the Yard construct the *USS Arizona* a generation before the war, which was sunk at Pearl Harbor on December 7, 1941, but it is also where the battleship *Missouri* was constructed, upon whose deck the formal surrender of the Empire of Japan was signed in 1945. Thanks to the efforts of its 70,000 workers, the Brooklyn Navy Yard became the world's busiest shipyard, earning the nickname "The Can-Do Yard" for its ability to patch up wounded ships and put them back in action." (From https://turnstiletours.com/tours/brooklyn-navy-yard/world-war-ii-tour-of-the-brooklyn-navy-yard/).

played against the Giants. Martin still has his car but has a little trouble with it. I think it is his battery. When you get your furlough I guess you will be able to give him some advice about his car. Unable to think of anything else. I will close.

Frank"

"Nov. 17, 1943

Dear John,
  Enclosed you will find $10.00. I am hoping you will receive it O.K. When do you expect to buy your train ticket? You will get another pay 1st of December and maybe that will help you out too. In case you feel when the time comes for your furlough that you will be short of money write in time and let me know so I will be able to help you out.
  Bet you are glad that the test is near a finish. Hope you feel all right after that dose of pills. I am rather anxious to know more about this test. But now that I am looking forward to your homecoming (in fact everybody in Edenwald knows it by this time) I will wait until such time to ask questions.
  I had a letter from Sonny. He seems to be making out all right. Was in an armistice parade[154] and said all the girls were admiring them. He said he thought of his father as he marched along. How Dave would like to don a uniform and expand his chest for all the ladies to admire him. I was thinking, "Leave it to the Lucas family for their big opinions of self." I guess Sonny has worked hard to get where he is. Told me he visited Niagara Falls one weekend.
  Did you get Ritchie's letter? Mrs. Bernabe told me Ralph wrote to you last week. Did you receive his letter? I am going to the Rosary Card Party tonight. Yesterday I spent over in Staten Island with Mrs. Hull, Mrs. Mooney and Mrs. Regan. We had a great day. Ate lunch in a classy restaurant and then took a bus around Staten Island and finally landed in Mrs. Hull's house, where she served a chicken dinner and everything that goes with it. Staten Island is one of the busiest places I have been in. The ferry boat was filled with people in all kinds of uniforms. It was 12 o'clock when I got home. Poor Mugs almost licked the face off me. We had a nice half cup of tea and went to sleep. Since Dad is working nights Mugs is my companion and she and I can almost talk together.
  I think I told you Buddy Mooney is home. He has had some great experiences. Was in that invasion of Italy. He expects to be home until December 8th. Why don't you send him a card while he is at home? His name is Robert. Bet he would like to hear from you. By the way, George Stanley

---

[154] November 11, now called Veteran's Day, was originally called Armistice Day.

was made Chief Petty Officer, so Mamie tells us. I think he is on an invasion boat.

When Neppie Bernabe heard you were coming home, he started jumping up and down with delight. Started asking a hundred questions - how you would be dressed and etc. Said he doesn't believe in Santa Claus because he found out he was a fake. Well John I will have to close now. Will be waiting to hear from you. Love from all.

Mother"

℘

NOVEMBER 21, 1943 - NBC RADIO

Drew Pearson, NBC Radio correspondent, gets a leak of the Patton slapping incidents from Ernest Cuneo, a liaison officer in the Office of Strategic Services (OSS), precursor to today's Central Intelligence Agency. He announces it on nationwide radio, bringing Patton's career almost to a halt. Eisenhower stops short of firing Patton. He needs him, warts and all.

℘

"Nov. 22, 1943 [Monday]

Dear Son John,

This is Monday morning and instead of doing the family wash I am sitting down writing. I have about a dozen letters to answer if I ever get them on their way it will be a miracle. So far I got a letter written to Mrs. Hull. By the way, I wish you would send her a card. She always asks for you. Also one to Tommy Lucas and Richard Simmons. Dad gave me orders to write one to you too. I wish you could see him and Muggsie sound asleep in bed. He had Saturday off so he treated me to the movies. We saw Abbott and Costello. It was very funny. "Come Home Lassie" is coming to Mt. Vernon so we intend to see it. I treated myself to a new hat and coat. Your father likes them so they must be nice. He and I went through the stores Saturday. They are beginning to decorate for Christmas. My heart warms up at the thought of your homecoming. If you heard Dad, I think he is going to invite the parish in for the holidays. I told Ritchie I hope he is home with you. Mom and Duke met Father Broderick yesterday. He told them he had a letter from you. Duke told him that he is putting extra weights in the house pinning it down, for fear you would "come home in one of them tanks and knock it down."

I was saying a few extra prayers for you Friday, hoping the test was a success. John, don't you think they will compensate you boys for that? Say by giving you a little extra time added to your furlough? Father Foley told me they should. He is great, John. His whole heart is concerned with the boys in service, maybe because he was a war chaplain. George down at Edbling's wanted your address to send you a Christmas package, but Dad told him you were coming home.

Well John, between tanks and taking over German villages I guess you must be quite a soldier by this time. As far as tommy guns are concerned, I can't picture you using it. But then I suppose it all goes with the training. Dad said it teaches you to take care of yourself. We suppose you got a big thrill out of the fact that the Generals were watching.

Thursday will be Thanksgiving Day. The big game will be at the Mount with Cardinal Hayes[155], and the winning of the $500. I will let you know more about it later. Turkeys are scarce this year but we are told the boys in service are going to get them. So enjoy the day John, and don't eat too much. My writing paper is all gone so I will close. Thursday morning (18th) I sent your bag and etc., also a letter with $10.00. Hope you received all. Write soon.

Love,
Mother"

℘

"Nov. 27, 1943 [Saturday]

Dear John,

This is Saturday night. Mary Ann is spending the weekend with me. She is asleep in bed now and Mugs is next to her. Well we saw the picture "Lassie Come Home" this afternoon. It was wonderful. I couldn't tell you at times whether I was laughing or crying but it seems to me the entire audience were blowing their noses. Didn't it make you think of Mugs? She understands so much too. I was wishing Dad could see it. He couldn't get there on account of work. There are a lot of ships in now so they are very busy. Well John I have so much news to give you I don't know where to start. But I want to tell you the Navy is just perfect now. Walter Cubita blew in town yesterday. He paid me a visit. The Ford girl was with him. His hat was on the back of his head and I tell you to see him coming along you would think Admiral Nimitz had arrived. He looks fine. I was really surprised at his appearance, but he got taller too. In fact I think he looks better than Robbie did. Have you been hearing from him? He tells me he has been writing to you and wants to know

---

[155] The Mount St, Michael - Cardinal Hayes Thanksgiving Day football game, played every year since 1943, continues to be one of the premier challenges between Catholic high schools in New York City.

why you write U.S. Army on your address. His one hope is that you and he will be home at Christmas together.

Last Saturday Peggy Regan was married. She is a SPAR.[156] Looks swell in her uniform and is secretary to the Commander of the whole outfit down at Palm Beach. She is here on furlough, married some soldier who is going overseas. Mary's boy - you remember him - is at some boarding school outside Washington. I was talking with Mary. Today the Jennings girl was married. Her brother said the Mass.

Well yesterday I got rather a surprise. I received a letter from Richard Simmons from the naval hospital. He has been sick with a cold. It made me feel bad when I read it. Do you recall John how he wrote about the cold weather? I think now this sick spell was coming on him and that is the reason he felt it so cold. His mother is rather worried and told me she is going up there tonight to see him. He tells me how he wrote to you and you never answered. I am surprised at that. Get busy and write to him. I am enclosing his letter for you to read. Write to the hospital address.

John my dear boy I didn't receive the letters you sent Sunday and Monday until Friday 26th. That means I had no word from you before Thanksgiving. I was a little disappointed. Well John I can say we had a very nice, peaceful Thanksgiving, a good dinner, chickens not turkey. Couldn't get it. Mom, Duke, Dad and I ate together. Dad had to go into work so we had dinner about 2 o'clock and although your absence was felt by us all and gave us a little ache in our hearts, I would say Thanks Be to God for it all.

I hope John the mess sergeant kept his word and gave you all a good feed of turkey and trimmings. We were wondering where you would be eating Thanksgiving dinner. That ammunition you speak of certainly is costly. Keep your head down Sonny Boy when it is flying. Did you read the story of General Patton slapping the soldier? In my opinion I think they should have kept that story under cover for the good of all.[157]

Dad thinks Walter McGowan is in that raid on the Japs. Mamie doesn't expect George or Walter for Christmas.

About Mrs. Hubbard's pictures, I haven't seen her yet to tell her. I was thinking John would you be able to call that picture place on the phone and explain the matter to them, telling them who you are and where located and maybe they could send the pictures to you or else get in touch with Mrs. Hubbard. Or would you suggest me telling Mrs. Hubbard to write to them. In fact I don't know why she didn't get in touch with them a long time ago. When you write to me again tell me what you decided. I leave it to your judgment.

---

[156] The U.S. Coast Guard (USCG) Women's Reserve, known as the SPARS, was the World War II women's branch of the USCG Reserve.
[157] The incident she is referring to is the "slapping incident", news of which has just recently hit the airwaves in November 1943.

John I have a surprise for you. We got a classy French telephone installed at last. The number is FAirbanks 4-4113. Write it down in your notebook. Dad wants you to call and reverse the charges. He said, "Tell John to call just so we can hear his voice." Next Saturday night (Dec. 3rd) Dad will be home. It is his night off so if you want to call then or if you would rather wait until you are sure when you get your furlough you could call up say the night before you are to leave and give us the particulars.

Anyway I want you to know the phone is here. Duke is in clover now, he can call Staten Island, etc.[158] *He still walks around the house surveying it. We have lots of fun now. Mrs. Windell's mother is here now during the day taking care of the children and she opens all the windows. Duke stands out in the back staring up at the house. "By George, that woman will have the house frozen!" And then he runs down to measure the oil.*

Well John I am going to finish up this letter and start on another to you. I can't send it all in one envelope. Love from Mother.

P.S. The mailman to us is the most important one who comes to the door these days."

℘

NOVEMBER 28, 1943

In Teheran, Iran, the first meeting of the 'Big Three' occurs. Soviet Union leader Josef Stalin, U.S. President Franklin D. Roosevelt and British Prime Minister Winston Churchill meet to discuss several topics during the four-day conference, including the decision to launch an invasion of Western Europe in the spring of 1944; the invasion of southern France; and a promise on the part of Stalin to enter the war with Japan militarily as soon as Germany was defeated. This last item is frankly something Stalin never intends to do.

---

[158] The call to Staten Island would probably be to Gallagher relatives, from the Duke's mother's side of the family (Bridget Gallagher McGowan).

SIX: "HOSPITAL LEAVE"

"Dec. 1, 1943 [Wednesday]

Dear John,
 This morning brought your letter telling me about you being sick with a cold. Well thank God John it is only a cold. Don't let it get you down. Because it could be a hundred and one things worse than that. Just take it easy and rest.
 I am not going to let your father see the letter so he won't have to know about it. If there is anything special you want to tell me write it on a separate piece of paper. I told you in my last letter about the telephone. So if you are able give us a ring. I suggested Saturday night because Dad expects to be off, but you call when you want to. Reverse the charges (FAirbanks 4-4113).
 In regards to your furlough, well John, there is no use saying we will all be mighty disappointed, but then if you don't get it you will have to make the most of it. Don't give up hope. Let you and I start on a prayer crusade especially to the Blessed Mother and maybe you could receive Communion. This will be First Friday and I am also on the altar work this week and there isn't anything like prayer, it will move mountains, and if it is God's will you will get home. After all John, I think they owe you a special break after that test, and you didn't see home since you left. If you get a chance, speak up for yourself. Don't worry, everything will come out O.K.

         Love,
         Mother

P.S. John I will write more later. I want to get this mailed. 10:30 a.m."

And the second letter of the day, going out in an afternoon mail pickup, or the following day.

"Wed. Dec. 1, 1943 [Wednesday]

Dear John,
 This morning I received your letter stating you were in the hospital sick with a cold. I mailed an answer to that immediately. In the afternoon mail I received your letter telling me you were back in the barracks feeling fine and that your furlough was assured. Well I certainly thanked God for that good news as it was a great relief to know you were all right again and coming home for Christmas.

Dad doesn't know you sent those letters or anything about your being ill. Although he is always asking if there is any letter from you. Frank was in last night and told me he had a letter from you. I told your father that you must be O.K. when Frank heard from you. That kind of satisfied him. You know John he comes home early in the morning on night work so there isn't much chance for him to go traveling. Every place is closed. He said to me today (Schultz) we better get in a lot of can goods - juices and that - for John when he comes home. I said O.K., but he didn't realize the feeling I had inside of me at that time.

Well John let us thank God in our prayers everything is fine. Receive Communion when you get a chance. Remember Dad and I in your prayers.

I wrote a letter to R. Simmons tonight. His mother visited last Sunday. He is getting along very nicely now although I think the poor fellow was mighty sick from what his mother told me. Yesterday I saw one of the finest looking army men I have ever seen, he got in on the Mt. Vernon bus and when he sat down Lo and Behold his insignia was a tank with a silver oak leaf on each shoulder. Dad said he was a Lieutenant Colonel. If all the tank men look like him, they must be fine. Take good care of yourself. Rest.

Love,
Mother

P.S. Write when you can. I am always waiting for your letters."

Another letter from friend Walter Cubita, written on the second anniversary of the Pearl Harbor attack.

"Tuesday, Dec. 7, 1943

Dear John,

Just a short letter to let you know where I am stationed now. I am here for six weeks after which I go to a hospital to strike for my rating as a pharmacists mate. When I was home I had quite a swell time. I spent some time in Hickey's talking with Tom Farrell and some of the fellows. I went up and had a nice talk with your mother for a few hours one afternoon. Well I will close now as I haven't anything else to say.

Your pal,
Walter"

"Dec. 8, 1943 [Wednesday]

Dear John,
  Today is the feast of the Immaculate Conception. Dad went to 6:30 Mass on his way home and I went to 7:30 and received Holy Communion so even though you may not have attended Mass you were remembered in our prayers and petitions to the Blessed Virgin.
  Last night Archbishop Spellman spoke on the radio. He would certainly touch your heart in his praise of the boys in service and their sacrifices and courage. In our uncertain times he told the world what the Catholic's attitude is toward God and country and finished by saying, "If need be we will fight and die for the ideals."
  Your father was disappointed he didn't speak to you on the phone. I didn't tell him about your cold but in my mind I have never stopped wondering how you were getting along in the battle maneuvers with that cold. I have been praying like I never prayed before that God would bring you through O.K. I told your father when you come home I am going to keep you in bed for a couple of days to rest and if your cold isn't better, you can visit the doctor's. I had a letter from Ritchie. He is getting along nicely. He won't be home for Christmas.
  I don't know when you are going to receive this letter John but I am sending it anyway. Oh! How I miss your letters. I look for the mailman even though I know he hasn't anything for me. I must write to Aunt Kitty. Love from everybody. Hoping to hear from you soon.

Mother

P.S. Are you prepared financially (fare) to come home?"

℘

For the rest of December the letters dried up, evidence that Private McGowan finally gets his extended furlough, maybe aided by the illness he contracted, and the volunteer work he has performed as a U.S. Army "guinea pig." So we can imagine a good end to his first calendar year in service, and turn the page to 1944.

SEVEN: "A NEW YEAR"

"Jan. 9, 1944 [Sunday]

Dear John,
    We were saying today your furlough passed so quickly that it seems like a day. Dad and I took the Christmas tree down the day after you left and the house is now in order and looks comfortable and nice. Of course the house seems very quiet and lonesome after you went, but we are getting back to the old routine again. You know Dad would never let you have many dull moments when he is around and the clocks as a rule are always stopped so we don't worry much about time.
    You should hear Father Broderick at nine o'clock mass today telling how Cardinal Hayes beat Michael's[159] in the basketball game down at the Garden - score 57-26. He said the coach up at St. Michael's let that score go up and up even though he knew the Hayes boys were licked before they started at the football game at Thanksgiving but he wanted a show. Whereas the Cardinal Hayes coach was very charitable at the basketball game and only let the boys score up 57 against St. Michael's. He told the children that was the $10 question of the morning, who won the basketball game? Everybody was laughing in the church. When he was about to leave the pulpit he came back and asked who won that game yesterday and a little fellow up front stood up and said Cardinal Hayes. Father said, "What was the score?" Boy said, "57 to 26." By the way, Father O'Hare's father died. He was 86 years old.
    Well John when your father woke up yesterday and I told him the news from you he put on a big smile and said, "That will be a little more news for Hickey's paper." I said, "I knew you would think of that." Today, Sunday, Dad met Peter[160] down at church. I suppose he gave him all the news. Duke met Walter[161] yesterday. He said he expected to go in some hospital to work, so Duke tells me.
    Mamie[162] told Duke the next time he comes up to her house with Mugs to bring a long rope with him and tie her outside. The Duke said, "By George, and do you forget the big cats you had running around here. You don't need to worry, that is a clean dog that sleeps in a bed."

---

[159] Mount St. Michael.
[160] Possibly Peter Hickey.
[161] Walter Cubita.
[162] Mary ("Mamie") McGowan, the Duke's sister-in-law.

He expects to have a good time tomorrow night voting for Mr. Mooney at the Holy Name meeting.

We will try to get a watch for you as soon as possible as I am sure it is a necessary article.

I suppose you will start on your new routine tomorrow. I am hoping you will be satisfied and happy with your new assignment John. In fact I think God was good to you so don't forget to show your gratitude for his blessings and if you get in a tight spot once in a while just put confidence in prayer by asking God to guide and enlighten you. I think John you are the kind of a boy that if he makes up his mind to succeed and master a thing he will do so. From what you have told me I think there is plenty of opportunity for you to learn a lot and observe from the contacts you will make. Don't forget to keep neat and clean and be polite. Dad said take good care of your feet. I am happy John because I think you are. So write a long letter and tell us all about yourself. Goodnight and God bless you. Regards and love from all.

                          Mother

P.S. Send your new address to those you write to. Did you find your knife?"

℘

"Jan. 16, 1944 [Sunday]

Dear John,

This is Sunday afternoon. Everybody seems to be taking their afternoon sleep. Your father and Mugs are both snoring over in the big chair. Frank and his family are gone home. They were here since early morning. So now that they are no longer here the house is very quiet and a good time to write a few letters.

When you called on the phone Frank and Dad were down in the cellar with a part of Frank's car trying to fix it up. It seems to me though judging from all the hammers they took down with them that they intended breaking it up. Duke was down with them to see that they did the job right. It was too bad John that you didn't wait until the evening to call. We could have had a longer conversation. You could have talked more to Dad. Those hours from 7 p.m. to 10 o'clock are reserved for servicemen to call home and I believe you also get special rates. So hereafter if possible call between those hours. I like to have you call because it breaks that distance between us as Dad said. It makes you feel nearer home. If you don't call again until after the 20th of the month it will bring the charge in on a latter bill.

We went to the 10:30 Mass today. Father Broderick was there. He gave a very fine sermon telling about the difference between the Eastern Orthodox Church and the Roman Catholic. It was the best explanation I heard on that subject. In fact I never remember hearing it explained before and there *are a lot of people who are confused about these churches as they all called themselves Catholic.*

I saw Bobby Mahon across at Butlers having his picture taken with Roberta. Dad said it looks as if he is Seaman 3rd Class from the marks on his sleeve. He looks good - improved a lot. But poor Walter[163] looks so thin and pale. He needs to get a little common sense and stop trying to be what he isn't, a big shot. If he would get back to serving God more and staying home with his father and mother once in a while and giving them a little happiness he might improve a whole lot more in body and soul. When you write to him give him some hints after all like yourself and the other boys he is only a kid. So he shouldn't rush in where angels fear to tread.

Well last Monday evening after the Novena I was coming out of church and someone put their arm around me and who was it but Mrs. Springer with tears flowing down her face. She wanted to know how you made out and of course she was so happy to hear your good news. Said to tell you she was asking about you. You are one of her special boys who she is always praying for. I felt sorry for her. She was so disappointed about Richard.[164] He was supposed to be home around the holidays and didn't arrive and she got no word from him which made it worse. Everybody has been asking for you. I had a letter from Sonny[165] yesterday. He is very anxious to hear from you and to know how you made out. So I am going to write and explain all to him. He said he is halfway finished with his course and about March expects to go to Nashville Tennessee. If you were near enough maybe you could get together.

Reading Richard Simmons's letter from Christmas again. He stated he would write again and let me know his correct address so I think I will wait. When I get in touch with him I will tell him to drop you a few lines, also Bobby and Walter. I don't know their addresses. What you want to do is get a notebook and write the addresses in it and also little notes and names you want to remember. If you don't do this you will lose all your friends addresses. Now that you have so much leisure time you should be able to attend to all these things and John you have a lot to be thankful for so get into Mass when you can and receive Communion. Thank God for his blessings. I expect a visit from Andy.[166] Will tell you more later. Don't get a swelled head now mingling with the officers. Keep a level head. Polish up on your good English. Dad is yelling for tea. Tell us something about your experiences when you write. Write to Aunt Kitty. Love from all.

Mother"

---

[163] Walter Cubita.
[164] Richard here may refer to Mrs. Springer's son.
[165] Sonny Lucas, John's first cousin.
[166] Andy Garbarini.

"Fort Knox, Kentucky

Jan. 18, 1944

Dear Mother,
I received your letter today and was glad to hear from you. The reason I didn't call Sunday night is because the lines are so busy that I would have to wait several hours before getting connected with you. Mother when I called you Sunday I asked you for Red Gibbons's address but you did not send it to me. Please send it as soon as possible so that I might write to him.
Today I was out at the 37 MM range and I scored the officers on the hits they made. After the firing we had to take the targets down and bring them back to the warehouse. I will be out on the range all this week so if I don't write again this week you will know that I did not get a chance to do so on account of I got in later or had to go out. The next time I call I will write a few days before and find out if Dad will be home and then you can tell me and I will call when he is home. Well Mother that's about all for now. Love to all.
Love,
Son John"

P.S. Remember to send me those addresses and I will write again."

"Fort Knox, Kentucky

Jan. 21, 1944 [Friday]

Dear Mother,
Well how's everything? Today is Friday and we have just finished scrubbing the floor so we are all set for tomorrow inspection of the barracks. Please excuse my writing as I cut my finger and it is hard to write well. Well Mother we are on another secret mission. We are out testing new American and English smoke bombs. It will take a week till the test is over so if you do not hear from me you will know why. I will have to work Sunday so that means I miss mass. There are supposed to be some big shots and scientists to watch us Sunday as we demonstrate the smoke bombs. It seems to be something important and they tell us this will revolutionize warfare if a success. I hope it is because we may get a three day pass out of it. I will go home on it. Well

how's Mugs making out with the Duke? Did they go up to McGowans on the hill[167] again? I think I have told you all and will close. Love to all.

                                                             Love,
                                                            Son John"

JANUARY 22, 1944

Allied forces land at Anzio in Italy.

Only two pages of the next letter are extant (pages 3 and 4), the rest unfortunately missing. The envelope is postmarked "Wakefield Station, New York, N.Y. Jan. 25, 1944, 8 PM". It is in pencil, in Anna's handwriting. From it we learn that John has been given an opportunity to attend officer training, but has turned it down, undoubtedly to his mother's chagrin. The opportunity he has turned it down for may be to join the Instructor's Regiment, and remain for some time at Fort Knox instructing new recruits in the intricacies of tanks.

    John recalled years later the events that led to his being selected for the Instructor's Regiment.

    "I was on the tank crew, and we were doing target practice. I was up top, helping the tank commander with coordinates to give the gunner down below so he would hit the target. After a while the tank commander dropped down into the tank, and gave me command. I was now in charge of everything. I kept feeding the gunner information on elevation, range, direction of fire and such, and every time he followed my instructions and fired, the shell would hit

---

[167] "McGowans on the hill" referred to another McGowan family, that of the Duke's deceased brother Frank, who passed away in 1935. They lived at 2132 Edenwald Avenue, which is on top of the plateau where Edenwald Avenue attained its highest elevation as it journeyed in a straight line eastward from E. 233rd Street and crossed the city line into neighboring Mt. Vernon in Westchester County. At the time this letter was written (January 1944), only Frank's widow, Mary McGowan ("Mamie"), lived "on the hill", renting two apartments in the sturdy brick house her late husband Frank had built in 1925, while she herself lived in the basement apartment. Her home was one of the first houses built on Edenwald Avenue, on lots they had purchased in 1905, when the area had been but recently woods, farmland and diminished country estates. Mary's eldest son John was married and living in White Plains, New York; her daughter Margaret was a Sister of Mercy (Sister Mary Albert); and her youngest child, Walter, was serving in the U. S. Navy in the Pacific. George Stanley, who Mamie had virtually adopted as a son when he was a young boy and suddenly orphaned, was also serving in the Pacific. The Duke apparently visited his sister-in-law often, always with his dog Muggsie in tow.

the target dead on. I could tell the tank commander was happy with my work, as he stayed down below and had a big smile on his face every time I could see him. After a while we were done with the exercise, and I turned around and noticed there was a knot of tank officers a short distance behind us, close enough that I could see one scribbling something on a clipboard while the others seemed to nod their heads at something one of them was saying. It didn't take long before the knot of officers had come up behind the tank. I was still the commander, and the officer with the clipboard waved up at me and asked 'What's your name, Private?'

'McGowan, sir,' I replied. 'Private John F. McGowan.'

'Nice job directing fire, son,' the officer said. 'You've certainly learned how to get the best out of this beast.'

'Thank you, sir.' I saluted, they returned the salute, and that was it for the day. I felt pretty proud at that moment.

Now, this was around the time when we would be getting our final assignments as to what combat tank division we would get assigned to, and the rumors were already flying about the different campaigns looming ahead, and how some would go to the Pacific, and others to Africa, but ultimately we thought we would probably be in battle in Europe. There was already speculation as to where in France the Allies would make a landing, and it was no secret that the German tanks were probably superior to ours, and there would be a lot of us there in that camp that day who might be dead a few months down the road, when we were finally deployed. And it wouldn't be long before we would know where our next assignment would be.

The day came, and the lists went up. All of us gathered around the bulletin board where the assignments were posted, and each time a G.I. found his name, there would be either a cheer or a downright curse. But my name wasn't on the lists, no matter how hard I looked for it. After a while I went to one of my officers and told him. 'Sir, I'm not on the list, sir,' I said.

He smiled slightly. 'You're on another list, Mac,' he said. 'Over there.' He pointed to another bulletin board a short distance away, with only one list posted, rather than the dozen or so that held our combat division assignments. I walked over to that list, wondering what sort of assignment it could be, and saw across the top the title *Instructor's Regiment*, and there right near the top was my name. It was then I realized that I wasn't going into combat, at least not yet. I'd been assigned to the Tank Training Division, and would be an Instructor at the camp, teaching raw recruits and officers just how to get the best out of the tanks I had just spent six months learning the ins and outs of.

While I had some mixed feelings about it - we were all still wet behind the ears when it came to the realities of war - it dawned on me pretty quickly what a gift I'd been given. I knew my time would come, and when it did I knew I would do my duty, no matter what Uncle Sam decided that would be. But for now that duty was going to be turning raw recruits and green officers into the best tank men the Germans or the Japs would ever face, and I was damned proud of what my role would be in that effort."

[Jan. 25, 1944][Tuesday]

"...*house when the telephone started ringing. People inquiring if he had any old antiques he wanted to sell. He was also asking about you and he said he wished he knew you had an offer to go into Officers school. He would have advised you to think it over before you refused but maybe this appointment may lead to something better. He said to tell you to take advantage of any opportunity you get and he also wanted to know if you visited the Chalk family.*[168] *Did he tell you one of the daughters is secretary to the Mayor of Louisville, Kentucky? There were eleven children in the family. The oldest boy died in the World War*[169] *and he attended him. That is how he got to know them. You ought to look them up. He would like you to and tell them he told you to call. They have a son in service somewhere.*

Well John your long awaited letter arrived Saturday although I notice you wrote it Tuesday. Your father and I were beginning to think we were waiting for the letter that would never arrive. You didn't give us much information about yourself. Now that you have more time we expect to hear from you often. How are your feet?

Dad was sick for a few days but he is feeling all right now. Your letters kind of boost his morale. I write to David and Aunt Kitty and George. Well John write more to us and don't get too smart with the guns.

Love,
Mother"

Enclosed is a small scrap of paper with John's friend "Red" Gibbons's address, now that the family has moved from Edenwald to City Island, another Bronx neighborhood.

"Harry Gibbons Jr.
461 Minifet Street
City Island, N.Y."

JANUARY 27, 1944

---

[168] The Chalk family were apparently a prominent family in Louisville, Kentucky.
[169] The First World War.

The city of Leningrad in Russia is relieved after suffering through a 900-day siege by German troops.

§

The young write also. The following letter is enclosed with one from his mother, and is written by John's pre-teen first cousin, Mary Ann McGowan.

"*January 30, 1944 [Sunday]*

Dear John,

Do you like your oranges? Did you sleep on the train? How are you? When are you coming home? Do you get your hankies dirty? I cannot get your hankies clean. Do you get good food? Do you have fun? Come home when you can. Muggsie is all right.

Love,
Mary Ann McGowan"

And the letter above is enclosed with...

"*Jan. 30, 1944 [Sunday]*

Dear Son John

This is Sunday afternoon as I write this letter. I realize you must be still on your journey many miles from here. I hope you enjoyed the little lunch I packed for you. If you are able to observe the sights as you ride along John. This traveling should be an education in itself. Did the train pull through the flood areas O.K.? When you write tell us how you made out on the trip.

Dad arrived home safe and sane. He is working as usual. Mary Ann is here with me. She is great company. I wish you could hear her sing - Pistol Packin' Mama and My Pin-Up Girl, etc. She knows all the verses. She and I had a little concert here, with Muggsie snoring out loud. And speaking of Muggsie, if she don't stop shedding that hair around here, she will have to look for a new abode. Today is a good, clear, cold, windy day so I kept Mugs out in hopes the strong wind would relieve her of some of her burden as it took me all morning cleaning the chairs.

Today Mary Ann and I went to nine o'clock Mass and being almost late Mr. Mulholland ushered us up to the very first pews. I thought he was bringing us up on the altar but being that I was away up front I had a very good chance to observe the flowers and etc., and I really felt good as everything look so beautiful. Father O'Hare asked the people to pray for the Supple boy. Mrs. Simmons and Richard received Holy Communion. I was talking to them outside of church. Now that it is coming near time for Richard to leave like all the boys he is getting a bit choky. They said they were so surprised to see you. The Jennings boy was there too, he makes a splendid Marine. Loretta Pierce took me down to church in her car this morning. She was asking for you. Said you ought to make a good officer, you had such a fine appearance. What a compliment. By the way I saw a young fellow coming out of church today with a tank insignia and T. Sergeant marks. I wonder who he is. I think he had a div[ision] number. You should keep an eye out for Johnnie Murray. Maybe you could get together now and have a chat.

    Well John everybody thinks you look swell, Thank God. In fact I thought you looked good on the first furlough but this time you looked better and heavier. So take good care of yourself. Here are some don'ts, even though I credit you with good sense. Don't indulge, because that is the one thing that leads us into temptation and weakens our wills - spoils our nervous system. Don't smoke too much. Get into bed early and get plenty of sleep. And above all, say your prayers. Never mind what the other fellows think. You keep close to God and it would please me very much John if it were possible for you to get to confession and Holy Communion this First Friday and if not receive Sunday if you can and ask God's blessing on you and your work. Sometimes John your actions may be observed by your superior officers when you least think about it and who can tell John maybe your good church attendance was watched before and helped to put you where you are. Everybody speaks so well of you John and you yourself have made me feel very happy. I only thank God for it all and hope he will continue to take care of you.

    Don't think I am trying to preach a sermon John but there are so many temptations in this world of ours that a young boy needs to be on his guard all the time. So in the words of the Commander who gave his life, be a good Catholic and you will be an honorable soldier.

    Aunt Kitty sent me Tom's address and John's too. I will enclose them. Did you ever write to Sister Mary Albert? You should John. Would it be possible for you to send her some kind of souvenir from there? Look around and maybe you could buy something suitable for her. Buddy Mooney is leaving for Philadelphia tomorrow. Mom said Johnnie Murray just passed by. He must be here yet. Aunt Kitty is coming to visit soon. I will tell Martin send the Tower. Be a good boy. Love from all.

                                                     Mother"

EIGHT: "INSTRUCTOR"

"Feb. 4, 1944 [Thursday]

Dear John,
I must tell you I got a great surprise when I received your money order Wednesday. Thanks a lot. I wondered if you left yourself short. I was looking for a few lines that I thought you might send to tell us how you made out in your traveling back but I take it that you at least reached there safe and sound.
Today being Thursday of course is Dad's big day. But thank the Lord he arrived home early as usual and O.K. He is now sound asleep and snoring. We had our throats blessed today and I went to confession for tomorrow is First Friday. Did you get a chance to get to church?
John that Marine I saw on Sunday was the Mansfield boy. Mrs. Mahon told me Bobby has a A.P.O. number. Mrs. Savage said she felt disappointed you didn't get to see her when you were home. The Rosary Society had a card party last night. That is when you get all the news.
Martin is going to send the Tower to you. Mom said he may go to Fordham instead of Manhattan. It is almost 11 o'clock John and I will close for the time being. Mary Ann went home tonight. I miss her chatter and singing. I will write more later. Send a little news when you can.
Love,
Mother"

℘

FEBRUARY 4, 1944

The Bronze Star Medal is established by Executive Order 9419. The medal, designed by Rudolf Freund (1878–1960) of the jewelry firm Bailey, Banks & Biddle, can be awarded to any person who, while serving in any capacity in or with the Army, Navy, Marine Corps, Air Force, or Coast Guard of the United States, after 6 December 1941, distinguishes, or has distinguished, herself or himself by heroic or meritorious achievement or service, not involving participation in aerial flight, while engaged in an action against an enemy of the United States. Private McGowan will become a proud recipient of this award, along with 690 other members of the 65th Infantry Division, the unit in which he is destined to go to combat with thirteen months down the road.

℘

"Feb. 7, 1944 [Monday]

Dear John,

The mailman brought your letter this morning Monday. I had been wondering for the last few days why we didn't hear from you as we were anxious to know how you made out on your journey.

I am glad to know you got down there safe and sound. You mentioned in your letter about moving to a smaller section. You didn't say why the change was made. Tell us more about it and what it means to you when you write again. Do you think you will remain in this Instructor regiment as a permanent place? Is there a chance that it will lead to a higher rating for you? You answer these questions in your next letter and then you will have something to write home about. Like all mothers John I am interested in you getting to the top and along with that I am also concerned about you taking good care of your body and soul. That above all is most important.

I just heard a beautiful sermon given by a priest over the radio on "Home" and he started by saying, "Mid pleasures and palaces there is no place like home." And he went on to tell how on every train you will see young soldiers and sailors traveling for hundreds of miles sometimes without an hour's sleep just to get home to spend a few hours out of two or three day furloughs and it made me think of you and Ritchie and John Lucas, how much he rushed home all the time just for a night and as Kitty said put up really with hardships to get there.

I met Ritchie's sister Saturday down at church. She said they heard from him and he told them he would have 48 hours off over the weekend but the time was too short to come home on so he was going to spend his leave with a fellow in Albany who resides there.

They have received no word so far about the Supple boy.[170] The Simmons girl told me that the Dumser boy[171] who was Johnnie Supple's pal sent home money for flowers to put them in front of the Blessed Mother as an offering for the Supple boy. I saw the flowers yesterday in the niche. They are beautiful. Wasn't that a nice thought of the Dumser boy?[172]

---

[170] John ("Johnnie") Supple, "the Supple boy", who had been declared Missing In Action, and feared dead.

[171] The Dumser family lived at 3565 Ropes Avenue. The father, Sebastian Dumser, Sr., 57, was a "metal spinner" in a machine shop. His wife, Margaret, was 38. They had three children: Sebastian, Jr., 17; Charles, 17; and Louise, 11. The reference to "the Dumser boy" could be to either of the two brothers, both the same age. Perhaps they were twins.

[172] The depth of faith evident throughout these letters is astounding. This example is really profound. Here is a young man, the Dumser boy, believing that an offering of flowers to the Blessed Virgin, along with prayer, may help determine the fate of

Dad was off yesterday Sunday so we went to the movies in the afternoon, saw "Old Oklahoma" and "Idrood Street".[173] *Your father started to take instruction is school today on fighter content over at the Navy Yard. He looked real nice yesterday going to Mass. I used a little elbow grease and soap around his head. He almost threw a fit but I accomplished it anyway. We went to 10:30 mass and was ushered up to almost the front pew. So I was glad I insisted on doing what I did. I saw Father Broderick but didn't get a chance to talk to him.*

Georgiana Lenahan's husband Bob is home. He has a 21 day furlough. Helen[174] *informs me that they are changing the rules about boot training. Mrs. Mahon called over to tell me she received an A.P.O. address for Bobby so she thinks he must be gone out to sea.*

Martin[175] *started in Manhattan College today. He is studying chemistry. Mom said he brought home papers for his mother and father to sign, something to do with taking the Navy V-12 test.*[176] *But Rose said they were not going to let him take it.*

Did you hear from Sonny Lucas? I must write to Aunt Kitty. She told me in her last letter that Dave was home for two weeks. He wasn't feeling well. If I can arrange it with your father maybe I will go over to visit her for a few days and get all the latest news.

---

his friend, for whom the worst, obviously, is feared. Would that such a faith existed today. The world might be a better place for it.

[173] "In Old Oklahoma" was a 1943 American Western film directed by Albert S. Rogell starring John Wayne and Martha Scott. The film was nominated for two Academy Awards, one for Music Score of a Dramatic or Comedy Picture and the other for Sound Recording (Daniel J. Bloomberg). "Idrood Street" remains a mystery.

[174] Helen Butler.

[175] Martin Moynihan.

[176] The Navy V-12 test qualified those who passed to enlist in the V-12 Navy College Training Program, designed to supplement the force of commissioned officers in the United States Navy during World War II. Between July 1, 1943, and June 30, 1946, more than 125,000 participants were enrolled in 131 colleges and universities in the United States. Numerous participants attended classes and lectures at the respective colleges and earned completion degrees for their studies. Some even returned from their naval obligations to earn a degree from the colleges where they were previously stationed. The V-12 program's goal was to produce officers, not unlike the Army Specialized Training Program (ASTP), which sought to turn out more than 200,000 technically trained personnel in such fields as engineering, foreign languages, and medicine. Running from 1942 to 1944, the ASTP recruits were expected but not required to become officers at the end of their training.

Joey Roda's mother was asking for you. Joe went back to the seminary. I often think of poor Andy.[177] I have been looking for his brother around church but never seem to see him. Father O'Hare was threatening all kinds of things yesterday if the boys don't attend the Junior Holy Name meeting. He said, "The boys tell their mothers they are going to the meeting but it seems they never arrive there." So he is going to do F.B.I. work and catch a lot of them at the game.

Well John they say that the best part of the story is left until the end, so here goes. Saturday morning the telephone bill arrived and lo and behold the amount of it nearly sent me spinning. It is only $26 and 11 cents. One of the day calls was $6 and some cents and the other was $5 and some cents and the other calls were $2 and $3 etc. Those two afternoon calls before you came home will be listed on next month's bill. So John I think we will have to give up calling for a while and resort to letter writing. Unless you think it necessary John don't call until after the 20th of February. That will give me a chance to get the bills adjusted. Try to call in the evening between 7 and 10 o'clock. It won't amount to so much and then you could arrange to call at least twice during a month. We don't want to be giving all our money to the telephone people. Maybe you will be getting another furlough later on and we want to save for that.

Next month the 27th will be your birthday. If you get home at that time we will have to have a nice cake with candles and etc.

By the way John were you ever able to get in contact with the people who had Mrs. Hubbard's pictures? I don't suppose you got to visit the people Father O'Hare told you about. Why don't you take some nice boy with you and look them up when you have a day off. Know your place John but don't be too shy either.

I saw Mrs. Springer and her son in church Friday morning. I had a letter from Mrs. Hull thanking me for the nice time she had here. Told me I was a charming hostess. Wait until I tell her you were home on another visit that very week and she missed you. Tonight is the Rosary meeting so I will have to clean my ears out to hear all the news. Muggsie is busy cleaning her paws. She has a friend now outside, a big dirty-looking cat that you would be afraid to touch. The cat insists on sitting by the gate so Mugs never stops barking.

*Love,
Mother*

P.S. Write!"

---

[177] Probably Andy Garbarini.

"Fort Knox, Kentucky

Feb. 10, 1944 [Thursday]

Dear Mother,
    I received your letter today and was glad to hear that you received my money order okay. I went in Louisville over the weekend and really had a good old time and while I was there I met some sailors and boy did we paint the town red. Mother I did not get a chance to get to church on First Friday but I expect to go this week.
    How is everybody around the neighborhood? Did you see any more of Walter Cubita or Red Gibbons around? If Dad sees Red he ought to invite him up because I think he is going into service soon. I am getting along fine over at the gunnery school. The fellows I am with are swell and we have a good time together. Well Mom that's all for now. Love to all.
                                Love,
                                Son John"

"Fort Knox, Kentucky

Feb. 13, 1944 [Sunday]

Dear Mother,
    Well today is Sunday and I got to confession and communion at the 11 o'clock mass. I was going to go to Louisville but it got very cold. It was 10 degrees above zero so I thought I would stay in camp and go to confession. But today is a very nice day. The sun is shining and it is nice and warm. I think I will go with the fellows for a walk around and then go to the show tonight.
    How is Dad and Mom and Duke? Is the flag still flying as usual? Did you hear anything from Richie Simmons or Walter Cubita? If you do send me their addresses so I can write them and also send me Red Gibbons's address again. I did not hear from Father Broderick as yet so I will write to him in a day or two. Mother I wonder if you could get me a small camera because I can get all the films down here easy. That's about all for now. Love to all.
                                Love,
                                Son John"

FEBRUARY 15-18, 1944

Allies bomb the historic monastery at Monte Cassino in Italy.

"Feb. 16, 1944 [Wednesday]

Dear John,
Received your letter Monday and also one today. I am glad to know you like the new section and that it may give you an opportunity to better yourself. Mrs. Windel was telling me today her sister's husband who was a 2nd Lieutenant in North Africa has been advanced to a 1st Lieutenant and is now at Oxford University studying. I don't think he ever was in real action. Mr. Goldberg the insurance man was asking for you. His son is now at Yale studying the Japanese language. So that proves John there is a chance for further education. And take my advice John if opportunity is offered to you for more education take advantage of it. Nothing worthwhile is ever got easy. As the priest said, these boys 18 or 19 should look beyond the present war days and try to prepare for the future when they will take their place in the world.

It must have been very cold down there over the weekend but in a way I am glad otherwise you would be off having a good time and would have passed up getting to confession and communion. You should try to receive at least once a month. Duke was down to the Holy Name meeting Monday night and I had a good laugh the next day listening to him telling about what went on. He said, "That fellow who uses the big words made a speech and he talked so long he put Mr. Trainor to sleep and I am a son of a gun if anybody knew what he was talking about. Mr. Roosevelt wouldn't understand him, he was using such jaw breakers." Well it seems they bought a pen and pencil to give Fr. Jordan and they were up in arms about someone writing to Fr. Jordan informing him how the Society was going to give him a present. Duke said, "They have more committees down there now than the President has in Washington." He said there was no talk about having a March 17th day.

I heard that the Supple boy was taken prisoner by the Germans. I spent last Saturday afternoon in Mt. Vernon with Mrs. Miller. We met on the bus so shopped together. She told me Ritchie Simmons was going to be stationed at Sampson for a few months yet he is going in to study for signalman like Tom Lucas I guess. Haven't seen any of the family to speak to. If I should I will tell them to ask Ritchie to write. I will be on the lookout for Peter and see if I can obtain information about Walter. Will enclose Red Gibbons' address and also an address book for you to keep.

Next week the 22nd will be Washington's Birthday. Do you recall John how you and I visited Aunt Kitty and that was the last time we saw Sonny. He sent me a nice letter with his picture which I am going to send to you and you can return it later. Judging from his picture I think he got very sober looking and older too. He told me they were to take their first flight in the planes last week but there were such bad weather conditions and snow, it looks like they were grounded. I think he is supposed to leave Buffalo the end of this month. I sent him a Valentine. Did you receive the one I sent to you?

John did you have your teeth attended to? I hope so. Don't neglect them. We had a big snowfall here last Friday and Saturday. Plenty of sled riding on Strang Avenue. Since then we had a heavy rain fall and it swept all the snow away. Duke was kept busy cleaning the street and the rain pipes. Today he took Mugs up to Mamie's house and I wish you could see Muggsie when she came home. Such a sight as you never saw, her paws were mud up to her ears. When Duke came in he said, "Look at the sight of that dog, is it any wonder that nobody wants to let one in when she is with me?" Poor Mugs stood looking so guilty, shaking her tail. She is taking a good sleep now. When the snow was on the ground I went out with her and made her run for the ball. How she loves the snow.

I am going to try to get a camera for you - maybe I will go down to Bloomingdale's and see what I can do about getting one. I want to get you a watch too. We'll have to save up some money and see what I can do.

John when you have time sit down and write a few lines to Sister Mary Albert. She was so kind to you. Write and tell her you are sorry for not writing before this and tell her about your present position.

I think Father Broderick writes in spells. He told me one time he had 12 letters to write. I put in your name the other night for a vigil light. I gave the envelope with money to Father Foley. He said the day you called at the Rectory he must have been out. I said, "Yes, Father." I didn't want to say, "No, you were in bed."

John, everybody wants to know why you don't have your picture taken. Do so if you can but be sure to smile and put your cap on straight. I take it John you are having great times down there. But know the limit and pick your company. You were a good, clean, wholesome boy when you left here. John everybody admired you and that is how I expect you to return home again someday so take care of yourself and always hold to what is right and good. Mr. Gold was asking for you - told me you were a smart lad. Mrs. Gold was in here one day crying to Mom all her troubles. You never heard such a line in your life.

Dad is coming in for supper. Write soon.

Mother

P.S. It is almost 7 p.m. now. I will write more later."

℘

An always-welcomed box of fudge and fruit is sent, along with a mother's heart-felt ambitions for her son's advancement in the ranks.

"Feb. 20, 1944 [Sunday]

Dear John,

    I hope you will enjoy the contents of this box. I wanted to send you the Catholic News as there are a few items in it that I am sure you will be interested in - especially Fr. Sheehan's write up on answers to Russia. In your spare moments sit down and read them. When you are finished try to pass them on to some other Catholic boy.

    Along with the papers you will find a letter from Ritchie which arrived on last Thursday morn. And Walter's came the next day, Friday. I thought you would enjoy reading them. It looks like Ritchie is going to stay at Sampson for a few more months. Tom Lucas studied the same along the same line. Didn't he?

    I was surprised to receive Walter's letter as he never wrote before. Duke said "He must be a doctor now that he is taking care of the patients in the ward." I am going to give Roberta[178] your address to forward to Bobby.[179] She tells me he seldom writes now. She isn't sure just where he is but he seems to be very busy. It occurs to me he got out in the midst of things very quickly. Mr. Mahon is making out fine - was able to get downstairs.

    Enclosed John you will find a book for addresses and see that you take time off to copy them all in it.

    The doorbell just rang and it was Roberta wanting your address. She told me Bobby is a 3rd class seaman now. Wears a red stripe on his arm. She hasn't received any mail from him in over a month.

    You know John I have been trying to figure out in my mind, how is it you never get a higher rating? I am sure being picked for an instructor was really a promotion and was based on your merits. Do you understand about this, if not why not consult some officer who might explain? Some day you might have a chance to do so. Of course I wouldn't discuss it with the boys in the barracks but just find out for yourself.

    I can hear you say, "There is my mother again, wanting to push me up first." You said in one of your letters there is plenty of chance for advancement. Just what did you mean by that? Tell us in your letter a little more about yourself. Dad is having a great sleep - snoring like an engine.

    Well I attended 9 o'clock Mass this morning. Fr. Broderick was the celebrant and as usual he was asking the children questions and ended by telling them as a special news item that Hayes High School won the basketball game yesterday making them the champions of N.Y. You should see the big smile on his face. I didn't get a chance yet to speak to him.

---

[178] Roberta McIntyre.
[179] Bobby Mahon.

We have Mary Ann with us for a few days. The schools are closed until Wednesday including the holidays. What did you think of David's picture? Send it back when you can. I must get busy and write to all my soldier and sailor boyfriends.

Well John Wednesday is Ash Wednesday, starts Lent so don't forget to do a little penance and say an extra prayer for me. I will have to close now hoping you will enjoy the fudge and fruit. I will write more later. Write me a nice long letter.
Love,
                Mother and Dad

P. S. *Am enclosing an air mail stamp."*

"Fort Knox, Kentucky

Feb. 25, 1944 [Friday]

Dear Mother,
 I received your nice package and was glad to receive it. I also got the letter that you sent Wednesday. First of all I will answer some of the questions you asked in it. I do know the fellow that was in the phone booth ahead of me. He was trying to get Maryland. You see Mother there are so many calls that everybody gets a minute in the booth to place their calls and then they get in again when their call comes through. Well Martin Moynihan wrote me but he did not mention anything about films. Maybe you could find out about them. Martin in your letter you mention Red Head that came up with Eddie Kenary (sp?) well to tell the truth I can't seem to place anyone Red Head except Walter McGowan. By the way do they hear anything from Walter or George? Well I am getting along fine down here. I think that I will go to town this weekend. That's all for now because it is getting late and the lights will go out in a little while. Love to all.
                   Love,
                   Son John"

NINE: "THE VISIT"

"March 1, 1944 [Wednesday]

Dear John,
    I started to write this letter yesterday Wednesday but I am finishing it up today. Tuesday I received a letter from you which you wrote last Friday. I was looking for a few lines from you today but nothing arrived. Tomorrow being First Friday always brings back memories of you and your departure. Speaking of First Friday John makes me wonder if you are doing a little extra penance for Lent. When you get the opportunity go to confession and communion and say a few extra prayers. Don't be persuaded too much by what the other fellows do. Keep close to God. That is what will give you strength and courage most when you need it. Did you remember your birthday is this month?
    Now to change the subject. Last Wednesday night a week ago last night the telephone bell rang and who was calling but Aunt Kitty. She wanted me to meet her and Dave the next day at the Roxy Theater.[180] Well I went down Thursday morning and met them. We saw the picture "The Five Sullivans".[181] It was very good - rather sad. Dave seemed to be using his handkerchief a whole lot. I couldn't tell if it was to wipe his tears away or if his chewing gum was catching in his teeth. We really had a very enjoyable day together. Aunt Kitty and I as usual had a great chat. She told me Tom got a Presidential Citation for serving on this certain ship. She said he is making out O.K. when he can even send Bobby home a dollar for helping her. She said, "The only work Bobby does is taking care of the neighborhood cats. The last cat he got, it took six kids to carry it home." It was a monster, so Kitty tells me, and that it didn't even have a tail on it. Her John is in England and from what he writes, she said he must have a girlfriend there. But as she said, being a good cook must be the attraction. We really did have a good laugh. Dave brought us in a place for something to eat and he got in a conversation with a red-headed

---

[180] The Roxy Theater was a 5,920 seat movie theater located at 153 West 50th Street between 6th and 7th Avenues, just off Times Square in New York City. It opened on March 11, 1927 with the silent film *The Love of Sunya*, produced by and starring Gloria Swanson. The huge movie palace was a leading Broadway film showcase through the 1950s and was also noted for its lavish stage shows. It closed and was demolished in 1960.

[181] "The Five Sullivans" was a film based on one of the more tragic events of World War II, the death on a U.S. Navy vessel of five brothers, the Sullivans, during and following a Japanese attack.

sailor, a nice-looking boy from Chicago. He was alone so Dave invited him to join us and have some ice cream with us. Half the audience in the theater seem to be boys in all kinds of uniforms and oh my, how the streets are crowded. I went home on the 7th Avenue subway, made good connections. It was about seven o'clock and Dad came in about one hour later. I also saw that picture "Madam Curie." It was wonderful, the best I have seen since "Mrs. Miniver." See it John if you can.

Well now for the news of the day. Ritchie Simmons was home for 48 hours over the weekend. I didn't see him but his mother said he looks fine and is getting on O.K. Mrs. Mahon told me she thinks Robbie is somewhere around Scotland. He is a 3rd Rate Petty Officer. She said he volunteered for overseas duty and she was going to crown him for doing so. Willie Mahon is on his way for overseas and Dickey who is in Australia gives a hint he may get back to the States for a furlough. By the way John I got a notice to file for Jury Duty again.

Do you recall me telling you about Robert Faurenback receiving the Air medal? Well last Sunday at church the priest read out a broadcast that had been given over W.Q.R. last week explaining about the courage and etc. of a crew on a bomber who with 400 flak holes in her sides and with her two gunners lying bleeding on the floor of the plane - the plane already burning - was brought almost miraculously to a safe landing. And it went on to say how the crew said they prayed like they never prayed before. And the navigator of that plane was Robert Faurenback. Father O'Hare told us he had received a letter from Robert that week and he told him partly as a secret that when they start out on a bombing mission every Catholic boy receives Holy [illegible][182] so they are prepared in case of trouble.

Did you write to Walter? I must send him a few lines. I met the Nebiolo fellow. He is looking dandy. Studying at Washburn University, Kansas, but from what he tells me I don't think he is so much in love with it. I read where Camilla Sforza[183] is gone into training for the Nurses Corps.

---

[182] The illegible word is not Communion as one might expect, but seems to be more of a synonym for "Unction", essentially last rites in case the plane goes down and they should die.

[183] The Sforzas lived at 3527 Delavall Avenue. Camilla is listed on the 1940 Census as Carmina. The family in 1940 consisted of the father, Crescenzo Sforza, 44, a mechanic in a gas station, and born in Italy; his wife, Antoinette, 36; and children Lena, 16, John, 14, Carmina, 13, and Michael, 9. While Carmina went off to become a nurse, her brother John Sforza joined the Army Air Corps in August 1943, and was stationed at Greensboro, N.C.
The United States Army Nurse Corps (ANC) was formally established by the U.S. Congress in 1901. It is one of the six medical special branches (or "corps") of officers which – along with medical enlisted soldiers – comprise the Army Medical

Buddy Mooney is gone out again. Dick is home on furlough for a week. I saw the two Hurley boys Monday night at the Novena. The McCullam boy[184] who graduated with Martin enlisted in the Navy. He is up at Sampson. There is some fellow who was working in the Safeway Store, kind of a thin face. Mom said he used to ask her about you and told her his brother was a Corporal in the Tank Division. We don't know his name but Mom said you must know who he is.

Duke built another bird house and painted it white. It is already occupied. Muggsie and he take their afternoon walks as usual. Eleanor Walsh's boyfriend who is in the Air Corps is reported missing. Did you know who he was? Jackie Walsh will be 18 the 4th of March.

John do you know how much tax Dad paid in since last July 1st? $355, and I still have to make a payment of $46 by 15th of March to square our income tax. Frank figured it out and by the way if you can send Frankie a nice card for his birthday the 17th of March I would like to remember him. He has been very kind. In regards to the camera John, Dad paid a deposit on one someplace down town and he wants me to meet him some night so I can decide on it before he pays for it. So we are going to try to get it to you soon as possible. Do you miss your watch? Well John I will have to close now. Don't forget to write. Give us a little more information about yourself.

Love,
Mother"

Department (AMEDD). At the start of World War II in December 1941, there were fewer than 1,000 nurses in the Army Nurse Corps and 700 in the Navy Nurse Corps. All were women. Vastly expanded afterward, recruits had to be unmarried women aged 22–30 who had their RN training from civilian schools. They enlisted for the war plus six months, and were discharged if they married or became pregnant. With over 8 million soldiers and airmen, the needs were more than double those of World War I. Fearing a massive wave of combat casualties once Japan was invaded in late 1945, President Franklin D. Roosevelt called on Congress early in 1945 for permission to draft nurses. The draft was not needed and was never enacted.

[184] The McCullums (as spelled on the 1940 Census) lived at 3822 Harper Avenue. They were Douglas and Elizabeth, both 46; and their two children, Evelyn, 18, and Douglas, Jr., 14. Mr. McCullum was a bookkeeper at a bank, and earned a princely $3,000 a year. "The McCullam boy" refers to Douglas, Jr., who in 1943 would be 17 years old.

"Fort Knox, Kentucky

March 1, 1944 [Wednesday]

Dear Mother,

    I have a lot to tell you of my doings since I last wrote you. Well I went to Louisville over the weekend and on Sunday I went with a friend to a fellow's house that works with me for a chicken dinner. The dinner was very good and after that meal we did not eat any more till Monday morning because we ate so much. I also went to 9 o'clock mass on Sunday. Last night Tuesday I went to a dance over at E-town which is a town near the fort. The dance was swell and I had a good time. The only good thing about being down there was I met a fellow that used to live on Secor Avenue. He is stationed down here and said he knew the Murray fellow and was going to tell him to visit me some day.

    Tell Dad that I got the Dyre Avenue News but they still got the wrong address so tell Dad to give Bill Hickey my right address. By the way is there anything new around town? If there is write me about it. Love to all.

Love,
Son John"

John's father Ed decides to make another unauthorized trip down to Fort Knox, neglecting to tell his son anything about it in advance.

"March 7, 1944 [Tuesday]

Dear John,

    I was sorry I was not at home when you called Monday night. It was about eleven thirty when I got in and Mom told me all you had to say over the phone. I had a feeling you were going to call. Thoughts sometimes seem to travel. We had a gay time down at the meeting. A great attendance - lots of gossip - all about my son, your son and the other fellows. I not only got wished in to be a hostess for a card party but picked if you please to be a high power salesman - selling a little talk to old Rosarians and new ones to come back and attend the meetings. If Father O'Hara had his way he would have me on all the committees in the church. Mrs. Plufer on Pratt Avenue here came to the meeting with me last night. She made a beautiful altar cloth - all kinds of finger towels and purification and what not for the church so she is certainly an asset to the Society. The latest announcement was Barney Farrell[185] wants to start a dramatic club and he is going to seek for talent among the members of the Society. Well that started some fun. Everybody started singing and

---

[185] Barney Farrell was one of the driving forces behind the *Dyre Avenue News*.

dancing to see if they had talent. Mrs. Donaldson started singing - she has one of them high voices that would be heard down at South Ferry.[186] You would think you were at the old fashioned opry house. Everybody had a good laugh. Even poor Mrs. Supple who is so worried enjoyed the fun. Mrs. Mooney said she is going to put me up for singing. Judging from ages I think Barney Farrell wanted to start something or else he expects to produce Uncle Tom's Cabin with Duke the oldest-youngest man in the Bronx playing the leading man and Mrs. Shea playing opposite him. I don't see much of Mrs. Springer these days. I wouldn't doubt but she takes a leading role. You should hear Father O'Hara with the women saying, "We know you all have talent now so don't be making excuses to keep out of this." By the way John he was asking for you. Did you ever get to visit his friends? You should try to get there. Maybe you would be treated to another chicken dinner. It looked like you boys had a feast the Sunday you went visiting. You must have had a taste of southern hospitality. Who was the boy you mentioned from Secor Avenue? Did you find out what his name is?

Well John the least said about your father's action is the best. I just shivered when I thought of him going down there again and the state he was in. He sent me a telegram saying he was going down. If there was any way to prevent him from going I certainly would have stopped him. I prayed he wouldn't reach the fort. I certainly hope John you sent him home in a hurry. He came home Monday afternoon - sober - but with empty pockets. He must have had about sixty or seventy dollars when he started out Thursday night.[187] I can't understand what on earth he does with it all. There would be no use telling you John, how much his visiting you pained and grieved me. I told him many times above all he must never go down to bother you again. But it seems at times he is so sunk down with liquor that he loses all sense of shame and pride. There is an example of what drink can do when it controls all your senses. That is why John I have such a fear of a boy like you getting the habit which is very easy acquired. How happy we could have been if Dad controlled himself instead of being a nightmare where I was concerned. So John, take my advice, always keep clear of it. Have the strength of character to be strong where it flows. For it is a true saying, there never was a curse like it. I want you to forget about your father's visit and don't worry too much about him. He doesn't say much about the trip. Perhaps he got enough of traveling experience to last him for a while. Did you write to Richie and Walter? Jackie Walsh enlisted in the Navy a week ago Monday. His mother called me on the phone last Friday to tell me. Mrs. Mooney was saying last night that Jackie took a test for radio since then and if he passes he will go to school, I think for

---

[186] South Ferry, almost the southern tip of Manhattan Island, and a far cry from the Northeast Bronx and Edenwald.

[187] $70 in March 1944 would be equivalent today (2019) to roughly $1,100.

ten months. Mrs. Supple had a note written in pencil from her son. It was marked with a big German name on top. I read it. He told her not to worry, he was well and eating good. Sent his regards to all and his name. She receives everything through the Red Cross and the poor thing was so happy with his note her hand was shaking holding it. She could hardly talk with emotion.

Mrs. Faurenback didn't receive a word from Robert yet. From what I see all around me John when I go down to church with all those good mothers praying for the safety of their boys, I am only more convinced than ever that there is nothing stronger or deeper than the love of a mother for a child. Boys should thank God for it and pray God may spare them. Did you hear from Father Broderick? I would appreciate it John if you would write more often and add a little more news to your letter than just saying you had a good time somewhere. How are things going down at the school? Any chance of you being promoted to Major? Do you realize you are down there eight months already? I ask you questions in my letters John but you seem to forget to answer them. Of course I am interested in your progress. That is why I ask you questions. Answer them and then you will have a whole lot to write about in your letters. Did you ever inquire about a higher rating? On your merits John, I think you deserve it. It pays to speak up sometimes. I read in the armored news a list of fellows, names from the instructor regiment who were made sergeants. How about being a Private First Class? That is the Irish, always wanting to push ahead. Go on strike for a raise in pay, like the war workers. Putting all joking aside John we should thank God you are as well off as you are. God has blessed you. Well Muggsie and Duke just returned from Mamie's house. It has been raining here and you can imagine what Mug's paws looked like when she got up there. Duke said it took Mamie a long time to open the door, wondering whether she should let them in or not. While Mamie and Duke were talking Mugs was investigating around the house and when Duke looked for Mugs where was she but in the bedroom? Duke said, "By George, it is a good thing she didn't get up in the bed." Mamie would have put them out. There is no word from Walter.[188] George[189] wrote a card and said he saw Walter someplace. I think it must be in his dreams.

I am sending you a letter from David.[190] Say a prayer for him once in a while John. His great task lies just ahead of him. Well write me a long letter with a whole lot of news and answer all questions. Remember me in your prayers. Say one for the traveler, too.

Love,
Mother

---

[188] Walter McGowan.
[189] George Stanley.
[190] David Lucas.

P.S. Any talk of you getting a furlough for Easter?"

And the letter from David Lucas.

"March 5, 1944 [Sunday]

Dear Aunt Anna,
    Hello, and how are you? Thank you for the swell letter and remembrance. I am enclosing the clipping.
    John seems to be part of a novel but notable experiment. I was glad to hear that it was so successful. John should feel pretty proud of his part. How is he making out in his new job?
    I completed my ten hours of flying last week. As you know it was the first time I had ever flown, and I enjoyed every hour of it. I don't remember any notable first impressions because I was constantly watching my plane or the instrument panel. Flying the Army way is a real job. I only hope that I shall be able to continue on in my future training as a pilot. Of course I shall know more about that in the near future.
    When I last wrote to you we believed that we were going to Nashville, Tennessee, but our plans have been changed since then. We shall leave Saturday 11th March for San Antonio, Texas, and classification. That trip promises to be quite interesting, and I shall certainly be wondering what will happen next. In all probability, my next letter to you will come from Texas, or some other place in the deep Southwest. I'll let you know about that, as soon as I am able to write from the new base.
    My mother[191] told me of the very pleasant afternoon which you spent in N.Y. I know what such an experience means to them and I am glad that they do get out. We haven't heard from John very recently, and now we haven't been hearing from Tom.[192]
    Things at home are very fine. Here in Buffalo things are drawing to a close. This will probably be our last week and our week will be very full. It is going to be tough to leave this town. School has been fine and I have enjoyed every day that I spent here. People have been very fine to us and we really appreciated it. This evening I am sitting here and being thankful.
    Remember me in your prayers for I shall need them in the days ahead. I am hoping that everything will go O.K., and I shall drop you a line from my new address. Give my regards to Ed and John.

                                            Regards,
                                            Dave

---

[191] Aunt Kitty.
[192] John Lucas and Tom Lucas, Dave's brothers.

P.S. Please send letters to this same address until I send a new one. Dave"

℘

"Mr. Harry Gibbons
461 Miniford Street
City Island, N.Y.

March 8, 1944 [Wednesday]

Hello Bottle Nose (Rummy),
  I was sure glad to hear from you. I just wrote to Murphy and sent him your regards. Well how's the women treating you?
  I'm looking forward to your next furlough, for we have a date for a good time. I haven't much time to write and when I do get around to it I can't think of nothing to say. I want you to pay strict attention to the arrangements and words used. I learned this from Molly. She's my old gal. Molly won't go nowhere without her Mother and her Mother would go anywhere. Molly was the silent type, also big and strong. She taught ju-jitsu to the Marines at the barracks. Molly had to leave her original hack as a Boiler Maker. She was too rough. So she took up welding. A real lady was my Molly.
  Next week tune in and hear more about Molly O'Toole, the girl who shot the hole in Murphy's beer can after 20 years good standing.
  I hope you are feeling well and I will stop up and see your Mom when the immigrant office signs my passports.
  Tell that bum Richey that he at least could have called me.
  My family sends their best regards and wants me to bring you over the next time you're in.
  Write soon. I remain,

              Dry Dock Gibbons
Note - *The humor used is strictly fictitious and any similarity to any persons living or dead are better off dead."*

℘

"Fort Knox, Kentucky

March 13, 1944 [Monday]

Dear Mother,
  Well I received your letter Saturday and I was glad to hear everything is going along okay. Mother I didn't worry when Dad was down because he was okay and he was with me for only a few hours. The only trouble was if he had told me earlier in the week that he was coming down I could have met him

when he arrived but when his message did come I was out on pass in Louisville and I just happened to meet a fellow from the company and he told me that my father was coming down. If I hadn't met this fellow I wouldn't know that Dad had come down at all because I was on pass till Monday morning.

Now I will answer some of your questions. You wanted to know why I am not being advanced. Well, that's a long story. First of all the ratings are frozen here at the school because we need a general to okay them and they haven't been Okayed yet. And secondly a lot of the fellows that have been here for some time are supposed to ship out and there is a lot of trouble over that. Well Mother you also want to know all about the religious side too. Well I get to Mass every Sunday and I try to get to communion at least once a month. You know that Sunday is the only day off so Saturday night we like to go out and have some fun.

I went to Louisville over the weekend and I went to mass as usual and at the service club I met a girl that had lived in Kearney, N.J. She is now living in Louisville and goes to Mount St. Mary's School for girls. We had quite a talk about New York and Jersey.

By the way Red Gibbons wrote me and said he was going to visit you folks someday so get prepared. Well how are things? Why don't you go into the dramatic society? It will do you good. Mother I wouldn't be too hard on Dad. You know everybody's got their faults and he tries to do his best. That's about all for now. Love to all.

Love,
Son John"

March 14, 1944 [Tuesday]

Dear John,

    I don't know whether it is your fault or my fault but somehow or other we don't seem to exchange many letters lately. When you consider that you have much more leisure time now you should be able to write a whole lot more. You may not realize it but your letters mean just as much to us now as when you first left home. We are always looking for them.

Now that I gave you a little lecture I will start on the news. To begin with I just finished writing to Mrs. Hull - Walter Cubita. I sent them a card for St. Patrick's Day and enclosed a note to Walter. I also wrote to Richard Simmons. His mother told me she had a letter from him and he wanted to know why I didn't write.

Yesterday I received a card from Aunt Kitty telling me she was in Buffalo spending a few days with Sonny before he left for Texas. Dave was with her.

Muggsie is sound asleep. I believe she is snoring lying at your father's feet and he too is asleep in the big chair. So far he has been on very good behavior since his journey south. He is working as usual. There is such a demand for manpower these days they let employees get away with a whole lot. I think when he arrived home that Monday afternoon Mugs gave him such a greeting you would think the King of England had arrived. I guess if it were possible he would take Mugs along on his travels. He told me you got fatter and that everybody down there likes you. I couldn't tell you all what. The half of it I take with a grain of salt.

Did you hear all the trouble Erin is having? You should hear Mom and Duke. They are on the war path blaming it all on England. There are two sides to the question and only time will tell the truth. I may go to see the parade Friday. Frank may get tickets for the grandstand. He was here for supper tonight and told me Ack[193] may be able to get me a camera for a reasonable price. So I will have to wait John and will let you know how we make out about it.

Last night coming home from the Novena Mrs. Mooney was telling me Buddy's girlfriend Marie was down at Trainor's and they told her Henry Wiedbe across the street is expected to be coming home. He received the Purple Heart, and they were notified he is wounded. They don't know just how badly but he is being shipped home. Mrs. Mooney said Marie said he was in the air corps, that he received his wings which he sent home. That news surprised me as he was an officer in the Infantry when he left the States and last fall Mrs. Koch told me he was in the anti-aircraft. Perhaps he trained in Europe for a pilot.

Mrs. Harenback told me she received a couple of letters from Robert since his thrilling experience. His plane called the "Bag of Bones" was pictured in the news. She was showing it to me in the paper. I don't think Jackie Walsh was called yet. I hear Gerard Diemer enlisted too. Tommy Cotter went away yesterday. 700 men left Mt. Vernon. If the draft keeps up we will have only women and children left. Dad said the Navy Yard is cleared out. I told Walter every time I wind the clock it brings memories of him. The Kerwin boy is in the Navy. Well John I will have to close. It is 11 p.m. Sit down and write me a nice long letter. Be a good boy. Remember me in your prayers. Mom and Duke send their regards.

Love,
Mother

P.S. Excuse writing in this letter John. It is getting late and I am tired."

---

[193] Salem Ackary, family friend.

MARCH 18, 1944

British bombers drop 3,000 tons of bombs on Hamburg, Germany, during an air raid. Hamburg is a continual target of Allied bombing, with over 40,000 civilians killed during one such attack.

"March 19, 1944 [Sunday]

Dear John,
This is Sunday evening. Dad is off today. We have just finished eating and sat down to listen to the radio and read the papers. Your father suggested I should write to you. If it was left to him he would have me writing all the time.
Somehow or other when evening shadows fall, it seems to bring thoughts of those who are far away. Of course as far as you are concerned I am always thinking of you. I received a letter from you last Thursday and I must say it was one of the nicest letters you ever sent me, with plenty of information. That is what I like John - a long newsy letter.
Wednesday morning I was just home from Mass about an hour when the front door bell rang. On the way out to answer it I said to myself I bet this is Mrs. Gold. You know she runs in here very often now to talk with Mom, especially when she and Mr. Gold are on the war path. Duke calls Mom "Lawyer Fillpots", giving advice to the neighbors. Well to come back to answering the door bell, when I opened the door who stood there but Agnes from Millbrook. What a surprise we got. She looks grand - got a bit older. She left Saturday morning and we really felt lonesome to see her go as her, Mom and I, including Duke, had great chats during the time she was here, and of course Agnes can tell you a lot of interesting events. One of the topics discussed every couple of hours was about Ireland's situation. Agnes went through the Irish history as far back as when the Druids ruled before St. Patrick got there. Mom, Agnes and Duke went downtown Friday to see the parade. Frank got tickets for the grandstand. They wanted me to go but I wanted to have my hair done so I remained home. It was raining heavy most of the day. They got drenched and cold, so coming back where does Duke land them but in Hickeys and got them each a drop of the creature. Agnes got a great kick out of that. We had a lot of fun when they came back, telling about what a great sport Duke was.
Agnes was asking for you. She said the Higgins often asked her how you are. Betty is married. Her husband does research work for the

government. They are living away out west. Stephen - the son - is a Captain in the Air Corps. He is what you call a liaison officer. Flies on special missions and carries big shots to important places. He is now stationed at some camp in Texas. You know he was a mining engineer before he went into service. He got interested in the Air Corps and studied for a pilot. From his rank it looks like he made good. Of course he was a college man and that helped him a lot. Agnes said he expects to make aviation his work after the war. She said to tell you take all the advantages at learning you can get because you are a young boy and have a great opportunity to help yourself. Her son is 26 years old.

   Dad met Peter today after Mass and he, Peter, said, "I hear you were down to visit John." Did you write and tell that to any of the boys? Dad wondered who told Peter. He said he hoped you would be home before he goes into service. Is there any chance of you getting home for Easter?

   You said to be prepared for Red's visit. I had to laugh about that. Do you mean eats? Well we had a swell dinner today. But no Red showed up. Did you hear from Robbie Mahon? I hear he is getting so fat his pants don't fit him.

   Eileen Hickey sends her regards. While I think of it John, did you have that tooth filled? Don't neglect your teeth! Take good care of yourself. Keep your clothes in good condition and your body clean, and do take care to have your shoes mended and shining. Appearances is what counts. Last but not least remember to pray and keep close to God. Next week I will be busy. I am on for the altar work but will write more during the week. Fred Allen is on the radio. Write soon. It is snowing out and very cold. Love from all.
                     Mother

P.S. Dad said he is going to start a victory garden.[194]"

℘

Undated, postmarked March 20, 1944, this next letter gives some insight into the training offered by the Instructor Regiment, and the clientele for that training, apparently officers who will need to know the workings of tanks.

"Fort Knox, Kentucky

[March 20, 1944][Saturday]

Dear Mother,

---

[194] "Victory Gardens" were a hallmark of the home front effort during World War II to supplement home-grown food supplies and make more food available to the soldiers on the front lines.

I received your letter and I thought I better answer it as it has been some time that I last wrote you. Well everything is getting along okay. We got a new officers class Thursday and I hope to have them done sometime in April. And speaking of April I may get another 3 day pass around the first week of the month. I will write more details on that later on. I didn't go to town this weekend as I have to work tomorrow afternoon putting up some explosive targets for the Major. Next week I will stay in camp too because my funds are kind of low and I want to save my money for that pass.

I am glad to hear that Dad is back in form again. Keep him that way. Well St. Patrick's Day was kind of quiet. They had a big party at the club but we had to scrub as it was Friday night. Today being Saturday it is raining as usual. It seems that on every Saturday it rains.

Well about Henry Wiedbe, I don't think he is a pilot but he might have been attached to the Air Corps. I think that if they sent notice to his family recently that he is coming back to the States that fast he must not have been hurt bad. By the way you didn't hear anything about Pete Thomas lately? I wrote to him but he did not answer me. Find out.

Did the Duke start to turn the dirt over in the garden yet? And tell him to plant tomatoes because when I come home later on I want some. Well that's all for now. Love to all.

Love,
Son John"

"Fort Knox, Kentucky

March 24, 1944 [Friday]

Dear Mother,
I received your letter and the church booklet which I found most interesting. I was sorry to hear that you did not see the St. Patrick's Day Parade because I read it was very nice. Well you must have been very much surprised when you saw Agnes[195] walking in. From what you wrote she must have had much to say and I was surprised to hear that the Higgins's were asking for me. I wonder how they are. Did she say much about them? Things have been getting along fine. I have been spending a lot of my time driving a jeep around for the Major. We are also going to move into new barracks in the next few days. Mother I didn't write anybody telling them that Dad was down to see me. He must have told somebody down at Hickey's and that was

---

[195] Uncertain who "Agnes" refers to. May have been a friend of John's grandmother Bridget.

how Peter[196] found out. By the way Mother when is Peter going in to service? Is it very soon? I was also wondering if the Dyre Avenue News was coming out soon. Tell Dad to give them my right address so it will not take so long to get here. How is everybody at home? Is Martin still going to college and how is his car getting along? Tell Duke to take good care of Mugs because she must be getting old now. That's about all for now. Be good and give my regards to all.

Love,
Son John"

℘

"March 29, 1944 [Wednesday]

Dear John,

    This morning I received your letter which was written very nice. You are improving John as a writer. Watch the spelling and keep the good work up. Dad got a kick out of your driving a jeep. Take it easy - don't drive too fast. Be nice to the Major. How is his dog?

    Well John we were hoping you would enjoy your birthday. Did you receive the package and Dad's remembrance? I would like to have sent you a camera but Frankie promised to try to get one reasonable. I am still waiting.

    I had a great deal of news stored up to tell you John but half of it I guess I have forgotten. Jackie Walsh is up at Great Lakes so his mother told me. I don't think he passed that test for radio tech. Did you read in the paper about what happened to all the [illegible] cadets being put in the Infantry? That must have been a great disappointment to them. I had a War Department notice of David's[197] transfer with his new address. He is at San Antonio, Texas. Tommy Cotter is somewhere down in Texas too, I guess in the Infantry. News of Pratt Avenue - Mr. Walsh over at Bernabe's is going into the Navy. They took him, flat feet and all. His wife was telling me. Mr. Lang was called up too but he is deferred for a few months on account of his work. Slow but sure they are all going. Ritchie Simmons was home over the weekend. His mother told me Gerard Diemer enlisted in the Navy and Bobby Wittaker is going into service too. She said every one of your club is in the armed service. Hickey was in today and told me Peter expects to go away soon. So I asked Hickey to tell Peter to come in to see us. Mr. Webber was home. He looks

---

[196] Peter Hickey.

[197] War Department Notice of Change of Address of David G. Lucas, A/S, Serial Number 32918108, Squadron 116, Barracks #5813, c/o AAFCC SAACC. Postmarked San Antonio, Texas, March 16, 1944. Prior address listed as Sect. 41, 23 C.T.D., U. of Buffalo, Buffalo 14, N.Y. Addressed to "Mrs. Ed. McGowan, 4030 Pratt Ave., Bronx (66), New York".

good in his uniform. Johnny Murray was home last week for three days. Do you ever see him? Father O'Hara told me there is a fellow down at Ft. Knox by the name of Nolan from Duryea Avenue. Perhaps you know who he is. I saw the McCallum boy. He looks good. George Diemer is down in Mississippi. Bob Bishop is down at Norfolk. I often think of Andy, John. The poor kid, I wondered how he is. Must keep an eye out for his brother and get a little information.

Last but not least of all the news items is the following, so brace yourself and take a good deep breath before you read this. We had primary election here yesterday and your father Edward J. was a candidate with his name on the ballot for County Committee. How he was chosen is still a mystery. It seems the Chippewa Club picked him at any rate. I think he was elected with the rest of the party. You should hear Duke about my husband being a politician. I made your father wear his glasses and get all dressed up to fool Duke who said now he knows why the country is going crazy, sure (?) looked the men they are putting to vote for. Mrs. Mooney and I laughed so much this morning coming up from church listening to Duke's comments we could hardly walk.

It is surprising John to know how interested Duke is in your letters. He watches every day for the mailman. Today when I read your letter he wasn't here so I had to read it again for him. When I got finished he said, "Hmmh, he is all business." Muggsie and he still take their daily walks as usual. Walter McGowan is coming home on a furlough. In fact he is supposed to be on his way. I will give you more information in my next letter.

Don't mind all the mistakes I made in this letter John, as Duke has been here talking, Dad is asking me questions and the radio is blasting away with Sam Kaye. How about you coming home? You didn't mention it in your letter. Let me know when you get your pass. I was thinking maybe you would be home this week. Did you take care of your teeth? I was wondering John how your shoes are for traveling. Do you need a new pair?

Duke has gone into a new business - making bird houses. He didn't start on the garden yet. Mom hasn't been so well for the last week or so. She has a bad cold and is just recovering from it. The Moynihan family seem to be getting on well as far as I know. Martin likes college. I think the Doctor's daughter wants him to take her to another dance. Perhaps she wants him just to accommodate her.

Well John it is a very stormy night outside raining and hailing and it is just eleven o'clock so I will have to close. Write soon again. Sometimes I wonder why you don't write more often. Be a good boy. Take care of yourself. Remember me in your prayers.

Love,
Mother

P.S. Did you hear from Walter Cubita? His mother told me he is in Florida now."

℘

"Fort Knox, Kentucky

March 29, 1944 [Wednesday]

Dear Mother,
    I received the package and the money and I want to thank you and Dad a lot. I and the fellows really enjoyed it. The money came in very handy because it was what I just needed. I might be home Sunday night for a day or two on a three day pass but I am not sure that I will come. The only way you will know if I will come is when I arrive. I got the Dyre Avenue News and I read in it where Pete Thomas and the Barker fellow are going into the army in three weeks. I also received a letter from Aunt Kitty and she told me how she went to the movies with you. She also said that she was up to see David for a few days. We get payed Friday so I will be okay. I was thinking if I get home I want steak and chicken all the time. Well that's about all from here for now. Love to all.

                                            Love,
                                            Son John"

TEN: "MEASLES"

This next letter, postmarked April 12th from New York, is redirected on April 13th to the Camp Hospital, where John is laid up with an ailment foreign to most of us in this day and age, save when the occasional outbreak unsettles our nerves - the measles.

"April 9, 1944 [Easter Sunday]

Dear John,
    It is almost the end of Easter Sunday and a busy day it was. We all went to eight o'clock Mass and received Communion. In fact as long as I have been attending Sunday Mass in our church I never saw such a crowd as this morning and almost everybody received. Why who paraded up the aisle but Mr. Bernabe with Neppie and Ann. Was I surprised? They say every church in the city was crowded. It must be the war that is bringing so many to church.
    Frank came down this morning and took Duke and Mom up to his house for dinner. They are not back yet so I guess they are giving them a royal time. This invitation surprised me and more so because it was accepted. But then there are some things you have to mark with a question mark to it.
    Well this noon about 1 o'clock the doorbell rang and who was at the door but Harry Gibbons.[198] He looks fine. The dinner was just ready to serve when he came in so I invited him to join us. I had pork and sauerkraut and I think he enjoyed it. We had lots of fun. Of course your father and Red discussed all the doings in the Navy Yard. He told us he will be eighteen soon and that he would like to apply as machinist for the Navy Air Corps. I told him about Peter's party so he called up Barbara Gueth[199] and I wish you could hear the line of talk he gave her. I imagined I could hear you laughing if you were here. Anyway he made a date with her to call on her before he went home so he left here about three o'clock. He said to tell you he expects a vacation and maybe he will arrange to visit you for a few days. How would you like that?
    He was gone about a half an hour when Helen and Dorothy Moynihan arrived, and did they look nice - some style! They spent the afternoon with us.

---

[198] Harry ("Red") Gibbons.
[199] William and Barbara Gueth lived at 2162 Strang Avenue. In 1940 he was 41, and she 34. They had three daughters: Barbara A., 12, Patricia, 6, and Catherine, 2 years old. Barbara Gueth referred to here was Barbara A., apparently a popular neighborhood girl, 15 years old in 1943. Mr. Gueth was a repairman for the telephone company.

Saturday morning I received a letter from Agnes telling me she received the beads. She doesn't know where her son is now. He is away off on maneuvers. She didn't see him or Betty in over a year. I also received a letter from Mrs. Hull. She is coming to pay me a visit. Aunt Kitty sent me a beautiful card for Easter. I am going to try to arrange to visit her for a few days if possible.

I sent all the boys cards. Did you receive the one I sent to you? I wanted to tell you John, Wednesday the day after you left, we woke up to see almost a blizzard. I never saw so much snow. Did you get any of it down there? Yesterday they cut down the old cherry tree in Bernabe's yard. It looks kind of lonesome over there without it but I guess it was getting rotten. Duke met Fr. Broderick and he was asking about you. Too bad you didn't see him. He told Duke he was going to visit us. Well John I hope you are taking care of yourself. Don't forget to get to confession and communion. Did you take any pictures? Write soon.

Love,
Mother

P.S. Helen's camera takes film 116."

℘

"April 11, 1944 [Tuesday]

Dear John,

It is after 10 p.m. Bob Hope just started his program. So I will have to write this letter in a hurry. Dad is now sound asleep in bed. I didn't want him to read what I wrote in this letter as I thought it best not to tell him about you calling yesterday.

Well how are you and the measles getting on? Hope you are feeling better. Mom said sometimes those little sicknesses clear your whole system out. Take whatever medical care you get and stay in the hospital until you feel better. It will give you a chance for a good rest in bed.

I received your letter today. Dad read your letter a couple of times. I think he was trying to make out what you wrote concerning him. Duke said, "How well he remembered the hole in the fence." He spent the whole day cleaning up the garden. I guess he was tired out when he came in.[200] Now that the spring is here the children are all out playing. You should hear Duke. "By George, if I can keep those childers[201] out where they belong!" Even the Johnson twins come in now.

Last night at the Novena Father O'Hare asked the people to pray for Robert Faurenback who is now reported missing. I feel sorry for his poor

---

[200] Bear in mind that in 1944, the Duke is 84 years old.
[201] "Childers" - a classic Irish pronunciation of "children".

mother, she must be worried stiff. I am praying he is safe, at least taken prisoner.

Yesterday Walter and Claire[202] were in to see us. Walter said he was sorry he didn't see you. He left last night, had reservations made for the plane to California. That is if he wasn't ordered out on the way for somebody with priority. Sometimes, he said, he thinks that priority business is a racket with some of the travelers. He has to get to his ship at a certain time or he will be left stranded and he was rather worried about getting through all the way on the plane. It only cost $3.25 fare. He was all interested asking about you and the tanks. All your precious possessions were on exhibition so he examined them all. I had to let him draw his own conclusions about what they were and etc. The only thing I know about that big one is that it is so heavy I can't even lift it. Hope it never falls or it will be just too bad.

Martin Moynihan took the V-12 test and passed but I think he is going to remain in college until June.

Today the telephone rang and who was calling but Sr. Mary Albert. She told me she is coming up to visit us Thursday afternoon with another nun. So I will have to get all polished up. Muggsie will surely have to stay in the dog house until they leave.

How is the weather down there? Yesterday it was lovely but tonight it is cold and rainy. The trees are all budding. Last night what jumped in front of Mrs. Mooney and I but a little frog. The first one I saw in a long time.

Tomorrow night is the Rosary Card Party so I guess I will attend it. Maybe I will be lucky and win a prize.

Dad was saying tonight on account of the new draft laws, he doesn't think Mr. Walsh will have to go now. He told me he was to leave April 19th.

Well John it is now 11:15 so I will close. Take good care of yourself and write and let me know how you are. I will be expecting to receive some pictures soon. Don't forget to take a few when you are well again. I will write more later in the week.

Love,
Mother

P.S. They are now telling about a terrific storm in the south. Did it hit your place?"

---

[202] Walter and Claire McGowan, relative newlyweds. Walter was John's first cousin, Mamie McGowan's son.

The illness that has laid Private McGowan low, measles, is a secret kept among the women of the family.

"April 15, 1944 [Saturday]

Dear John,
   I have been wondering and watching for word from you. So today Saturday I received your letter and from what you wrote I guess you are getting along O.K. Don't be in a rush to get out again. The rest in bed will do you good. Just relax and take good care of yourself. How are the eats? Any better than at the barracks? They keep telling us over the radio about the great surplus of eggs on the market. I was half tempted to sit down and write a letter to the O.P.A. and tell them if they are so anxious to use them up, in heaven's name why don't they feed a few fresh eggs to our boys in service? Walter told me if they saw a fresh egg or milk they would pass away. John you should have received two letters.
   You know John I have kept your sickness a secret to myself. The only one who knows about it is Mom. Duke don't know anything about it otherwise he would be apt to tell everyone who came along. Dad would surely hear it. And I think it best not to let him know at present. So if you write to the boys don't let on about your trouble or Dad will be bound to get the news.
   I would suggest that you write a letter home. Write it as if you are on duty as usual even if you have to use your imagination. And enclose an extra note for me about your condition and etc. I will keep it and let Dad read the letter. Otherwise if he don't see a letter from you he will wonder why you are not writing. Every night he comes in - the same old question: "Any news from John?" Put a stamp on your letter. It will come quicker.[203] *Maybe toward the end of the week if you find it convenient call on the phone in the evening. I had to laugh about the fellow from Brooklyn. Has he got the measles too? What you want to do is start talking about the Bronx. See if you can outdo him.*[204] *Did any of your friends come down with the measles?*
   Well John last Thursday was sure a busy day here. For two days before I was cleaning and polishing so that by Thursday noon everything was shining and I was more than delighted that the house looks so good as you will find out the reason why after you read the rest of the story.
   About 2:30 Thursday afternoon Margaret[205] *and another nun and Mamie*[206] *arrived. They had a lovely visit here, spent a couple of hours. During the time I showed them your possessions. They were greatly interested.*

---

[203] Mail from servicemen was free, but apparently went quicker if it was stamped.
[204] Age old rivalry between Brooklyn and the Bronx is revealed here.
[205] Sr. Mary Albert McGowan (Margaret McGowan).
[206] Mary McGowan, Sr. Albert's mother.

Couldn't understand how you ever carried the weight home. I told them if they ever hear of an explosion in the Bronx, they will know it is us gone up in powder. The nun who was with Margaret said judging from your picture you look like a boy with plenty of good character. Because you have a strong looking face and not the kind that his mother needs to worry about. Think her judgment was correct in your mind?

Poor Margaret, she was so sorry you didn't pay her a visit. She would love to see you in uniform. I think you ought to compose a nice letter and send it to her with your present address. Tell her how I wrote and told you she was to visit. She said she feels Walter[207] made a great mistake by rushing into marriage before the war was over. Just loading himself down with more worry and responsibility than he can carry.

She was anxious to see how I had the place here arranged so I took her and the other nun through. They thought it was lovely. Margaret said everything looks so nice. On their way home from here they were to stop to Mahon's.

It was about four o'clock when they left. So afterwards I felt kind of tired and I went inside to read. My feet felt as if they could stand some freedom, having on my good shoes. So I removed them. I was just relaxing when I see a car driving up to the door and a woman got out, opened the back door of the car and out emerges two nuns making way for our door. Well if ever I put my shoes on quick I did then and flew to the door. Here stood Mrs. Ford, your girl-friend's mother and two Dominican nuns, and the one nun stood and looked at me and said, "You know me, don't you Anna?" I said, "Yes sister, but I just can't recall your name." She said, "Catherine Malloy[208], Mrs. Malloy's daughter." Mom's lady friend.[209] So Mrs. Ford said, "I am sure you must know who I am. If you don't," she said, "John does." Of course I knew who she was. And then they introduce the other nun who had come to visit Mrs. Ford's mother and brought Catherine with her. While they were at Ford's, Catherine asked them if Pratt Avenue was nearby and said she knew McGowans on that street. So Mrs. Ford said, "Oh, yes, I know McGowans," and she brought them down here to visit. Mom and Duke got a great surprise. Catherine is a lovely nun. You couldn't help but like her. She teaches school. Has degrees from Fordham. We all had a great talk while they were here. Mrs. Ford was telling about her daughters and etc. She also said Peter was leaving the next morning for service (Friday). His mother was taking his going away so hard, poor thing.

---

[207] Walter McGowan, Margaret's younger brother, Mamie's youngest son, at the time a sailor in the U.S, Navy off fighting in the Pacific.
[208] Who Mrs. Malloy was is uncertain.
[209] "Mom" being Anna's mother-in-law, Bridget McGowan.

They had to get home at six o'clock so they couldn't stay very long. Catherine said now that she knows where the place is she is coming up on a Saturday afternoon. Well, after they all left I said to Mom we should have a priest to visit and that would complete a perfect day. Now you know why I was so happy that the house was in perfect order. Muggsie wanted to get next to the nuns but I kept her outside in the yard. I couldn't start brushing the hair off their clothes like I do with the sailor boys.

I wondered if Red[210] got to the party. Did you hear from him? Mrs. Ford told me her daughter got a letter from Jackie Walsh and he said everything is O.K. where he is, only the eats. He is half starved. I owe Walter a letter. I must get one off to him. I haven't heard from Richard Simmons in some time. I think I wrote to his old address.

Aunt Kitty will think I passed away if I don't soon write to her. Uncle George expects me to visit him. I am supposed to let him know when I will get over there. Some one of these days with God's help I am going to surprise myself and get to see a dentist. Do you think that fellow you went to on Dyre is worthwhile? He is near home.

Dad is taking his Vitamin A. Maybe he will turn into Superman. Only cost $3.00 for a small bottle of capsules. They ought to contain vim and vigor for that price. You know the doctors now can give you vitamins by injection. H. Butler[211] got them. Now I know why she could fly in and out so quickly with the broom. Do you remember? Maybe that is what I need. I could get a job as a welder with Dad. How he would like that! Write.

Love
Mother

P.S. John would you like me to mail some papers to you? How is your financial account?"

"April 18, 1944 [Tuesday]

Dear John,

Tonight after you called I realized that I had money put away for the telephone bill so I am going to enclose $5.00 of it to you. So use it wisely. Last week I had to pay the State tax and Dad's pay for his sick leave wasn't paid yet. That left me kind of short.

I was glad that you called on the telephone. Dad asked if there was any mail from you tonight when he came home. So rather than keep him under any more suspense I said, "Yes, John called this afternoon and I had to tell

---

[210] Red Gibbons.
[211] Helen Butler, Vincent Butler's wife.

him a lot of news." News I made up in my own mind but I didn't dare look at him straight in the face. I was afraid he would detect I was making believe.

So when you called tonight he couldn't understand it all. So I told him the truth and he was satisfied. When he didn't see any letter from you Monday he said, "Gee, John must be so busy over the weekend he don't take time to write home anymore." But I kept making excuses.

Well John this is just a short letter as it is late and time to get in for a sleep. Be a good boy and take good care of yourself. When you are in town eat good wholesome food. By the way Mr. Walsh isn't going away now. This draft business has everybody so mixed up they don't know whether they are coming or going. Did the tornado hit Kentucky? Write.

Love from all.
Mother

P.S. Let me know if you receive this O.K. Duke is building a nice fence around the garden."

"Fort Knox, Kentucky

April 26, 1944 [Wednesday]

Dear Mother,

I am sorry I did not write sooner but this is the first chance I had. Saturday I went to town and Sunday I went to Mass and after that I was invited with a friend to a girl's house for dinner and boy what a time I had. This week so far I did not hear from you but I guess the mail is slow due to the floods down here.[212] *This week so far I have been out on the range practically all week. Friday we fire all night and I have to stay out at our base camp at Cedar Creek for two days so if I don't write until Saturday you will know why. Well*

---

[212] The spring of 1944 saw some wicked flooding along the Mississippi River. The Mississippi has flooded with regularity since recorded history, but no flood was greater than that of 1927. Beginning in March, for six continuous weeks, numerous levees broke along the Mississippi River from Illinois to Louisiana, inundating numerous towns in the Mississippi Valley. Heavy spring rains caused a second major flood in the same region in June. In all, 28,400 square miles which were home to more than 931,000 people were inundated. To avoid flooding the city of New Orleans, the governor of Louisiana allowed engineers to create the Poydras cut, which saved the city but led to the flooding of St. Bernard and Plaquemines parishes instead. Millions of acres across seven states were flooded. Evacuees totaled 500,000. Economic losses were estimated at US$1 billion (1927 dollars), which was equivalent to almost one-third of the federal budget at that time.

how are things at home? How is Dad? Is he being a good boy? Tell him we are having a beer party this week. Did you hear anything from Pete Thomas lately? I didn't hear from him yet. Well that's about all for now. Regards to all.

Love,
Son John"

℘

"April 27, 1944 [Thursday]

Dear John

Today is a cold rainy day. It seems we have had a great rainfall during the month of April. Last Monday, it looked as if we were going to have a flood. But just the same everything is budding and Spring is in the air even though it is rather cool. The children are all out again, playing and laughing. Duke said he doesn't know where they all come from. They must be under cover all Winter like the groundhog. And speaking of Duke he has the whole garden dug up and a fence built around it. That you would need a step ladder to climb over it. He changed some of the bushes too. Last night he planted grass seed and the birds were down early this morning eating it all up. He built a bird house for Neppie and now Bobby Walsh wants one too.

Duke went out to the mail box this morning and when he came in he said, "No mail. Sure that fellow down in Kentucky is so busy in Louisville that he doesn't have time to write." You would laugh if you heard Duke talking to Muggsie. He went up to Mamie to ask her if she wanted to buy a bird house.

Mom is feeling better now. Her high blood pressure has come down. She was up to Doctor Kent's office again and she thinks he is a good doctor.

Dad is O.K. Working every day. Taking his Vitamin A pills and etc. By the way John, he wants me to tell you to not go out on them phony passes because he said if one fellow was caught up it would implicate you all. So don't take a chance, it isn't worth it and beside I want you to get the good conduct medal at the end of the year. After all John our good name and character are our most priceless possessions. You are young now, perhaps you don't value them for what they are but as you grow older in life you will find no matter what happens if you have been honorable in your dealings and a gentleman you need fear no man. No matter what sacrifices I have had to make John you have always been a source of satisfaction and pride to me - in other words a consolation, and I think Dad feels the same as I see his face light up when your name is mentioned. So John whenever you are tempted to do anything that isn't just right remember what I have told you and no matter what the cost do the honorable thing.

Well John the Dyre Avenue News is out for the month of April so I suppose you will be receiving it and will read all the news from Edenwald. I *tried to get some information regarding Peter but I didn't get where he is. Hickey told me he was going to let me know.*

I wrote a letter to Walter today. It is long overdue. I am hoping he didn't move from the address I have. I guess you will be surprised when you hear that Ritchie Simmons is very sick from pneumonia again. His mother expected him home over the weekend of the 23rd. Instead I understand she got word to go up to Sampson. I haven't heard yet how he is. Sunday at Mass Father O'Hara called his name out to pray for him. I don't think he is such a strong boy John. He needs to take very good care of himself.

From what you say John I don't think you appreciated The Catholic News. *Well I didn't send it to make you any holier as you seem to think but because I regard* The Catholic News *as a good wholesome paper and you can depend upon it to publish the truth. Dad said we should send you* The Daily Worker *or the P.M. as just a load of funny sheets. Speaking of* The Catholic News *have you been to Communion since Easter? Remember your Easter duty. Why not go to confession and communion when you are in Louisville? It would please me very much John if you could get to the Novena on Monday night at the Fort chapel. If you do I would like a few special prayers said for me.*

Last week I received a letter from Aunt Kitty which I am going to enclose. Poor Sonny, I can imagine how he feels after trying so hard. But God knows best. Maybe it was for his own good. Dad said he was lucky he wasn't put in the infantry. Mrs. Windel's husband is going down tomorrow for his exam for the draft. He is over 26 so maybe he won't be taken. Helen Butler told me George Deimer's parents wrote to the Red Cross and wanted him to come home before Gerard left. But it seems it didn't work. I don't think he is gone into service yet. Bob Bishop is an M. P. down in Norfolk Virginia and Helen says he hates the job. He said it is one of the worst places he ever saw or heard o and he is going to ask for a transfer into another branch of the service. She said he is really sick with disgust. He would like to go out to sea where the air is clean and wholesome. When you think about these places, I come to the conclusion that Edenwald is next to Heaven.

Martin Moynihan expects to join the Marines, so Mom tells me. Helen thinks her boyfriend is shipping overseas. He sent her and Dorothy nice gifts for Easter. I think he is a nice kind thoughtful boy. Well John I don't know what you do with your time but I must say you don't spend it writing home. So just get busy - you wonder why you don't hear from us. We wonder too what is wrong when you don't write. Dad wants to know if you still drive the jeep. According to your armored news John there are no ratings frozen. That is a lame excuse. Speak up for yourself John. Do you read about Gen. Patton?

Love from all,
Mother"

ELEVEN: "DUKE'S GARDEN"

The following letter is undated, but the envelope carrying it is post-marked May 1, 1944.

"Fort Knox, Kentucky

[May 1, 1944][Sunday]

Dear Mother,
    Today is Sunday and I have just come back from mass and communion. I went to confession before mass. This week I stayed in camp instead of going to Louisville. Tomorrow being the first of the month we will get payed and that's what we have been all waiting for. Mother I am sorry I don't write so much but I don't know what to say. When I wait a couple of days I have something to write about. Friday night we had firing all night so yesterday Saturday I had off to catch up with my sleep. I was sorry to hear about David Lucas but maybe it is better that way. Anyway he has gone to college and got that training. Boy was I surprised to hear that Richie Simmons was sick again. Write and tell me how he is and try and get his address. When you get Pete Thomas's address, send it too. Tell Dad I will try and get home for the 5th of June and tell him and Duke to get plenty of stuff for it. The weather down here is swell. It is very warm but at night it gets quite cool. Mother are they going to have a barn party this year? Well Red Gibbons ought to be getting along swell with his women now that everybody is gone away. Well mother I will close now. Give my regards to all.
                                                          Love,
                                                          Son John"

"May 9, 1944 [Tuesday]
11 o'clock P.M.

Dear Son John,
    This morning I received that sweet little letter with its flowers and Mother's Day greetings. Dad thought it was so nice. In fact we were both delighted to hear from you. He wanted to know all you had to say over the radio telephone. You must be very busy from what you tell us. Dad said you should put in for overtime. Are you driving the jeep yet?

Last week we had the Catholic Charities Drive. They say it was very successful. I think they missed you boys this year. Mrs. Mooney and I were hostesses for them one night serving coffee, sandwiches and cake. It seems everything Father O'Hara wants done now he calls on us. We had our meeting last night and Father put us all on the spot by holding a quiz on Christian Doctrine. You should hear Mrs. Donaldson making up answers. She is a scream. Tomorrow night Mrs. Mooney and I are the hostesses for the card party. There was a little write-up in the home news tonight about it.

Father Foley was asking me about you. I told him that you were an instructor and etc. I said I am hoping John will be here for the duration and he said, "Well he did his share, he did plenty for them." I wondered at first what he meant but then I realized it must be the test he was referring to.[213]

Last Thursday I mailed a box filled with fruit and candy to Ritchie[214]. I didn't hear from him yet but I hope to soon. Walter Cubita writes frequently to us. I think he likes to receive mail. Do you write to him? One Saturday night Victor[215] came in to visit about two or three weeks ago. He feels rather bad about poor Andy.[216] They seem to ship him over so quickly, within five or six months. I am going to enclose his address so you can write him a few lines.

Mr. Ford told me Peter was in the Air Corps but didn't say where he was stationed. I hope he won't be thrown down in the end like David[217] and the other cadets. I haven't heard from Aunt Kitty in a couple of weeks.

Dorothy Moynihan[218] came out second in her exams and she won a scholarship.

Did you receive Hickey's paper? No word has been heard from Robert Faurenback[219] yet. His poor mother is almost gone to a shadow. Mrs. Supple told me her son received a citation. It was sent home to her.

John when you write again ask Duke how he is getting on with his garden. You would be surprised to know how he watches for mail from you. I had to laugh the other day. Mom read Hickey's news to him and when she

---

[213] A rather cryptic comment from Father Foley, in answer to a mother's understandable sentiment, hoping that her son will stay stateside until the war's end; which, in the event, he will not. In fact, at this point (May 1944), he is a short while from being transferred to the Infantry, and a little more than seven months from going overseas into the European Theater of Operations (ETO). The "test" that Anna is referring to is probably the Atabrine test.

[214] Richard Simmons.

[215] Victor Garbarini.

[216] Andy Garbarini.

[217] David, probably David Lucas. This must refer to his earlier trouble.

[218] John's first cousin, daughter of his aunt, Rose McGowan Moynihan.

[219] No 1940 Census record found under this spelling.

finished I heard him say to her, "What, not a word in it about John?" Mom said, "Do you want them to be writing about the McGowans all the time?"

Duke is getting the screens ready to put up and as usual we won't get much time to wash the windows. Here is where I miss you John, helping to get the windows shined up.

John you spoke about getting a pass for three days. Dad said to tell you to be sure it is official. We will all be glad to see you if you can come. Get your shoes. If you are short of funds, I will try to help you out. Write soon again and let us know how you are. Love and regards from all.
Mother

P.S. John it is rather late so excuse writing. I had to hurry."

Undated, post marked May 12, 1944 [Friday].

"Fort Knox, Kentucky

Dear Mother,

Well I received your letter today and was glad to hear everything was okay. I was glad to hear that the Duke is taking good care of the garden. Tell him I'll help him plant the tomatoes and put the seed in when I get home again. From your letter I see that you are starting to run around a lot now, going out to card parties and things and leaving poor Dad at home to take care of Mugs. This week I went to a dance Monday night and I expect to go to Louisville for the weekend. Mother I won't buy my shoes yet because if I get a pass I save my money and send to you for some money to pay for my way home. Well how are things around the neighborhood? Did the Mount have its graduation for this year yet? And when is the Holy Name going to have their beer party? The weather down here is getting awful warm. All we do is drink watery beer at the P.X. to cool us off. The food is getting very good now. We had steaks and beef this week. Well that's all from here. Love to all.
Love,
Son John"

"May 15, 1944 [Monday]

Dear John,

How surprised and delighted I was Saturday morning when I received that beautiful remembrance for Mother's Day. It has been on exhibition. I think Dad was as happy over it as I was. Thanks John and God bless you for being such a thoughtful boy.

Well Sunday was certainly a beautiful day in every way. The weather was perfect and everything growing is almost on full bloom. The lilacs are all out too. The bush seems to grow larger each year.

Duke's garden looks fine. He has planted kale, spinach and a few other things. It is all fenced in like an estate. He left a patch of ground for Dad to plant. If we thought you would be coming home soon Dad would let you do his plantings as he only has Sundays to do his work. I believe he expects to plant tomatoes and string beans. So if you want to plant the seed let us know.

The card party we were hostesses for last week was very successful. We are having the forty hours devotion at the present time. It happens to be my week on the altar with Mrs. Mooney. We just got back after doing a little work down there. I really like to help around the altar as I don't know of anything that gives me a greater feeling of satisfaction as that work. I said to Mrs. Mooney after this card party business I am going to count myself out as I didn't have time to do my spring house cleaning. Well it seems instead of getting out of action it is that I am getting into it. Father O'Hara wants me to become secretary for the Rosary Society. I will take over in September. I don't know whether I should or not because it entails a lot of work. Mom said I should, but as she said all my poor boys in service will not get many letters. By the way Walter wrote again. His mother and father told me yesterday they would like you to visit them when you come home again. I had a nice letter from Richard which I am enclosing. Yesterday Victor came in to visit me. He said they had mail from Andy, also a beautiful Mother's Day card. Victor was to go down today for his physical exam. If he passes he will leave soon for the Navy. He gave me Peter's address. Did you write to Andy?

Mrs. Ford told me to let you know her Margaret Mary won a four year scholarship to college, I think Mt. St. Vincent. It is worth $800. Duke said it is what the mothers want now to be writing to tell the boys what smart daughters they have. Did you get Hickey's paper? I don't know if the Holy Name will have a party in the woods this year but I hear we are in for a lawn party in June.

The girls gave Buddy Mooney's girlfriend a shower in Talbot's house last night - friend of the Trainor girl. Latest news bulletin - Joe McGovern has a new baby son. She didn't see her husband since last summer. He is with the Marines away off some place. Did you know that Johnny Murray from your Fort is in England? The Farrell girl told me last night. It looks like a change was made down there. He was there about 2 years.

Well John I received a letter from you today Monday and I noticed the classy way your address is printed on it. I was so glad to hear you are getting good eats again. I was a little worried about that part.

I had a letter from Aunt Kitty. She said Sonny is getting over his big disappointment. I do hope Peter won't meet with that fate. David may be home on furlough next month. Tom is now stationed in Staten Island. John is still in England. She told me they were in N. Y. to see "Going My Way" with Bing Crosby. It is a very good picture.

Well John we have all the windows cleaned and the screens up. You should see Duke holding the ladder while I cleaned the windows. You would have had a good laugh I bet if you could see me shaking on one leg on top of the ladder.

Frankie told me he sent you a letter? Did you get the papers I sent? Would you like me to send anyone in particular? I forgot to tell you John a week ago I received a letter from the Mount from Brother Louis asking for your address in service and etc. The idea is to keep in touch with their boys and to send you the Tower, also to place your name on the Honor List. So I sent a nice letter back with the information they wanted. Guess you will be hearing from them soon.

Write a few lines to Ritchie when you can. How is the Major? John I want you to get the shoes if you can. If you need money I will send some on to you to help pay your way home, but shoes are a necessity. Dad would have a fit if he thought you needed them and didn't get them. I suppose you had a good time at that dance. Enjoy yourself but don't overdo it. Take care of your heath. Did you take any pictures yet? Enclosed are pictures of Duke's pedigree dogs. Do you remember Beanty and her mother? Rover too.[220] Write soon.

*Love,
Mother"*

℘

Every now and then a letter slips in from someone else, whether referenced in one of the more usual letters or not. A letter from a friend of John's, or in this case from a cousin also in the service, John Lucas, addressed to John's mother, John Lucas's "Aunt Anna". The letter is a "V-Mail".

*"Pvt. John Lucas
BATXD377 AAA/AWL BN
APO 230 c/o P.M. N.Y. N.Y.*

May 23, 1944 [Tuesday]

---

[220] Beanty and Rover - long gone dogs of the Duke.

Mrs. Ed. McGowan
4030 Pratt Ave.
Bronx, N.Y.

Dear Aunt Anna and Ed,

    Well it is about time I wrote to you. I am very sorry that I have not written to you. Well how is John making out? I hope he makes good for yours and Ed's sake. Well the weather over here is very nice right now and I hope you are having good weather home too. Well someday when we all get home we will all get together and have one big time at our place home. I hope you are getting mail from the two brothers of mine. Till I write again. Thanks for the medal. God bless you all.

Love,
John"

MAY 25, 1944 - ITALY

German forces, despite having counter-attacked the Allies several times, are forced to retreat from Anzio. The Allies push northward through Italy. Destination: Rome.

"May 30, 1944 [Tuesday]

Dear John,

    Your letter arrived yesterday. I was glad to know you arrived back safe and sound. We had cool rainy weather all week after you left. In fact Saturday was the first day we saw the sun and then in the evening we had a big thunderstorm. But Sunday was a beautiful day, just perfect. Speaking of last Sunday we all attended the eight o'clock Mass which was said in honor of Mom and Duke's 50th wedding anniversary. We are not going to have any party here but Sunday we are all invited up to Frank's for the day. I believe Johnny McGowan[221] is going to be there too so as Duke said we can prepare for lots of hot air.

    Dad met Jackie Walsh and he said he looked fine. He gained 14 lbs. - said he may go on an L.I.R. boat. Told Dad he was going to pay us a visit but I haven't seen him yet. Ritchie Simmons didn't get home for the weekend.

    Well today was Memorial Day. They had a big parade down in the city, otherwise it was a quiet day here. Did you have a parade down there or

---

[221] Mamie McGowan's eldest son, my father, John James McGowan. -Ed.

any celebration? I put the film in to have it developed so we should be getting the pictures soon. Did you get your new shoes?

I hope John you are attending to your teeth. Don't neglect them. How is your hair growing? I was talking with Mrs. Bernabe today. She thinks you got so tall. Ralph is painting Walsh's apartment. You should hear Duke kidding him that it was about time he got to work and stopped bluffing. Mrs. Walsh is moving tomorrow and she has been so excited over going that she is out yelling over everything and yesterday Bobbie fell off his bike and broke his arm, so now she will have to change all her plans, she told me, and stay with her mother until Bobbie is well. Mr. Walsh wrote he wanted to be remembered to the McGowans. He liked this place around here very much.

Father Foley's brother, a priest, is very ill. He lives in Ohio. Father Foley is out there with him for the past week.

A girl just sang that song "I'll Be Seeing You". It is a lovely song. Did you hear it? That is why I am making so many mistakes, trying to write and listen to the radio at the same time. You know John I often think of you talking about the Major and the hammer and I have a little laugh to myself. Dad and Muggsie are fast asleep. Mugs is snoring like an old man. I think she misses you after you left last week.

I owe about a dozen letters so I will have to get back to sending out more mail again. John would you like a box with oranges and etc.? If so, let me know. The rose bushes are right on time this year. Little roses are beginning to show their heads. The garden looks good too. As the Duke would say, everything is blooming. Don't forget to send Duke and Mom a card for June 3rd. Well John I will close. Write soon. It is almost 10:30. Bob Hope is going off.

*Love,
Mother"*

P.S. Had a laugh over the knockout drops. Indeed that is what they are."

§

A postcard serves to convey some convivial jesting from a neighborhood friend, Victor ("Vic") Garbarini, about which is the better branch of the service - Navy or Army?

"Victor C. Garbarini
Co. 1208, USNTS
Great Lakes, Illinois

May 30, 1944 [Tuesday]

Hi Mac!

The Navy is the nuts! We got it all over the Army. Why, we even wish we had mess duty so we don't have to dress up in whites. This place is lovely. They treat us like kings, as long as we drill and keep clean and neat satisfactorily. I'm not even lonesome. There's 139 other swell guys in my company. The CO's a swell guy too. Write.

Regards,
Vic"

Mt. St. Michael Academy, Bronx, NY Graduation Invitation, Class of 1943; John, flanked by his parents, Edward and Anna McGowan

John turned 18 on March 27, 1943, while still in high school. It did not take the Local Draft Board long before they reminded him to be ready.

John as a baby in the yard of 4030 Pratt Avenue, with his mother, Anna McGowan.

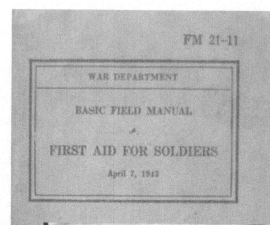

First Aid Manual, one of the first things soldiers would learn.

The "Dyre Avenue News", Vol. 1, Issue 3, August 1943

John's Air Warden Service Honorable Discharge, given when he entered the military.

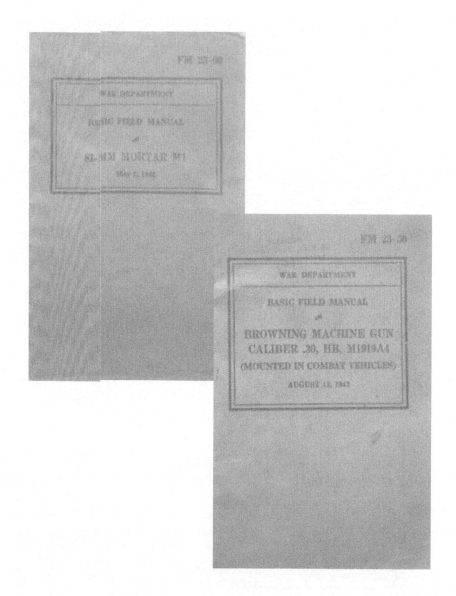

Manual for the .30 Caliber Browning machine gun and the 81 mm Mortar, both of which John would demonstrate great proficiency in.

Anna McGowan's Ration Book and Ration Card, which would go inside her Ration Book for safekeeping.

Home on furlough, in front of 4030 Pratt Avenue, Edenwald, the Bronx.

INNOCULATIONS

1. SMALLPOX—Date 8-21-43
2. TYPHOID—Date 9-4-43
3. TETANUS—Date 9-4-43
4. _____

ORGANIZATIONAL SUBJECTS
HOUR FOR HOUR BASIS

1. SEX HYGIENE __3__ hrs.
2. PERS HYGIENE __1__ hrs.
3. ART OF WAR __2__ hrs.
4. ORG OF ARMY __2__ hrs.
5. PROT OF MIL INFO __4__ hrs.
6. ORIENT COURSE W/FILMS __2__ hrs.
7. CW & GAS CHAMBER __12__ hrs.

ARTC
FORT KNOX, KY.
INDIVIDUAL TRAINING RECORD

Important — Retain This Card

NAME: John F. McGowan
ASN: 32985511
DATE OF BIRTH: 27 March 1925
B CO. 5TH BN. 2nd REGT.
RECOMMENDED ASSIGNMENT: DRIVER
SINGLE __X__ MARRIED ____
EDUCATION: High School Graduate
CIVILIAN OCCUPATION: Student
TESTS: CA-1 2-117 MA-1 3-109
AGCT 3-99 OTHER ROA 4-81

PERSONAL AFFAIRS
INSURANCE: 10,000 WAR
ALLOTMENTS: FAMILY ____ BONDS/18.75

PHYSICAL CHECKS
GLASSES—Prescription ____ Prs. ____
PHYSICAL EXAM—Latest Date: 12-29-43
BLOOD TYPE: O
IDENTIFICATION TAGS: Yes

WEAPONS INSTRUCTION

	INSTR FIRING	RECORD FIRING	SIM'D FIRING TSC	MINIATURE RANGE	FIRE PROBLEMS	FAMILIARIZATION	TRANSITION	FINAL RATING
RIFLE CAL .30	S	S						S
CARBINE CAL .30	S	S						S
TSMG CAL .45	E	E						E
MG CAL .30	S	S						S
MG CAL .50	E	S						S
37-MM TN GUN								
75-MM TN GUN	S	E		E				S
105-MM HOW SP								
GRENADES, HAND	S	S						S
ROCKETS 2.36"								
81-MM MORTAR								

P—POTENTIAL INSTRUCTOR
E—EXCELLENT (OVER 85)
S—SATISFACTORY (OVER 60)
U—UNSATISFACTORY (UNDER 60)

Pvt. McGowan did well at the ARTC, so well that he was asked to remain as an Instructor.

> Dear John   Jan 30 1944
> Do you like your oranges.
> Did you sleep on the train
> How are you. When are
> you coming home. Do you
> get your hankies
> dirty. I can not get
> your hankies clean.
> Do you get good food.
> Do you have fun camp home
> when you can Muggsie
> is ok right.
>
> love Mary Ann McGowan

Letter from Mary Anne McGowan, Private McGowan's young cousin.

Home on leave, John and his mother, Anna Cecelia McGowan.

A Sunday in the Bronx: Cousins Martin Moynihan and John McGowan, with grandparents Bridget and Dennis ("the Duke") McGowan.

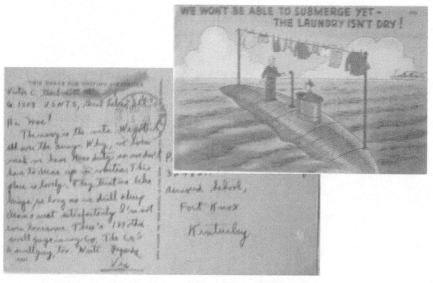

A post card from a friend serving in the U.S. Navy, with obvious bragging as to which branch of service is the best.

ENLISTED MAN'S PASS
Fort Knox, Kentucky

John F. McGowan   Pvt.   32985511
   (Name)   (Grade)   (Army serial No.)

is authorized to be absent from his post—

From 1700 15 July 1944

To   1700 18 July 1944

To visit New York City, New York

Signed *Cecil C. Brady*
       CECIL C. BRADY   Company commander
       1st Lt., F. A.,
       Comdg. Co. D, Instr. Regt., TAS.

Enlisted Man's Pass, issued to Pvt. McGowan, and good for 72 hours. Be back at Fort Knox by 1700hours (5:00 PM) on July 18th or be AWOL!

ARMY SERVICE FORCES
New York Port of Embarkation
Brooklyn, New York

METHODS OF ABANDONING SHIP

1. GENERAL

When disasters at sea occur, it is important that personnel upon receipt of an "Abandon Ship" order, (as provided in the ship's standing orders) abandon the stricken vessel by the fastest and safest means available. To insure speed and safety a uniform method of utilizing the means of getting off the ship is necessary.

   a. The following are methods of abandoning ship.
      (1) Debarkation Nets
      (2) Man Lines
      (3) Jacob's Ladders
      (4) Fire Hose
      (5) Boom Ladders

Instructions on how to effectively "abandon ship" were shared with all departing soldiers, should they fall prey to a German U-boat.

Notice of Address Change - Mail to Private McGowan will no longer be going to Camp Shelby, but to an overseas APO address, for eventual delivery wherever he may be deployed.

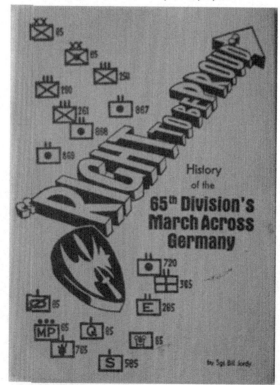

Cover to Jordy's book chronicling the travels, trials, travails and triumphs of the 65th Infantry Division.

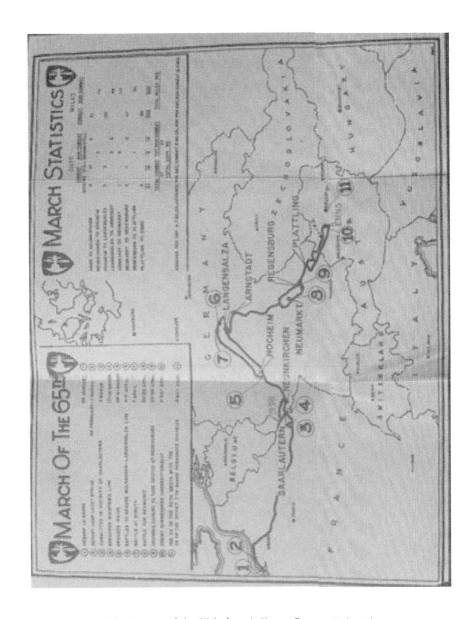

The Journey of the 65th, from LeHavre, France, to Austria.

John, on the left, and a pal beside one of the many rivers the 65th will cross on their march through France, Germany and Austria.

Amid a lull in fighting, this photo of John, left, and a pal atop a foxhole is snapped. A few moments later the GI bending over in the left background will be killed by a German mortar shell.

"Somewhere in Germany". With the end of hostilities in Europe, the American GIs quickly assume the role of tourists eager to see what remains. And not every square inch has been bombed to oblivion.

John, second from right, and some pals on a junket through some German town. Note the GI to John's left, the only one with a wedding band on, glad to not be leaving a widow behind.

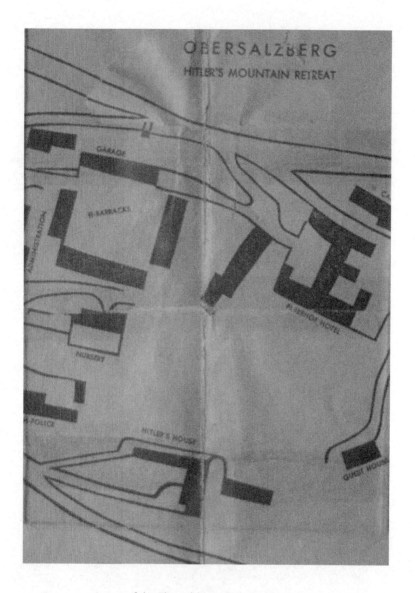

A map of the Obersalzberg, *Hitler's mountain retreat, which John and his fellow GIs explored in the aftermath of Germany's defeat.*

Snowball fights and shirtless skiing in August, and an Identification Card to be presented at any time upon demand to the Military Police. MPs had their hands full keeping restless GIs in check in the months after the war. Football leagues organized around Division lines helped relieve some of the pressure. John became manager of one such team.

War-weary GIs in line and finally boarding at Le Havre, anxious to begin the long trip home.

John, center, and two pals, all glad to be part of the Troops Embarked for the Good Old U.S.A." at LeHavre.

John on board the USS Hood Victory, *homeward bound.*

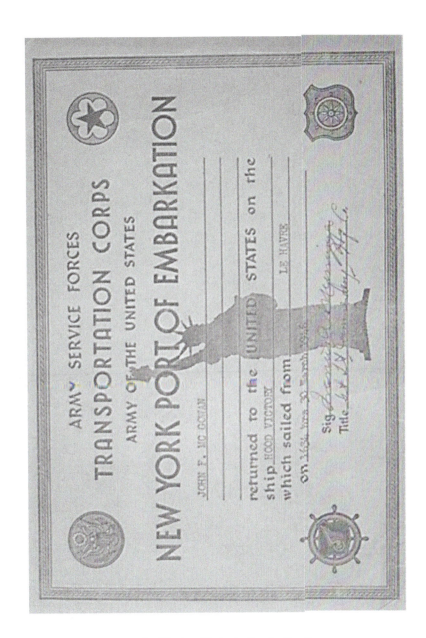

Certificate of Embarkation for Home.

Friends and neighbors Elizabeth (Betty) and Thomas (Tom) Cotter, from just over the City Line on Kingsbridge Road in Mt. Vernon, NY, with their sons Tom, Jr. and Jack. Friendships were forged among many of the families mentioned in this book in the 1920s and 1930s. Some continue to this day, in the "Baby Boomer" generation and beyond, though the principals have moved far from their Edenwald roots; Cotters, McGowans and O'Keefe's, to name several.

Raymond O'Keefe, Sr. and his wife Margaret (Marge). Ray, along with Tom Cotter, braved the flames of the Nativity Church fire in 1958 to save the carved wooden statue of the Blessed Virgin from destruction. The O'Keefe's were more friends with the Edenwald Avenue McGowans (the branch of the family "up the Hill"), with several mentions in diaries and other records of social visits between Mary ("Mamie") McGowan and Mrs. O'Keefe, Ray's mother, in which Ray O'Keefe's return from the Pacific Theater of Operations is frequently spoken of. Marge O'Keefe, now 99, is still going strong, a vibrant connection between our times and that of "The Greatest Generation", of whom it has been written: "Everyone served."

TWELVE: "WHEN THE ROSES BLOOM"

JUNE 5, 1944 - ROME, ITALY

Allied troops enter Rome, the Eternal City, a major objective in the quest to liberate Europe from the south. Their victory, however, will be eclipsed by events in Northern Europe the following day.

℘

JUNE 6, 1944 - NORMANDY, FRANCE

D Day - the invasion of Normandy in France begins.

℘

"June 6, 1944 [Tuesday]

Dear John,

How glad I was to receive your letter, especially today, D Day, although we would never know it was any different from the other days here except the radio is blasting with excitement. Frank was in for supper tonight and he was telling us all the Department stores were closed downtown and Mayor LaGuardia had called for a prayer meeting at Madison Square. Dad couldn't get a Journal. All the papers were gone. Duke's friend was broadcasting this evening, Gabriel Heater, and he was actually crying. I believe he has a son or two in the war. I never saw the people of our nation so stirred up before. Well John I thank God you are not in the invasion but I pray that God will protect all our boys everywhere and bring them home soon. Roosevelt has just delivered his prayer and now they are singing hymns. There is one thing sure - this is no time for atheists in our midst with so much faith in God being shown.

I was sorry that you didn't get a card to Mom and Duke. I watched for it. I realize now how hard it is to get those kind of cards and you are excused. Last Thursday I went down to confession for First Friday and Fr. O'Hara called me in to speak to me. He told me that Fr. Foley and he had planned to have a special ceremony at the eight o'clock Mass Sunday 4th for Mom and Duke but I was not to let them know a word about it. So I kept the secret only to tell Rose and Frank and a few others. So Sunday we went to the Mass. It was First Communion Sunday and also the Rosary Society were there to receive, and all in all it was a crowded church for the 8 o'clock Mass. Well, Fr. O'Hara started talking from the pulpit about the little girls and boys who were receiving First Holy Communion and the first thing you know he started up with, "We have with us today a couple who are celebrating their 50th

wedding anniversary, Mr. and Mrs. Dennis McGowan." And he went on and on about them, how faithful they were and what an example they were to the divorced today. After the Mass was over everybody was told to remain and Fr. O'Hara came down and took Duke and Mom out of the pews and up with him to the top step of the altar where Fr. Foley was waiting to give them thankful blessing and Duke was presented with a silver rosary and Mom with a miraculous medal on a gold chain. Fr. O'Hara escorted them down the middle aisle and Marie played the wedding music. I am telling you it was lovely. Everybody was laughing and crying together. Everyone was running up to them outside the church to congratulate them. They got such a surprise, it was a shock to them. Duke said, "By George if I knew what I was doing when I got up to that step." Fr. Foley wanted Duke to kiss Mom like a regular bride and groom. Duke shook his head no and you should hear everybody laughing. They found out I knew all about it and didn't tell them. Dorothy said she heard a woman say to another, "You know that woman, her grandson is a soldier."

    Rose and family were here for breakfast and we were just about finishing when Fr. O'Hara arrived and we had a lot of fun with him. About one o'clock Fr. Broderick was on the scene. He gave them his blessing. I explained to him about you - what you were doing - he seemed very much pleased about it. That afternoon we went to Frank's and had a very nice afternoon. Came back about ten o'clock. I understand Ritchie was here with his mother and father when we were out. I was sorry to miss him. His mother expects him home again in about two weeks. Gerard Diemer is home too. Last week Jackie Walsh visited us and I wondered if he could come in the door, he looked so tall. He told us he likes the Navy very much and may go into signalman's school now.

    I was thinking of John Lucas today. I suppose he is going in with the invasion. I owe Aunt Kitty a letter. I must get it off to her. Last night we had one last rosary meeting of the season so I had to accept my secretary job. We are going to have one bazaar the latter part of the month. Buddy Mooney got home Monday. He is going to be married Sunday at the Sacred Heart Church, Mt. Vernon. It can't be that Hickey's paper won't contain social news this month after all these events taking place. Martin Moynihan went down to enlist in the Marines but they told him to wait until he was drafted. I wondered if he really knows what the Marines go through with their training. Although it looks as if the kids in the infantry are putting up the real fight now and as Dad said Patton has shown what the tanks are worth in battle. They certainly carried the victory to Rome, from what we are told. A letter came from Agnes. Her son was home for a week. He is now as she told us Major King and is going overseas with 15,000 men. So now you have a 42nd cousin a Major in the air corps. She was asking about you.   I am enclosing the pictures you took. My, those close up ones look as if your faces were blown up like balloons. Answer these two questions. Did you get your shoes? And did you have your teeth attended to?

The garden is coming along fine. We got a new bird bath for the birds. The roses are in full bloom. Sunday was graduation day at the Mount. Be a good boy John. Get to Communion. Call us on the phone some evening. Write soon.

Love,
Mother"

"Fort Knox, Kentucky

June 7, 1944 [Wednesday]

Dear Mother,

Well we are interested in the invasion as you probably are. We took things easy down here and everything went along as smooth as possible. Mother did you receive the letter I wrote Sunday in which I told you I couldn't get a card for Mom and Duke. Last weekend I had a good time in town. I went to the Club Madrid and boy what a time we had. Today guess who I got a letter from, but no one but Andy. He told me all about his training in the Anzio[222] beachhead and how he was up to the front. When I get a chance I must write him and give him all the news. Martin Moynihan also wrote me and said that he was going down to the Marines soon to try and get in. Don't let his Mother know about this because he said not to. Things here at camp are very quiet except for some fellows that are shipping out for overseas.

How's the Duke making out with the garden? Did he take any more of Dad's ground? Tell the Duke to take Mugs out for a walk up to Mamie's. By the way tell the Duke also that I go with a new blond in town and that she is very nice. How's Dad getting along? I want to ask him one thing. Some fellows said that we had 18" guns on some battleships but I said we only had 16". Please write and tell if, and which one has 18" guns. I will close now. Love to all.

Love,
Son John"

JUNE 10, 1944 - ORADOUR-SUR-GLANE, FRANCE

---

[222] Anzio, often referred to as the forgotten invasion, was a bloody, bitter, hard-fought effort to break through German defenses in Italy, and allow the Allies to penetrate Europe from the south.

A Nazi SS Division surrounds the village of Oradour-sur-Glane in France and orders everyone in the town, 652 persons in all, to assemble in the town square. Once there, they are told by the Nazi commandant that they are suspected of hiding explosives. As a result there will be a search and a check of identity papers. The entire populace is then locked up, the men in barns, women and children in the church. The Nazis then set fire to the entire village and begin shooting the villagers with machine guns, then set the barns and the church on fire, burning the men, women and children alive, and shooting anyone who survives. A total of 642 townspeople -- 245 women, 207 children, and 190 men - are massacred. Three days after the massacre, a Catholic Bishop finds the charred bodies of fifteen children in a heap behind the burned out altar inside the church. The village of Oradour-sur-Glane is never rebuilt, forever standing as a silent monument to Nazi atrocities.

§

In this letter Anna's capability with words comes in full force, with her description of the roses in bloom. You'll see what I mean.

"June 13, 1944 [Tuesday]

Dear John,

I received your letter written on June 7th. I mailed a letter to you on the same date. You must have received it since. I was glad to hear you had mail from Andy.[223] Don't forget to write him a nice long letter. Send him a few pictures if you have them and give him my regards. By the way I had a card from Victor[224] and he told me Andy is some kind of a gunner now. Said he wrote to you and he likes the Navy very much.

Had a letter from Ritchie[225] too. I will enclose it for you to read.

Robert Fauerback[226] is reported taken a prisoner. Everybody here is rejoicing that he is alive after such a long time of waiting. The news traveled

---

[223] Andy Garbarini.
[224] Victor Garbarini.
[225] Richie Simmons.
[226] The Fauerbachs lived at 3723 Rombouts Avenue. In 1940 the family consisted of Felix, 55, and his wife Elizabeth, 51; Robert, 22; Donald, 11; and Mrs. Fauerbach's mother, Mary McGuiness, a widow of 88. Mr. Fauerbach was born in Germany, his mother-in-law in Northern Ireland. He was a bookkeeper in a building and trust company. His son Robert was a clerk in an insurance company.

like wildfire. Even Mrs. Orback[227] down the street rushed out to ask me if I had heard about Robert.

Jackie Walsh is going to train for some kind of work in the school for the time being. His cousin the parachute fellow is in the invasion they think. Helen Butler said Bobby Mahon must be in the invasion boats. They expect George Diemer home tomorrow.

Georgiana and her baby left for Norfolk, Virginia to stay with her husband Bob. The Walsh's have moved. I guess Mrs. Lang misses Mike. Dad said his position is in some state hospital.

Bernabe's have a new tenant in a young couple with two little boys who can cry and yell like sixty. Poor Bobby was mild toward these gents. Your old friend Mrs. Springer was asking for you. She is very much worried about her son. She didn't hear from him in such a long time. He is out at sea.

Well John we are going to have the bazaar for three nights the end of June and as usual they are looking for gifts and boosters. I got a card asking me to attend the meeting but I didn't go down as I am into so many things now. I am wondering how I will be able to do it all. The roses this year John are beautiful. They are in full bloom. Everything looks its best now. We have a lot to be thankful for the beauty, peace and quiet we have here. It makes us all feel rather sad now when our thoughts wander across the seas to that terrible invasion. Maybe with God's help our boys will be home again when the roses bloom.

I wrote to Aunt Kitty. Am still waiting for her answer. I would like to know how the boys are making out.

Last Saturday here we had a very heavy rainfall all day along with lightning and thunder.

Sunday was a busy day. The Holy Name had their Communion Breakfast. Dad didn't go but Duke was there and they made a great fuss over Duke and his 50th wedding anniversary. They had the Police Glee Club there and Duke tells us they had a great time. They sang "When You and I Were Young, Maggie" for Duke.

When Duke came back from the breakfast, Frank took us up to Mr. Windell's mother's home. His sister died - 23 years old. She was buried Monday. We were back about one hour or so when Val Lenahan came in to visit us. He looks fine. Is here taking up firefighting. He is stationed at a submarine base at Brazil. You should hear him tell tales about the jungles and people of Brazil. He has a 15 day furlough and then he is going down there

---

[227] Bernard, 54, and Lillian, 50, Orbach lived at 4006 Pratt Avenue. He was from Russia. She was from Austria. Children living with them in 1940 were Elaine, 24, and Melvin, 21 years old. Mr. Orbach was a salesman for a paper and twine distributor. Elaine was a stenographer for a retail fur shop. Melvin was a clerk in a retail china shop.

again. In answer to your question John regarding the guns on ships, Valley and your father both say there are no 18 inch guns. 16 inches is right. So you win.

Sunday at 5 o'clock we went up to see Buddy Mooney married at the Sacred Heart Church.[228] One side of the church was Little Italy, little ones and big ones, and on the other side was the Irish.[229] Buddy looks well but he is very thin. His run was from Canada to South America. I guess he must be making plenty of money. I think he is a shrewd fellow.

Well John the garden is coming along good. Duke is slowly but surely moving into Dad's garden. He said if you were here you would be out measuring it. He said he guesses the blondes are taking up all your time and that is why you can't write. How did you like the pictures? Dad expects to get a vacation in July. It is 11:30 p.m. John so I will close for now. Take care of yourself. Write soon. Take care of your teeth.

Love,
Mother

P.S. John I am going to mail some pictures of tanks. I thought you might like to read about them. They are getting great praise in the newspapers for their great work."

---

[228] Sacred Heart Church in neighboring Mount Vernon was the original parish for the Roman Catholics of Edenwald, before the establishment of Nativity Parish in the 1920's. The original Nativity church was erected in 1924 (just across the street from its current location) where the playground area of The Nativity of Our Blessed Lady School (3893 Dyre Avenue) is located. The grammar school opened in 1953 and has seen different orders of educators, including the Sisters of Mercy, the Sisters of Charity, and the Dominicans. While the original church was being constructed, masses for the community's primarily Italian, German, and Irish parishioners were conducted at Brienlinger's Hall, a popular party and dance hall, at the corner of Boston Post Road (Route 1) and Dyre Avenue. In the summer of 1923, a huge tent was erected on the corner of East 233rd and Secor Avenue, where the present Nativity church now stands, and Masses were held there. The original church opened in 1924. There were movie nights and minstrel shows inside the original church during the 1920s. The original Nativity church was destroyed by fire in 1958. During the fire, two or three men rushed into the church to climb up into the niche above the altar and rescue the beautiful wood-carved statue of the Blessed Mother and carry it out of the church before it burned. For the next twenty years it remained in a school janitorial closet, before being disposed of. The identities of two of these men recently came to my attention: Ray O'Keefe and Tom Cotter.

[229] Sounds like Buddy, clearly an Irishman, must have married a nice Italian girl, in an age when this was close to being considered marrying outside your race - on both sides of the coin!

JUNE 13, 1944 - LONDON, ENGLAND

The first German V-1 rocket attack is launched against Britain. *The History Place: World War II in Europe*, tells us about them: "The 'V' came from the German word *vergeltungswaffen*, meaning "weapons of reprisal". The V-1 was developed by German scientists at the Peenemünde research facility on the Baltic Sea, under the direction of Wernher von Braun and Walter Dornberger. They were nicknamed "buzz bombs" by the British due to the distinct buzzing sound made by the pulse-jet engines powering the bombs, which overall resembled a small aircraft. Other British nicknames included "doodlebugs" and "flying bombs." Each V-1 was launched from a short length catapult then climbed to about 3,000 feet at speeds up to 350 miles per hour. As the V-1 approached its target, the buzzing noise could be heard by persons on the ground. At a preset distance, the engine would suddenly cut out and there would be momentary silence as the bomb plunged toward the ground, followed by an explosion of the 1,870 pound warhead. The first V-1s were launched against London on June 13, 1944, a week after the D-Day landings. During the first V-1 bombing campaign, up to 100 V-1s fell every hour on London. Over an 80 day period, more than 6,000 persons were killed, with over 17,000 injured and a million buildings wrecked or damaged. Unlike conventional German aircraft bombing raids, V-1 attacks occurred around the clock in all types of weather, striking indiscriminately, causing suspense and terror among the population of London and parts of Kent and Sussex."

"Fort Knox, Kentucky

June 14, 1944 [Wednesday]

Dear Mother,
    This is the first chance I have had to write you this week. Well everything is going along as good as possible. But first I will answer your questions. I didn't get my shoes yet but I expect to as soon as possible. I didn't go to the dentist yet because we are very busy and they can't have none of us off. I was glad to hear of the nice surprise you had for Mom and Duke. I bet they were surprised where they had that little affair at the 8 o'clock mass.
    Things are pretty quiet down here except for the weather. It is warm and boy do I sweat. How's Dad making out? Is he still being a good boy? While writing we are having a little discussion in the barracks about Little

Butch LaGuardia of New York the Negro lover.[230] *We are starting to get a lot of new men from overseas so I guess that we might be moving out in the next*

---

[230] This reference to LaGuardia is very interesting. It could stem from his sympathetic reaction to the Harlem Riot of 1935, which took place on March 19, 1935 during the Great Depression. It has been described as the first "modern" race riot in Harlem, because it was committed primarily against property rather than persons. The rioting was sparked by rumors that a black Puerto Rican teenage shoplifter was beaten by employees at an S. H. Kress "five and dime" store on 125th Street, across from the Apollo Theater. That evening a demonstration was held outside the store and, after someone threw a rock through the window, more general destruction of the store and other white-owned properties ensued. Three people died, hundreds were wounded, and an estimated $2 million in damages was caused to properties throughout the district. In the aftermath of the riot, Mayor LaGuardia set up a multi-racial Mayor's Commission on Conditions in Harlem, headed by African-American sociologist E. Franklin Frazier and with members including Judge Hubert Thomas Delany, Countee Cullen, and labor leader A. Philip Randolph, to investigate the causes of the riot. The committee issued a report, *The Negro in Harlem: A Report on Social and Economic Conditions Responsible for the Outbreak of March 19, 1935*, which described the rioting as "spontaneous" with "no evidence of any program or leadership of the rioters." The report identified "injustices of discrimination in employment, the aggressions of the police, and the racial segregation" as conditions which led to the outbreak of rioting. The report congratulated the Communist organizations as deserving "more credit than any other element in Harlem for preventing a physical conflict between whites and blacks." Whereas previous race riots had been characterized by violent clashes between groups of black and white rioters, subsequent riots would resemble the riot in Harlem.

A subsequent race riot took place in Harlem, New York City, on August 1 and 2 of 1943, after a white police officer, James Collins, shot and wounded Robert Bandy, an African-American soldier; and rumors circulated that the soldier had been killed. The riot was chiefly directed by black residents against white-owned property in Harlem. It was one of six riots in the nation that year related to black and white tensions during World War II. The others took place in Detroit; Beaumont, Texas; Mobile, Alabama; and Los Angeles. In Beaumont and Mobile, the riots were white defense industry workers attacking blacks. In Harlem, Bandy had witnessed a black woman's arrest for disorderly conduct in a hotel and sought to have her released. According to the police, Bandy hit the officer, who shot the soldier as he was trying to flee from the scene. A crowd of about 3,000 people gathered at police headquarters, after a smaller crowd had followed Bandy and the officer to a hospital for treatment. When someone in the crowd at police headquarters incorrectly stated that Bandy had been killed, a riot ensued in the community that lasted for two days and resulted in six deaths and hundreds injured, with nearly 600 arrests. The riot had a pattern mostly of vandalism, theft, and property destruction of white-owned businesses in Harlem, resulting in monetary damages, rather than attacks on persons. New York City Mayor Fiorello H. La Guardia ultimately restored order in the borough on August 2 with the recruitment of several thousand officers and volunteer forces to contain the rioters, and the enlistment of African-American community leaders to aid in quelling the disturbance. City units cleaned up and repaired buildings. The mayor also supplied food and goods afterward to compensate for the closed businesses. LaGuardia's sympathy with the disadvantaged, and his overriding desire to right wrongs may have earned him the sobriquet.

A third riot in Harlem in 1964 repeated the pattern. The Harlem riots of 1964 occurred between July 16 and 22, 1964. They began after James Powell was shot and killed by police Lieutenant Thomas Gilligan. The second bullet of three fired by Lieutenant Gilligan killed the 15-year-old African American in front of his friends and about a dozen other witnesses. Immediately after the shooting, about 300 students from his school who were informed by the principal rallied. The shooting set off six consecutive nights of rioting that affected the New York City neighborhoods of Harlem and Bedford-Stuyvesant. In total, 4,000 New Yorkers participated in the riots which led to attacks on the New York City Police Department, vandalism, and looting in stores. Several protesters were severely beaten by NYPD officers. At the end of the conflict, reports counted one dead rioter, 118 injured, and 465 arrested.

But all of this pales when compared with the Draft Riots of 1863. The Draft Riots, which convulsed the city between July 13–16, 1863, were violent disturbances in Lower Manhattan, widely regarded as the culmination of white working-class discontent with new laws passed by Congress that year to draft men to fight in the ongoing American Civil War. The riots remain the largest civil and racially-charged insurrection in American history. U.S. President Abraham Lincoln diverted several regiments of militia and volunteer troops after the Battle of Gettysburg to control the city. The rioters were overwhelmingly white working-class men, mostly Irish or of Irish descent, who feared free black people competing for work and resented that wealthier men, who could afford to pay a $300 (equivalent to $9,200 in 2017) commutation fee to hire a substitute, were spared from the draft. Initially intended to express anger at the draft, the protests turned into a race riot, with white rioters, predominantly Irish immigrants, attacking black people throughout the city. The official death toll was listed at either 119 or 120 individuals. Conditions in the city were such that Major General John E. Wool, commander of the Department of the East, said on July 16 that, "Martial law ought to be proclaimed, but I have not a sufficient force to enforce it." The military did not reach the city until the second day of rioting, by which time the mobs had ransacked or destroyed numerous public buildings, two Protestant churches, the homes of various abolitionists or sympathizers, many black homes, and the Colored Orphan Asylum at 44th Street and Fifth Avenue, which was burned to the ground. The area's demographics changed as a result of the riot. Many black residents left

six months but I am not sure of this because the Major told me that I will be here for quite a while yet. Well that's about all from here. Love to all.

Love,
Son John"

℘

"June 19, 1944 [Monday]

Dear Son John,

    Perhaps when you see the insignia on this paper you may think I have joined the WACs. But the truth of the matter is I suddenly discovered every piece of my writing paper is gone. Even the box I had from Mrs. Hull for Christmas is all used up. So now you can't say I don't do a whole lot of corresponding. I searched around and found this sheet in a box with your letters.

    Today is Monday, and my, what a storm we had this morning. Lightning and thunder - the rainfall was so heavy about 11:00 A.M. you couldn't see across the street. It is clear this afternoon, but we needed the rain as we just got over a very hot spell.

    Your father wants me to thank you for that nice remembrance you sent him. For the last few months your father has been having Sunday off each week. But it just happened that this week he had Saturday off and it was he who went out for the mail Saturday morning which brought your letter. Of course John we all look for your writing on the envelope. Dad came in from the gate yelling to me, "Here is mail for you from John," and not getting any word from you in over a week your father didn't notice that one was addressed to him until I went to open it and I gave it back to him so he opened it himself and I am telling you John it would have done you good to see how delighted he was with it. For a minute I couldn't tell whether he was going to laugh or cry. He said, "John just sent this in time. Today is the Holy name picnic in Seton Falls." Well, Duke and he went to the picnic and between you and I they had a good time. Although (thank the Lord) they both got home safe and sound, Dad fell asleep and that was the end of a perfect day. From what Duke tells me, they were all playing cards and that kept them busy. They had two barrels of beer. It was a very warm day. A big crowd was there. Duke said as usual all the kids in Edenwald came to eat the frankfurters, so there wouldn't be any left for the men who spent their money. Duke is a scream. If anything he is getting wittier every day. He told us Fr. Broderick was over at the picnic and he got so hot he removed his collar and belongings along with his big prayer book and left them in somebody's car and when it came time for

---

Manhattan permanently with many moving to Brooklyn. By 1865, the black population fell below 11,000 for the first time since 1820.

him to leave the car he left his things in was gone and he had to sit down waiting and praying it would return and who was it but Roger's car, he drove off someplace to get another barrel of beer and discovered he had the collar and belongings when he came back. So I guess a good time was had by all. Dad I guess informed one and all how he received the card and contents from you. I often miss you John, to sit down and talk things over for a good laugh. Your father said Saturday Schultz here is where you are going to miss John to play cop after me. I said yes, but now he is able to play an M.P. thank God. Dad somehow or other as Mom remarked isn't as foolish as he used to be. He seems as if he got a good deal more serious and is content to stay at home. Thank God. But with all his faults and weakness just the same way down deep inside of him there is a great source of affection for you and it appears John you are a great source of pride and satisfaction to him. While I think of it, he wanted me to send you a big book explaining all about 16 inch guns on the ships so you would be sure to win out in the argument.

 Friday night Helen Butler invited me to attend a social with her up at St. Michael's lawn. So I went with her and it was very nice. In fact, I enjoyed it a whole lot. It was crowded. They had dancing. W.J.Z. broadcasting company put on a whole program of entertainment. We also were treated to ice cream soda cake. Martin tells me they are going to build more. They have the plans drawn out. Did you receive the Tower yet? George Diemer came home last Friday on a 15 day furlough. Looks good and said Mississippi is a very hot place. Helen expects to give them an engagement party.

 You mentioned in your letter about new men coming in from overseas. Dad wants to know are they going to take your places down there if you people move out, and if you should go across John would it be in tanks? Did you hear about the new order for more tanks? Answer this? Dad is interested. In regard to your shoes John well I would like you to get them when you can. In hot weather especially you need a few pair of shoes for changes. Take care of your feet. Change your socks as much as possible. That is necessary on account of perspiration. I want you John to have your health attended to if necessary. Ask the major for time to have it done. It wouldn't take long. They perhaps have better dentists there than you would find at other places. So get busy. Your teeth are part of your health. Get on the ball (as you say) and get them fixed up. Duke wants to know how the blonde is. Do you ever see the girl from Jersey?

 Mugs is lying beside me. She was kept busy chasing squirrels and pigeons out of the garden. But I suddenly discovered now we have another guest - a cat with a bell ringing on it. Roberta expects to graduate from St. Barnabas next Saturday. There has been no word from Bobby in some time. Roberta thinks he must have been in the invasion boats. Yesterday they told down at church that Sgt. Lawrence Cody was killed in action. Did you know him? He belongs to the parish. Mrs. Mooney told me she went into the movies the other day and not knowing they were showing pictures of the invasion she said she was actually sick when she came out. That the people were not only crying around her but sobbing out loud. I was going in to see "Buffalo Bill" but changed my mind after her story of the [illegible] news. Although today we got very encouraging news from Churchill. He predicted the European War may be over before the summer months are gone and as Mom said when she heard the news, "Thank God and may Japan blow up with them." So who can tell? Maybe this Christmas with God's help we will have real peace on earth.

John, by the way, I forgot to say Dad didn't get that nice dollar you sent. I took care of that and put it away for a remembrance. I know this will make you laugh.

I just looked out the window. Neppie is playing ball and at every turn he is blessing himself. Maurice may come back in the fall. Duke has made a new invention for watering the garden, a cooling pot tied to a long pole. Well John the paper is gone and the time is running away fast. Novena tonight.

Love,
Mother

P.S. John I am enclosing a letter from Walter. He should be here now. I see every clock in the house is stopped. Will write more later ([illegible] soon).

Mother and Dad

John, this little poem about answers the description of our garden.

WHOSE GARDEN?

Young Peter had a garden he called his very own,
But Fido claimed a corner for burying a bone;
And Pussy thought the plum tree belonged to her because
It was exactly suited for sharpening her claws.
The robins came for breakfast, the grackles called at noon,
The oriole and bluebird brought their supper with a tune.
A toad took up his lodging beneath a mossy stone,
For there are bugs in plenty where garden things are grown.
A rabbit came there nightly; when folks were all asleep.
A garden snake explored it, and not so very deep.
A mole had made a tunnel close into the parsnip bed;
It's all my own, my garden, young Peter proudly said."

"Fort Knox, Kentucky

June 19, 1944 [Monday]

Dear Mother,
    Well today is Monday and boy is it warm. It was about 96 in the shade yesterday. Over the weekend I stayed in camp so yesterday being Sunday I went to Mass and Communion at the 11 o'clock Mass. They had a new priest and he gave a very nice sermon about going to church and keeping up Christian ideas. Things are pretty quiet down here but there is a lot of trouble between the Italian prisoners and fellows from overseas. They had a riot here yesterday and things are really very hot. The MP's are going around with machine guns and the fellows from the 1st Armored from Africa said that they fought and were killed by the "ginnies" and then when they come back to the States the "ginnies" are in the army and are better off than we are. You won't see anything about this in the papers because they are trying to kill the story and make peace.[231]
    Well how are things going with the bazaar? You know Mother you ought to get into this and make a name for yourself then you can throw your chest out and go up to the first pew like the rest of the McGowans. How are Dad and Muggsie getting along? Are they getting their sleep? Well that's all for now. Love to all.

                                                          Love,
                                                          Son John"

A letter from Dick Simmons, U.S. Navy Seaman 2nd Class, mentioned in many letters throughout as "Ritchie Simmons".

"U.S. Naval Training Station
Sampson, New York

Wednesday, June 21, 1944 [Wednesday]

Hi John,
    I received your letter and it was swell. Say, that girl hasn't written to me yet. When you see her tell her I am still waiting. I was home last week on a forty eight hour pass. Gerard Deimer and Bobby Whitaker was home also. Saturday night I stayed in and played cards with my mother, father and sister

---

[231] In developing this memoir of World War II, John intimated that there were plenty of items kept from the public during the war, and many not revealed until decades later, if revealed at all.

Marge. We were supposed to go out to Coney Island but Joan was sick and we didn't go. And Sunday afternoon it was so hot out I put on my whites. Deimer, Whitaker and myself went to the show at Proctors. I am going home this coming weekend on my graduation weekend leave. It starts Friday night at 5:30 and I will hit Penn Station at 2:30 AM Saturday morning. Me and another fellow are going to stay downtown until about seven or eight Saturday morning and then I will go home and go to bed. I am going down to Saks, where I used to work, Saturday afternoon and then that night I am going to Coney Island with my mother, father and two sisters. Sunday, I don't know what I will do. Visiting, most likely. I want to see your mother and Mrs. Miller and a few more friends. I was over to see Deimer last night. He is one unit away from me. He is in O.C.U. waiting to be shipped out. He was going to try and get home again this weekend so we could be home together again, but he isn't allowed two weekends in a row. We had all our graduation exams and I passed them all. We will get our average on the exams in a day or two. It is this average that decides where you will go when you ship out of here. If I get fleet replacements, it will be a long time before I get home again. You know where Jack was sent to. Well he is at Illinois State Signal College. Pretty nice. I miss the bazaar this year. I go home this weekend and it is the following weekend. I wanted to be home for that too. You know plenty of meat at the bazaar. I will get my S ½ stripe in one week. I will be glad to get that on. Three looks better than two. It is also an increase of 12 bucks a month. Hey, you know who signed up with the Navy for six years? Red Gibbons. He leaves in one week. Sonny Mitz goes into the Navy this October. Freddy Muller is in the Navy and is over at North Africa. James Henessey is on an aircraft carrier and has an F.P.O. Junny Kerwin is in the Navy and is over. Gerard's brother, George, was home on a long furlough last week also. You remember Tony Russo from Harper Avenue. Well he was in last week. He is third class cook. You remember Bernie Curtin that I used to go around with. Lived on Strang and Amundson. Well, her brother Eddie, an aerial gunner on an Army bomber, was missing in action but his mother was notified that he is a German prisoner of war. Roy Miller from Secor Avenue next to the church is in the Navy and is at Brooklyn Naval Hospital with a touch of pneumonia. He got it while on a weekend pass from Sampson. Well John, there is a little news for you. I will be saying so long for now. Hoping to hear from you soon, I remain,*

*Your pal,
Dick"*

JUNE 22, 1944 - RUSSIA

The Soviets launch their summer offensive, code-named Operation Bagration.

"June 22, 1944 [Saturday]

Dear John,
I was more than glad to hear your voice over the telephone. Somehow or other I had a feeling you might call. I guess thoughts travel sometimes. Speaking of telephone calls the tax on toll calls is now 25%. So John when you call try to do so at night, as the day calls knock your hat off.

By this time you must have received the letter I sent you Monday night. I forgot to tell you that last Sunday afternoon we attended Dorothy's graduation[232]. It was a very solemn affair as it was held in the church. Dorothy won two medals and a partial scholarship. Her girlfriend won a 4 year scholarship to Mt. St. Ursula and a partial to some other private school. She seems to be a very smart kid.

I received your letter today. It certainly must be hot down there. So far up here we can't complain, because one day the temperature is down to 50 degrees and next day up to 80. The night you called you needed to wear a coat outdoors and tonight it is warm again.

Yesterday was a rainy day. Mom and I visited the McGoverns and saw Joe's new baby. They think he is very much like you when you were a baby. I think you were twice as fat. Everybody thought you were a grand looking baby. Don't get a swelled head now.

Going back to your letter John I was surprised when I read of all the trouble down there. But then it surprises me that prisoners and boys from overseas are quartered in the same place. When you think of these Italians John, after all they had to do what they were ordered to do so after all you can't be too hard on them. International law, you know, requires that all prisoners be taken care of, and much patience and common sense I am afraid will have to be used in dealing with our boys coming home. A great many of them will be nervous and short-tempered. It is best to have no argument with them. There are more Italian boys in service than any other nationality in this country.

I was glad to see you got to Holy Communion. Stay close to God John and all other things will take care of themselves.

This morning I received an announcement of Catherine and George's engagement and an invitation to attend a party Saturday night in their honor. Isn't there class to that? Mom said to tell you the sidewalks are being swept already. I understand Catherine got a swell ring. I wonder how poor George could afford it. Victor tells me he is having great experiences on all kinds of

---

[232] John's first cousin Dorothy Moynihan, graduating with honors.

boats.²³³ *He seems to like it very much. After all Dick Mooney's study they are not going to be commissioned. He is very disappointed. June 24ᵗʰ is their graduation.*

Enclosed John you will find a little money. I don't like to think of you being without a penny. Write soon. Dad and Mugs are snoring.

Mother"

P.S. *John, your father wanted me to tell you he expects to have his vacation during July and he would like you to save your trip home until then. That is if you can do so. This is new writing paper, supposed to be air weight paper called stratosphere. It feels like tissue paper to me. Mrs. Reynolds called me on the phone this morning to ask me if I would make out a list of names for her for the bazaar. I heard Duke upstairs asking Mom who was calling and when she told him he said, "Hmm, to be sure. Well, her son wants her to be a big shot now and take a seat in the front pew." Mom said, "Indeed I give him credit." And so the conversation went on.*

Nothing interests Duke more than your letters. Regardless of what hurry I am in, he likes me to sit down and read what news you write to us. That is one reason I like you to mention him in your letters.

I am enclosing John some little articles about different weapons that were in the newspaper. I thought you might be interested in them. We had lettuce from Duke's garden today."

℘

A letter from John's cousin, Martin Moynihan, a student at Mount Saint Michael, and one of the editors of the school newspaper, "The Tower". Why he addresses his letter "Dear Bill" is an unknown. Perhaps it was a nickname he had for his cousin. And he closes with a jestful "Love and kisses", this soon-to-be Marine.

"4268 Barnes Avenue
Bronx 66, New York

June 27, 1944 [Tuesday]

Dear Bill,
I just received my yearbook from the Mount and although it's one of the best, it still isn't as good as the previous ones.

Your letter about not receiving your "Tower" was not a shock here for I live only about ten blocks away from the school and I haven't received

---

²³³ Victor Garbarini.

one as yet either although I have read the last one over in Woodlawn.[234] *It's pretty good too. In the center it shows all the pictures of the year of '44 and the largest picture in the group is one by an artist showing what the school is supposed to look like. They say they intend to continue to build the Mount after the War.*

There's a girl over in Woodlawn who claims she knows you or met you someplace - that is by looking at your picture. Her name is Lois Plunket and she lives around 238th Street over there. In case you should happen to remember her, tell me in your next letter because she wants to know. If I had a picture I would send it but I haven't.

Say, by the way, is there any chance of you getting me a fatigue suit? You know, those green overalls. If possible, try to pick me up an old one. I can use it.

I have to register the twenty-first of July and I expect to go to the Marines. I have my heart set on it, so don't be trying to dissuade me please.

My car is running fine since I corrected the starter. Everything would be fine if I could run it on water.

Expect to hear from you soon.
Don't forget about the suit if possible.

Love and kisses,
Cousin Mar T"

℘

JUNE 27, 1944 - FRANCE

After a hard-fought struggle that lasts a solid three weeks following the Normandy invasion, U.S. troops finally liberate Cherbourg, France. This deep-water port is deemed essential to the success of further Allied inroads into Northern France, because it will allow direct transport of men and materiel from the United States without first having to be offloaded and then reloaded in Britain for eventual delivery to Normandy. Though the Germans have bitterly contested the ground, and ultimately destroy most of the harbor, reconstruction efforts will complete in August. Once up and running again the harbor will prove vital to allowing the Allied advance into France to continue at a pace the Germans have neither expected nor planned for.

---

[234] Woodlawn was the Bronx neighborhood adjacent to Wakefield, where Martin Moynihan lived, which was next over from Edenwald, John's neighborhood.

THIRTEEN: "WINDS OF CHANGE"

"Fort Knox, Kentucky

July 2, 1944 [Sunday]

Dear Mother,
    Well today is Sunday and I am spending this weekend in camp. I got done late Saturday so I thought it was better that I stay in because I would get into town too late. Well how's everything? I was expecting to hear from you but I didn't receive any mail from you since last Sunday. Is there any trouble at home? How did the bazaar go over? Was it a success? And how did you make out in getting all the names? I guess that Dad had to sample the beer which they usually have down in the back of the church. I wonder if the Duke got anything out of his garden yet. The string beans ought to be coming up soon. I am supposed to get home soon but I don't know when. I will write you and tell you when. Did you hear anything more from the fellows? And Mother, could you send me Cubita's address so I could drop him a few lines? Things are very busy down here. We have classes in day and at night so you can see that we are at mass production. There is a little Frenchman from Canada that sleeps next to me so during my spare time I brush up on my French with his help. He was in Africa[235] and boy what stories he can tell about the Germans. We also got some boys from Guadalcanal[236] and you ought to hear the stories they tell. They were telling us that the Army saved the Marines and how they didn't get any credit for it. They also said that the picture that we saw in the movies was mostly army troops and not Marines as they said in the movies. So I was thinking about Mr. Goldberg and his son that was killed there. Do you remember how we wondered how he could have been killed when the Marines were supposed to have defeated the Japs? The truth of the matter is that the Marines only held a small part of the beach and Henderson airfield and that the Japs were pushing them back when the army arrived. If you see Mr. Goldberg tell him and also tell him that I met a fellow that said he knew a

---

[235] The war in Africa, often overlooked, is where Patton had his first successes against the Germans.
[236] Guadalcanal, fought between August 7, 1942 and February 9, 1943, was one of the fiercest battles in the Pacific, and the first decisive Allied victory in the war. But it came at great cost. Allied (read U.S.) casualties were 7,100 killed, and 7,800 wounded. The Japanese lost almost 20,000 killed, and 1,000 captured, and suffered a major blow to their aura of invincibility.

Lt. Goldberg from New York and that he was in the Infantry. See if I am right Mother. Well that's all from here. Love to all.

Love,
Son John"

ఞ

JULY 3, 1944

The "Battle of the Hedgerows" is fought in Normandy. On the eastern Front, the Soviets capture the city of Minsk.

ఞ

Of interest, the following letter was not mailed from the Bronx, but from Brooklyn instead. "Brooklyn NY 7, JUL 4 8:30 PM." John's father Eddy must have mailed it on his way to work at the Brooklyn Navy Yard.

"*July 4, 1944 [Tuesday]*

Dear John,

I will have to make this rather a short note as it is already 10:45 P.M. You know how quick the time goes on Novena night.

Well it seems to me we didn't get much out of that call last night. The door bell rang and the telephone bell together. Frank[237] and family were coming in from the bazaar[238] and there was so much noise I guess that is one reason why I couldn't hear what you said. Everybody was talking at once and it seem to me you weren't talking at all.

The bazaar ended last night, Sunday. I couldn't tell you who won all the prizes but I know we didn't. I won a pair of pillow cases playing bingo. Some of the booths charged a quarter a chance. Try and win. Father Foley[239] set the goal at $5,000. I doubt if he made that amount. He called it the School Fund Bazaar and told us two weeks ago he doesn't owe one penny debt and has $30,000 cash to start a school after the war.[240] Isn't that good management?

Well we had that big engagement party and I am telling you it was a social affair. About 100 people attended it. The guests were packed in like sardines. Catherine received beautiful gifts. Had her picture in the Daily

---

[237] Frank McGowan, John's uncle.
[238] A church bazaar, Nativity of Our Blessed Lady.
[239] Father Foley was the Monsignor.
[240] The school would be built, and opened in 1952, on bustling Dyre Avenue.

Argus[241] *with a write-up all about the party and the announcement. George returned to Mississippi last Thursday. You should hear Helen raving. But with it all John she is a good hearted person. Buddy is working since last week. He was sixteen last Friday.*

The other day I had a V-Mail letter from John Lucas. Aunt Kitty told me in her letter which I am enclosing that he is in England.

You know Mom and Duke left this morning to spend a week with Agnes and I must say the house seems very lonesome. I wrote to Aunt Kitty last week and asked her to come over and spend a few days with me. It would be an ideal time but she is to let me know later. I am hoping she will come.

I understand Jackie Walsh is making out O.K. His cousin the paratrooper is in Italy. I see in your armored news that a lot of cadets visited down there. Did you see any of them?

You know John every store I look in I see cherries and peaches and I see your face as I look at them. How you liked peaches! I would send you a box but the man told me he was afraid they might spoil before you received them. Tell me something about your furlough when you write. Dad was angry last night because I asked you about the raise the infantry will get. But I said "Why shouldn't John be interested when it means more money for him?" And for goodness sake I hope that you get that roll of newspapers and an old navy book your father sent or he will throw a fit. It looks to me he wants you to be as smart about the navy as the army. Maybe for fear you won't win out in an argument. Remember Dad how he liked to argue.

Did you hear Clare Booth Luce's speech at the convention, all about G.I. Joe and his demands? I think Dewey will have a strong fight to defeat Roosevelt. A great many people think the European war will be over before elections. Do you think so? Is the trouble settled down there? John I like to receive mail from you too. So write more often.

Love,
Mother

P.S. *Write a few lines to John Lucas if you can."*

૭

"*July 8, 1944 [Saturday]*

Dear John,

By this time you must have received the letter I sent you last Tuesday. I was rather amused with what you had to say about brushing up on your French. Well keep the good work up. There is nothing like gaining knowledge

---

[241] *The Daily Argus*, neighboring Mt. Vernon's daily newspaper, was very popular throughout the Edenwald section of the Bronx.

- the more the better. Education is going to be one of the strongest weapons a boy will have after this war is over which we hope will be soon.[242] Perhaps you would like your French dictionary. Has your friend ever been in New York? Why not invite him for a visit?

I was interested in that fellow knowing Lt. Goldberg. As soon as I see his father I will tell him and find out what regiment he was in. Do you remember Mr. Goldberg let me read the letter - his son's friend a doctor sent? He was there when the Lieutenant died. He went in on the island with the army to relieve the Marines. Both his legs were machine-gunned. They flew him by plane back to a hospital where he died.

Mom and Duke are still away in Millbrook.[243] We think they will be back Monday. Everything went along O.K. Dad was a model man. He is now asleep in the chair. He starts his vacation from tonight on for a week. We were wishing you would be home during that time. Did you get any more information about your furlough?

I saw The Song of Bernadette[244] the other day. It is wonderful but rather sad. Well the latest news on Pratt Avenue is - sorry to say - Mr. Bernabe has put his house up for sale. He is getting a very good job in Detroit. From what he told me I think he is going to be manager of sales for some corporation. He

---

[242] In the weeks after the Normandy Invasion there was increasing optimism that the war might be brought soon to a successful conclusion, and the troops would be home before long, much of it reminiscent of the prior war's prediction that 'the lads would be home before Christmas.' Such was not to be.

[243] Millbrook, a town in Dutchess County, New York, was home to the woman Agnes, often referred to, who appears to have been an old friend of the Duke's wife, Bridget Kenney McGowan, perhaps from their days as maids when fresh off the boat from Ireland.

[244] *The Song of Bernadette,* a popular movie produced in 1943 and starring Jennifer Jones in the title role, is a biographical drama film based on the 1941 novel of the same name by Franz Werfel. It tells the story of Bernadette Soubirous (later canonized Saint Bernadette) who, from February to July 1858 in Lourdes, France, reported eighteen visions of the Blessed Virgin Mary. The film was directed by Henry King, from a screenplay written by George Seaton. The novel was extremely popular, spending more than a year on The New York Times Best Seller list and thirteen weeks heading the list. The story was also turned into a Broadway play, which opened at the Belasco Theatre in March 1946.

was telling me tonight that he learned from a very good source that the war with Germany will be over in about three months.[245] What do you hear regarding that? He was asking about you. I guess he would like to see you before he leaves New York. We hate to see them leave. Mom is afraid Italians or some clan will buy the house. I told your father I think I will make a bargain with Bernabe and run opposition to Duke. It might not be such a bad investment. If a person was shrewd enough.

Speaking of Duke the garden is coming along fine. We had lettuce and now the string beans are grown. I expect to cook some for dinner tomorrow.

Mrs. Gleason was telling me her son is in that fight in the Mariana Islands.[246] She didn't hear from him in a long time. The other fellow is on guard over at the navy Yard. I see him quite often. Did you write to Andy? Don't forget to write a few lines to John Lucas. I haven't heard from Kitty since she wrote the letter I enclosed. Did you receive the papers? I suppose you heard of the fire in Hartford, Connecticut.[247] It was terrific. I am hoping Mrs. Hull's people weren't there.

We have had a very hot spell here this week. It is still hot tonight. Mugs is here sleeping beside me. She is waiting for you to come home to go walking. Walter's[248] mother informed me that Walter is going on to be a surgeon. I had to swallow hard after that jaw breaker. He didn't finish this course yet. So I was very polite about it and told her that was fine.

It is almost eleven o'clock John so I will close for now. Write soon.

Love from all.
Mother

---

[245] Three months would have put the war's hoped-for end sometime during October 1944, just as Hitler's great offensive, the Battle of the Bulge, was gearing up. Hitler hoped to stall the Allied advance on the Western Front and force them to come to terms, so that he could then turn his forces against the Russians encroaching from the East.

[246] The Mariana Islands were in the Pacific Theater of Operations.

[247] The Hartford circus fire, which occurred on July 6, 1944, in Hartford, Connecticut, was one of the worst fire disasters in the history of the United States. The fire occurred during an afternoon performance of the Ringling Bros. and Barnum & Bailey Circus that was attended by 6,000 to 8,000 people. The fire killed 167 people and more than 700 were injured. The cause of the fire remains unresolved. Investigators at the time believed it was caused by a carelessly flicked cigarette; however, others suspected an arsonist. Several years later, while being investigated on other arson charges, Robert Dale Segee (1929–1997), who was an adolescent at the time, confessed to starting the blaze. He was never tried for the crime and later recanted his confession.

[248] Walter Cubita.

P.S. May Cotter was telling me about a soldier from this parish who was attending Mass some where and when the priest turned to bless the people who was it but Father Jordan. He got some surprise."

JULY 9, 1944

British and Canadian troops capture the city of Caen, France.

"July 10, 1944 [Monday]

Dear John,

 Well I had Ritchie and another sailor friend of his here to visit me. The boy with him was from Delaware. They were both traveling tonight to the West Coast, it looks like. So they said, as if they were bound to see the Japs.

 I was glad to know you heard from Andy. Keep writing to him John. It means so much toward their morale. Yesterday I wrote to John Lucas. Did I tell you I received a V-mail letter from him? He dated it May 23rd and I got it June 26th.

 Martin Moynihan is leaving Wednesday for the Marines. He certainly was anxious to join up. I hope he won't be disappointed.

 Dick Mooney is stationed down at Asbury Park at some naval station. Buddy is out to sea again.

 Mom and Duke arrived home this evening. They had a fine time with Agnes. Duke is still raving about the farm. Their son Major King is now stationed at Fort Dix. He flies, so Mom says, Grasshoppers. Did you ever hear of that unit? Tonight Mr. Lang, Mooney's Mom, Duke and I all had a great talk out at the gate. It was ten o'clock when we got in. Mr. Lang was asking for you. Dad has everybody told about you coming home. Even Mugs was informed, Ed said. He was going to give her her annual bath so she will look nice when you get home.

 Well I thought you would be coming home soon because as usual I am working in the altar this week and somehow or other you seem to arrive when I am working down at church. Mrs. Mooney even mentioned that to me. She noticed it. God is good to us. That must be the answer. The bazaar was a great success, the best they ever had. I am enclosing the money as you ask me to do, praying that it will arrive safe in your hands. It is taking a chance this way. I will close John. Hoping with God's intention to see you soon.

               Mother

P.S. Write soon and let me know if you receive money. Put a stamp on letter. It will come quicker."

JULY 18, 1944

U.S. troops reach St. Lo, France. They will consolidate forces here, and between July 25th and 30th, in Operation Cobra, they will break out of this position and begin a steady push across France.

JULY 20, 1944

An assassination attempt is made on German Fuhrer Adolf Hitler. A handful of top-ranking generals, among them Field Marshall Erwin Rommel, famed tank commander and victor of El Alamein, have plotted, or acquiesced in, an attempt to eliminate the Fuhrer, and seek peace terms with the Allies. Families of the conspirators are not spared. Ultimately more than 7,000 - innocent men, women and children - will be arrested for the crime of being related to the conspirators. Almost 5,000 will be executed.

"Pvt. A. L. Garbarini 2999604
2628 Central Postal Directory
A.P.O. 698 c/o U.S. Army

Italy

Saturday July 22, 1944 [Saturday]

Dear John,
Just a few lines to know how you are coming along with your instructing in Fort Knox. I am feeling fine and I hope that you are feeling the same way. I wrote [illegible] another letter today and I hope he is O.K. over there in England. Did you get my letter I wrote to you a month ago? Have you been teaching any more allied generals down there? How do you get along with them while you are teaching all that brass that comes down there for instruction on our tanks and guns? How are you making out with your new girlfriend down there? I hope that you got the cream of the crop. By the way, have you heard from Hughes yet? Let me know if you move to another camp. I'll end this letter wishing you lots of luck in your instructing. Answer soon.
Your pal and buddy in army,
Andy"

JULY 24, 1944

Soviet troops liberate the first concentration camp Allied troops have encountered, at Majdanek.

JULY 28, 1944

On the Eastern Front, Soviet troops take Brest-Litovsk, site of Russia's humiliating surrender to Germany in 1918, during the First World War.

FOURTEEN: "A DROWNING"

AUGUST 1, 1944 - WARSAW, POLAND

The Polish Home Army begins an uprising against the Nazis in Warsaw. In Normandy, U.S. troops reach Avranches.

AUGUST 4, 1944 - AMSTERDAM, NETHERLANDS

An informant for the Gestapo, whose name will never be known, provides tip as to the location of a Jewish family who have been hiding in an attic for the past two years. It is less than a month before Amsterdam will be liberated by the Allies. Otto Frank, his wife Edith, and his two teenage daughters, Margot and Annelies, also known as Anne, are packed off to Auschwitz. Anne's diary, later made famous, records her last entry on August 1, 1944. All but the father, Otto Frank, will perish at the hands of the Nazis.

℘

"*Aug. 7, 1944 [Monday]*

Dear John,
I received your letter with five dollars last Thursday. Thanks a lot. I will return it soon. Well, from what you stated, I take it you expect a change. Perhaps it will be for the best. I guess you get restless being in one place such a long time. Everything here at home is O.K. Dad is working nights, so that leaves Muggsie and I to take care of each other. Frank is back with his family, so the house is quiet and peaceful, maybe a little lonesome too now that all our boarders are gone on their way, including Rusty. He was such a wild animal.
I suppose you will be surprised when you read the following. Mamie McGowan up the hill went down to Rockaway with her brother to spend a week there. They went a week ago today on a Monday. Tuesday morning they got ready to go for a swim. Mamie sat on the beach and her brother Johnny went on into the water and was only in the swimming a short time when he was drowned. Some girl first aider pulled him in to shore and he died on the beach. Mamie almost died from the shock. He was buried last Saturday morning. The poor fellow didn't get much time for his vacation. They said he was so anxious to get down to the water. One of George's brothers attended the funeral. He is home on a furlough for some time now. He was on a ship that was blown up. I think he is a Chief Petty Officer and a big man - picture of George.

  Father O'Hare came back from his vacation. He told me he was in New Mexico with friends of his on a ranch. He traveled by plane. Said he wished he could stay for the summer, he liked it so much. John Alan is home on furlough for two weeks. Martin got a job with the American Express. It seems he has to be up four o'clock in the morning to be on time for his work and is finished at 2 o'clock in the afternoon.
  Tom Cotter is home on furlough. We are invited to visit Mrs. Cotter tomorrow afternoon, so maybe we will see Tom. I must get busy and write to all the boys. I forgot to tell you I had a nice letter from Ritchie, said California is a beautiful place.
  Well John your letter after you were gone a whole week was rather short but then I suppose you don't have much time to write home. I am getting very tired so I will close now. Would you like a pair of those sandals?
Love,
Mother"

℘

AUGUST 7, 1944

The Germans, determined not to allow the Allies another foot of French soil, begin a major counterattack toward Avranches.

℘

"Fort Knox, Kentucky

Aug. 8, 1944 [Tuesday]

Dear Mother,
  Well I was waiting for word from you as to whether or not you got the money I sent you? I have been transferred to the training company and I am awaiting shipment to a new camp. I might get home for a few days so if I give you a call you can probably be sure it's for some dough. You see Mother all the fellows that have been at Fort Knox for a year or more have to be rotated to a new camp in order to let fellows from overseas get easy jobs. While I am here in the training company they go over things that we had in our basic training such as map reading and the disassembly of small arms.
  Well how are things at home? How is Dad making out? Keep him on the ball. I was thinking if I get home this time we ought to go out to see Aunt Kitty because I might go to Arkansas or Mississippi, so it will take me about two or three days to get home and I won't get home for another six months. How's the Duke making out? Tell him he might have to put the flag up quick if I get home. Well that's about all for now. Love to all.
Love,

Son John"

℘

"Victor C. Garbarini S 1/C RT
713-38-75 O.G.O.P.O.
USNTC, Great Lakes, Illinois

Hi Yardbird!
    Hear you've been home again. Did you get my letter? I've been here in the hospital for the last three weeks, recovering from a scalded ankle (spilled hot water on it). Tomorrow I go back to O.G.O. and wait around until August 18th to go to school.
    Boy, if you ever met any of the Waves and Navy nurses here, you'd have wished you'd joined the Navy!
    I'm enclosing a clipping of some GI's "in action" in Normandy. What do you think of it?
    Andy's been in a hospital in Italy recovering from a rash. I think he's out now. He writes home every day, but very little mention of fighting or the hospital.
    I notice that Jack Walsh is at the University of Illinois here in Chicago (Dyre Avenue News). If you know his address, I'd appreciate having it.
    Take it easy and drop me a line sometime.
                                              Your pal,
                                              Vic"

℘

AUGUST 15, 1944

Operation Dragoon kicks off. The Allies invade southern France. The war is now coalescing to a Western Front, and an Eastern Front.

℘

"Aug. 15, 1944 [Tuesdsay]

Dear John,
    Today is August 15th. I just got back from 7:30 Mass and Holy Communion. I have been watching for the mail man as usual but have found out he left no letter from you.
    Of course that leaves me a little disappointed. When you first left home you wrote every day and I guess that kind of spoiled me. I think it was last Wednesday (9th) night you telephoned. The next morning I received a letter from you and not a word since then. I wondered why you didn't write a few lines to let me know if you received the Western Union checks.

In case you don't need to buy your train ticket for some time yet, be sure to put the money away safe for it, as I can't very well send you that amount again in a hurry. You know after Dad's performance last month, it left me rather low for several weeks.[249]

You know John, I always gave you credit for being a good sensible boy with a level head on your shoulders especially where the question of money and its use were concerned. I know you can't have good times without spending but don't overdo it. Thank God you have a good, healthy body, the greatest treasure man possesses. So take care of yourself both in body and soul. Keep close to God. He is your best friend.

Well I had Tom Cotter in to visit me. He had a delay enroute furlough. He was with the tank destroyers in Texas and now he was transferred to the Combat Engineers to Camp Robinson, Arkansas. I told him you might go to Arkansas too. So he wants me to let him know. He said perhaps you two could manage to get together sometime.

I think David Lucas is in an Officers Training School again. Leave it to him. He means to get ahead in the world. Mrs. Simmons told me last night, Richie wrote her and said he has all his equipment and will sail out in about three days. She is worried stiff. He is going out to fight the Japs.

Martin Moynihan is working for the American Express. Mom said he is making out fine, only the hours are awful. He has to arise at 4:00 a.m. to get there. His mother received a certificate from the Marines all about how Martin was accepted for enlistment. John Allan went back a free single man. God help him. Mom said it would be better if he would forget about taking a big burden on his shoulders and take care of himself and gain a few more pounds.

We haven't seen Mamie up the hill since the funeral. Mom said she doesn't have to run home now to put the radio on for Johnnie any more.[250] *"She has a free foot now to trot all over," Duke said. "Yes and to see the style of her with the long black beads like a merry widow. No doubt she will be wearing three pair of glasses now instead of two."*

Barney Farrell sent me some pictures he took of you and everybody is raving over them. They came out so swell. If you want me to I could send you the pictures and you could return them later.

You know Gately who keeps his car in the garage here, well I hear he is going into the Navy as an ensign - something to do with firefighting. Dad told me he was picked for it.

I am away back with my mail. I owe letters to all the boys. It has been very warm here without any letup. In fact it is the hottest summer I remember

---

[249] Anna is referring here to Ed's surprise trip to see John.
[250] The funeral referred to is that of John ("Johnnie") McGloin, Mamie's brother who had drowned just a few weeks earlier at Rockaway Beach.

in a long, long time. Everybody is rather exhausted from it. I hope when you get home again it will be nice and cool.

John I suppose you didn't get any more information about your destination. Is the major going out too? I am hoping you will find the change satisfactory. Perhaps it will give you an opportunity to advance in rank. Don't work too hard but keep on your toes. Get plenty of rest. Take care of yourself and your appearance. That is what counts. How are your teeth? Dad said to write more often. Mom and Duke send regards. Kiss from Mugs.

Love,
Mother

P.S. I forgot to tell you I gave Mugs a good scrubbing by myself. Lured her with candy."

AUGUST 16, 1944 - FRANCE

General George S. Patton complains in his diary about a decision made by his commander, General Omar Bradley, whom Eisenhower had earlier chosen to lead the Normandy Invasion, while Patton languished in England with his Third Army, not being allowed to enter the fray until two months later. The blunder, Patton notes, is "of historical importance," and involves Bradley ordering Patton to halt a lightning-quick advance he has made from the Normandy salient. Writes Bill O'Reilly, in his book *Killing Patton*:

"Eisenhower's pick quickly proved costly. Bradley's decision to halt Patton's troops instead of allowing them to attack prevented the encirclement of fifty thousand Wehrmacht soldiers and SS troops in mid-August. The Germans took heavy losses, but many more quickly escaped through what was called the Falaise Pocket. If Patton had had his way, his tanks would have slipped the noose around those trapped German troops, taking thousands of their best soldiers prisoner and seriously damaging the Wehrmacht's ability to wage war. 'We're about to destroy an entire hostile army,' Bradley noted of the opportunity. 'We go all the way from here to the German border.' But in the end Bradley grew timid. He ordered Patton's tanks to halt at the town of Argentan, leaving a gap between the American and Canadian units that would have encircled the Germans - a gap through which the Germans soon escaped."

AUGUST 19, 1944 - PARIS, FRANCE

A popular uprising begins in Paris, fomented by the ever-active French Resistance movement.

AUGUST 19-20, 1944

The Soviets enter the Balkans, and begin an offensive against Romania.

AUGUST 20, 1945

The Allies have the Germans almost encircled in the Falaise Pocket, but a senior-level command allows them to escape.

By the time this next letter is received, Private McGowan has been transferred to a new unit, the 65th Infantry Division, stationed at Camp Shelby, Mississippi. He serves in Company K, where he will stay until the Division is disbanded in Europe following the Allied victory there and against Japan, in August 1945.

"Pvt. Melvin A. Mickiewicz 33697340
Co. B 16th Tank Bn.
A.P.O. 412
Camp Chaffee, Ark.

Aug. 25, 1944 [Friday]

Dear John,
  I guess it is about time I should write. Well how is everybody getting along at Knox or did you move out too? The trip down was slow but we sure did have some fun. We had a 24 hour layover in Memphis. We painted the town red. When we hit Fort Smith[251] we were all set to get on the train and go back to Knox. The girls in Smith would break their faces if they would smile. I was first assigned to the 69th Infantry. After working all the time for 4 days straight I was transferred to the 16th Tank Battalion. Boy was I glad to get out of there. Another week I would have gone over the hill.[252] I stayed at the 16th for 5 days. Then I was told I was soon to go to P.O.E.[253] The next days were spent in clothes checking, shots and processing and more physical examinations. I believe that I am okay. Well Mac did you volunteer for

---

[251] Fort Smith, Arkansas.
[252] "Over the hill", a jocular term for deserting or going AWOL (absent without leave).
[253] "P.O.E." refers to "Port of Embarkation" for overseas duty.

paratroops or was you scared? Ha! Ha! Just kidding. How is Vinnie? Tell him I said hello. I'll send my new address as soon as I can.

Your pal,
(Jap) Melvin"

℘

AUGUST 25, 1944

Paris, the City of Light, is liberated.

℘

"Camp Shelby, Mississippi

Aug. 30, 1944 [Wednesday]

Dear Mother,
    I arrived here after my long trip and everything is going along okay. They say that we will be here for about 9 weeks in order to take some training. Boy remember when I was home and we had that hot spell? Well it is twice as hot down here and it rains practically every day. The trip down here was all right. We had an air-conditioned car all the way from Louisville to this camp. We arrived here yesterday about 12 o'clock and I didn't get a chance to write till today because I just got my bags which had my writing equipment in. They split all the fellows that came down here with me. There are only four of us together out of the whole gang, but at least we are together. This camp is very big and it is built in a God-forsaken place away from everything. Tell Dad that they sell quart bottles of beer down here for 15 cents. Well mother that's about all from down in the sunny south for now. Love to all.

Love,
Son John

P.S. My address is
    Pvt. John F. McGowan
    Co. K, 260 Inf. A.P.O. 200
Camp Shelby
Mississippi"

℘

AUGUST 31, 1944

Soviet troops capture the city of Bucharest, capital of Romania.

FIFTEEN - "NINE WEEKS TRAINING"

"Sept. 1, 1944 [Friday]

Dear John,
    Your letter arrived this morning, First Friday. I met the mailman as I was coming in from Mass. How glad I was to receive news from you. Everybody in the house gathered to hear me read the letter.
    Well I am glad that you arrived in Mississippi safe and sound. Dad said he guessed they brought you in an air conditioned train to cool you off before you felt the heat of the Deep South. I guess it must be different in a whole lot of ways than Fort Knox. But you stood through heat there and intensive training too, so I guess you are soldier enough now to take it too.
    John you wrote in your letter that you would be there for nine weeks training. We would like to know what you are training for, to be a private in the infantry or for some special work. You didn't give us much information regarding that. Dad is interested.
    They are predicting the war in Europe will be over in 60 days from now. If that is so by the time your training is finished you will be getting your honorable discharge.[254] The man on the radio was just telling the story of how the flame thrower came into use. They found out that the Japs were terribly afraid of fire, and that was their weak spot in the war on nerves. So they scared the life out of the Japs when they used the flame thrower and they now have them mounted on tanks.
    I had a card from Betty and John Lynch.[255] They are down at Camp Springs, Washington, D.C. They were asking for you, and said they would like to see you.
    Well yesterday I got the monthly cards out and believe me my hand was almost paralyzed when I got finished writing addresses.
    Mom was over to visit the Moynihans Monday and she said there were so many letters from John Allan in the mail that the mail man asked if that was all John had to do in the army. It doesn't look as if Martin will don a uniform.
    Social news - Helen Butler and family left their residence a week ago today to visit Georgianna at Norfolk, Virginia. They haven't arrived home yet.

---

[254] A mother's wishful thinking, amid the optimistic predictions of a quick victory in the heady days following the Normandy Invasion and subsequent advance through France. The war, of course, would not end by November 1, 1944. Some of the worst fighting - the Battle of the Bulge - would occur following that time.
[255] Betty and John Lynch, relatives of Anna. John was her brother.

   Dad's hours are going to be changed from 9:15 p.m. until 7 o'clock a.m.
   You know I forgot to give you some candy from that 2 lb. box of candy. Mugs and I are just enjoying a piece of it. I saw some nice apples today. How would you like me to send you a box of fruit?
   We are going to have a Triduum in church next week from the 6th to the 8th which is the Blessed Mother's birthday and mine is the 7th so I am celebrating too. Well John take good care of yourself. Get plenty of sleep. You will need it now for training. Remember to say your prayers. Write soon. Love from all.

                      Mother
P.S. Read the enclosed. How are the moccasins?"

℘

SEPTEMBER 1-4, 1944

The Allies roll up an impressive tally of victories in the first four days of the month, liberating the cities of Verdun, Dieppe, Artois, Rouen, Abbeville, Antwerp and Brussels.

℘

"Camp Shelby, Mississippi

Sept. 3, 1944 [Sunday]

Dear Mother,
   Today is Sunday and I have just finished coming back from lunch. This morning I went to the 11 o'clock mass and it was very crowded. At mass they had music and singing and all together it was very nice. Tomorrow Monday I am supposed to start my training so I think that I will be kept quite busy taking my training. This camp is very big. It is somewhat larger than Fort Knox in men and area. The other night I went to the movies and saw Abbott and Costello in "Society". It is very good. You will get a lot of laughs out of it. So if you get a chance Mother you and Dad should go and see it. Well how's everything at home? Is Dad behaving himself, and how is Duke and Mom doing? And forgot to [give] my regards to Mugs, of course. How's the weather up there? Boy down here it is warm. All you do day and night is sweat and sweat. I was surprised when I got down here to see so many young fellows around my own age. I think that about 90% of this camp are all young kids like myself. Well Mother that's all for now. I write again in a few days and I hope to hear from you. Love to all.

                       Love,
                        Son John"

"Camp Shelby, Mississippi

Sept. 6, 1944 [Wednesday]

Dear Mother,
  I received your letter and I was glad to hear from you. Well everything is going along okay. I am attached to a mortar section. Dad can tell you what they are. The work is very interesting so I guess I'll be satisfied for a while.
  Last Sunday I went to the Service Club with a bunch of fellows from Knox. While we were there we went to see a Variety show. Well during the show a girl was dancing and then she asked for someone to get up and Jitter Bug with her, so the fellows made me get up on the stage and dance with her. Boy did I feel funny in front of all those people but they liked our dancing and gave me a big hand and after it was over a lot of people told me how good I was. So I guess my stage career has started down here (oh yeah).
  Tomorrow guess! I have been given an opportunity by being a member of the K.P. so I guess I'll be pretty busy for the day.
  Well Mother I am getting tired and it is getting late so I will close now. Love to all.

Love,
Son John"

"Sept. 7, 1944 [Thursday]

Dear John,
  Our three day Triduum closed tonight down at church. The priest who conducted it is the chaplain from City Prison, a very good speaker.
  Well this has been a very busy week for me. Working on the altar and Wednesday night we had our Rosary meeting and of course it was my first night as secretary. But I made out okay (Thank the Lord!). I was talking to Mrs. Simmons. She is very much worried not having heard a word from Richard in a long time.
  Mike Fury was telling me that Andy was transferred to France. He was in the invasion of southern France. Do you write to him? If you don't you should. I heard today the Vogel boy is home from overseas. The Savage boy is on Saipan Island.[256] I read a letter from Dick Mooney to his mother today. You know he is down at Annapolis Academy for four months. Well

---

[256] Saipan Island is in the Pacific.

according to what he states believe me he is going through plenty. By the way, did you hear that they are going to have the big football game at Annapolis?

Dad is still working nights and behaving very well, thank God. He is always looking for mail from you. Somehow or other your letters don't come very often these days. Why not write more often, if you have time to do so. We are always eager for news from you.

By the way that letter you sent Sunday arrived here Thursday. I am beginning to make mistakes. I am getting so tired. John do you remember the word "mite", or is it "might"?

Well John I take it that Camp Shelby must be a very large place. I think it is better for you to be with boys your own age. You will have more in common. Your news will be more along the same line.

I suppose you are sweating it out with your training. Get plenty of rest. That is important. When you write again give us more details about your activities. What do you do with your time off there? Is any town near the camp? Are you near Kessler Field? That is where George Diemer is. Mrs. Miller told me she is positive the Murphy boy is at your camp. Keep a lookout for him.

The Bernabe family got back from Maine. Mrs. Bernabe was saying she doesn't care to go to Detroit. She likes it here.

Maurice is coming back to St. Michael's this fall. The brothers have so many boys to board this year they had to refuse to take a great many in.

I gave Mugs a haircut. She is a great old dog. I guess I would be lonesome at times if it wasn't for her.

It is very cool here tonight and dark at 7:30 p.m. If you were here I am sure all the lights in the house would be on long before that hour.

Well the other night we got a great surprise blackout. All the whistles and sirens from one end of N.Y. to the other started to ring. I think in two minutes every house was in blackness but it proved to be a test in the end. I read in the paper that the lights in Coney Island[257] for some reason or other blazed on during the test, and the Little Flower[258] said he would put them out of order for good if it happened again. Leave it to him.

Well John it is about 11:30 p.m. and I have one eye closed so I will close for now. Take good care of yourself. Get to communion if possible. Would you like me to send you anything? If so let me know. Did you get paid? Write more often.

---

[257] Coney Island, a perennial New York haven.
[258] "The Little Flower" was a nickname for N.Y.C. Mayor Fiorello LaGuardia, who served as mayor from 1934 until 1945. Under his administration the City began to abandon one of the most extensive streetcar networks of any city in the world, in favor of gasoline powered buses. A sad day for streetcar buffs and former motormen.

> Love,
> Mother"

§

This V-Mail is from John's cousin, Tom Lucas, to John's parents, Tom's Aunt and Uncle. Tom is a sailor aboard the U.S.S. Gandy.

"Tom Lucas 3 3/E SM
U.S.S. Gandy (DE764)
c/o Fleet Post Office
New York, NY

Sept. 11, 1944 [Monday]

Dear Uncle Ed and Aunt Annie,
    Please forgive me for not showing up that night. But when I found out that I was shoving off soon I wanted to spend the last night home although I would have liked to have seen John. Where is he now? I haven't been over here too long. This is my fourth time I have been across.
I spent a weekend with [illegible name] while I was home. First time I had seen him in sixteen months. I believe it's a year today since I saw John. I was certainly surprised to see Ed in N. Y. I guess that's the first time I've seen him in over a year.
    I wish your John a lot of luck. Hope to make up for that night [illegible] soon.

> *Love,*
> *Your nephew,*
> *Tom*

P. S. Went to church here yesterday!"

§

A little more about the *USS Gandy*, on which Tom Lucas is serving, is in order. She was a Cannon-class destroyer escort built during the war, and served in both the Atlantic and Pacific Oceans providing escort service for Navy vessels, and particularly convoys, protecting them against attacks by enemy submarines and air forces. She bore the name of Seaman Second Class Andrew Jackson Gandy, who served as a gunner on board the *USS San Francisco,* a heavy cruiser. Seaman Gandy died heroically at his post during the Battle of Guadalcanal in November 1942, guns blazing against Japanese torpedo planes, and was posthumously awarded the Navy Cross. His namesake ship was launched on December 12, 1943, in Tampa, Florida. Gandy's sister Ruby was present at the launching. Commissioned February 7,

1944, the *Gandy* was placed under the command of Lieutenant Commander W. A. Sessions, and joined Escort Division 22 at the port of New York.

On April 15, 1944 *Gandy* set sail from New York as part of the escort for a convoy of ships bound for Northern Ireland. Two days out, on April 16, 1944, shortly past eight o'clock in the morning, German U-Boat U-550 launched a torpedo towards the tanker *SS Pan-Pennsylvania*, sinking it. Survivors were picked up by several ships in the convoy, including Gandy. At about 10:00 AM, one of these ships made sound contact with the U-Boat, and launched a depth charge which forced the submarine to surface a mere 600 yards off *Gandy's* starboard bow. Commander Sessions ordered the ship hard to right, to open fire and get ready to ram the enemy vessel now coming dead ahead of them. *Gandy* hit the sub solidly 30 feet from its stern, and then pulled clear to assess damage to her bow. Meanwhile the crew of U-550 quickly abandoned their sinking sub, and 12 of the crew were rescued by another escort vessel, the Joyce, who had launched the depth charge that flushed U-550 from its lair. Shortly thereafter, a muffled explosion shook U-550, and she sank beneath the waves, never to threaten Allied shipping again.

Gandy continued on with the convoy, encountering no further difficulties, and reached Lisahally, Northern Ireland on April 26, 1944. She would escort nine more convoys from New York to Lisahally, and Liverpool as well, before the war ended in Europe in May 1945. U-550's wreckage was discovered July 23, 2012 some 70 miles south of Nantucket, Massachusetts. *Gandy's* days ended in 1971, by which time she was a ship in the Italian Navy under the name of *Altair*, and suffered the inglorious fate of being sunk as a target.

Whether Tom Lucas was aboard *Gandy* on this, her second voyage, is not known, but his letter above does state that the September 1944 voyage was his "fourth time across", so perhaps he was.

℘

"Sept. 12, 1944 *[Tuesday]*

Dear John,
　　Looking out the window today you would certainly think the fall was here to stay. There is a cold rain falling along with a strong wind blowing the leaves to the ground.
　　The doorbell rang about twenty minutes ago. It was Mrs. Gold calling to have a conference with Mom. She was all excited. It seems her and Mr. Gold had a quarrel over spelling a word correct. It got so hot and heavy between them that she ran down here to cool off. I wish you could hear Duke's

comments. *You would scream. He said, "Mom is letting the spuds burn black in the pot listening to that woman and her silly notions!"*

Duke is down here now with me listening to the news over the radio. It is just 6 p.m. We heard them just tell that Gen. Eisenhower announced that the battle for Germany is about to begin. Judging from what some of these men tell us over the radio John I sometimes wonder if it isn't a race between the U.S.A. and England against Russia's invasion of Germany. Time will tell all.

Yesterday I received your letter written on the 6th. Well John I don't really understand what mortar guns are. But I suppose they are powerful weapons.

Well I did have a good laugh, in fact we all did, when I read how you danced on the stage. How I would like to have seen you. It looks like you all had a good time anyway. Duke said, "By George, when the war is over instead of that fellow coming home it is what he will want to go traveling with the moving picture people." He even told Mrs. Mooney how smart the McGowans are. You should hear her laughing.

Martin was here yesterday. His car isn't running yet. Well at least he is leaving to join up on Wednesday 20th for Parris Island.[259] *I guess you will be hearing from him. Do you receive the paper from Mt. St. Michael's? They were supposed to send out copies every month to all the boys in service.*

Last night when I came out from church who did I meet but Walter Cubita. He is here on a five day furlough. His grandmother died so he got home for a few days. He looks well from what I could see of him in the dark. He is still stationed in Florida. He said he heard all you were doing was traveling from Fort Knox to Pratt Avenue and back again. "Well," as I said, "it takes a smart man to hold down a good job." You know John I would never want to confide or tell a secret to him. He is very outspoken.

I wish John you were here to just take one look at Muggsie. She is all wrapped up in blankets in the big chair. You can just see her nose and ears. She is after coming in from outdoors soaked to the skin from the rain so I rolled the old blankets around her to keep her warm.

Those pictures you had taken when you were home I sent down to Margaret[260] *in the convent to see and she kept them to show to a nun who taught you in school. Margaret was transferred down to 81st Street. An orphanage and boarding home is there.*[261]

There is an old nun friend of Margaret's who I have met several times. She attended the funeral. It seems every time I meet her, she tells me I should

---

[259] Parris Island is one of the major Marine Corps camps.
[260] Sister Mary Albert McGowan.
[261] Much of Sr. Mary Albert's life as a devoted nun would be spent working with orphans.

have been a nun. I can see you smiling at that. But then there would be no John F. McGowan.

     Did you get Dad's letter. After he finished writing he asked me to read it and I laughed so much, he got angry. Did you notice the air mail stamps he enclosed? He was sure to send them as he thinks your letters will arrive sooner. Write more often John, for his sake, if you can. He wakes up in the morning and asks if you sent a letter. Some fellow who lives near here takes him back and forth to work and so far (thank God) it has proved very satisfactory. He gives 50 cents a day but I guess it is worth it as traveling by train costs 30 cents a day.

     I am enclosing a little clipping. Sometime take it out and read it. I am sure it will prove interesting to you.

     Be a good boy John. Don't forget to pray and remember us all in them. Take it easy on the jitterbug dancing. You will have all your shoes worn out. Muggsie just sat up like a queen. Write soon.

Love,
Mother"

SEPTEMBER 13, 1944

U.S. troops reach, for the first time, the Siegfried Line in western Germany. But it will be some time before the Line is breached, as events will take a turn against the Allies in a very short while.

Training at Camp Shelby intensifies as the date of overseas deployment seems to draw inexorably nearer, though no one knows exactly when that will be.

"Camp Shelby, Mississippi

Sept. 14, 1944 [Friday]

Dear Mother,

     This is first time I had to write you this week since we have been so busy. I received your last letter and I want to say that I will write as much as I can when and if I get the chance to do so.

     Well this week was really rough. We really got into the swing of things. Monday night we had a night problem[262] *and we had to crawl through mud and swamp and boy was that rugged. But when we got back to camp they*

---

[262] "Problems" were simulated combat situations the soldiers might find themselves in, and the solution was something they had to work out on their own.

had hot coffee and doughnuts waiting for us. We also had the next morning off so we could sleep. Tuesday and Wednesday we were out in the field all the time working on problems and we are kept busy on these problems running from position to position and also crawling with full field packs.

By the way you asked me if I got paid well yes and everything is going along okay. How's everything at home? Give my regards to all. I will have to close now as they are putting out the lights so love to all.

Love,
Son John"

SEPTEMBER 17, 1944

While U.S. forces opposite the Siegfried Line cool their heels, impatient to be given the order to advance into Germany, another offensive begins to the north, led by British Field Marshall Bernard Montgomery. Operation Market Garden begins with an Allied airborne assault on Holland.

"Camp Sholby, Mississippi

Sept. 20, 1944 [Wednesday]

Dear Mother,
I was sure surprised to hear about all the damage the hurricane did up there. We didn't get much of it all but for a couple of days of continuous rain and boy did it rain. Well how is Walter? I guess he got together with Robbie Mahon, didn't he? The Butlers must have put on some style for that occasion. I guess he had all his ribbons on and what did he have to say about everything?

How are things going along with you Mother? Did you have to send out cards again yet and how are things in general with the society and Father O'Hara, how is he? I was going to write Father Broderick tonight but I didn't get a chance. But I will write him tomorrow. Well Martin went into the Marines today. I wonder how his mother is taking it. I hope he makes out okay in them. Last night I went to the movies and I saw a picture "Since You Went Away". It was very good. I personally thought it was better than "Going My Way". Mother if you get a chance you should go and see it. You will enjoy it immensely.

Mother you can send me some oranges and apples if you can get them. I was also wondering if Dad could have The Daily News sent down to me. You *know all we get down here is southern papers and I don't hear much what's happening up North. Tell Dad I might call up but it takes about two to three hours to get a call through, so I much rather write than call. Give my regards to Duke and Mom, and ask Duke how Tommy is getting along with the garbage. Love to all.*

Love,
Son John

P.S. The food here is okay."

SIXTEEN - "SOLVING PROBLEMS"

"Camp Shelby, Mississippi

Oct. 1, 1944 [Sunday]

Dear Mother,
    Well this is the first chance I had to write to you and Dad in more than a week. When I called you up I told you I was going to be kept busy for about a week. You see, we were out on a week's maneuvers.
    Last Sunday I went to mass and communion at the 7 o'clock mass. Monday morning we started out by a ride in trucks for a few miles, then we had to get out and walk about 10 miles. After walking this distance it was almost dark so we camped for the night. It was about 1:30 Tuesday morning that they got us up. There was no lights or talking. We had to grope around in the dark but in the meantime before we got up it started raining and we all got good and wet. We ate a quick breakfast and started on our way. We walked about 9 miles in two hours. We got to our destination and waited around a half an hour before starting a dawn attack. This problem[263] lasted until about 10 in the morning. We then took trucks to a new camping area.
    At this area we set up tents and Wednesday and Thursday we didn't do much but Thursday they told us to get ready to leave about 11 o'clock. We got ready and started out on a 10 mile hike. While walking it started raining and we all got soaked to the skin. When we got to where we were going they told us to catch a few hours sleep. We couldn't light any fires to dry out or light a cigarette. I took all my wet clothes off and went to sleep in my blanket. Some of the fellows just laid in their wet clothes on the ground. In the morning it started to rain hard after I put my wet clothes on again so everybody was feeling kind of wet. The cooks made us some good hot coffee and fried eggs. After we ate we didn't feel so bad. Well the rest of Friday we ran a few problems and Saturday we came in and had to clean our guns. Today we had to get up at 5 in the morning to go on a 3 hour problem. I had to miss mass as we got back about 1 in the afternoon.
    Well mother from what you have read you can see that I was kept pretty busy. I received your apples and oranges and they were swell. The fellows and I enjoyed them immensely. Well how's everything on the home front making out? How's Dad? I guess he wonders why I didn't write. By the

---

[263] "Problem" was the term used for the overall drill, e.g. the dawn attack was the problem, or objective, of that morning's exercise.

way I had a letter from Martin Moynihan from Parris Island. He didn't say much but I don't know. Well will close now. Write soon. Love to all.

                Love,
                Son John"

OCTOBER 2, 1944 - WARSAW, POLAND

The ill-fated Warsaw Uprising ends. The Polish Home Army surrenders to the Germans. A total of 200,000 civilians are killed during the two months of the Uprising. Casualties among the rebels number 26,000, including 10,000 killed in action. German losses are 25,000, with 9,000 troops killed in action. In the aftermath of the abortive attempt to throw off German domination, almost a million civilians are forced to flee the city, with many hundreds of thousands subsequently dying from starvation, murder and the elements.

"Oct. 6, 1944 [Friday]

Dear John,
  I arrived home last night, which was Thursday, after spending a few days with Aunt Kitty. Dad met me over at Hoboken and we traveled the rest of the way together. Only instead of riding on the ferry, we traveled by bus to 43nd Street. That was a new discovery for me as I had never traveled that way. When we left the bus we continued on the 8th Avenue subway and on home. When I got here I found you had written while I was away. Of course I was anxious to know how you were getting on. When you telephoned I understood you to say that you were going on a month's maneuvers, but I see from what you say it was only a week, which I guess was enough at a time. You call your maneuvers problems. Well John from what you tell us all you have to endure I would call them little crosses plus problems. I hope you didn't get cold from that wet underwear. I said to your father can you picture that? And he said, "Well, what do you suppose they do in foxholes?" But it made me think how I couldn't bear to think of you getting wet feet when you were home. Have you any idea when your training down there will be over? I heard Tom Cotter is going overseas. His two little boys are pictures.
  I was glad to know you heard from Martin. Did he tell you about taking a test for radio? According to what Mom tells me he is taking all kinds of tests and coming out 100% in them all. Of course you know his parents want him to get a No. 1 job right away. You remember how Rose was when he was in school wanting him to be on top all the time. That is why I expect you to be aide-de-camp to Gen. Patton.

John do you remember Martin Moynihan who lived in the Bronx, he was commander of a P.T. boat, a cousin of Tim's. Well he was home on a short furlough and while in N.Y. through some mysterious circumstances met his death. I am going to send you The Catholic News. There is quite a write up in it about him.

I am glad you all enjoyed the fruit John. I like you to say we all eat it. Likewise I think you enjoy it more by sharing it with the boys. Now how would you like another box? The Lucas family gave me a carton of cigarettes for you, a big box containing candy and chewing gum, etc. If you want another box write and tell me what you would like in it.

I intend sending a nice fruit cake to John Lucas. He is now in Germany. Tom was home for one night while I was there. Kitty tells me he has had some great experiences at sea. Sonny is still in Virginia. The rest of the family are getting along fine. Bobby still has his family of cats - big ones and little and for fear of them living lonesome brings in all the cats belonging to friends who are out of town. Kitty said if the cats were any good around she wouldn't mind that they are the kind that the mice can play tag around them.

Morgan is still a Philadelphia lawyer when it comes to making speeches about everything that happens. There is a very interesting little incident that happened out there connected with him while I was there. I haven't time to tell you now but I will in a later letter as I think you will get a good laugh out of it. They had their place all done over since we were there and it looks very nice. Theresa is expecting to graduate this year and of course the family manners don't suit her at all now as she wants them all to wear the high hat. But I am afraid you couldn't change them very much, especially Dave. Kitty and I were getting ready to go out so Dave got all dressed up to go with us and I wish you could see the style of him. Talk about Andy! I had to laugh and laugh. Well his chest keeps on expanding as Kitty said with all the hot air inside of it. It will explode someday. His coat will only button once on him. I mean with one button. And now he wears a big ring and a wristwatch. He told Kitty he was going out for a few minutes and she said to me, "You know where he is going?" And I said, "No." She said, "Well, indeed, he is going out to get his big cigar to complete his appearance."

They were all asking for you. I really enjoyed my visit. It all struck me so funny. Theresa is coming out to spend a weekend with me.

I met Mrs. Mahon today. She told me Robbie is leaving tomorrow night. Dickie who is in New Guinea expected to be home for Mary's wedding Nov. 11th but now he can't come. Did you receive Hickey's paper? Or the paper from the Mount?

Sunday they are going to have the Holy Name Rally at the Polo Grounds, so I guess we will all be over there. There isn't much happening in the neighborhood John. Everything is about the same. Of course Mr. and Mrs. Gould are still battling it out. They were in and out of court every other day it seems but still the turmoil remains with all the violations. He told Mrs. Gould if she would give him $500 he would move. Who wouldn't if they could put it over?

Do you people hear any speeches over the radio in regard to politics? Or have you formed any opinions on the subject? How are things going on down there? Do you find any difference in the officers? Are they better or worse?

John, I was wondering when you are finished down there, will you be regarded as an infantry man or a tank man? Give us some information on the subject.

I was glad to know John that you were to confession and Holy Communion. By keeping close to God it will give you courage to endure many difficulties, especially when the going gets hard. Many of the boys of other faiths say when they come back here that there is something the Catholic boy has to give him courage that no one else can understand.

It has been very cool up here. Duke had to put on the heat, in spite of what he intended to do. Tonight it is raining and warm outdoors. By the way, Jack Hickey bought Ramona's house. Can't say the egg and butter business isn't profitable. Well John it is almost time to get Dad's supper ready, so I will close. Write soon. Did you write to Father Broderick? Love from all.

Mother

P.S. How is the weather down there? Did I tell you R. Simmons wrote home?"

℘

A V-Mail from John's friend, Andy Garbarini, who writes from Italy, where he is recovering from what appears to be the second time he has been wounded.

"P.F.C. A. L. Garbarini
CO H 5*th* Inf. APO#3
c/o PM NYC

Oct. 9, 1944 [Monday]

Dear John,

I am back in Italy again in a different hospital. This time I got wounded in France where I was fighting since August 15, 1944. It isn't very serious. How are you making out in Knox? I will be getting the Purple Heart soon. I got hit by a piece of shrapnel from a Jerry A.P. gun. I hope this letter finds you in the best of health. This is all for a while.

Your pal,
Andy

P.S. Regards to your family."

The next letter is from John's younger friend "Buddy" Butler.

"Oct. 9, 1944 [Monday]

Dear Mac,

 Since this is the first letter I have written to you prepare yourself for quite a lot of news. To begin with, I'm a junior now and have reached the mature age of 16. I gave Butch's address and got my junior license this summer. Crazy Mahon came home from England without telling anybody and Pee Wee almost fell over when he came loping in as he usually does, almost taking the door with him. I joined the Civil Air Patrol 2 weeks ago and went up yesterday. I went up in a Piper Cub and it was a little windy. I had a little excitement going up to the airport. We started out with Boay, that big tall kid and myself. Then we picked up a kid and while we were blowing the horn he yells out the attic window to stop that infernal racket. All this happened about 8 o'clock. We were testing the car for speed, my father's little coupe, and it hit 69 M.P.H. On our way up we pushed a car for about a mile with our emergency brake on. Finally we got there, went up in the plane and then started for Ossining to be a color guard. The sergeant gave us a C gas stamp and bought five gallons of gas. We started out for Ossining and after we came down a long curving steep hill and the tee rod broke and we couldn't steer the car so we had to stop. We got the tie rod back and drove through Pleasantville, Harrison, Rye, White Plains, Armonk, New Rochelle, Tuckahoe, Bronxville, and Mount Vernon.

 To get back to Mahon he painted his house and just went back yesterday. The team played 3 games and lost the last one to White Plains 20 to 12. What the heck, you can't win them all. Well, so long for now, write soon.

Your pal,
Buddy Butler"

A welcome break in "The Big Easy", where the following letter is mailed from, postmarked "NEW ORLEANS, LA OCT 11 7:30 AM 1944".

"Camp Shelby, Mississippi

Oct. 10, 1944 [Tuesday]

Dear Mother,
　　　Well I am spending a few days down here in New Orleans. The place down here is very nice. There are a number of French here and the city itself is very old. You see that this is one of the oldest cities in the U.S.[264]
　　　I was very sorry to hear about Muggsie[265] but we can get a new dog. There are plenty of them. I guess Dad's taking it bad. Tell him she would have died anyway and that she lived her life well.
　　　When I called you up the last time I said that I was going out for a week and not for a month in November. You can write me Mother because it is 1 class and the army gives it out in the field. If I don't write so much you can tell that I am kept busy in the field and will write when I get the chance. Well this is about all from here. I will write again when I get back to camp and please excuse the writing as I am writing with a bad pen. Love to all.
　　　　　　　　　　　　　　　　Love,
　　　　　　　　　　　　　　　　Son John"

"October 11, 1944 [Wednesday]

Dear John,
　　　By this time I guess you are back at Camp Shelby. How did you like New Orleans? I expect that you will write and tell us all about your trip. We thought it was very nice for you to serve as altar boy. Your father had a big smile when I told him. Your telephone call was rather a surprise. I thought you were on your way home when you were calling at that early hour. Both your calls from Mississippi, Camp Shelby and New Orleans will come in on the next bill. So like a good boy don't call again this month, unless you find it necessary. We want to recover from this one first. You can get a whole lot more information in a letter, I think. Except of course we like to hear your voice. It brings us closer together.

---

[264] New Orleans, on the mighty Mississippi, was founded by the French on May 7, 1718.

[265] Poor Muggsie has met her end at the hand of a careless driver. But she would not be the end of the line. There would be a Muggsie II, if not a Muggsie III. I know because I played with them as a young boy growing up in Edenwald in the 1950's and 1960's. - Editor.

Well John I guess you were surprised to hear about poor Muggsie. Poor thing, she went quick. I couldn't tell you how badly Dad and I felt. I guess we were crying a couple of days over her. I didn't tell Dad she was struck with the car. It happened in the afternoon. He wasn't here. So I told him that she just took a spell and died. Of course it was a great shock to him but I think it was really worse on me because I saw it all and she was such a companion to me especially when I was alone. Even yet when I come in I imagine she is going to greet me. I guess we all really loved Mugs. She is part of a chapter of life it seems that has closed for us. Everybody misses her on Pratt Avenue, perhaps for her barking. The house doesn't seem the same to me, it is so lonesome.

Your father tells me he is going to get a puppy for me. But maybe it is best not to get another dog. You get so attached to them it almost tears your heart out if something happens to them. Of course I know you would like a pup, at least Dad said. He knows you would like one.

Did I tell you John that Dad got all the cards out for me last month? That is, he stamped them. Richard Simmons wrote to his mother he is on some island off the Pacific. He crossed the Equator on his way there. No one seems to have heard from H. Gibbons. Jackie Walsh is expected home on furlough. His course is finished. Robbie Mahon came in Sunday afternoon to say goodbye. Headed for San Diego. I was talking to Rick Cotter today. He was telling me that he was stationed at Camp Shelby for 14 months during the First World War. I suppose they have made a great many improvements down there since he was there.

When you first went down to Mississippi, you wrote that you would be there for nine weeks, which according to that would end in a few more weeks. Do you have any idea if you will move out then or are you going to have any connection with the armored force again? You know John you don't give us much information at all regarding what is going on down there. Mom tells me since Martin is away he writes and describes the island he is on and everything they do, even all about the nice sergeant he has. He has to take a radio test today and if he passes I believe he will take a course in radio and radar. It may be a great opportunity for him if he is successful. Do you hear from him? Frankie told me he had a letter from you.

I sent a nice Christmas package to John Lucas today. I fixed it all up with Santa Claus and all the trimmings. I put a small fruitcake in it and a lot of other little things. Dad rolled up some newspapers for you. I mailed them today too. You should receive them in a few days.

Your father is fast asleep. He is working in Bayonne now. It is such a long journey for him that he falls asleep before he has the paper read. The weather here is almost perfect. I get out for a walk almost every day. Here is a little social news. Claire Trainor is going to be married in a few weeks. Her boyfriend I hear is taking instruction from Father Broderick to become a Catholic. That rather surprised me. He must be stationed nearby because he seems to be here so often.

There is great cleaning and washing going on across the way. Georgianna and her husband are coming up from Norfolk to spend his furlough here. Sonny Lucas wrote his mother that he is going in to Washington, D.C. for a visit and while there would try to locate John Lynch at Camp Spring.

The Holy Name Society expects to have a barn dance the end of October. They are going to have all kinds of tickets and chances out for it. Well John it is growing late so I will close for now. See if you can't write a good long letter like this to me. October 15th was our 23rd wedding anniversary.

Love,
Mother"

OCTOBER 14, 1944

The Allies liberate Athens, Greece. In Germany, Erwin Rommel commits suicide for alleged complicity in the July plot to kill Hitler.

"Camp Shelby, Mississippi

Oct. 15, 1944 [Sunday]

Dear Mother,

I received your letter that you wrote last Wednesday. Mother I think that you and Dad ought to get a pup because it will be a companion to you when Dad is away. I was wondering did Dad see Muggsie when she was dead and who buried her.

Well yesterday night we got big news. We had a company meeting and they told us that we are going overseas and that we are going to leave Camp Shelby next month. I don't know where we are going or when and if I did I couldn't tell you anyway. I don't want you and Dad to get worried now because everything will be okay. Tell Dad not to start traveling down here because we are restricted and no one can get in. They also told us that our mail will start getting censored starting Monday. By the way, I am now a First Class Private (P.F.C.) and I get 4 more dollars a month in pay. Well you wanted to know my job down here. I am now No. 1 gunner in a machine gun squad.

Mother I also want to tell you that starting January 1945 I will have $10 sent home. I want to save this money for me or use it if you need it. I am having this done because they told us we don't need much money overseas. I will also be sending home in a few days the black suitcase with some of my extra clothes and things in it. They have been working us pretty regular. We even had to work today, Sunday. They said that we are ready for combat. The weather down here is changing. It gets very cold at night but during the day it is warm. Tomorrow we change and start wearing woolens. That's about all I can think of at the present time so I will close now. Love to all.

Love,
Son John"

OCTOBER 21, 1944

At the Wolf's Lair in East Prussia, Hitler convenes his remaining generals, now that those disloyal to him have been largely eliminated, and unveils a new plan to reclaim the initiative in the war: Operation Watch on the Rhine. "The goal of the offensive," writes Bill O'Reilly in his book "Killing Patton", "is to split the British and American armies. It helps that his tank commanders will not have to face George S. Patton and his Third Army, because the secret offensive is deliberately being launched too far north for Patton and his sharp tactical mind to reach the battlefield in time to engage."

On this same day the Allies take the German city of Aachen, the first German municipality to be taken. Optimistic minds predict that the war will be over by Christmas. More realistic assessments argue it will last far longer. General George Marshall, Chief of Staff of the United States Army, has set New Year's Eve as the last day he will accept continuation of the war. General Dwight Eisenhower, supreme commander in the European Theater, is left trying to figure out how to achieve that ambitious goal.

At Camp Shelby, the impending departure overseas looms nearer and nearer for the soldiers of the 65th Division, and Europe begins to gel as their likely destination. The predictions of an early end of the war made so boastfully by Allied leaders just months ago have proven false, and a fresh German offensive is about to be launched which will go down in history as the Battle of the Bulge. It will catch the Allies largely by surprise, and make the need for reinforcements and replacements a foremost concern. For the first time in a letter home, John intimates the possibility that he, like many other soldiers in this war, may not return. It is a sobering thought for all.

"Camp Shelby, Mississippi

Oct. 22, 1944 [Sunday]

Dear Mother,
    I think we didn't have good telephone connections last night but it was good to hear yours and Dad's voice. Mother I was trying to tell you that when I was in New Orleans I bought a crucifix and I had it sent home. Tell me in your next letter if you got it or not. I wish you would write more often too. It takes about four days for a letter to get here and it's good to hear from home.
    Mother, I might get home so don't count on it and don't get expectations. You know what I mean. I would like you to send me a watch because I need it for my job down here. We are going for sure sometime next month. I think we are going to Europe from all that I see and hear. I like those little speeches that you make up in your letters. Do you write them yourself or do you get it out of some book? Tell Dad to get a dog because he'll be great company.
    I found out about the bonds. They told me it takes about a month to a month and a half till you will get my bonds so don't worry about them. If I am overseas for Christmas I will send you official notice to my change in address.
    About saving my money I will have this ten dollars sent some starting in January '45 and I want you to invest it for me. I also think Martin is having a hard time of it. That's what he writes to me about but don't tell his mother or let this leak out. Keep it a secret. From what you said in your letter I see that you are stepping out. You should do it more often. It won't hurt you. By the way Mother, go to the dentist as a favor to me and have your teeth taken care of. Well Mother it is getting late and I will close now. Tell the Duke and Mom I was asking for them and tell the Duke I said to get better so if I get home he can put up the flag. If I get home. Love to all.

                                              Love,
                                              Son John"

"Camp Shelby, Mississippi

Oct. 28, 1944 [Saturday]

Dear Mother,
    Today is Saturday and at noon time I received a letter from you. But at supper time they called my name out for an insured letter but to my amazement I found a package and I couldn't imagine what it was. When I opened it what a surprise I got when I saw the watch you and Dad sent me. It

was swell of you to send me one. The watch itself is okay. It works all right, but thanks a lot.

In your letter you sent me the Dyre Avenue News and I saw how you had Dr. Cubita in quotation marks out. You think he was Bishop General of New York the way he has his sentences phrased. Do you ever hear from him or see his parents around down by the church or at some meeting? By the way I forgot to tell you that I just went to confession and I expect to go to communion at the 7:30 mass tomorrow.

Last night I went to the movies and saw "Irish Eyes Are Smiling".[266] It's very good. They play all the old time Irish songs. I got a kick out of it. I was glad to hear that the Duke was up and around. Maybe that's all he needs is a drop of the creature, or hot stuff. Mother I got a letter from Andy Garbarini and he wrote that he was wounded in France and now is in a hospital in Italy. I thought it would be nice if you could write him a few lines because they say you get awful homesick when you're in a hospital because you have nothing to occupy the time. Enclosed in this letter you will find the letter he wrote to me. So drop him a line.

From the looks of things I think that this is going to be a close presidential race.[267] I would like to see Dewey get it because I think another term in the White House would kill Roosevelt.[268] From his pictures he looks pretty far gone now. I was reading an article which said that they couldn't take any more front views of the President because his face is flushed and has sunken in.

Mother is that official that Desmond Gleeson is missing in action? I bet his mother feels bad, first it's one boy, then the other. I hope they find him or he turns up some place okay.

Well I think I will close for now and I hope you win that 20 pound turkey. My mouth is watering for a piece of it now. Love to all.

                       Love,
                        Son John"

---

[266] "Irish Eyes Are Smiling" was a 1944 musical film which chronicled the life of popular Irish song composer Ernest R. Ball. The screenplay by Earl Baldwin and John Tucker Battle is based on a story by E. A. Ellington. The film was directed by Gregory Ratoff, and produced by Damon Runyon for 20th Century Fox. The film was nominated for the Academy Award for Best Original Score in 1944.

[267] The 1944 presidential election was between two New Yorkers: Franklin Delano Roosevelt, running for an unheard of fourth term; and Thomas E. Dewey.

[268] And it did. FDR won, and five months later, in April 1945, succumbed to an enormous brain hemorrhage at his retreat in Warm Springs, Georgia, at the age of 63.

OCTOBER 30, 1944 - AUSCHWITZ

The infamous gas chambers at this equally infamous concentration camp are used for the last time. Since its conversion from an army barracks to a death camp in 1939, Auschwitz has served as the execution place for some 1.1 million people, including Anne Frank.

SEVENTEEN - "FOURTH TERM"

NOVEMBER 4, 1944 - FENWAY PARK, BOSTON, MASSACHUSETTS

U.S. President Franklin Delano Roosevelt addresses a crowd at Fenway Park. It is just a few days before the election, and the race seems uncertain. The speech is broadcast on national radio. Frank Sinatra sings the National Anthem. Orson Welles warms up the crowd. And FDR wows them for 35 minutes. He is on the cusp of winning election to an unprecedented fourth term as President. And in a little more than five months, he will be dead.

But for now, it seems that victory, at least in Europe, will be relatively quick in coming. And Roosevelt is focusing more on the world after the war, and the cooperative roles both the U.S. and the Soviet Union will play in it. Roosevelt trusts the Russians, and their leader Josef Stalin, far more than his colleague, British Prime Minister Winston Churchill does. And FDR has entrusted his chief of the OSS, William "Wild Bill" Donovan, with making sure that any future confrontation with the Soviets be avoided.

General George S. Patton, on the other hand, detests the Soviets. He trusts them not at all.

୨

"*Camp Shelby, Mississippi*

Nov. 5, 1944 [Sunday]

Dear Mother,
I just received your letter that you mailed last Friday. I am glad to hear that you are still holding up your religion. I received Dad's letter also and I was glad to hear that he is making out okay and that he received my card. I know it wasn't much but it was the best I could get at the present time. Mother what happened to the Romanos? Did Louie ever get married and what happened to the old lady? I also want to ask you if you know how Mrs. Thomas is or how is Pete? I was wondering why you don't pay her a visit. I know that she would be more than willing to have you.
About the trains, I think we ought to save them for my kids and anyway, I think that some of them are broken. It's up to you Mother if you want to give them away. About that stuff I sent home, I think that some of those shirts will fit Dad. Tell him to wear them and if he doesn't give them to Duke he ought

to look sharp in them. But put those books away and don't let anybody have them. I am going to send some more stuff home soon, maybe this week.

I heard a good story on the radio, it's about Bing Crosby. Well happens in New Guinea it seems that this soldier was listening to Bing Crosby over the radio in his tent. He happened to turn around and there he saw a 10 foot snake. He didn't know what to do. But as he watched the snake he saw it didn't move. The soldier finally got by the snake and got an axe from another tent and killed the snake. It seemed that Bing Crosby singing happened to hypnotize the snake and it didn't move an inch. Believe it or not?

It's too bad about the Gleason boy. I hope they find out he is okay. I didn't hear from Martin in about a week but I hope to hear from him soon.

Things down here are about the same. I don't know when we are going but I expect it won't be for a couple of months. Well I will close now. Love to all, and tell the Duke should get a bottle and that I think you pet him up. Love to all.

Love,
Son John

P.S. Tell Dad to get a dog and not a cat."

℘

"Camp Shelby, Mississippi

Nov. 12, 1944 [Sunday]

Dear Mother,

I had to laugh about when you said I don't write. Well for last week I received a letter last Sunday and one yesterday, Saturday. There is a 7 day interval between letters. I try to answer your letters as soon as I get them. They give me something to write about. Well that's enough of that. During the week I have been kept pretty busy running problems and other teaming courses. Last night I went to town and had a good time. I didn't get back to camp until 3 in the morning. The town here is very small considered with Louisville. But there are a lot of clubs to go to and they have good dances. Today being Sunday things are pretty quiet. Most of the fellows are in the beer garden next to the P.X. drinking beer and soda. I expect to go to the movies tonight. They say there is a good picture playing there. Boy the weather down here is nice. It's just like an early summer day out. The sun is shining bright in a clear blue sky. But at night it gets cold enough to use a comforter. I was glad to hear that the Duke is up and around again. I guess he will make his daily tour of the house as he usually does, seeing that everything is in order. By the way how's that little cat that follows up from the church? Do you still see him? Tell Dad I want to know if he got a dog yet. He and the Duke ought to go fifty-fifty and buy one. From what you say in your letter things must be about the same around the neighborhood with the kids playing football in the street. Does Mom still yell at them when they hit the telephone wire and want them to move down and play in front of their own houses? Mother did you get the cross blessed yet and you ought to hang it up on the wall and don't put it in some box in the hope chest. If you don't get a letter next week you will know that I am out on a four day probe and can't get a chance to write.

  Well the election didn't mean much down here because the one thing the fellows are interested in is knowing when they are going to get out of this army. Well I think I have wrote enough for now. Love to all.

Love,
Son John

P.S. Ask Frankie what's the matter with [illegible]."

℘

"Camp Shelby, Mississippi

Nov. 19, 1944 [Sunday]

Dear Mother,
  The weather down here has been very miserable for it has been raining all week and today for the first time the sun has come out. It's good to see it. Yesterday I had to give a talk on Russia for our news class. We have one every week. The fellows told me my talk was good but what a time I had pronouncing those Russian towns.

  I received your letter Friday and I will try an answer and write to you as much as I can but there is not much to write about going on down here except for the training problems we run during the day. At night most of the time we go to the movies if I don't go to town. Yesterday being Saturday they had a big dance in town so I and the rest of the fellows took off in the rain. We were lucky for we got a ride in because there is a big crowd going on the buses. Well I stayed at the dance till 12 o'clock and then we went to get something to eat. After eating we got a ride in a G.I. truck going to camp. If we didn't get a ride in the truck we would have had to stand about 2 hours in the bus line. This morning I got to Mass as usual. The masses are conducted nicely here. They have someone play the organ and there is a fellow with a good voice singing.

  I received a letter from Martin Moynihan in which he said he expected to get home in a few weeks. I wish I could get a furlough too but we can't get one at the present time. Maybe I will get home later on. They aren't sure when we will move out but I think it will be in a month or two. The training we have been getting lately is really tough. I think they want to make us good and tough. One night last week we went out on a night problem and while we were marching there was a cloud burst and boy did it rain. We got wet to the skin, and boy was it good to get back to camp and get dried out.

By the way did you find out how the Wheate boy is making out, because in your last letter you said that a friend of his that was overseas with was at his house. I might be able to get down to see Victor Garbarini some weekend because he is only about 80 miles south of me and I can get there in about 4 hours. I had to laugh when I read your letter in which you said Dad didn't want to take the hairs off his coat because they were Muggsie's. Tell him to get a new dog and then he can clean up his hairs. Mother I just happened to think did you hear from Red Gibbons lately, if so send me his address. Well I will close now and don't be worrying why I don't write because I will soon again. Tell the Mom and Duke I was asking for them.

Love,
Son John

P.S. Any snow yet? How's the girls doing? Any new ones?"

℘

"Camp Shelby, Mississippi

Nov. 22, 1944 [Wednesday]

Dear Mother,
Tomorrow is Thanksgiving and we have to work but we are going to have a feast with turkey and all the trimmings that go with it. They told all the fellows that had their wives in town or friends to bring them as we will have enough to feed all.

I am glad that you are finally agreeing that I am not at fault for writing so much as you, because you know the civilians and families are supposed to keep up the soldier's fighting morale by writing him often as possible. I am glad to hear that Dad is making the mission. I wish I could make one but I might be able to make the next one. Don't tell me that all the women are falling for the missionary. What has happened to Father Broderick? I thought he had them all charmed. I was surprised to hear about Mr. Bernabe going to the mission but it might do him a lot in getting him to go to church again. I wonder if the Mrs. had anything to do with his going. Maybe? I had a letter from Buddy Butler in which he told me he's in something concerning aviation and how he has been up in airplanes and such. From what he writes he seems to get around quite a bit now. I had to laugh when I read that you were going to enclose a letter and some chance books from the Mount. Well you didn't enclose them in your letter. Mother I don't see why you have to send me some chance books. The fellows I know wouldn't buy any because they are all quite *broke and most of them don't believe in buying bonds. I think that your idea is okay but I know that it wouldn't work. Maybe I read your letter wrong on that. Please tell me when you write again.*

We are supposed to have a big dance this Friday night here at Camp and I expect to go. Saturday I also expect to go to confession and communion Sunday. Tell Dad we had an argument about if there was or wasn't any seaplanes on battleships off the North Carolina. Ask him to tell you and write me the answer. It is getting late and the lights will go off at any moment so I will close now. So till I hear from you again love to all.

*Love,
Son John"*

NOVEMBER 20, 1944

French troops drive through the 'Beffort Gap' to reach the Rhine. Four days later, on the 24th, they capture the strategic city of Strasbourg.

"Camp Shelby, Mississippi

Nov. 27, 1944 [Monday]

Dear Mother,

I received the letter you wrote on the 24th and was glad to hear that everything is okay. About these classes we have well we have one every week and they tell us the current news while during the class there are four fellows that every week talk on different countries so when my turn came I had to talk on Russia. That's how it goes.

From what you say about the missionary I think that you all are falling for him. We had a very nice Thanksgiving Day down here. I had plenty of turkey and all the trimmings that go with it. They had music and everything went along okay. Glad to hear that the Mount won their big game. I bet the brothers were glad.

I had to laugh about Frankie wanting to know if I shed tears over Notre Dame losing. What does he think, I am a kid? I was sorry to hear that they lost but maybe they will have a better team next year. Tell Martin I was asking for him and ask him to write to me and tell me his new address. I was going to write him but being that he's going home there's no sense writing to him.

Well I see that you are stepping out now going to visit all the neighbors and such. I bet Dad would like to go with you to go visiting. From all things I think we will be here for Christmas. They are planning to have a big time *for us. The Mess Sergeant plans to have an organ or piano and eat by candle light to make it just like being home. The fellows really get down in the mouth when a holiday comes.*

Tomorrow night we go on a twenty five mile hike we have to make in 8 hours and before we go on the hike we have to run a tough problem out in the field. The next day we go on a 9 mile speed march which we will have to make in two hours. From this you can see that we have a pretty tough week. Next week we are supposed to have a beer party. Most of the fellows are looking forward towards it, and so am I. The weather has been very rainy and there is much mud all around the place. Well Mother I am getting tired and I think I will close now. There is one thing funny about practically all your letters and that is that every time you write Dad is asleep. Boy he must get a lot of sleep. Love to all.

*Love,
Son John*

P.S. Please excuse writing."

EIGHTEEN - "THE BULGE"

DECEMBER 9, 1944 - THIRD ARMY HQ, NANCY, FRANCE

The Third Army is Patton's. With these men he made the first major breakout from the Normandy beachhead, and then raced across France knocking through stiff German resistance in his own form of blitzkrieg, the only Allied commander to successfully use the Germans' tactic upon themselves. He now sits poised in Eastern France, ready to spring into Germany and race to Berlin, and bring German Fuhrer Adolf Hitler to heel.

At Third Army HQ, Patton's senior intelligence officer, his "G-2" Colonel Oscar Koch, has a suspicion the Germans, far from being defeated, are up to something. His sources have detected a significant buildup of German troops in the area opposite the Ardennes Forest, a natural barrier to any troop movements that, as a result, has been left lightly defended. The Germans at present have a numerical superiority of two-to-one over the American First Army opposite them, commanded by General Courtney Hodges. 500 Panzer tanks have recently been moved into the area as well. And all of this has been done in complete radio silence. The Germans are broadcasting nothing over the airwaves.

Even Patton is reluctant to believe it, impatient to launch his own offensive directly into Germany. More than anything else, he wants to be the first Allied commander to reach Berlin and crush the German Reich. But he agrees with Koch, and orders that emergency plans be drawn up should Hodges's First Army be attacked. He is largely alone in this respect. The rest of the Allied command gives little credence to the possibility of a German counterattack.

℘

"Camp Shelby, Mississippi

Dec. 11, 1944 [Monday]

Dear Mother,
    This is the first time I had to write you all week for we have been kept very busy. For instance, we went on a night problem on Wednesday. The weather was cold, but I had enough of clothes on me including my overcoat and I kept very warm. Friday night I had to go on guard duty. I had to walk

guard from 10 till 2 in the morning. Yesterday I went to town and bought some Christmas cards. Boy were they dear. They cost 25 cents apiece. Last night I got a surprise when I got a box of candy and cookies from Aunt Kitty. I thought that it was swell of her to send them to me and I am going to send her a letter of thanks for it.

    Mother I don't want you to buy anything for me for Christmas because the only thing I can use is some money or something to eat. I was wondering if you could send me a cooked chicken. I mean by cutting the chicken up after you cooked it and put the pieces in wax paper and send it to me, the fellows and myself would appreciate it a lot so what do you say? Send it soon because I don't think we will be here for Christmas. I sent home my shoes and a new wool shirt for Dad. I wonder if you could have my shoes fixed so if I ever get around home I could drop in and wear them around. Don't build up any dreams now that I might be home though it could happen we will go to New York. The shirt that I sent I think will be good for Dad for working or around the house. It is perfectly new and hasn't been worn.

    It is raining very hard out, and the wind is blowing. Boy, what a dismal night out. By the way tell Dad I won the argument as usual, as if we could lose an argument with our line of bull.[269] Tomorrow I go on K.P. so I will be in for a hectic day. But there is one good thing about it, I won't have to be out slopping around in the mud as we usually do. I will close now for the present. It is getting late and I have to get up early. Love to all.

                                                                         Love,
                                                                         Son John"

DECEMBER 16, 1944 - GERMAN FRONT LINES

At 0530 hours the order is given. Along an 80-mile wide front the German artillery unleashes a barrage of shells that falls squarely in the laps of the Americans, ten miles to the west. "Screaming Meemie" rockets and shells from 88 mm guns rouse the American troops under Hodges to an unexpected nightmare. At the same time, a group of English-speaking German soldiers, garbed in American uniforms and schooled in American slang and customs, has infiltrated the American lines with the mission of spreading rumor and falsehood, and inflicting whatever damage they can upon the unprepared defenders standing in the way of the German onslaught. And an onslaught it is. Thirty German divisions are now streaming through the dense Ardennes Forest, Panzer tanks under Colonel Joachim Peiper racing to reach the bridges across the Meuse River, beyond which they will have relatively unbridled

---

[269] A good "line of bull" seems to be a family trait among the McGowans, and overall not a bad quality to have.

freedom to surround major American armies, and force the Allies to come to terms. With the Western Front safe, Hitler can then face the mounting threat from Russian armies slowly pushing his Eastern Front inward, and perhaps still win this war.

DECEMBER 17, 1944 - MALMEDY, FRANCE

By morning the breakout of the Germans is complete. Peiper and his Panzer tanks roll through the Ardennes, taking U.S. soldiers prisoner as they go. At Honsfeld 17 are captured sleeping, marched out into the bitter cold in nothing but boxer shorts, and executed, one by being tossed in front of a Panzer tank. At Malmedy a larger group is captured around noon, and marched into a field. There the SS turn their machine guns on them, and in two minutes 84 U.S. soldiers lie dead in the snow, prisoners of war supposedly protected under the Geneva Convention, to which all civilized nations in the world have been signatories, including Germany. This will be known as the Malmedy Massacre, and news of it spreads through the American lines like wildfire. Over the next three days 350 more will share their fate, along with 100 innocent Belgian civilians. The word goes round, as the Germans push towards the Meuse River, beyond which they hope to complete breakthrough of the Allied lines. Take no SS troopers prisoner. Remember Malmedy.

DECEMBER 19, 1944 - VERDUN, FRANCE

The briefing at 12th Army Group Headquarters is a grim gathering. The U.S. First Army under Gen. Courtney Hodges is almost surrounded, and the Germans continue their advance towards the Meuse. Patton, whose Third Army is over 100 miles south, is tasked with coming to the rescue. He boldly - and perhaps brashly - states that his troops can be there, with three divisions, in two days - 100,000 men, material, ordnance and supplies; 100 miles, in 48 hours. The other commanders, including his immediate superior, Gen. Omar Bradley, and the supreme commander, Eisenhower, are incredulous.

To the northeast another German force attacks the 99th Infantry Division entrenched on the Elsenborn Ridge. Their attack will continue for five days without letup, and each assault will be repelled by the 99th, sapping critical German resources with every attempt at breaking through the American lines.

DECEMBER 22, 1944 - BASTOGNE, BELGIUM

In the Ardennes, the 101st Airborne holds the critical crossroads of Bastogne. Before long they are surrounded, and the Germans offer them the opportunity to surrender. Their commander, General Anthony McAuliffe, sends the two German emissaries off with his typed response: "To the German Commander, Nuts! The American Commander." It is a line that will be immortalized.

DECEMBER 23, 1944 - LUXEMBOURG CITY, LUXEMBOURG

Patton and his troops are 30 miles south of Bastogne, and not making the progress he had hoped for. The German bulge in the American lines is now 60 miles deep and 30 miles wide. Snow and cloud-covered skies hamper aerial operations, and the men of the Third Army, Patton at their lead, slog through mud and crusted ruts, marching without stop, going north as fast as men can possibly go, bent on one thing: to save their comrades in Bastogne, now solidly surrounded by the Germans, who have already proven their ruthlessness ten times over.

DECEMBER 24, 1944 - OFF THE COAST OF CHERBOURG, FRANCE

Off the northern coast of France, a German submarine, U-486, waits patiently for prey. It is six minutes of six in the evening, and the light is fading. In her sights a troop ship, the *SS Leopoldville*, a Belgian vessel converted to a troopship, slowly chugs south with reinforcements for the ongoing Battle of the Bulge. In Southampton, England, she has been hastily loaded with over 2,200 U.S. troops from the 66th Infantry Division. But for a scheduling snafu, or other stroke of luck, these could have been troops of the 65th. The troops have been crammed onto the vessel as they arrived at dockside, irrespective of regiment or company, and confusion reigns. There are not enough lifejackets, and drills to familiarize those on board with using them and the ship's lifeboats fall mainly on deaf ears, if they fall at all. Southampton recedes behind them at nine o'clock in the morning, and the *Leopoldville* and another troopship, the *SS Cheshire*, are escorted by three British warships, and one French.

The passage is slow, and boring. The troops, mainly green, are nervous about what awaits them when they land. Rumors are rampant about the success the Germans have had since they broke out in a mad dash to split the Allied lines on the Western Front. Is another Dunkirk at hand?

Five miles off Cherbourg U-486 launches two torpedoes. One finds its target on the starboard side aft of the *Leopoldville* and explodes in its number four hold. Three hundred men are killed within moments as the compartments they are stowed in flood. "Abandon ship!" is shouted - but in Flemish, the language of the Belgian crew. Most soldiers opt to remain on the sinking vessel, thinking it will be towed safely into the port, not that far away. One of the British escorts, *HMS Brilliant*, takes five hundred men off the *Leopoldville* and heads for shore. The other escorts are on a search for the German submarine. Twelve hundred soldiers are still aboard.

There is little awareness of the disaster on shore at Cherbourg. Radio communications are hampered by the use of different radio frequencies and codes. There is minimal staffing available on shore, as most personnel have departed for Christmas parties. It is an hour before Cherbourg realizes that *Leopoldville* is sinking. Several hundred Allied vessels lie idle in the harbor, their engines cold, their crews elsewhere. At forty minutes past eight on the evening of Christmas Eve, *Leopoldville* sinks beneath the cold waters of the English Channel, carrying hundreds more U.S. soldiers to their deaths.

A cover-up follows. News of the tragedy is highly restricted, and all official documents remained classified until 1996. It will not be widely revealed until a documentary about it airs on the History Channel in 1998. Of some 2,235 U.S. soldiers aboard at the time of the attack, over 500 go down with the ship, and another 250 die from injuries, drowning or hypothermia. Their fate is shared by the Begian captain of the ship, Charles Limbor, and several crew members and accompanying British soldiers. Following the attack, all survivors in the 66th Division are ordered not to speak of the incident at all. Letters home are strictly censored to remove any mention of what they have gone through. When discharged from the service at war's end, they are told that any veteran's benefits they might be entitled to will be removed if they speak to anyone in the press or media about it.

With events in Europe deteriorating in the face of the surprise German offensive, the Battle of the Bulge rages on with no certain outcome either way. Preparations to move additional troops into battle accelerate, and the 65th Infantry Division gets ready to ship out.

"Camp Shelby, Mississippi

Dec. 26, 1944 [Tuesday]

Dear Mother,
 Yesterday was Christmas and things went okay. Of course most of the fellows were a little homesick but we didn't mind it. We had a very good dinner

with turkey and all the trimmings and it tasted alright. I went to midnight mass and also received. The mass was very good. There was about 5,000 attending. The priests were much impressed by the big turnout.

  Yes the chickens arrived and they were very good. I and the fellows enjoyed them very much. Mother when you sent me a Christmas card and I thought that you were going to include some money because I am flat broke but don't send it now because of the time being. Uncle George sent me a letter and he was glad to hear from me and he wants me to write. I think you ought to pay him a visit being now that his son John is overseas. He also said how Sonny (David) Lucas[270] was up to see him. I wish I could see him in his uniform. I had to laugh about you and Dad wanting me to advance just because a couple of relatives become officers. I tell you it isn't who you are in the army but if you can do your job and come out in one piece I think it's okay for a fellow to become an officer if his career is in the army or navy.[271] Mother I also sent another package home. Write and tell me in a few days. If you don't hear from me for about a week don't worry because I will be okay.[272] I will close now as I have a few more letters to write. Love to all.

Love,
Son John"

※

DECEMBER 26, 1944 - LUXEMBOURG CITY, LUXEMBOURG

At Third Army Headquarters the mood is somber. The German resistance to Patton's march to relieve Bastogne and the 101st Airborne is fierce, and U.S. tank crews find themselves in a standoff across a broad front, some 30 miles in total. The effort is taking far longer than Patton and his subordinates thought, and McAuliffe and his men are daily pounded by a relentless German assault. The battle for Bastogne has become the focal point of the Bulge.

---

[270] Sonny was David Lucas's nickname. "Uncle George" may have been another brother of Anna's, or otherwise related to the Lynches or the Lucases.

[271] John explained this sentiment to me personally on one of my visits with him while developing this book. He said that he was approached many times regarding going to officer training, and each time declined, because, as he said, "all I wanted to do was do my job, and do it well, and then go home."

[272] This comment refers most likely to the Division's imminent departure overseas, and the expected time it will take for a troop transport to cross the Atlantic Ocean. As it turns out in the end, it is a longer journey, as the Division, when it finally sails from New York, its first port of call is Bermuda, where they have to wait for a sufficient number of ships to assemble to warrant a convoy across the still-dangerous, U boat-infested waters of the Atlantic. The 65th is sent to Le Havre in France, their entry point into the European Theater of Operations.

Patton receives little help from the other Allied forces. Eisenhower has pulled several units back westward as reserves in case the Germans break through. To the north, British commander Bernard Montgomery, now bearing the title Field Marshal, and Patton's bitter rival in a war of huge egos, will not budge from his position.

The phone rings in Patton's headquarters. It is Major Hugh Gaffey, commanding the Fourth Armored Division, and he suggests his tanks make a last-ditch effort to break through the German lines and save Bastogne. At the spearhead of the Fourth is Lt. Col. Creighton Abrams, a 30 year old New Englander just eight years out of West Point. "Try it," Patton commands Gaffey, and before long Abrams, with twenty Sherman tanks rolling at their top speed of 30 miles per hour, is on his way to Bastogne. With fierce fighting at every village they roll through, they break their way through the encircling Germans, and clear a narrow pathway to Bastogne. From a foxhole outside the shattered village Lt. Webster of the 101st emerges. "Glad to see you," he casually remarks. The siege of Bastogne has been lifted.

DECEMBER 27, 1944

Soviet troops advance up the Danube River, heading westward. They besiege Budapest, capital of Hungary.

NINETEEN - "OVER THERE"

JANUARY 12, 1945

The 65th Infantry Division ships out of New York on January 12, 1945. The troopship sails first to Bermuda, where it joins a convoy to cross the waters of the Atlantic. Initially bound for Southampton, England, they are diverted to Le Havre, France, to help avoid a repetition of the *Leopoldville* disaster.

JANUARY 16, 1945

Troops of the U.S. First and Third Armies link up after a month being separated by the German assault in the Battle of the Bulge.

JANUARY 17, 1945

Soviet troops capture Warsaw, Poland.

JANUARY 20, 1945

FDR is sworn in for his fourth term in office, and gives the first Inaugural Address delivered in wartime since Abraham Lincoln's 1865 address. Reverend Angus Dun reads the oath of office, which Roosevelt swears to while holding his hand on his family's centuries-old Dutch language Bible, and open to I Corinthians 13. Rev. Dun will be called upon again to serve the President in a few short months, to preside at his funeral.

JANUARY 22, 1945

After 10 days crossing the Atlantic, the transports enter the much-bombed port of Le Havre on January 22, 1945. Sergeant Bill Jordy, in the first written history of the 65th's wartime experiences, called "Right to be Proud", describes the arrival of the 65th in France. "Ship-sick doughs, forbidden for security reasons to go topside, squeezed around port holes and open hatchways to get a first glimpse of the twisted ruins of what had been the great transatlantic port which docked most of the steamers bringing Americans to Paris." [273]

---

[273] Jordy, *Right to be Proud*, from which many of the details of the 65th's engagements have been sourced.

JANUARY 25, 1945

The famous Battle of the Bulge is in its final throes, though the German advance essentially stalled on Christmas Eve 1944, and never regained the momentum it had begun with. Through December and January Patton's troops have pushed the Germans back relentlessly, and by January 25 the Germans are back to where they had been when "Operation Watch on the Rhine" began.

JANUARY 26, 1945

Soviet troops liberate Auschwitz.

℘

The first destination for the 65th is Camp Lucky Strike, near the English Channel port of St. Vallery en Caux, which they reach on January 26, and where they will remain until February 25, preparing for combat. A treeless field with tents as far as the eye can see, covered with snow, Lucky Strike will be their home for the next few weeks. "Food, fuel and blankets were scarce," Jordy tells us. But things will get better, as the 65th does their part to improve their portion of the camp. Probably from Lucky Strike, Private McGowan pens his first letter home in over a month. And of course, he cannot divulge where he is now located, other than a vague "Somewhere in France."

"Somewhere in France

Jan. 27, 1945 [Saturday]

Dear Mother,
This is the first chance I had to write you and Dad. I am okay and am feeling fine after our long sea voyage. It was very exciting for all of us and I liked it a lot. While around I happen to visit Le Havre. It is a big city but has been considerably damaged.
How is everything going back home? How is Dad making out? Tell him to keep up the Navy. I am sorry I couldn't make it home that Saturday night but I think it was best that way.[274] *It is cold here very much and the weather is just like back home during the weather months. While I was aboard the ship I went to mass practically every day and also received at every mass. Andy Garbarini sent me a V-Mail Christmas card just like the one you got from John Lucas. I was wondering if you send me a package containing some can*

---

[274] Probably refers to a "last chance" furlough opportunity soldiers from New York had when they deployed to Camp Sampson to quickly visit home once again. Apparently John declined the opportunity.

goods because that stuff will not break or get broken. Well Mother that's about all for now. Write as often as you can. Love to all.

*Love,
Son John"*

JANUARY 30, 1945

Albert Speer, Hitler's chief armaments minister, goes on record with the Fuhrer that the war is lost. Germany now lacks the industrial capacity to produce armaments sufficient to defeat the Allies. Nor does it have the manpower required to do so. It is time to try and cut the best deal that they can with the Allies, and avoid the impending destruction of the homeland. His plea falls on deaf ears.

"France

Jan. 30, 1945 [Tuesday]

Dear Mother,
Being that I got the time I thought that I would drop you a few lines. This place is just like Canada for the people have the same customs. The French that I took in school is helping quite a bit when we go to town. It is very cold and has been snowing quite a lot. I haven't received any mail from you as yet but I hope to soon. The fellows were just talking how they would like a nice American steak but all we can do is just talk about it because we can't get any here. I will close now. Love to all.

*Love,
Son John"*

TWENTY - "CAMP LUCKY STRIKE"

The next letter is not a letter at all, but a small postcard of sorts, with the image of a young French boy writing a card to his father, who wears an obvious military uniform, and gazes fondly at the letter he holds in hand from his son, who smiles fondly at the recollection of "mon cher papa." Postmarked Feb. 2, 1945, so presumably mailed that day or more likely earlier, given the delay between the written word and the "on its way" letter.

"Feb. 2, 1945 [Friday]

Dear Mother and Dad,
This is a little souvenir postcard that I picked up in a small town. I hope you receive this okay. Write and tell me if you get it.
Love,
Son John"

℘

FEBRUARY 4 - 11, 1945

Over seven days, Roosevelt, Churchill, and Stalin meet at Yalta. The decisions made here over these seven days will shape the world for decades to come, and not necessarily for the best of humanity.

℘

"Somewhere in France

Feb. 7, 1945 [Wednesday]

Dear Mother,
This is Tuesday night and I am writing this letter by candle light so excuse some of the writing. I have been waiting for a letter from you but I haven't received any as yet but I hope to get one in the next few days. Mail call is as important as chow call here because everybody wants to hear from home. Sister Mary Albert wrote to me and thanked me for the Christmas card I sent her. She was also asking for you and Dad and wanted to know how you are. You and Dad ought to go down to see her because from the way she writes not many go down to see her.
Well how are things going at home? How are Dad and you? I don't want you and him to be worrying about me too much because I am okay and couldn't be in better health except for a cold. Did you hear any more about

Martin Moynihan? Give Rose[275] my address to send to him because I liked to hear from him and hear how he is making out. I wrote a letter to Father Broderick the other day so if you see him he will probably tell you he received a letter from me.

  I was reading in the Stars and Stripes, *the paper for Americans in the European theater,* that there is a big shortage of meat, oil and coal in New York. How are you and Mom making out with the shortages? Tell Duke the horses over here have their tails cut off so they can't get in the way of the manure. When you look at the towns and country around here you would think that you were in the movies looking at a travel talk film because it doesn't seem real. Mother when you write send most of your letters by air mail because that seems to be the quickest way of getting here. How is Frankie and his family making out? I will drop a few lines as soon as possible because we don't get very much time for writing except at night. Tell Dad I had some of that French wine and cognac and also some of that French bread. Ask him if he had any of this stuff when he was over here.[276] Also tell him we have some of that mud, and boy what stuff! It's up to your knees in some places and thick as pudding. I think I will close now so don't worry. I will write again and don't you forget to write. Love to all.

Love,
Son John"

℘

FEBRUARY 10, 1945

Despite the fact that of the 650,000 Allied troops involved in the Battle of the Bulge, 600,000 were Americans, Supreme Commander Dwight Eisenhower, in a bow to global politics, agrees to name British Field Marshall Bernard Montgomery as Allied leader of the next big push of the war, the assault on the German heartland. Patton and his victorious Third Army, heroes of the Bulge, are ordered to cease their eastward advance and go on the defensive. Patton seethes, but has no choice but to obey Ike's orders.

FEBRUARY 13-14, 1945

The German city of Dresden is destroyed by a firestorm following Allied bombing raids.

---

[275] Rose Moynihan, Martin's mother and John's aunt.
[276] John's father Ed trod these same fields as a doughboy in World War I, and doubtless told his son many tales of his days soldiering through France in 1917 and 1918.

"Somewhere in France

Feb. 14, 1945 [Wednesday]

Dear Mother,
  Today beginning of the week I thought I would drop you a few lines that I am okay and everything is fine. I had a letter from Red Gibbons and he said that he expected to ship out soon but he will try and drop by and see you and Dad. Tell Dad I had some of that French beer and it's just like drinking water that's colored. In my first letter I asked for a package from you. Try and send it as soon as possible. How are you getting along with your secretarial work? I was wondering if you got your cards out on time. What's the latest news around Dyre Avenue and the neighborhood? I will close now and I hope to hear from you as soon as possible. Give my regards to all.
              Love,
              Son John*"*

"Somewhere in France

Feb. 18, 1945 [Sunday]

Dear Mother,
  I received a V-Mail letter from you and Mrs. Hull. I was very glad to receive both of them. Please excuse the pencil but due that there is no ink to be got we have to write in pencil. After I write this letter I expect to go to 2 o'clock mass down in the chaplain's tent.
  I was wondering if you could send me a camera because I think it will become very handy in taking pictures of some of these foreign places. We have a half day off today so I will try and give myself a halfway decent cleaning up.
  I was wondering if you are getting my bonds okay. They told us that they might be a month or so late so don't worry about them. How has my mail been coming home? I have been writing about twice a week. Your mail has been coming here to me good. I would write more but due to the censorship[277] we are under we can't write much. What is Martin Moynihan taking up at

---

[277] At this point all mail home was censored to make sure that nothing of a military intelligence nature was being communicated. This letter bore on the outside envelope a rubber stamp stating "PASSED BY US ARMY EXAMINER 51122", and was signed "James C. Coleman, 2nd Lt." Lt. Coleman's job was to read every letter the soldiers under his domain wrote.

Princeton? Some kind of special course? From what you wrote I thought he was going to O.C.S.[278] to become an officer. When you write again send me John Lucas's address. I might be able to look him up. I saw some pictures in a paper here of the snowfall in New York. From what I saw and read you must have really had a winter this year.[279] Well how's Duke making out with his oil and the women? He ought to see some of the French women here. How's Dad making out at work these days? I will close now as it is time to go to church. Love to all.

Love,
Son John"

§

"Somewhere in France

Feb. 20, 1945 [Tuesday]

Dear Mother,
    I just got off of K.P. so I thought I would drop you a few lines to let you know that everything is going along okay. We have the radio tonight and the gang and I are listening to Glen Miller's orchestra and it sounds good. When I asked for a camera I forgot to tell you to send some film also because I don't think I can get any here. I had my hair cut short and all the fellows tell me my hair is turning red. Maybe the Irish is coming out in my hair. By the way I received The Tower, the Mount paper, and I was glad to get it. I will close now. Write as often as you can. Love to all.

Love,
Son John"

§

FEBRUARY 25, 1945

Beginning on February 25, and continuing until March 1, 1945, the 65th Division moves out of Camp Lucky Strike and the fields of Normandy, and travels across France, as Jordy tells us, "by truck and train." Through Beauvais and Compiegne they travel - Compiegne, where the Armistice ending the First World War had been signed a mere twenty-six years earlier, at 6:00 AM on the morning of November 11, 1918, bringing to an end "the war to end all wars." Through Soissons and Metz the trucks roll, "past the battlefields of

---

[278] Officer Candidate School.
[279] The winter of 1944-1945 was particularly brutal, with temperatures routinely plummeting below zero.

World War I." Private McGowan's thoughts must have dwelled on what his father had suffered through on those same battlefields, the trenches and the barbed wire, the stench of mustard gas. Between Metz and Thionville the Division halts, and the Division Command Post is established in a small farming village called Ennery. Major General Stanley Reinhart, commanding the 65th, must be wondering just how ably his well-trained but untested warriors will fare.

"Somewhere in France

Feb. 25, 1945 [Friday]

Dear Mother,
 I received a letter from you in which you said that you had received mail from me. I was very glad to hear that and hope that you receive the rest of my mail. In your letter you stated that two cats were crying in the yard and that Dad said that Muggsie would have chased them. I just knew he would say something like that. I was also glad to hear that Martin is coming home. Maybe his mother can finally give him some of her ham.
 This morning I went to 11 o'clock mass. It was very nice. We sang hymns all through the mass. The chapel tent was very crowded and I think it was a swell turnout being where we are. I don't think you will have to send me that French dictionary because I am picking up the French okay. Every time I go to town I pick up a few new words. There is one thing I would like to have and that is a pipe. Don't buy a real good one, just one that has a metal filter in it. They cost about a dollar.
 The other night I was wondering if Dad still goes down to the Holy Name Meeting and do they still have the good old beer which they all go for? How about the card game? Are they still going as strong as ever? Tell the Duke he ought to invest in a bulldozer to do the snow shoveling for him. As I write this letter I am munching on a big piece of French bread. The bread is good. They make it out of potatoes instead of flour because it is very scarce. You ought to see the shoes the average French person wears. The sole is made out of wood and is about 1 inch thick. The rest of the shoe is made out of cheap leather. The clothes are okay that they wear and they seem to have enough of them. In some towns little children run up to you and say, "Cigarette for Papa." They also know how to say "chewing gum". I get a kick out of them because they will follow you for blocks and just say four words, "Chewing gum, and cigarette for Papa." When I saw this it reminded me of the time in Canada when you and Dad gave those kids some candy for letting you take a picture of their dog and carriage.

The churches in small towns are like cathedrals in our large cities back home. Well mother I will close now. Hoping to hear from you soon. Give my regards to all. Don't worry.

Love,
Son John"

TWENTY-ONE - "IN THE FRONT LINES"

MARCH 4, 1945

By the 1st of March all units have left Camp Lucky Strike, and by the 4th of March the Division has fully assembled in the vicinity of Ennery[280], and begins its first mission - relieving the 26th Division in the Saarlautern bridgehead area, and continuing aggressive defense of the area against German attempts to blunt the Allied advance.

The 65th Division is comprised of three core infantry groups - the 259th, 260th and 261st regiments. Private McGowan is a member of the 260th, and moves with his unit to occupy the Saarlautern bridgehead, which takes up an eastward-facing bulge in the Saar River. From March 7th until the 18th there is a constant artillery battle going on between the 65th on the west bank of the Saar and the German defenders on the east. Foot patrols actively probe across the Saar, steadily engaging the enemy. The 13th and 14th sees increasing action on the part of the 260th, with missions that are initially characterized as "limited objective attacks", but which rapidly turn into fierce hand-to-hand, house-to-house struggles to gain precious space in the city of Saarlautern. But enemy resistance is strong, and the 260th, while acquitting themselves extremely well in their first real combat experience, are forced to pull back several times. Tellingly, the tenaciousness of the 260th's attempts at Saarlautern convince the Germans that they face a much larger action.

Private McGowan recalls one such night years later: "A rainy and eerie evening. Beams from enemy flares and tracers lit the sky. Machine gun and mortar fire appeared all around us. The unknown, combined with great anxiety, tension and nervousness set in. We had to cross an open bridge over the Saar River[281], being aware of enemy fire, then follow engineer tape to avoid

---

[280] Ennery (German: Ennerchen) is a commune in the Moselle department in Grand Est in north-eastern France.
[281] The Saar River (French: Sarre; German: Saar) is a river in northeastern France and western Germany, and a right tributary of the Moselle. It rises in the Vosges Mountains on the border of Alsace and Lorraine and flows northwards into the Moselle near Trier. It has two headstreams (the Sarre Rouge and Sarre Blanche, which join in Lorquin), that both start near Mont Donon, the highest peak of the northern Vosges. After 126 kilometers in France and 120 kilometers in Germany, the Saar flows into the Moselle at Konz (Rhineland-Palatinate) between Trier and the Luxembourg border. It has a catchment area of 2,869 square miles.

mine areas. Saar Lautern[282] was heavily guarded by pill boxes and bunkers of the Siegfried Line[283]. My friend and comrade Walter Moore[284] was hit and died from mortar wounds. There was also great stress when going out at night patrol. A barrage of screaming meemie[285] made everyone nervous."

MARCH 6, 1945

The last German offensive to be launched in World War II takes place in Hungary, with the objective of defending strategic oil fields from capture or destruction by the advancing Soviet Army.

℘

The next letter, like many others, is addressed in compliance with requirements of military secrecy from "Somewhere in France", is written just a few short days after Private McGowan's first combat experience, about which he mentions nothing at all.

"March 6, 1945 [Tuesday]

Dear Mother,
I thought I would drop you a line as this is the first chance I had to write you in about a week. Everything is okay and I hope things at home are going along as good as possible. Today I went to confession and communion in an old French church. We had an American chaplain hear confessions and say the Mass. It seemed strange to see the way the French people act during the Mass. They sing the Latin all the way through, and answer the priest instead of the altar boys. By the way, I received the Dyre Avenue News. *It was good to read about the happenings around the neighborhood and vicinity. Well I will close now. Love to all.*

Love,
Son John"

℘

---

[282] Saar Lautern is today called Saar Louis.
[283] The Siegfried Line was a string of concrete barriers strung for hundreds of miles throughout the western reaches of Germany. Referred to as the "West Wall", it was thought by the Germans to be impenetrable by tanks, a notion General Patton and his Third Army handily dispelled.
[284] Walter Moore was an early casualty in the 65th's campaign.
[285] "Screaming Meemie" was a nickname for the Nebelwerfer, a piece of German World War II rocket artillery.

MARCH 7, 1945

Operating north of the 3rd Army, the 1st Army takes the city of Cologne and secures a still-standing bridge across the Rhine at Remagen.

By March 7th the transfer of "front ownership" is well under way between the 26th and 65th Divisions, and Major General Reinhart assumes command of the sector. Jordy tells us "the entire relief was completed by March 9. On this date the 65th Division, as a whole, was a 'frontline' outfit, although some units had already been in combat for four days."

Jordy gives us the context of events at this time, just six weeks after "the Bulge" has concluded, and the path to victory in Europe once more seems assured, but not before significant sacrifices will be required. "The Division," he tells us, "went into the line at a time when the great 'spring offensive' was already well underway on the northern end of the Western Front. Four Allied armies had closed the enemy into a series of narrow pockets along the western bank of the Rhine. This offensive steadily spread southward to reach the Third Army at a time when General Patton's troops were already advancing slowly on a broad 50 mile front from Prum[286] on the north to Saarburg[287] on the south. The key city of Trier[288] fell two days prior to the commitment of the 65th Division. Seventy-two hours after the capture of Trier, armored units pushed

---

[286] Prum is a town in the Westeifel (Rhineland-Palatinate), Germany. Ninety-two percent of the town was destroyed by bombing and ground fighting during the Second World War. In 1949, it was wrecked again by an explosion on the Kalvarienberg hill caused by a fire in an underground ammunition bunker. Twelve people were killed, 15 injured and 965 left homeless.

[287] Saarburg is a city of the Trier-Saarburg district in the Rhineland-Palatinate state of Germany, on the banks of the Saar River in the hilly country a few kilometers upstream from the Saar's junction with the Moselle. Now known as a tourist attraction, the Leuk River flows into the town center and makes a spectacular drop of some 60 feet before joining the larger Saar River that bisects the town. The waterfall is the result of a 13th-century project to redirect the Leuk through the city center. The area around Saarburg is noted for the cultivation of Riesling grapes.

[288] Trier, heavily bombed in 1944 and evacuated by most of its inhabitants, had been declared by the German Reich a "fortress city" in January 1945, with a military commander assuming power there. But the upgrading of Trier as a "fortress" proved to be impossible, and it fell without heavy fighting on March 2, 1945, to advancing US tank troops.

across the Kyll River[289] to advance swiftly to the west bank of the Rhine north of Koblenz."[290]

But it is on March 7 that the 65th begins to prove its worth as a combat unit, in the defense of what is referred to as the Saarlautern Sector. Jordy relates that this mission "marked the baptism by fire for the 65th Infantry Division. At Ennery there was peace. A few miles up front - abruptly - there was war. Suddenly, training, and men, and fortitude met their first test. Almost immediately, the Division shed its first blood. It was especially hard to think of a man coming so far for one, two, or three days of combat."

Private McGowan's regiment, the 260th, "moved into a small bridgehead which had previously been forced across the river at Saarlautern." The next ten days will be "characterized by aggressive holding actions, intensive patrolling, and the extensive use of artillery fire against enemy personnel and installations on the east bank of the [Saar] river." But more than artillery occupies the minds of the soldiers of the 65th. "Patrols actively probed across the Saar…where one patrol consisting of four EMs captured a German pillbox and returned with its twelve former occupants on March 10 to merit the Division's first battlefield awards."

ʂ

A day later, now addressed from "Somewhere in Germany", Private McGowan writes home.

"March 10, 1945 [Saturday]

Dear Mother,

I am dropping you a few lines to let you know I am now somewhere in Germany and everything is okay. I received a letter from you which you wrote Feb. 11. I was glad to hear that the Sullivan fellow called you up, he told me

---

[289] The Kyll River, noted by the Roman poet Ausonius as Celbis, is a river in western Germany and tributary of the Moselle. It rises in the Eifel mountains, near the border with Belgium and flows generally south through the towns Stadtkyll, Gerolstein, Kyllburg and east of Bitburg. It flows into the Moselle in Ehrang, a suburb of Trier.

[290] Koblenz, spelled Coblenz before 1926, is a German city situated on both banks of the Rhine where it is joined by the Moselle. Koblenz was established as a Roman military post around 8 B.C. Its name originates in the Latin *ad cōnfluentēs*, meaning "at the confluence" of the two rivers. The actual confluence is today known as the "German Corner", a symbol of German reunification that features an equestrian statue of Emperor William I. The city celebrated its 2000th anniversary in 1992.

he would. How is the new priest? Is he old or very young? And by the way, does Father Broderick still come up to the church? Talking about church, I served Mass for a French priest in his country church. It was very nice and I got a lot out of it. I was also wondering if Dad had got a dog yet. In some of your letters you said he was going to get one. I will close now. Love to all.

*Love,
Son John"*

MARCH 10, 1945

At 0300 hours the XX Corps, of which the 65th Division is a part, launches a major offensive on the Siegfried Line. Pushing on the line from the west are the 94th, 80th and 26th Divisions. The 65th, on the southern flank, begins attacking in the area of the Saarlautern bridgehead to prevent the Germans from reinforcing their positions along the Line.

"Somewhere in Germany

March 12, 1945 [Monday]

Dear Mother,

This is the first chance I had to write you in over a week. We have been very busy and don't get a chance to write. I have visited the city of Frankfurt[291] which you must have read about in the papers. Things are moving along fast now so I don't know where I will be next. I received the package you sent with the pipe and I want to thank you and Dad very much. I am sure

---

[291] Frankfurt (officially *Frankfurt am Main*) is a metropolis and the largest city of the German federal state of Hesse, and its 746,878 (2017) inhabitants make it the fifth-largest city of Germany after Berlin, Hamburg, Munich, and Cologne. On the River Main (a tributary of the Rhine), its urban area has a population of 2.3 million. Like France and Franconia, the city is named after the Franks. Frankfurt is the largest city in the Rhine Franconian dialect area (West Central German dialects). Frankfurt was severely bombed in World War II (1939–1945). About 5,500 residents were killed during the raids, and the once-famous medieval city center, at that time the largest in Germany, was almost completely destroyed. It became a ground battlefield on March 26, 1945, when the Allied advance into Germany was forced to take the city in contested urban combat that included a river assault. The 5th Infantry Division and the 6th Armored Division of the United States Army captured Frankfurt after several days of intense fighting, and it was declared largely secure on March 29, 1945.

the fellows and myself will enjoy all that was in the package. I think you said that you had another box on the way too! If you send me any more packages see if you can put a few oranges in it because we rarely see them over here. I received the Dyre Avenue News and I saw the write-up they had about me. I had to laugh about them saying I was rated expert infantryman. Because now we are all combat infantrymen and we are supposed to get $10 more a month. Mother when I was in France I sent some money home. Tell me in one of your letters if and when you received it. By the way give Mom and Duke my thanks for the nice birthday card that they sent me and tell them I appreciate it very much. I also want to thank you and Dad for your Easter card. And about that cablegram you were supposed to send me I didn't receive it yet. I think due to all my movements that it will take some time to reach me. I hear that there is a lot of trouble in New York over the 12 o'clock curfew on beer places. What does Dad think of it? Of course he mustn't like that. Tell him I read that buck beer is coming and in the states now. By the way ask him if he ever had any of this German wine. It seems that they go in a lot for wine and such. Their wine is much stronger than ours and it has a much better taste than ours. How are things going in the neighborhood? Anything new of interest happen around there? I will close now. Hoping to hear from you soon. Love to all.

Love,
Son John

P.S. You can probably see that I have changed the date on my letter[292]. The reason is that we can write but we can't mail them because of being on the move or that we have no time to write. So I don't want you and Dad to worry if you don't hear from me regularly. Everything is okay and going along as fine as possible.

Love,
Son John"

ς

MARCH 13, 1945

With all of these actions, General George S. Patton's Third Army is finally on the move again, after being stalled by orders from above. Though British Field Marshall Bernard Montgomery has been selected to lead the massive Allied push into Germany, and thinks Patton's Third Army will be a small cog in that

---

[292] Indeed, the date of March 12 is overlaid on an earlier date, perhaps March 7.

massive wheel, events will prove otherwise. Bitter rivals, Patton is determined to be the first to cross the Rhine into the German heartland.

The immediate objective: the Siegfried Line, a defensive perimeter erected by the Germans and snaking across the farmland and forest of far western Germany, allegedly impervious to tank attack, and which will form the western wall of Fortress Germany.

At 0300 hours, a night-time offensive consisting of the 94th, 80th and 26th Divisions surges forward with the objective of smashing through the Siegfried Line. The 65th, to the south of XX Corps, pokes and probes in the Saarlautern bridgehead to prevent German reinforcements from going to the aid of those units under ruthless attack further to the north.

The 260th Regiment, Private McGowan within its ranks, proceeds with "limited objective attacks inside the Saarlautern bridgehead in conjunction with XX Corps' three-division offensive to the north of the 65th Division. Both times several city blocks were taken, but both times the 260th was forced to withdraw in the face of strong enemy resistance."

MARCH 14, 1945

The attacks by the 260th Regiment upon the entrenched Germans continue. They serve a strong purpose, confusing the Germans, who think the ferocity of these "limited objective attacks" indicates a far larger force attacking them than a single regiment. Indeed, the German High Command speaks of the difficulties encountered in "repelling fierce offensive action in the vicinity of Saarlautern."

℘

Post-marked "U.S.POSTAL SERVICE NO. 1 MARCH 31, 1945 10 PM". Word is hard to get home.

"Somewhere in Germany

March 16, 1945 [Friday]

Dear Mother,
Well tomorrow is St. Patrick's Day and I am spending it here somewhere in Germany. I guess Frankie[293] will drop down with the kids with

---

[293] John's Uncle Frank.

a big green tie on as usual. I received the air mail letter you wrote March second. It was a long letter and I enjoyed it. I wonder if you can send all your letters air mail because you can write more than a V-Mail. I try and write about once a week so if you don't receive mail so much from me don't worry because we don't have much time to write. That was really something about the bus helping Dr. Cahill[294] when he was in trouble. Maybe they will stop kicking when the bus is late. I want to congratulate you on staying in office as secretary. I hope I receive the box okay because I am sure the fellows and myself will enjoy it. Will close now. Love to all.

Love,
Son John"

MARCH 17, 1945

Active probing of the east bank of the Saar River by reconnaissance patrols of the 261st Regiment pays a big dividend. The regiment puts parts of two battalions across the river. Their first landfall is a little hamlet called Menningen. From there it is two miles march to the larger town of Merzig.[295] These advance units of the 65th succeed in capturing the dominating high ground south of the town.

MARCH 18, 1945

At 0600 hours the XX Corps, all Divisions involved, including the 65th, begin a "smashing" assault on the Siegfried Line. Millions of Allied troops comprising six Allied Armies are involved in making a relentless push which they hope will bring them to the Rhine River, the final obstacle to entering the German heartland.

The assignment given to the 65th is "to smash through the Siegfried Line in a wedge-shaped area between the southeastwardly advancing 26th Division to the north, and the northeasterly advancing 70th Division to the south." To the 260th Regiment is given a narrow sliver in the middle of the Division's objective area, which includes the northern half of Saarlautern and

---

[294] The bus in reference is the Bronx 14 bus, which at the time of these events ran from White Plains Road and 233rd Streets to Dyre Avenue and Boston Post Road. It was discontinued sometime after 2000.

[295] Merzig is the capital of the district Merzig-Wadern, in Saarland, Germany with about 30,000 inhabitants in 17 municipalities. It is situated on the river Saar, south of Trier, and northwest of Saarbrücken.

Saar-Louis-Roden.²⁹⁶ The 259ᵗʰ Regiment is given as its objective the southern part of Saarlautern, and all of Fraulautern and Saarwellingen. There is some shuffling of troops among the Regiments. 1ˢᵗ Battalion, 260ᵗʰ is attached to the 259ᵗʰ, while that regiment's 3ʳᵈ Battalion goes into reserve. 1ˢᵗ Battalion, 261ˢᵗ, shifts over to the 260ᵗʰ, within whose "objective area" the main drive against the Germans is to occur. The initial goals of this assault on the Siegfried Line are "Dillengen and Saarwellingen, and three areas of high ground which lay along the rim of a semi-circle between 3,000 and 5,000 yards out from the Saarlautern bridgehead."

The attack by the 259ᵗʰ and 260ᵗʰ Regiments jumps off at 0430 hours. The 261ˢᵗ pushes forward at 0600, against light enemy opposition, and by 2400 hours has seized Dillingen and the high ground east of the city. The 259ᵗʰ and 260ᵗʰ are not so fortunate. Operating in the Saarlautern bridgehead, by nightfall they have gained only 1,500 yards. The 260ᵗʰ, with Private McGowan in its midst, succeeds in capturing just a few city blocks inside Saarlautern, with fierce house-to-house combat against the defending Germans. They sleep that night in defensive posture in the beleaguered town, wary of a German counterattack, licking their wounds.

MARCH 19, 1945

A change in battle plans shifts 1ˢᵗ Battalion, 261ˢᵗ Regiment back to its home regiment, which will march on Saarwellingen, originally the objective of the 260ᵗʰ, with the 259ᵗʰ pursuing a parallel path to the south of them. The 260ᵗʰ, battered but not beaten, is moved to reserve.

In the action that follows the 65ᵗʰ takes Saarwellingen, Piesbach, Bilsdorf, Fraulautern and Ensdorf.²⁹⁷ They are part of a giant pincers movement between Patton's Third Army and the U.S. Seventh Army²⁹⁸ to the

---

[296] Saar-Louis-Roden is a city in the Saarland, (Germany), capital of the district of Saarlouis. Saarlouis, as the name implies, is located on the River Saar. It was built as a fortress in 1680 and named after Louis XIV of France.

[297] Piesbach, Bilsdorf and Ensdorf are small villages in the district of Saarlouis, in Saarland, Germany, on the right bank of the river Saar, opposite Saarlouis, approximately 12 miles northwest of Saarbrücken.

[298] The U.S. Seventh Army was a United States army created during World War II that evolved into the United States Army Europe (USAREUR) during the 1950s and 1960s. It served in North Africa and Italy in the Mediterranean Theater of Operations and France and Germany in the European theater between 1942 and 1945. Originally the I Armored Corps under command of Lieutenant General George S. Patton, it made landfall at Morocco during Operation Torch as the

south to capture the Saar Basin. The Germans, confused as to which direction further attacks will come from, begin a rapid retreat. In its sector, the 65th follows in equally rapid pursuit, toward Neunkirchen.[299]

MARCH 20, 1945

Jordy's words describe it best. "During D-Day-Plus-2, the 65th captured or killed such delaying groups as had been left behind by the enemy. Once the Wehrmacht turned tail, there was nothing for it to do, but to continue scampering until the Rhine was put between the conquerors and the conquered. The 'overhang' was toppling toward the 'base', and in the military avalanche Germany lost her third greatest industrial area."[300]

MARCH 21, 1945

The 65th halts and regroups in the area of Neunkirchen, taking a well-earned respite. With little exception, they have seen action almost every day since the month began, and have gone from "green" to "blooded" soldiers. And many casualties have been suffered.

℘

Western Task Force, the first all-U.S. force to enter the European war. Following successful defeat of the Wehrmacht under General Erwin Rommel in North Africa, the I Armored Corps was redesignated the Seventh Army on July 10, 1943 while at sea en route to the Allied invasion of Sicily as the spearhead of Operation Husky.
[299] Neunkirchen is a town and a municipality in Saarland, Germany. It is the largest town in, and the seat of the district of Neunkirchen. It is situated on the river Blies, approximately 20 km northeast of Saarbrücken. With about 50,000 inhabitants, Neunkirchen is Saarland's second largest city. On 10 February 1933, an explosion of a giant gas tank at the ironwork caused 68 casualties, and 190 injured. The damage spread over a part of the factory and also hit a nearby residential area and a school building. The duration of repair work and temporary closing of the damaged parts of the iron works was about nine months. This event caused worldwide media attention. Having a big ironworks complex right in the town center made the town a target for Allied bomb raids in the Second World War. In 1945, an air raid destroyed about three quarters of the town center. Due to that, there are many malfunctioning WW2 bombs that didn't explode and can be found even today.
[300] The other major German industrial areas included the better-known Ruhr valley.

The following day, Private McGowan gets a chance to write home.

"Somewhere in Germany

March 22, 1945 [Thursday]

Dear Mother,
    I am now at the present time living in a house in Germany. This is only for a few days. You see the army takes over these houses for us soldiers instead of us living out in the fields. I am now part of Patton's Third Army[301] and I was in the battle of Saarlautern. You must have read about it in the papers. At the present time I am somewhere in the Saar. Things were hot for a while, but now things are rolling along okay. I don't want you and Dad to worry. All you can do is say a few prayers for me. I think that everything is going to be all right in a few months. Tell Dad I wish I could send him a few cigarettes because we have more than we can smoke. There is one thing I must say and that is if the people back home could see the stuff that they are giving up back home to send over here I think that they wouldn't kick so much. Today I received a letter that you wrote on March 7. About that camera, I don't think you better send it because I can't carry it around. You will have to excuse me for not writing to all those people who you tell me to write to because I don't have the time. I will close now. Regards to all. Write as much as possible.
                                                    Love,
                                                    Son John"

Post-marked "U.S. POSTAL SERVICE NO. 1 APRIL 8, 1945 10 PM".

"Somewhere in Germany

March 23, 1945 [Friday]

Dear Mother,
    I received the letter you wrote on February 28. It seems it got here later than the one you wrote on March 8. Well how did you enjoy St. Patrick's Day? I guess Dad had a few beers to keep up with the day's celebrating. Today I took a nice shower. It felt very good because that's the first one I had in several months. To top it all off our platoon had a big barrel of beer. I do mean it was good. Tell Dad I was thinking of how he would have liked a glass

---

[301] Patton's Third Army was one of the most storied U.S. armies, led by their fabled commander, General George S. Patton.

of it. Everything is going along okay. We are getting a few days rest for a while and I am in perfect health. Tell Duke to get to work on the garden.

Love,
Son John"

℘

The following letter is from Richard ("Dick") Simmons to Anna McGowan, sometime after he has entered the service.

"March 25, 1945 [Sunday]

Dear Mrs. McGowan,

    Well here I am again. First of all I want to thank you very much for John's address. I got it last week in a letter from Mom. I wrote to John the very next day. I wrote him a nice long letter. I figure I owe him at least another letter, so I intend to write to him again tomorrow. It will get the ball rolling again between us. He will have plenty of questions to answer. I can't wait till I hear from him.

    And how are you, Mrs. McGowan? Fine, I hope. And Eddie, I hope he is fine. How is Mr. and Mrs. McGowan who live in your house? Fine, I hope, and tell them I was asking for them.

    As for me, there isn't much new, Mrs. McGowan. Still stationed on the island and having everything okay.[302] I am getting my mail steady which makes me very happy. Today is Sunday and my day off. In a little while I will be going for my Sunday dinner. The food is very good here, especially for an island base. The only thing I miss is my ice cream. We don't get it here. The last time I had any was back in the first week of January and I was on the ship then. Although there is a cigarette shortage in the States we still get them. We are rationed to a carton a week. And that is plenty for us.

    Well I guess by this time the snow is all gone and the air is warmer. And people looking for their Easter suits.

    Well Mrs. McGowan, I just came back from dinner, and what a dinner. Turkey. Can you imagine that? It sure surprised me. But it was very good. And we got plenty. Well I will be saying so long for now, Mrs. McGowan, and will write soon again. Give my regards to Eddie. Until next time I remain,

Your friend,
Dick
R. T. Simmons"

℘

---

[302] Not sure what "island" Dick is referring to, probably somewhere in the Pacific.

MARCH 27 - 29, 1945

Slogging eastward across Germany, the 65th assembles at Bockenhausen on the 27th, and Schwabenheim on the 28th. The 27th marks Private McGowan's twentieth birthday. He wonders if he'll see another. At Schwabenheim the division awaits its turn to cross treadway bridges hastily built across the Rhine River by earlier divisions at the shattered German cities of Mainz and Oppenheim.[303] On the 29th the 65th begins its crossing. As Jordy tells us, "The broadly curving arc of the bridge at Oppenheim represented the longest pontoon bridge in military history."[304]

MARCH 30, 1945

Soviet troops capture Danzig, the modern day city of Gdansk in Poland, but in 1945 a major German port city.

MARCH 31, 1945

From Jordy: "By the last day of the month…the 65th Division, along with a vast part of United States' striking power, had attained the overall objective of

---

[303] Mainz is the capital and largest city of Rhineland-Palatinate, Germany. The city is located on the Rhine river at its confluence with the Main River, opposite Wiesbaden on the border with Hesse. Mainz is an independent city with a population of 206,628 (2015) and forms part of the Frankfurt Rhine-Main Metropolitan Region. Mainz was founded by the Romans in the 1st Century B.C. It served as a military fortress on the northernmost frontier of the Roman Empire and as the provincial capital of Germania Superior. Mainz became an important city in the 8th Century AD as part of the Holy Roman Empire, becoming the capital of the Electorate of Mainz and seat of the Archbishop-Elector of Mainz, the Primate of Germany. Mainz is famous as the home of Johannes Gutenberg, the inventor of the movable-type printing press, who in the early 1450s manufactured his first books in the city, including the Gutenberg Bible. Historically, before the 20th century, the city was known in English as Mentz and in French as Mayence. Mainz was heavily damaged during World War II, with more than 30 air raids destroying about 80 percent of the city's center, including most of the historic buildings. Today, Mainz is a transport hub and a center of wine production.
Oppenheim is a town in the Mainz-Bingen district of Rhineland-Palatinate, Germany. The town is a well-known wine center, being the home of the German Winegrowing Museum, and is particularly known for the wines from the Oppenheimer Krötenbrunnen vineyards.
[304] The pontoon bridge crossing the Rhine at Oppenheim stretched 1,100 feet from shore to shore.

the 'spring offensive' - the east bank of the Rhine. It was charged with the mission of continuing the pursuit of the enemy, in a zone which ran northeastwardly from the Frankfurt area, to bring the 65th to the bitter battles at Langensalza and Struth. Behind…lay Germany's Frontier Defenses and two of her greatest industrial areas. Ahead lay the heart of the country, and…more than five weeks of fighting for Major Stanley E. Reinhart's now-tested division."

Once over the Rhine, part of the division (the 261st Infantry) is assigned to move forward with the 6th Armored Division.[305] Moving ahead of the tanks, the 1st Battalion of the 261st seizes a bridge over the Fulda River near Malsfeld, and then holds it against a strong German counter-offensive during the night.[306]

---

[305] The 6th Armored Division ("Super Sixth") was an armored division of the United States Army during World War II. The division was activated on February 15, 1942 at Fort Knox out of "surplus" elements of the reorganized 1st and 2nd Armored Divisions, with Brig. Gen. Carlos Brewer assigned as its first commanding general.
[306] The Fulda River is a river of Hesse and Lower Saxony, Germany. It is one of two headstreams of the Weser (the other one being the Werra). The Fulda is 137 miles long. The river arises at Wasserkuppe in the Rhön Mountains in Hesse. From there it runs northeast, flanked by the Knüll Mountains in the west and the Seulingswald in the east. Near Bebra it changes direction to the northwest. After joining the Eder River it flows straight north until Kassel, then changes direction to the northeast, with the Kaufungen Forest east and the beginning of the Reinhardswald forest northwest. The north end of the river meets the Werra in Hannoversch Münden, Lower Saxony, where the Fulda and the Werra join to form the Weser River.

TWENTY-TWO - "GERMANY"

APRIL 1, 1945 - EASTER SUNDAY

The German attack continues into the early morning hours of Easter Sunday, repulsed at every turn, and finally the Germans retreat. In short order the 261st and the 6th Armored are on the east bank of the river, and continuing forward.

The rest of the 65th follows. They are assigned a zone running northeastwardly from Frankfurt straight into the heart of Germany. They will take the lead in XX Corps' push to seize the major German cities of Weimar and Erfurt. Near Hattenbach, the 65th's assembly point west of the Fulda, the order to advance is given.[307]

APRIL 2, 1945

At 0600 hours the two remaining regiments of the 65th (259th and 260th Infantry Regiments) advance over the Fulda bridge and push eastward. By midnight that night they have pushed seven to ten miles east of the crossing site. Reconnaissance units are even further east.

APRIL 3-4, 1945

---

[307] Weimar is a city in the federal state of Thuringia, Germany. It is located in Central Germany between Erfurt in the west and Jena in the east, approximately 50 miles southwest of Leipzig, 106 miles north of Nuremberg and 106 miles west of Dresden. Weimar is well known because of its large cultural heritage and its importance in German history. The city was a focal point of the German Enlightenment and home of the leading personalities of the literary genre of Weimar Classicism, the writers Johann Wolfgang von Goethe and Friedrich Schiller. In the 19th century, famous composers like Franz Liszt made Weimar a music center and later, artists and architects like Henry van de Velde, Wassily Kandinsky, Paul Klee, Lyonel Feininger and Walter Gropius came to the city and founded the Bauhaus movement, the most important German design school of the interwar period. However, the political history of 20th-century Weimar was inconsistent: it was the place where Germany's first democratic constitution was signed after the First World War, giving its name to the Weimar Republic period in German politics (1918–33), as well as one of the cities mythologized by the National Socialist propaganda.

The 261st Infantry, still attached to the 6th Armored, is given a night assignment to capture another bridge, this one in the center of the city of Muhlhausen. This they do, "in wild west fashion", and keep the 6th Armored rolling. They continue to push eastward, and advance as far as Schlotheim, ten miles east of Muhlhausen.

The rest of the 65th continues to put pressure on German defenses, encountering "scattered, but frequently stubborn, enemy opposition." On April 3rd the 65th advances thirteen miles, and takes up position east of the Werra River.[308] The Division, for its continuous forward progress, has been given the nickname of "the Spearhead Division". Indeed, it is around this time that they also achieve the distinction of being the closest American unit to Berlin. What a prize that will be, they all think, when they roll into Berlin and capture the Fuhrer's principal city!

APRIL 4, 1945

The 65th finds itself temporarily assigned to VIII Corps, and the 260th has to wait for the 6th Armored Division to roll through with their tanks, which have been given priority of travel in the sector, the east bank of the Werra. The 259th proceeds towards Langensalza, and the 260th catches up when the 6th Armored has rumbled through. Erfurt and Weimar are still the Division's objectives, and they are the U.S. division closest to both of these centers. But both of these cities are given to other divisions to claim. The 65th is then ordered south, to a new sector. But for the next four days they will remain in this zone. And they will do serious battle with the Germans.

APRIL 5, 1945 - LANGENSALZA[309]

---

[308] The Werra River forms the right-source of the Weser. The Werra has its source near Eisfeld in southern Thuringia. After 182 miles the Werra joins the river Fulda in the town of Hann Münden, forming the Weser. The Werra Valley (German: Werratal) forms a natural border between the Rhön Mountains and the Thuringian Forest. Local attractions include Eiben Forest near Dermbach, the fairytale sandstone cave at Walldorf, the deepest lake in Germany formed by land subsidence (near Bernshausen), and the "Krayenburg", the ruins of a castle.

[309] Bad Langensalza (until 1956: Langensalza) is a spa town of 17,500 inhabitants in the district of Unstrut-Hainich, Thuringia, Germany. It was first mentioned in historical records ca. 932, as a village named "Salzaha". The town's name was changed to Langensalza ca. 1578, and "Bad" or "Bath" was added to the name in 1956. In 1075, Langensalza was the site of a battle, in which Emperor Henry IV defeated the rebelling Saxons and Thuringians. The town was plundered and damaged by fires during the Thirty Years' War (c. 1632). Fires again destroyed large

The 259th Regiment of the 65th approaches the Germans entrenched in Langensalza from the southwest, and it is evident that the Germans are prepared to defend this city strenuously. A railroad embankment faces the Regiment, and the only underpass through it is firmly barricaded. Heavy Sniper fire greets them as they make their way up the main road through neighboring Ufhoven. The Germans are slowly flushed from their positions, and tanks from the 748th Tank Battalion force their way through the barricaded underpass. The assault continues throughout the day, and into darkness, and a narrow corridor is carved through the city to its City Hall, which is reached at 2300 hours. A German counterattack is expected at every street intersection along this path through the city, but none ever materializes. The Germans, battered throughout the day by U.S. artillery and mortar fire, cut their losses and fade into the night. A number, however, remain behind, waving white flags of surrender.

APRIL 7, 1945 - STRUTH

The 3rd Battalion, 261st Infantry has located their command post at the hamlet of Struth, where they have holed up since the previous day. They form the left flank of the Division, and are in a somewhat exposed position. A force of 1,000 Germans lie in wait, with armor and SP guns,[310] about to begin an attack

---

parts of the town in 1711, including complete destruction of the town hall, which was rebuilt between 1742-1752. War again affected the town from 1756 to 1763, during the Seven Years' War; it was the scene of a battle in February 1761. In 1815 Langensalza became part of the Prussian Province of Saxony. In 1866 it was again the site of a battle between Prussia and Hanover during the Austro-Prussian War. American troops occupied the town in 1945.

[310] An SP gun was a "self-propelled gun". At the outbreak of World War II, virtually all artillery was still being moved around by artillery tractors or horses. While the German Blitzkrieg doctrine called for combined-arms action, which required fire support for armored units, during the invasion of Poland and France this was provided by the Luftwaffe using Stuka dive-bombers effectively acting as artillery. Conventional towed howitzers followed. As the war progressed, most nations developed self-propelled artillery. Some early attempts were often no more than a field gun or anti-tank gun mounted on a truck—a technique known in the British Army as carrying portee. These were mobile, but lacked protection for the crew. The next step was to mount the guns on a tracked chassis (often that of an obsolete or superseded tank) and provide an armored superstructure to protect the gun and its crew. Many of the early designs were improvised and the lessons learned led to better designs later in the war.

which has the goal of rolling through the 65th and ultimately retaking Muhlhausen, six miles to the east.

The first detection of enemy movement comes at 0230 hours, when an American picket manning an outpost north of Struth detects a "shadowy figure" moving stealthily about in the darkness. He fires a BAR[311] at the figure, who quickly disappears. A moment later a German grenade comes sailing over and explodes in a foxhole. Then all is quiet, until 0500, when the Germans unleash a tank attack west of the town, which quickly threatens to overwhelm L Company of the 261st. A German infantry attack simultaneously sweeps into the town from the north where it is met by K Company. Reinforcements are quickly called for, and two companies of the 260th swing into action as the two companies of the 3rd Battalion hold their places against the German advance, essentially checking it. L Company, 260th moves in from the west, while B Company, 260th circles around the town from the east. The 261st Infantry also gets into the fray, attacking the Germans from the south. L Company, 260th captures a group of German paratroopers who have hidden in a farmer's field under piles of hay. I Company, 261st stalls another German advance heading from neighboring Dorna. By mid-morning the battle has been raging on for five hours, but the outcome seems certain, as the 65th slowly pushes the Germans back from Struth. By 1300 hours the Germans are in full retreat, eleven of the sixteen tanks they began the battle with destroyed.

APRIL 9, 1945

The 65th assembles near Berka, about twelve miles to the southwest of Langensalza. It is assigned to VIII Corps as a reserve unit, behind the 87th and 89th Divisions. Over the next week the 65th will be involved in a number of "mopping up" actions behind the front-line assault divisions, ferreting out rogue German emplacements, and accepting surrendering German troops. The division's movement is generally to the southeast, with assembly points at

---

[311] "BAR" - Browning automatic rifle. The BAR is a family of American automatic rifles and machine guns used by the United States and numerous other countries during the 20th century. The primary variant of the BAR series was the M1918, chambered for the .30-06 Springfield rifle cartridge and designed by John Browning in 1917 for the American Expeditionary Forces in Europe as a replacement for the French-made Chauchat and M1909 Benét–Mercié machine guns that US forces had previously been issued. The BAR was designed to be carried by infantrymen during an assault advance while supported by a sling over the shoulder, or to be fired from the hip. The BAR never entirely lived up to the original hopes of the war department as either a rifle or a machine gun.

Waltershausen and Arnstadt.[312] It is clear now that they will not be going to Berlin. Berlin has bee reserved for the Russians.

APRIL 12, 1945 - WARM SPRINGS, GEORGIA

U.S. President Franklin Delano Roosevelt, while having his portrait painted by artist Elizabeth Shoumatoff, suffers a cerebral hemorrhage. "I have a terrific pain in the back of my head," he says, and slumps forward. It is a little past 1:00 PM. Aid is summoned, and doctors work feverishly on the President, but to no avail. At 3:35 PM, FDR dies. He is just 63 years old, but looks at least ten to fifteen years older. Harry S. Truman, FDR's Vice President, succeeds him.

On the same day, the concentration camps at Buchenwald and Belsen are liberated by the Allies.

APRIL 13, 1945

The Soviets take Vienna, after almost two weeks of constant battle.

℘

"Somewhere in Germany

April 15, 1945 [Sunday]

Dear Mother,
I thought I would drop you a line being that I got the time to do so. Everything is going along okay. I had a cold and bad cough but I am getting over it. The other day I gave my feet a good washing in some hot water. It was the first time I had the chance in about three weeks. This afternoon I expect to get to mass if the chaplain gets around. You see we have only two Catholic chaplains for our Regiment and he has to travel from town to town saying mass and sometimes he can't get to every town so we are just hoping he hits our town today. We were just talking about the difference of time between here and New York. There is six hours difference. It is 10:30 in the morning and it is 4:30 in the morning back home. So you can see that you will

---

[312] Arnstadt is a town in Ilm-Kreis, Thuringia, Germany, on the river Gera about 20 kilometers south of Erfurt, the capital of Thuringia. Arnstadt is one of the oldest towns in Thuringia, and has a well-preserved historic center with a partially preserved town wall. The town is nicknamed *Das Tor zum Thüringer Wald* ("The Gateway to the Thuringian Forest") because of its location on the northern edge of that forest.

be still sleeping while I will be eating my lunch. Mother I was wondering if you could send me some air mail stamps. I am out of them and all the fellows are too so everybody is writing home for some. Well how are you making out? I guess you probably bought a new Easter bonnet and Dad is raving over it as usual. What do you think about Roosevelt's death? It was all a big surprise to us. I thought that he was going to kick the bucket sooner or later but I didn't think he would do it so soon. I wonder what kind of president Truman will make. Some of the fellows think he will be all right being that he was in Congress for such a long time. Tell Dad that I really had some good wine yesterday. It seems it came from South America and boy it was good. I know now Mother you will be saying that I shouldn't be drinking because it isn't good for me. How are things doing around the house? Did Duke get the screens up yet? Over here I didn't see any and I don't think that they use them. I will close now. Love to all and I hope I hear from you soon.

Love,
Son John"

APRIL 16, 1945

Soviet troops on the outskirts of Berlin begin their final assault on Hitler's capital city.

American troops enter Nuremberg, the city where in several months a war crimes trial will commence to mete out justice to key Nazi perpetrators.

APRIL 17, 1945

At Arnstadt, the 65th Division is transferred back to XX Corps from VIII Corps. It will remain a unit within XX Corps until Germany surrenders, on May 7, 1945. The entire direction of the Third Army is changing, much to General George S. Patton's chagrin. His troops, continuing their drive across central Germany push into areas where forces of the First and Ninth Armies have been building. XX Corps is lopped off the Third Army and redeployed towards southeastern Germany, where rumors of a "last ditch" stand by the German Wehrmacht are rampant. Taking a long ride southward, the 65th passes through Coburg, Bamberg and Altdorf, where it relieves the 14th

Armored Division.[313]   A new objective zone is given to the 65th: continue southeast through Neumarkt[314] and cross the Danube[315] to Regensburg.[316]

---

[313] Coburg is a town located on the Itz River in the Upper Franconia region of Bavaria, Germany. Long part of one of the Thuringian states, it joined Bavaria by popular vote only in 1920. Until the revolution of 1918, it was one of the capitals of the Duchy of Saxe-Coburg and Gotha and the Duchy of Saxe-Coburg-Saalfeld. Through successful dynastic policies, the ruling princely family married into several of the royal families of Europe, the most notable being Prince Albert, who married Queen Victoria in 1840. As a result of these close links with the royal houses of Europe in the late 19th and early 20th centuries, Coburg was frequently visited by the crowned heads of Europe and their families. Coburg is also known as the location of Veste Coburg, one of Germany's largest castles. In 1530, Martin Luther lived there for six months during which he worked on translating the Bible into German. Today, Coburg's population is close to 41,500. Since it was little damaged in World War II, Coburg retains many historic buildings, making it a popular tourist destination.

Bamberg is a town in Upper Franconia, Germany, on the river Regnitz close to its confluence with the river Main. A large part of the town has been a UNESCO World Heritage Site since 1993.

Altdorf is a municipality in the district of Landshut, in Bavaria, Germany. It is situated 4 km northwest of Landshut.

[314] Neumarkt is a Landkreis (district) in Bavaria, Germany. It is bounded by (from the north and clockwise) the districts of Nürnberger Land, Amberg-Sulzbach, Schwandorf, Regensburg, Kelheim, Eichstätt and Roth.

[315] The Danube River rises in the town of Donaueschingen, in the Black Forest of Germany, at the confluence of the rivers Brigach and Breg. The Danube then flows southeast for about 1,700 miles, passing through five capital cities (Vienna, Bratislava, Budapest, Bucharest and Belgrade) before emptying into the Black Sea via the Danube Delta in Romania and Ukraine. The Danube, known by various names in other languages (in German: Donau), is Europe's second longest river, after the Volga. The Danube was once a long-standing frontier of the Roman Empire, and today flows through 10 countries, more than any other river in the world. After Germany, the Danube passes through or borders on Austria, Slovakia, Hungary, Croatia, Serbia, Romania, Bulgaria, Moldova and Ukraine before draining into the Black Sea. Its drainage basin extends into nine more countries. Since ancient times, the Danube has been a traditional trade route in Europe, nowadays 1,501 miles of its total length being navigable.

[316] Regensburg is a city in south-east Germany, at the confluence of the Danube, Naab and Regen rivers. With more than 150,000 inhabitants, Regensburg is the fourth-largest city in the State of Bavaria after Munich, Nuremberg and Augsburg. The city is the political, economic and cultural center and capital of the Upper Palatinate. The first settlements in Regensburg date from the Stone Age. The Celtic name *Radasbona* was the oldest given to a settlement near the present city.

The 65th advances rapidly in this zone, despite stiff Wehrmacht holding actions defending this rugged territory. Division artillery plays a big part both in transport, as well as reducing German pockets of resistance.

"Somewhere in Germany

April 18, 1945 [Wednesday]

Dear Mother,
I received the telegram that you and Dad sent. It came a little late although I was glad to get it. It seems it has been over a week since I heard from home. Mother if you don't hear from me write anyway because I like to hear that everything is okay home. It is starting to get hot now so I think summer is not far off. How is it at home? I was wondering if Duke still has that old rocking chair, the one that used to fall apart when I sat in it? How is Martin Moynihan making out now? Do you know when he will be finished with school? Tell him to stay there and don't be looking forward to combat because he will get a big surprise when he sees what it is like. Mother if you send another box put some tea in it because the tea in the last was very good. How are you making out in the Rosary Society? I will close now. Love to all.
Love,
Son John"

APRIL 20, 1945

In Berlin, Adolph Hitler marks his 56th birthday. He has contemplated making a retreat to the Eagle's Nest, a redoubt high in the mountains of Southern Germany, and there make a last ditch stand with other stalwarts of the Nazi Party. But he has changed his mind, and instead remains in Berlin, his crumbling capital.

In Neumarkt the Germans make a stand. The 259th and 260th Infantry Regiments hit the outskirts of the town, and their initial progress is smooth. But soon enemy SP, nebelwerfer and artillery fire stop the 65th's advance.

Around AD 90, the Romans built a fort there. It is nicknamed "the most Italian city north of the Alps." The medieval center of the city is a UNESCO World Heritage Site.

Also on the 20th, units of the Division overrun a subcamp of Bavaria's Flossenberg Concentration Camp. At its high point in March 1945, just a month earlier, Flossenberg and its subcamps held almost 53,000 prisoners. Executions of Russian prisoners of war was routine. On March 29, 1945, the SS officers commanding the camp hung 13 Allied POW's, including one U.S. soldier, who had been taken prisoner during the Normandy invasion the previous June. On April 9, 1945, the SS hung prominent German prisoners linked to the abortive July 20, 1944 assassination attempt on Hitler's life. Admiral Wilhelm Canaris, Major-General Hans Oster, and Pastor Dietrich Bonhoeffer met their end at the hangman's noose.

As U.S. forces approach the camp, the SS begins evacuating prisoners towards Dachau. 7,000 die on the journey. When the main camp is liberated by the 90th U.S. Infantry Division, only 1,500 prisoners remain. In all, while in operation from 1938 to 1945, over 30,000 prisoners will have died in Flossenberg and its subcamps. And this is a relatively small death camp.

APRIL 21, 1945

The Soviets reach Berlin, the prize denied General George S. Patton by political considerations and deal-making among the three major Allied powers - the United States, Great Britain and the Soviet Union.

The Third Battalion of the 260th, Private McGowan's battalion, continues to push through the town of Neumarkt, driving out German defenders in house-to-house combat. The First Battalion of the 259th circles around the town to the southeast, and captures retreating German defenders who are being pushed out of the town by the 260th. Fighting continues while the town begins to burn down above its defenders heads.

℘

"Somewhere in Germany

April 21, 1945 [Saturday]

Dear Mother,
I have been waiting for a letter from you for more than a week but I haven't received any as yet. I am writing this letter on a table in a beer tavern in which we are billeting. I was wondering if you had Red Gibbons's address because I want to write to him but I lost his address. How is Walter Cubita doing? I read he was sick in the Dyre Avenue News. *Do you know how he is getting along? Do you know who I was thinking of? Robbie Mahon, the last I heard of him he was somewhere in the Pacific. Can you give me a little*

information on him? Tell Dad he would be at home in this tavern for there is plenty to drink. I am enclosing some German money as a souvenir. This is Nazi money. We get paid in German money put up by the Allied governments. Mother how is Frankie's gang getting along? You said he wrote me but I haven't received his letter as yet. How is he getting along with all his neighbors up on the hill? I am going to close now and to let you know I am okay and don't worry. Love to all.

*Love,
Son John"*

APRIL 22, 1945

With bayonets and grenades the 260th digs out remaining individual German snipers from their hiding places in the rubble that remains of Neumarkt. The town is declared cleared, and the path to the Danube lies ahead.

APRIL 25-26, 1945

Three days later the Division is on the north bank of the swiftly-flowing Danube River, assembling for the push south across this historic landmark. At 0200 on the 26th, in the darkness of night, the crossing commences. The 65th crosses the river west of Regensburg, with orders to then swing around the city and attack it from behind. The 71st Division crosses to the east of Regensburg, in similar fashion. The first units to cross for the 65th are 2nd Battalion, 260th, and 1st and 3rd Battalions, 261st. The 259th has been placed in Division reserve, to follow later. The care, precision and secrecy of the crossing is attested to by the fact that enemy outposts on the southern bank, near Matting, the landing site, are taken completely by surprise by forward elements of the 260th. German sentries awaken to find bayonets pointed at their throats, and quickly surrender. They are glad to be surrendering to American troops, knowing that Russian troops would likely not have given them the option.

The 260th quickly fans out on the morning of the 26th, though they run into heavier opposition later that day. The 261st, who have landed near Kapfelberg, have a hotter time. They battle their way through Lengfeld, push on towards Abbach, encountering heavy enemy fire all the way.[317]

Meanwhile, the rest of the Division continues the Danube crossing, which lasts well into the next day, the 27th. Engineers work feverishly to ferry troops

---

[317] Bad Abbach is a municipality in the district Kelheim, Bavaria, Germany. Due to its sulphurous springs it has the status of a spa town.

across, now under fire from German 88s. By 2100 hours a treadway bridge[318] is finished across the river, and the heavy trucks and equipment make their way onto the far bank.

Unknown to the Americans, the German commander in Regensburg has taken to his heels the morning of the 26th. He has been replaced by another commander, who mulls over the wisdom - or lack thereof - of continued resistance.

APRIL 27, 1945

The struggle for Abbach continues, and 1st Battalion, 260th goes to the aid of the 261st and carves a path through the defending Germans. The Germans begin to melt away, and the 260th and 261st move on towards the city of Regensburg. A message is received from the newly-appointed German commander in Regensburg. He wishes to surrender the city. At 1030 his offer is accepted by General John E. Copeland, Assistant Division Commander, and Colonel Frank Dunkley, Commander of the 260th Infantry. By day's end, patrols from the 260th are walking the streets of this cathedral city, vigilant as ever for rogue snipers, but confident that in this city, at least, they have little to fear.

By day's end the 261st is deployed south of Regensburg. The 259th protects the right flank of the division, west of the city. Remaining elements of XX Corps, having crossed the Danube behind the 65th, continue onward into Austria, while the 65th, battle weary but victorious, goes into Corps reserve once more.

APRIL 28, 1945

In Italy, Benito Mussolini, Il Duce, is captured by Italian partisans and hung. Venice is captured by the Allies.

§

Post-marked "U. S. ARMY POSTAL SERVICE MAY 6, 1945 8:00 PM".

"Somewhere in Germany

---

[318] A "treadway bridge" is a type of pontoon bridge, designed to carry medium tanks. It had steel treadways for runways, which were emplaced by means of a truck mounted crane. It used special rubber pontoons.

April 28, 1945 [Saturday]

Dear Mother,
Being that I got the chance I thought I would drop you a line or two to let you know that everything is going along okay. We have been on the move a lot and have crossed a big river.[319] I am writing this letter on a desk in a German apartment and boy what a time we are having. We have all the whiskey and liquor that you can drink and plenty of eats. It's just like being back home with all the comforts that are here. I received two letters that you wrote in April and they are very interesting. I am glad to hear that Dad is working on the garden. Tell the Duke to keep him at it. The Duke ought to be in this town I am in for he would have a good time. There is a whole railway yard filled with cars of stuff and everybody is down there breaking into the goods that are in the cars and carrying it off. He could have a time investigating all the stuff that is around here. I was talking to a Catholic priest today and he said that they were very glad to get liberated by us and he was surprised at all the Catholics that were in the American army. He said he would like us to come to church any time we wanted for he would say mass for us. I received a letter from Richie Simmons whom I was glad to hear from. He gave me all the news about himself and told me of some that was about the neighborhood. I will have to drop him a line when I get the chance. Mother you said in one of your letters that John Lucas was going to try and look me up. Do you know what Army he is in and A.A. battery he is in? I am in the 65th Infantry Division in the 3rd Army. So if you want to send him my Division number and Army number maybe we could find out the whereabouts of each other. When is Martin Moynihan going to get his commission? I guess that will be a big day. I will have to close now being that I go on guard in five minutes. Love to all.

Love,
Son John"

APRIL 29, 1945

Forces of the U.S. 7th Army liberate the Dachau concentration camp.

---

[319] The "big river" is the Danube, but John is prevented from disclosing any information about their movements, other than the fact that they are "somewhere in Germany".

APRIL 30, 1945 - BERLIN

In Hitler's underground bunker in Berlin, newlyweds Adolph Hitler and Eva Braun, married for one day, ingest hydrocyanic acid, the liquid form of cyanide. Death comes quickly. A smell of almonds pervades the chamber, characteristic of the poison. Hitler's Reich, which he swore would last a thousand years, is crumbling outside under the Russian onslaught.

TWENTY-THREE - "THE REICH FALLS"

MAY 1-2, 1945

The 65th Division is taken out of reserve, and leaves Regensburg and vicinity to advance to the southeast, with the south bank of the Danube on their left. They follow the 13th Armored Division across the Isar River at Plattling, and then pass through the 13th Armored to continue driving towards the Inns River.[320] The Isar is crossed at midnight on the first day of May. The Inns is

---

[320] The Isar River is a river in Tyrol, Austria and Bavaria, Germany. Its source is in the Karwendel range of the Alps in Tyrol. It enters Germany near Mittenwald, and flows through Bad Tölz, Munich, and Landshut before reaching the Danube near Deggendorf. At 183 miles in length, it is the fourth largest river in Bavaria, after the Danube, Inn, and Main. It is Germany's second most important tributary of the Danube after the Inn. It is quite likely that the Isar was used as a trade route, even in prehistoric times, to transport wares from the Alps and even Italy towards the Danube with rafts. An existing trade road from the Inn valley across Seefelder Pass into the northern foothills of the Alps was built up and called Via Raetia by the Romans. The town of Mittenwald thus became an important trade post.
Plattling is a town in the district of Deggendorf, in Bavaria, Germany. The town is situated on the river Isar, 9 km southwest of Deggendorf, just before the river enters the Danube. Near the city-center in the river there is a wave/hole which is one of Europe's best play spots for freestyle kayaking. Around the time of World War II, the regions around Plattling became a conservative base of Nazi support, producing top-ranking SS officers like Leo Grasmeier and Heinrich Himmler. Until 1993 both Heinrich Himmler and Adolf Hitler earned places on Plattling's list of 20 Honorable Citizens.
On April 26, 1945, concentrated fire from small arms and automatic weapons pinned down K Company of the 65th Infantry Division's 260th Infantry Regiment as it entered Plattling. First Lieutenant David Ewing Ott from the 868th Field Artillery Battalion, a future Lieutenant General, served as attached forward artillery observer. Because of his exceedingly precise fire direction, three small bursts silenced the enemy. Under hostile observation, Ott preceded the most forward elements by 1,000 yards to direct artillery fire from a high ridge. It resulted in 150 enemy casualties, and the surrender of a German infantry platoon. On May 1, 2011, the city of Plattling hosted veterans and relatives of the 65th Infantry Division. The delegation joined local representatives for the dedication of a Memorial Marker to the Division's humanitarian assistance provided to survivors of the Plattling concentration camp. Mayor Erich Schmid and members of the city council welcomed the Americans at St. Jacob Cemetery.

reached the next day. Between the two rivers a number of skirmishes take place, but none so serious as to delay the advancing assault units. Years later Private McGowan will recall one such event: "After crossing the Danube River our Company was marching in columns on a road to Passau when suddenly we were ambushed by machine gun fire. Some guys around me were hit. Thank God I rolled over into a ditch next to the road. It was a close call. I got up to help the medic with the wounded."

MAY 2, 1945

German troops in Italy surrender.

Passau is entered on the 2nd of May.[321] It is defended by 300 SS troops, the most diabolic of Hitler's legions, who have sworn a death oath to their Fuhrer. The 65th, along with artillery and tank destroyer battalions, annihilate the town's SS defenders. The few that remain alive after the U.S. assault surrender at 0030 on May 3rd.

On the 2nd, the 261st Infantry locates to a point some eight miles south of Passau, on the Inns River opposite Scharding, in the town of Neuhaus. A strategic bridge crosses the river there, the Neuhaus-Scharding Bridge. It is a long and impressive structure, and reconnaissance patrols of the 261st arrive there at 0515 on the 2nd, just as retreating Germans blow the bridge, in a dazzling spectacle of destruction.

When the rest of the Battalion arrives in Neuhaus around noon on the 2nd, they immediately set to establishing defensive positions both in and around the outskirts of the town. They receive reinforcements in the form of two companies of the 265th Engineer Battalion, who take up positions on the north bank of the river. It will be their job to enable the crossing of the Inns River, so that the Germans can be dislodged from their positions in and around Scharding.

A peace overture is made by the Americans. At 1430 an officer of the 261st, under a flag of truce, crosses the Inns River to Scharding and locates the

---

The Inns River is a river in Switzerland, Austria and Germany. It is a right tributary of the Danube and is 322 miles long. The highest point of its drainage basin is the summit of Piz Bernina, at 13,284 feet. The Engadine, the valley of the En, is the only Swiss valley whose waters end up in the Black Sea (via the Danube).

[321] Passau is a town in Lower Bavaria, Germany, also known as the Dreiflüssestadt ("City of Three Rivers") because the Danube is joined there by the Inn from the south and the Ilz from the north.

ranking German general. He asks him whether the Germans wish to surrender and avoid further bloodshed. The reply is that they are not ready to capitulate. The officer returns to the Neuhaus side. The Engineers, closest to the Germans, set up machine gun positions and dig in. Their action is just in time, for the Germans open up on the opposite shore with a burst of machine gun fire. For the next few minutes the Engineers step into the role of Infantrymen, and return fire, maintaining a brief but fierce exchange with the Germans, until the German guns go silent.

While this short battle rages, 1st Battalion, 261st, sends out a few scouting parties to locate some boats and a potential fording site to cross the Inns River to the German-held shore. They turn up a large-sized rowboat, and something more: the Judge Advocate Generals of both the German Army and Navy, who have found themselves stranded on the Neuhaus side when the Neuhaus-Scharding Bridge was blown. While these high-ranking prisoners are taken to the rear, the 261st prepares to begin ferrying men across the Inns in the rowboat, while the Germans entrenched in Scharding suffer through a massive barrage of artillery and heavy weapons fire for two and a half hours during the afternoon, ending around half past five o'clock. As a result, not a shot is fired at the 261st in their initial crossing. Transport continues throughout the evening, as additional craft are brought forward, this time consisting of four engineer assault boats. By midnight two companies of the 261st have crossed, and the rest of the Regiment follows by 0800 on the morning of the 3rd.

MAY 3, 1945

Scharding is quickly overrun. German troops holed up in its cellars to survive the artillery barrage of the previous day find the Americans solidly in charge of the ground floors, and quickly surrender. During the day, more units of the 259th and 260th are ferried over, and the bridgehead is consolidated.

With the assault regiments having pushed through, significant German troops are left behind and seriously harass the advancing U.S. troops. 2nd Battalion, 260th is deployed to the rear on the 3rd and effectively deals with a group of several hundred German diehards who they surround in a wooded area off the road. No more harassing of the units advancing behind the 65th occurs.

MAY 4, 1945

Engineers complete a pontoon bridge across the Inn at 0900, and the remaining units of the Division join their comrades on the far shore. Augmented in force, the 261st Infantry branches out from the bridgehead and moves rapidly southeast from the Division's right flank. The 260th advances north from the bridgehead, on the Division's left flank, and then turns southeast also, to run a parallel path towards Linz, the Division's next objective, and a key goal. Linz is Austria's second city, surpassed only by fabled Vienna. And eight miles southeast of Linz flows the Enns River, which has been decided upon by Allied commanders and politicians far above Division, Corps or Army level as the dividing line between U.S. and Soviet Union forces. The 65th picks up its pace, eager to be first to enter Linz.

MAY 5th, 1945

For the 65th, there will be some disappointment. The morning of the 5th is spent pushing forward on their last march through the German Reich, confident they will be the first American troops to enter Linz. They encounter some limited German resistance, but it is a half-hearted effort, and most of the German troops they encounter are intent on surrendering, preferring to surrender to U.S. troops rather than the Russians. But some advance elements of XII Corps, coming in from the Division's left flank, beat them to the prize and enter the city about noon on the 5th. Five hours later they are relieved by the 65th, as the 260th Regiment rolls into the city in force. The 261st moves on to the Enns River, beyond which they are forbidden to cross, lest the Russians be denied their slice of the Reich pie.

MAY 6TH, 1945

The next day, the 6th, the 259th Infantry takes its place to the right of the 261st, and the Enns River line is complete. Also on the 6th, the Germans on the opposite shore surrender unconditionally, and begin to cross the Enns River westward, by any means that they can, to avoid becoming prisoners of the Russians, who will show little mercy to the men who have ravaged their land since the war in the East began.

℘

"Somewhere in Austria

May 7, 1945 [Monday]

Dear Mother,
  Well I am still waiting on that second package you sent but it hasn't come as yet but your letters are coming okay. I get one about every three days.
  I am now somewhere in Austria but I can tell you that we made a bridgehead across the Danube River in assault boats. I helped paddle across. Little did I think back in civilian life that I would row a boat across the Danube.

From here we went to the city of Regensburg, which you can find on the map. Here we had a good time. In my last letter I told you about the place and how I went to confession to a German monk who could speak English. I later went to communion in the cathedral there. Boy, what a beautiful church. This is getting more like a sightseeing tour every day. Austria is a very pretty country. Sitting in the distance are the snowcapped Austrian Alps and what a sight it is to see them. At present I am in a big city where there has been considerable damage. I can't tell you the name of it but see if you can find it on the map. We are living in an apartment house and 7 of us have a whole floor to ourselves. The best thing of all is that we all have beds and are they comfortable. By the way I forgot to mention it but tell the Duke I got a brand new old fashioned pipe for him and when I get the chance I am going to send it home. Yesterday I went to mass and communion in the most beautiful church I ever saw. It looks as if the whole altar was made out of gold and it had some wonderful paintings above it. The thing that got me about this was that they have a martyr in a sealed glass casket in the side of the church. It was really something to see. Well how is everything getting along back home? Did you go out visiting Aunt Kitty again? I wonder if I told you that I received a letter from her and she put in her John's address so as soon as I get time I will drop him a line. Everything is going along okay with me and I think that this trouble over here will be over soon. I will close now. Give my love to all.
Love,
Son John"

MAY 7, 1945

A telephone call is received at the command post of the 65th Division. The German High Command has surrendered unconditionally, effective as of 0001 May 9th. The news is quickly relayed to the scattered units of the 65th.

THE GERMAN HIGH COMMAND SIGNED AN AGREEMENT FOR UNCONDITIONAL SURRENDER OF LAND SEA AND AIR FORCES AT ZERO SEVEN ONE FOUR ONE STOP. ACTIVE OPERATIONS WILL CEASE AT ZERO NINE ZERO ZERO ZERO ONE STOP. EFFECTIVE IMMEDIATELY ALL TROOPS WILL STOP MOVEMENT AND ACTIVE OPERATIONS STOP. DUE TO THE FACT THAT COMMUNICATIONS ARE SO POOR THERE WILL PROBABLY BE SOME ACTION ON THE PART OF THE ENEMY AND WE WILL HAVE TO REMAIN ON THE DEFENSIVE.

Major Stanley E. Reinhart, with several subordinates, travels 45 miles through the darkness, east to Erlauf, to meet his Russian counterpart, who has traveled

55 miles west from Vienna, which the Soviets took on April 13th, after a pitched battle of almost two weeks duration. There he meets Russian Major General D. A. Drechkin, Commander of the Seventh Guard Parachute Division, who began his journey westward from the ruins of Stalingrad in January 1943, when Private McGowan was still a student in high school. For them and the men under them, the war in the European Theater of Operations is over. The war in the Pacific Theater, of course, is another matter entirely. The Japanese seem as determined as ever to hold out until the bitter end, even if it proves suicidal for the bulk of their people.

MAY 9, 1945

Herman Goering is captured by troops of the U.S. 7th Army.

℘

"Somewhere in Austria

May 13, 1945 [Sunday]

Dear Mother,
Today is Mother's Day and I want to send you my love and wish you a Happy Mother's Day. You have probably heard the good news about the war being over. I knew it wasn't going to be long because the Jerries just kept falling back and we just pushed closer and closer until we met the Russians. I bet there was a lot of excitement in New York. Over the radio they said London and New York were going wild. As yet I don't know what they are going to do with us. There is a rumor that we may stay here as occupational troops and will be able to go to school. I think that it would be swell if we could go to school over here. I received a letter from Dad and two from you the other day. By the way I can tell you that I am in the city of Linz in Austria. If you look at a map you can see it is very near Vienna and is on the Danube River.
Yesterday was a big day here. General Patton met some Russian general and boy what a big show. There were more generals here than I have ever seen in one place. This afternoon I expect to go to mass in the cathedral at 2 o'clock. I expect they will have a big crowd being today is Mother's Day. You know mother, there isn't much to write about over here and I expect there will be less to write being that everything has quieted down. So don't expect too big a letter from me. You understand, don't you?
Tell Dad I heard about the English ship Dido[322] *that he talks so much about. It seems it was in on the Norwegian surrender. Tell him also that I*

---

[322] H.M.S. *Dido* was a British warship that saw extensive action during World War II. *Dido's* last mission in the war was to go to Copenhagen, firing the last naval shot in

could go for a good, cold bottle of beer. It is very hot here and the Austrians have some schnapps. It is just like our whiskey. A couple of drinks and you are flat on your back. Mother I want to thank you for the air mail stamps. They were just what I needed. I had to buy a few before receiving yours. Well I will close now. Give my regards to all and love.

Love,
Son John"

"Austria

May 20, 1945 [Sunday]

Dear Mother,

Well today is Sunday and as usual I am expecting to go to church. It is a very dismal day out for it is raining and I think I will go to movies this afternoon. Oh yes the army has taken over two movie houses in town and are operating them. They are also going to open a P.X. in a department store and is to have all the things like beer, cokes and etc.

We are still living in style. All I do is pull a little guard duty. In our house now we have a Polish working. He cleans up and makes the beds. You see he is one of those slave laborers and he can't get transportation home so we pick him up. All we give him is three meals like we get and he is very thankful. He comes to our house about 6 in the morning and shines all our shoes before we get up. This life over here is better than civilian life back in the states. All I do is sleep and eat, but I think it can't last forever.

How are things going along at home? How is Dad making out doing day work?

I received a letter from Frankie. He didn't say much but said everything was going along okay. By the way I also received a letter from Andy Garbarini. It seems he got wounded again. That's his second time and he is now back in the States. He says that he had some trouble with his liver and that he has trench foot.[323] I think that he will get a discharge from the army on account of the trench foot. It is a very serious thing in some cases. Fellows lose a whole leg or foot. I hope he pulls through anyway. Richie

---

the war in Europe on the way, for the surrender of the German *Kriegsmarine* which was signed aboard *Dido*. After the signing, *Dido* escorted the German cruisers *Prinz Eugen* and *Nürnberg* to Wilhelmshaven.

[323] Trench foot was a serious condition, which, left untreated, could result in gangrene of the toes or foot, requiring amputation. John's father Eddy would have seen much of it during his time in the trenches during the First World War, and no doubt had some stories to tell his son about it.

Simmons wrote and said that he received a letter from me and was very glad to hear that I was okay. He also said that he was getting along okay. Mother I am going to enclose a photograph of a buddy and myself taken at our foxhole when we had to dig in at Muhlhausen[324] Germany. After this picture was taken we were attacked by 9 Jerry planes. See if you can pick out our machine gun. If you wonder what I have on, it is a German winter jacket. It was very warm. I will close now. Love to all.

*Love,
Son John"*

MAY 23, 1945

SS-Reichsführer Himmler commits suicide. The German High Command and Provisional Government is imprisoned.

MAY 25, 1945 - PATTON'S HQ - BAD TOLZ, BAVARIA, GERMANY

Patton, in the aftermath of the German surrender, has been appointed military governor of Bavaria. His HQ is in the former commandant's office of what had been an SS officer's training school thirty miles south of Munich. Despite impressive creature comforts, Patton yearns for one last battle. He is itching for a command in the Pacific Theater, where operations against Japan show no

---

[324] Mühlhausen is a city in the north-west of Thuringia, Germany, 3 miles north of Niederdorla, the country's geographical center, 31 miles north-west of Erfurt, 40 miles east of Kassel and 31 miles south-east of Göttingen. Mühlhausen was first mentioned in 967 and became one of the most important cities in central Germany in the late Middle Ages. In the mid-13th century, it became a *Freie Reichsstadt*, an independent and republican self-ruled member state of the Holy Roman Empire, controlling an area of approximately 85 square miles and 19 regional villages. Due to its long-distance trade, Mühlhausen was prosperous and influential with a population of 10,000 around 1500. Because it was spared from later destruction, Mühlhausen today has a great variety of historical buildings with one of the largest medieval city centers remaining in Germany, covering a huge area within the inner city wall. There are eleven Gothic churches, several patricians' houses and a near completely preserved fortification. Johann Sebastian Bach worked as the city's organist in 1707-08. The theologian Thomas Müntzer, a leading person in the German Peasants' War, gave sermons here and was executed in front of the city hall. John A. Roebling, the constructor of the Brooklyn Bridge, was born in Mühlhausen.

sign of abating. His chief competitor is U.S. 1st Army's General Courtney Hodges, who almost suffered a nervous breakdown when the Germans burst through his defenses during the early days of the Battle of the Bulge. General George C. Marshall, U.S. Army Chief of Staff, will make the ultimate decision, and he bides his time. Aside from that, Patton argues to keep at least a third of U.S. troops in Europe, ready should an engagement with the Soviet Union be necessary, as he strongly believes it will be, and should be.

A visiting Russian general requests an audience with Patton, and is ushered into the general's office. Speaking impeccable English, he complains about the amount of Germans the U.S. is allowing to flee across the Danube River into the American Zone of Occupation, often using stolen Soviet boats. A demand is made for return of these craft to the rightful owners, the Russian Army.

Patton has had enough. He smashes his storied revolver on his desk, and instructs his aides to "Get this son of a bitch out of here!" He also issues an order to alert three divisions, including the 65th, to be ready to launch an attack against the Russians to the east, where they occupy what will become Soviet-controlled Eastern Europe during the Cold War. The Russian general departs, terrified, and Patton's order goes out to the three divisions. They should commence attacking the Russian lines as soon as practical.

A few moments later Patton rescinds the order, and a Third World War following closely on the heels of the Second is narrowly averted. "Sometimes you have to put on an act," Patton explains. "And I'm not going to let any Russian marshal, general or private tell me what I have to do. That's the last we'll hear from those bastards!"

℘

"May 26, 1945 [Saturday]

Dear Mother,
    Everything is going along okay and I am still in Linz. We do a little guard duty but on the whole we lay around most of the time. The only amusement is the movies and the pictures are ones that we either have seen in the states or ones that are very old. There is a lot of talk of us going back to the states and then on to the Pacific[325] but what I hear I think that we will be over here for about 6 more months.

---

[325] Having won one war in Europe, battle weary soldiers were now preparing to jump in feet first to the Pacific Theater of Operations, where the war with Japan, in most assessments, was expected to drag on for several more years. A bit of verse

I heard over the radio that there is a serious meat shortage back in the states. How are you getting on with the present situation? I was thinking that you ought to store up on can goods and other articles. Potatoes are another thing that you can keep for a long time. From what we hear the people in the states are going to tighten up their belts and go on a light diet. Oh yeah, that picture of you was very good. Who took the picture? I was showing it to some women over here and she said that American women were nice looking and dressed very well. Of course I thanked her for the compliment.

If you are wondering how many points[326] I have well it's on 37 so I think I will be in the army for some time yet. I had to laugh, we got a new fellow into our outfit and he only has 9 points. Boy, he'll be in for life. Well I just had to go downstairs to get a drink some fellows made up. Boy was it strong. Mother I was wondering if and when I hit home again if I could have the gang up and throw a real good party. The fellows say that they will chip in for everything. But let's wait till I get home. That's what I tell them. I will close now. Love to all.

Love,
Son John"

---

caught the typical soldier's sentiments pretty well: "The Golden Gate in Forty Eight." As troops prepared for the cataclysmic invasion of mainland Japan, casualty estimates ranged upwards of one million soldiers dead. Ultimately events would take a far different turn, in the aftermath of Hiroshima and Nagasaki, which finally brought the Japanese Emperor and his military advisers to their senses.

[326] The "point system" worked like this: points were accrued for months in service, time in combat, number of children under eighteen, and medals awarded (e.g. Bronze Star, Purple Heart, etc.) The more points a soldier could accumulate, the quicker he would be sent back home to the States.

TWENTY-FOUR - "WHERE TO NEXT?"

JUNE 5, 1945

The Allies - including now France, along with the U.S., Great Britain and Russia - divide up Germany and Berlin into four occupation zones and take over the governmental administration of each. It is one day less than a full year since the Normandy invasion, at which time the outcome of the war was still a gamble.

℘

"June 6, 1945 [Wednesday]

Dear Mother,

Today is a holiday here in Europe for it is the anniversary of D-E Day when we invaded France. We have started to drill and have calisthenics. It is just like being back in the States. Marching is our specialty. We have parades once a week and it is to impress upon the people that they lost the war and we are their conquerors. I am sorry that I don't write very often but we have been kept very busy with guard and such that I just forgot to write and time passes by so quickly that weeks seem to go by just like one day to another. Tomorrow we are expected to move up to a new place up near the Czechoslovakian border and it is 25 miles just north of Linz so I think we will be able to get off now and then. I have just come back from taking a shower in the public baths here. They are under army control now. They are very nice. Each fellow gets a tile room to himself with shower and all. It is just like being at home in your own bathroom. I expect also to go swimming for there are a great number of pools open here to soldiers. On the whole everything is getting better here. They are selling beer and Coca-Cola in the P.X. and the movies are good. They are also starting to get floor shows with movie actors and actresses and etc. I think that occupational army will be just like back in the States. The weather here is getting warm and sticky just like it does back home but it is nice and cool at night, enough to have a blanket on you. I am glad to hear that Dad's and Duke's gardens are getting along so good. What does Frankie have to say about their gardens? By the way Mother I received the oranges. They were swell. I got 7 good ones out of the box and the rest weren't any good so I think that is pretty good for the distance that they traveled, don't you? Mother in my letters that Rickie[327] wrote me he never mentioned a thing about

---

[327] Rickie probably refers to Richie Simmons. What might have been "the matter" with his sister is unknown.

his sister so maybe he doesn't know. I never mention anything in my letters about the matter. Well I think I will sign off for now. Love to all.

*Love,
Son John"*

℘

"June 10, 1945 [Sunday]

Dear Mother,
    Well I am now stationed just on the Czechoslovakian border and we are acting as border guards between Austria and Czechoslovakia. The weather has been rather miserable for it has been raining for three days straight and it keeps us indoors most of the time. We are staying in a school building which is right next to our post and the only thing wrong with this place is that we have to sleep on the floors for there are no beds to be found. It is healthy otherwise being away out in the country. We have a little swimming hole built and we spend most of our time playing around in the water and boy does it feel good to get in for a swim.
    This morning I walked about 2 miles to go to church in a small town. I was surprised to see such a big church as I did and also surprised at the nice altar they had inside. All the people think it strange when they see us going to church for the German radio used to tell them that all we were was gangsters and would kill everybody around. The Germans really told them some awful things about us. But they are quickly changing their minds about us. I received the letter in which you put the Honor Roll and list of the names of fellows in service. Too bad it had to rain and spoil it all. I think I know the brother that you said you met. His name is Brother Victor.[328] By the way if Andy comes to visit you tell him to send me his new address for I lost the one he sent me while he was in the hospital. I will close now. Give my love to all.

*Love,
Son John"*

℘

JUNE 13, 1945

Patton receives word that he has been passed over for a Pacific Theater command. Marshall has chosen General Courtney Hodges over Patton to be General Douglas MacArthur's right hand man in the continuing campaign against the Japanese. For Patton, both the war and his career in the military are over.

---

[328] Brother Victor, presumably one of the brothers at Mt. St. Michael Academy.

The United Nations Charter is signed in San Francisco.

The 65th receives news that they shouldn't expect to be going home any time soon. They are now part of the "occupational" army, being kept overseas in Austria to maintain order until the country can return to some semblance of normality. They will also be part of a ready reserve of forces available for shipment to the Pacific, if needed for the imminent invasion of mainland Japan, or to stand against Russia, should that become necessary.

℘

"June 26, 1945 [Monday]

Dear Mother,
 I just received two swell letters from you so I thought I would answer them now. Well the biggest news here is that our Division is temporary occupational troops here in Austria. So that means that we will probably be here for about six months or maybe longer than that. We don't know as yet where in Austria we will be stationed. I think we will stay here until they set up some kind of government or other.
 The other day we went on a boat ride up the Danube. It was very nice. It took 7 hours and it reminded me of taking a trip up the Hudson back home. They served two meals and boy did we eat. I guess the water made everybody hungry. Along the trip we saw many old castles and monasteries. They say that they dated away back.
 Mother about my bonds and such I am having a $50 bond taken out every month and I am also having a $10 allotment sent home too. Are they sending all of this to you? If not write me and I will try and see what the trouble is, but I think everything will be all right.
 It would be okay for you to send my camera but if you do, send some films for they are very scarce over here. If you can't get any films don't send the camera. About sending packages Mother, I am always glad to receive something to eat and so are the fellows. Usually at night we build a fire and then go around to the farms and hunt up some eggs. Then we come back and heat up some coffee and fry the eggs. This of course is our midnight snack after chow.
 Too bad Dad's garden isn't coming along so good. I bet Duke dug up all his seeds so Dad's garden wouldn't beat his. By the way, how is Frankie's garden getting along, and how is the family making out? Did he add a new one yet, "oh yea"? Oh, tell Martin to drop me a line when he gets a chance for I didn't hear from him in a long time. I didn't as yet receive a letter from the Mount for a contribution toward a fund. Boy from what those articles said that you sent me they really must have had some time in New York for the 86th

Division.[329] *I hope when we get there we get just as good a time. I also received a letter from Richie Simmons today. He said everything is going along okay and hopes it will be over soon.*[330] *I will sign off now. Love to all.*

Love,
Son John"

P.S. No more censorship."

---

[329] The 86th Division (the "Blackhawk" Division) was originally a New York unit raised during the Civil War, and had strong ties to New York. They followed a similar path through Europe as the 65th, just a little behind them. They were transferred back to the States shortly following the war's conclusion, and treated to a true heroes' welcome by the citizens of New York City.

[330] Simmons, somewhere in the Pacific, is talking about the still-ongoing war with Japan.

TWENTY-FIVE - "OCCUPATION ARMY"

JULY 1, 1945

American, British, and French troops move into Berlin, up to that point controlled in its entirety by the Russians. The city is carved up into four zones, beginning over 40 years as a divided city, East Berlin and West Berlin.

"July 2, 1945 [Monday]

Dear Mother,
  Today is Monday and I thought I would receive a letter from you today but I didn't. As a rule I get one in Monday's mail but it will probably come tomorrow. Well, yesterday myself and some of the fellows took off to town and went to 10 o'clock mass. It was very drawn out with the priest giving a half hour speech.
  You would be surprised at the weather here at present it is very cold and all it does day in and out is rain. I hope it gets warm soon so we can go swimming again in our lake here. Last night we got two bottles of drink, one wine and the other champagne. It was given to each squad by Gen. Eisenhower as a little reward to quench our thirst.
  Mother I was wondering if Dad could have the Daily News *newspaper sent to me every day because we like to hear news of home and what's doing around New York. I think Dad could do it. Ask him, will you?*
  From what we hear the fellows that are going back are having a hell of a time in New York and other cities. You ought to hear the fellows here talk about what they are going to do. You would have a good laugh, but it will sure be good to get back and talk to people that can speak English instead of using arm and hand signals or something.
  Oh, yeah, at present I have two battle stars and we expect a third. So that gives me 35 points. If we get this other star I will have 40. Mother, you would be surprised how they give medals out over here. It seems each Division is given so many medals and they give them out any way they want to. For instance, the "Purple Heart" is a joke. Some fellows who need five points to have enough to get them out and they didn't even get a scratch. About that "Bronze Star", I know in outfits they roll dice for them. So don't get fooled when you see a fellow with a lot of medals. Most of the time the ones who deserve them don't get them. Our Lieutenant wanted to give a bronze star for capturing four Germans one night when I was on guard. But I told him I didn't

want it because it was in the line of duty and I didn't really deserve it. You see after the war was over here our Division had a lot of medals left over so they just gave them to anybody they felt like.

  Well, how's everything doing around the neighborhood? Is there any new excitement that happened? How are you making out with your secretary job? Did you have to make any new speeches yet? Well, I will close now. Love to all.

Love,
Son John"

"July 10, 1945 [Tuesday]

Dear Mother,
  Well the biggest news here is that our Division is going to be broken up. So this means that we will all go to new outfits and may get home quicker than we thought. It seems that most of the fellows are going back to the Armored so I guess that's where I will go. Wouldn't it be funny when I get back to the States if they sent me to Fort Knox again? Oh yeah Mother don't send the camera because I don't think it will get here in time and I will probably get home in a few months or if you sent the camera already it's okay because I get in time to come.

  In this letter Mother you will find a money order. It is money I saved up, amounting to $70. Do you get my bond and allotment of $10 every month okay now? If not tell me in your next letter.

  I hear that you had a big heat wave around New York and vicinity. I bet you and Dad drink Mr. Edling dry in beer. "Oh, yeah!"

  Glad to hear that Pete Thomas was up to see you. From what you say he must like the Air Corps. Their work is much cleaner and they get the best in eats. Did Pete say anything about where Walter Cubita is or if he heard from him?

  Yesterday Andy Garbarini dropped me a V-Mail and said that he was back in the hospital again. He says everything is going along okay. Well that's about all I can think of now so I will close. Give my regards to all.

Love,
Son John"

"July 11, 1945 [Wednesday]

Dear Mother,

I just received two letters from you today so I thought I would answer them. I was glad you received a package from me. There should be another one soon because I sent two of them about the same time. About the pipe for Duke I didn't send it because I thought it would get broken with all the handling it would go through. I will keep the pipe and take it home with me.

I had to laugh and so did the rest of the fellows when I read to them how you said that they planned a big day for us on the fourth of July. Mother I think it's a joke about how they tell the people back home how all these movie stars are going overseas. The only places they go are to the big cities where they can live in comfort and have a good time. Since we have been over here we never saw one American show. The only ones we see are Austrians who try to sing American songs and such.

Well there isn't any new news on our moving as yet but I don't think it will be long before we go to a new Division. It seems like they are shifting all the fellows around to new Divisions.

How was the bazaar? Did you or Dad win anything, or did you spend all your money? I hear that they made out pretty good with the money end of the bazaar. They ought to be getting that church pretty soon now.[331]

I got a letter from Richie Simmons today and he said that everything is going along okay and that he wrote to Walter Cubita and sent my address to him. Well Mother that's about all for now. Love to all.

Love,
Son John"

₰

JULY 16, 1945

Detonation of an atomic bomb, under secret development by the U.S. and Great Britain since 1939, is tested successfully in the deserts of New Mexico. The nature of warfare has entered a terrifying new era, with the introduction of a weapon of mass destruction the likes of which the world has never before seen, or can even imagine.

₰

"July 20, 1945 [Friday]

---

[331] Not sure which church this refers to, since Nativity already had a church, but was planning on building a school at some point in time and raising money for that purpose. Perhaps it was another, neighboring parish, like St. Francis of Rome on Baychester Avenue.

Dear Mother,

Well yesterday I went on a very interesting trip since I been here. It was to Hitler's famous mountain retreat where he made all his famous decisions. I just can't describe the place because it is such a wonderful sight. His house is built up about 5,000 feet up and his other house is at 9,000 feet at Eagle's Nest. Up at the highest place you can see five countries and it looks as if you can reach out and make a snowball. I saw some of the highest mountains in the world, and boy, what a sight. We also traveled through Salzburg, Austria which is the biggest summer resort and the place is loaded with girls. In my letter I am enclosing a picture of Berchtesgaden and a diagram of the layout of Hitler's retreat. I am also enclosing a picture of the main plaza in Linz. By the view you can see that it is quite a place. There is also a picture of the Danube and a few of the boats on it. The Danube isn't blue, it is very green. Well, Mother I got to church Sunday and the priest was supposed to say mass here too but he never showed up. Things are about the same, all we hear are rumors. How is everything going back home? Tell Dad maybe he has a late garden. I think I will close now so that will be all for now. Love to all.

Love,
Son John"

JULY 24, 1945 - POTSDAM, GERMANY

The week-long conference of the big three - the U.S., the Soviet Union and Great Britain - is the first since FDR's death in April. Stalin is manipulative, Churchill is bitter, and Truman cannot be read. Pulling Stalin aside, he lets him know a little about the new weapon the U.S. has developed. Stalin, through his spies, already knows. Earlier agreements at the Yalta Conference (February 4 - 11, 1945) are reaffirmed. Germany and Austria will be carved up into four occupation zones and ruled by the Allies - the U.S., Britain, the Soviets, and France. But Truman, unlike FDR, totally distrusts the Russian dictator Stalin. The foundations of the Cold War begin to be laid. A further codicil of Potsdam is that former Nazis are barred completely from any role in helping the German nation rebuild. Patton, faced with a dearth of local administrative talent other than those who may have been aligned with the Nazis, even if out of sheer necessity, balks at this new policy. His animus towards the Russians increases. He seems to enjoy being a thorn in their sides.

"July 24, 1945 [Tuesday]

Dear Mother,
I just received a letter from you yesterday and this is the first chance I had to answer it. Last night we went to a stage show given by some Austrian actors. It was okay but their music was kind of corny. Next week we are going to have the Division swing band so that ought to be pretty good.

I was glad to hear that you have two packages on the way. I will appreciate receiving them. Mother how many packages did you receive from me so far, as you know I sent two of them?

About this fellow that is in my company, see if you can find his name out because there are about two hundred fellows in it. I will look around anyway and maybe I will find him.

I found out that we are going to be able to get a lot of fellows soon so it will be okay to send me the camera. From what I hear at present they think that we will remain here for some time yet but everything is so uncertain that you can't tell what will happen next.

Every weekend we are able to spend it in Linz and they have now opened a Red Cross Doughnut shop where we can get coffee and doughnuts and listen to a little jukebox music.

The other day I got The Tower. *I was glad to get it. I saw a few articles about fellows that used to be in my class at the Mount. I also got the* Dyre Avenue News *and read all the neighborhood gossip in it. I see that practically all the younger fellows are going into service. Well I will close now. Tell Duke to build a trap for that rabbit.*

Love,
Son John"

℘

JULY 26, 1945

Atlee succeeds Churchill as British Prime Minister. In a complete surprise, Churchill, who has guided his nation through six years of terrible war and privation, does not win re-election as Prime Minister.

℘

As the Allied victors begin the dismemberment of Germany into occupation zones, soldiers find themselves being transferred about like pieces in a chess game. American and Russian soldiers barter goods for trade, as both get accustomed to life in a former combat zone. Private McGowan's future career as a successful businessman begins to come into evidence as he turns a handy profit selling his wristwatch to a Russian soldier. And, dutiful son, the money is sent home.

"July 31, 1945 [Tuesday]

Dear Mother,
    I just received a letter from you yesterday so while I had the chance I thought I would answer it. Well since I last wrote you we have moved to a new place away out in the hills. It is supposed to be a guest house but is only an old farmhouse. We were wondering where they got the name guesthouse because all the roads that come here are only cow paths. We have no electric or running water. Boy what a hell of a place. All we do is sleep and go riding, walking or do a little fishing. We all hope in time to come that we will move. The place that we used to be in is now occupied by the Russians. Boy did the people hate to see us go. But the Russians will straighten them out because we were too easy with them.
    Mother I am enclosing a money order for $100. I got the money by selling my watch to some Russian. I thought it a good investment. What do you think? I also wonder if you and Dad could get me another watch and keep it till I get home. I don't know exactly how much you and Dad payed for my watch but I think I made about $50 profit and that's nothing to turn your back at. Did you get my last money order okay?
    Oh yes, I did receive the letter from the Mount and I'll leave it up to your judgement how much to send them. The other day I got a big surprise when I got the Catholic News, Sunday Visitor. *What things to send me. We all had a laugh over them. I would rather have some home newspapers where I could get a little news of home and in the States instead of spiritual news.*
    In your letter you said one of the Hurley boys got killed. Which one, the one that was in my class or the older one? About that night I was on guard I was on by myself and nobody else was around.
    I guess things are pretty quiet around Pratt Avenue now that Mrs. Gold's tenant moved. Did anybody move in yet? Tell Dad we don't need a radio where we are now because we have no electric and our mail comes by carrier pigeon.
    Well Mother I will close now. Love to all.

Love,
Son John"

TWENTY-SIX - "NO MORE PACIFIC PLANS"

AUGUST 6, 1945

The first atomic bomb is dropped on Hiroshima, Japan. 146,000 die, including 20,000 Japanese soldiers. The rest are civilians. The U.S. hopes this will bring Imperial Japan to its senses and force an immediate surrender, removing the need to invade mainland Japan, an invasion in which U.S, military casualties are estimated at one million American soldiers dead.

AUGUST 8, 1945

Soviets declare war on Japan and invade Manchuria, finally acting on a promise they were supposed to fulfill as soon as Germany was defeated, three months prior to their fulfilling it.

AUGUST 9, 1945

With no word on capitulation forthcoming from Japan, a second atomic bomb is dropped, this time on Nagasaki, Japan. 80,000 perish in this second attack. There are more atomic bombs in production. One will be ready for use by August 19. Three more will be ready in September, and three more in October. A list of candidate cities has been prepared. Japan seems destined to be wiped off the face of the earth, should they continue to choose not to surrender.

AUGUST 14, 1945

Welcome news is received - Japan has surrendered. Seven more atomic bombs will not be dropped, and no longer do the Allied troops in Europe need to worry about being sent to the Pacific for the invasion of Japan. But there is still the lingering uncertainty of what the Russians might do, now that they are poised at the very heart of a defeated Germany, from where they can fan out in any direction. Sad news as well - the Halberd Division, the 65th, is going to be broken up, and its men transferred out to other Divisions. Private McGowan is going back into an armored division, the branch of service he began in when first entering the service.

℘

A new Chaplain arrives, an Italian from Brooklyn who proves to be quite a comedian.

"Aug. 17, 1945 [Friday]

Dear Mother,
 Well we just received news over the radio that Japan has agreed to the surrender terms. The fellows are going wild shooting and yelling for it means that we will be getting home more quickly.
 I am sorry I didn't write but we have been so very busy getting ready to move that I just forgot to write. I didn't get your packages or the newspaper but I am on the lookout for them. Tomorrow we are moving to a new Division. Our Division is breaking up so we are all getting transferred to the 10th Armored Division[332] which is around Munich. Our company commander said that we are on our first leg home so that's okay with all of us. Every night we get to go to Linz[333] for a few hours so that means seeing a show or go to the circus where most of the GI's go.
 Every GI in town has a new rumor about us going home or ending up someplace else. Talking about going to Mass we got a new chaplain and what a guy he is. He comes from Brooklyn and is Italian. He told me he knew Father Quill very well and boy is he a lot of fun. He puts on a little show before he says Mass and you would die laughing at him. At the present time I just went out to get a glass of beer. It seems everybody got a couple of barrels.
 Well Mother I will close now and write as soon as I get my new address. Love to all.
  Love,
  Son John"

Address provided, another letter quickly follows, from Mittenwald, Germany, deep in the Alps and almost at the Swiss border.

---

[332] The 10th Armored Division, nicknamed the "Tiger Division", was an armored division of the United States Army in World War II. In the European Theater of Operations, the 10th was part of both the Twelfth Army Group and Sixth Army Group. Originally assigned to the Third Army under General George S. Patton, it saw action with the Seventh Army under General Alexander Patch near the conclusion of the war.

[333] Linz is the third-largest city of Austria and capital of the state of Upper Austria. It is in the north center of Austria, approximately 19 miles south of the Czech border, on both sides of the River Danube. Linz is well known for the Linzer torte, which is said to be the oldest cake in the world, with its first recipe dating from 1653. The city was founded by the Romans, who called it *Lentia*. The name Linz was first recorded in AD 799.

"Aug. 17, 1945 [Friday]

Dear Mother,
    Well Mother I am now in a new Division. It is the 10th Armored. But I am not in tanks. I am in the 61st Armored Infantry Battalion which is attached to the 10th Armored. We are stationed in a little town of Mittenwald[334] Germany deep in the heart of the Alps and only 3 miles from the Swiss border. Boy what mountains! It is really something to see, you just can't explain these towering giants that go right up into the sky.
    We didn't get any news on what we are going to do but we hope we get home soon for all the fellows like myself are starting to get a little homesick for the States. You see our whole Division broke up and our battalion got sent here. I don't know yet where the rest of the Division went. I did hate to leave Linz since we were there for such a long time and I was getting to like the place. When I get home I will tell you about my adventures there and of the good times we had.[335]
    By this time you must know that the war is officially over. I bet the people back in the States are having the time of their life. We heard over the radio how London went wild with excitement of the victory.
    How are things doing back home? Dad's garden must be in full bloom. Did you get any tomatoes out of it yet? How's the Duke making out? Is he still selling junk to the junky down on Kingsbridge Road?[336]
    You know Mother I am sorry I don't write to all these people you sent me addresses of but I really don't know what to say to them. For the most part it takes so long for a letter to go to the States and back over here that I lose interest in writing other people. Well Mother I will close now. By the way, I received your box. Thanks a lot. Well goodbye for now. Write soon.
                                                   Love,

---

[334] Mittenwald is a German municipality in the district of Garmisch-Partenkirchen, in Bavaria. It is situated in the Valley of the River Isar, by the northern foothills of the Alps, on the route between the old banking and commercial centre of Augsburg, to the north, and Innsbruck to the south-east, beyond which is the Brenner Pass and the route to Lombardy, another region with a rich commercial past and present.

[335] Linz must have been a good posting!

[336] The "junky" was not a drug addict! He was a tinker of sorts, who even into the 1960's would wheel his one-horse wagon through the streets of Edenwald collecting junk of all sort from the neighborhood residents - a precursor to the recycling movement. He would repair pots and pans, sharpen knives, repair leather goods, and so forth and so on. Apparently he must have had his home base somewhere on Kingsbridge Road, just over the border separating the Bronx from Mount Vernon, and Edenwald from the original settlement of Eastchester, where St. Paul's Church still stands in testimony to a proud past.

Son John"

§

"Aug. 20, 1945 [Monday]

Dear Mother,
  Well here we are away deep in the German Alps and nothing to do. I didn't get any mail here as yet but I think it will catch up with us in a few days.
  Yesterday being Sunday I was supposed to get to Mass but because we ate breakfast late and I had to walk about a mile to the church I didn't go. Next Sunday though I think I will be able to go. Practically every day now it has rained and I hope it will clear up. We had to laugh how the people in the States are sweating with the heat while we have it nice and cool all the time.
  The only activities they have around here is a movie house and a few beer gardens and the beer is awful. The movies are about two or three years old. Back in Linz they were getting to be new ones but who knows we may get some good ones yet.
  In my letter I am enclosing a few of the German marks and some of the American Occupational money. You said in one of your letters that Mr. Edling would like to have some.
  We didn't get any news on what we are going to do but this place is running wild with rumors. You can't tell what's going to happen from one day to the next because things change so much. The other night we were thinking how people all over the world payed a lot of money to see the scenery that we have around us and we just look at it and don't think nothing of it. Well Mother I will close now. I hope we get home soon.
                Love,
                Son John"

§

"Aug. 23, 1945 [Tuesday]

Dear Mother,
  I just got back from a U.S.O. show. The show was very good. This afternoon I went into the neighboring town and picked up a few post cards. It shows a little of the place I am stationed and of the surrounding country. Save the cards and add them to the ones that I have already sent you.
  Yesterday I received your box containing the sardines and etc. They were very good. We had a little midnight snack with them. If you get the chance send some more, and instead of soap send a few olives or pickles. Well I will close now. It is raining out again and I think I will go to bed again for the night. Love to all.
                Son John"

"Aug. 27, 1945 [Saturday]

Dear Mother,
 This evening I received a letter from you. So being that I just got back from the show, and having nothing else to do, I thought I would write you.
 Well Sunday I had one of the most exciting days that I have had over here. Two fellows and I went on a tour up to the highest mountain in Germany, which is 9,727 feet up in the air, and that's pretty high.[337] While we were up there we went skiing with our shirts off. Boy, people back in the States would think you were crazy if you told them we went skiing in August. While there we had a snowball fight. Boy what fun we had. It was something to be out in the snow with your shirt off. But it was very warm and we were sweating a lot. Then we went up to the top of the peak in a cable car. Boy what a sight. You can look down an 8,000 foot sharp drop down the side of the mountain. You can look for miles over the mountains and it is one of the greatest sights I ever saw. We all thought that it was much better than Hitler's home. On top of the mountain they have a large bronze cross. All the high peaks here have crosses on them. I am enclosing a folder in which you can read a little of my experiences. First we took a train up the mountain to the hotel and then by cable car we went up to the peak. The train goes through a 3 mile tunnel of solid rock up to the hotel. We expect to go up to another mountain this week.
 I was glad to hear that you all had a good time over the surrender of Japan. We just had a few drinks on it but there wasn't any great excitement. This Division is scheduled to go back in the States in October but I don't know how they are going to do about the points. Tell Dad he better stack up on the liquor because when I get home we will have a big bang up time to make up for lost time and we will get Mother a little drunk so she will start laughing.
 Good night. Love to all.

Love,
Son John"

---

[337] The mountain, called the *Zugspitze*, in Southern Bavaria, at 9,718 feet above sea level (9 feet less than its measurement at the end of World War II), is the highest peak of the Wetterstein Mountains as well as the highest mountain in Germany. The Austria–Germany border runs over its western summit. South of the mountain is the *Zugspitzplatt*, a high karst plateau with numerous caves. On the flanks of the *Zugspitze* are three glaciers, including the two largest in Germany. The *Zugspitze* was first climbed on August 27, 1820 by Josef Naus, his survey assistant, Maier, and mountain guide, Johann Georg Tauschl.

TWENTY-SEVEN - "WISHING FOR HOME"

SEPTEMBER 2, 1945

In Tokyo Bay, aboard the *U.S.S. Missouri*, Imperial Japan formally signs the surrender agreement. It is V-J Day, the long-awaited victory over Japan. World War II is over.

From the postmark we see that Private McGowan has found a home in Company A of the 60th Infantry Regiment, in the 9th Infantry Division, now that the 65th has been broken up.

"Sept. 7, 1945 [Friday]

Dear Mother,
    Well Mother I moved again and this time I am in the 9th Infantry Division[338] just outside of Munich. It seems as though we will bounce all over Europe until it is time for us to go home. This outfit we are in now is an "Occupational Division" so I don't know how long I will be here. All we get to do is sit tight and wait for our turn to go back to the States. There is only one thing I got to say about all this moving around and that is I am certainly seeing all of Germany, practically every town around. It will probably take some time for my mail to catch up with me through all my movements.
    Yesterday I met a fellow and I went to school with his cousin up at P.S. 68.[339] This fellow seems to know a lot about Dyre Avenue and vicinity and his cousin lives on Light Street. He is an Italian boy so I don't think you know him.[340]
    How is everything getting along back home? Are the gardens doing good and what's new around there? I will close now and will write in a few days because I think I will move again.
                                    Love,
                                    Son John"

---

[338] The 9th Infantry Division, nicknamed "The Old Reliables", was an infantry division formed in World War I, which saw extensive action in Africa and Europe during the Second World War.
[339] P.S. 68, at 4011 Monticello Avenue, was the neighborhood Public School for Edenwald. It was opened in the 1920's and is still going strong today.
[340] An interesting comment, in an age when European nationalities tended to cluster among themselves.

"Sept. 12, 1945 [Wednesday]

Dear Mother,

    Well today is Wednesday and I haven't moved out of this Division. I think maybe I will stay here for a while. Tomorrow some of the fellows are going to go to France to work on the docks and help with the loading of equipment.

    As yet I haven't got any mail but I expect it in a few days. You see with all my moving it will take time for my mail to get to me. Mother I was wondering if you could send me a camera because I could take some good pictures and something I could always look at and remember my stay over here. I am enclosing a few snapshots of myself and friends while we were skiing. In one picture a pal has just hit me over the head with a snowball. I hope you like them.

    I was just wondering if Dad got a dog yet. You said earlier he was but I haven't heard anything on the subject yet. I guess all the kids are going back to school now. Well maybe next year at this time I will be going to school also. I will close now. Look at my new address.

                                          Love,
                                          Son John

"Sept. 18, 1945 [Tuesday]

Dear Mother,

    Well here I am, still in Germany, and we don't know when we are going to get home. Since I have been here I haven't got any mail yet and neither has any of the other fellows. But we think we will. Our movements - that's the hold up.

    The outfit I am in now is okay. We get very good eats for the first time and when a guy gets pretty good eats he don't mind the things that aren't so interesting like marching and training. All we hear all day are rumors when we are going back to the States, but nothing seems to happen. The same thing with the newspapers, all they print are how fast the fellows are going home. Most of the fellows are getting mad at Truman and Congress with all their bungling around. They have more men over here than they know what to do with. There is one bill that is in Congress that looks pretty good to me and I might get out on it. That's the one that if you're in the Army 2 years and have overseas service you will get out. The fellows over here think that the people back home would put a kick into Congress and make them settle this discharging right.

    Well that's enough of my bitching. Mother, if you get me a camera tell Dad maybe down on the Bowery he could pick up a 35 millimeter camera?

Sunday I went on a visit to Munich. The city is very much destroyed by our bombing. The one thing that surprised me was all the churches there. I later learned it was the seat of Catholicism in Germany. I will close now. Hoping you are all in the best of health.

Love,
Son John"

SEPTEMBER 28, 1945 - FRANKFURT, GERMANY

Patton is called before Eisenhower, for what does not promise to be a very pleasant encounter. He is relieved of command of the Third Army, his army, and given a "paper" job. Disheartened, he complies, but knows in his heart that he will be better off resigning from the army and returning home, where he can speak his mind about the pitfalls facing the U.S. now that the war with the Germans and Japanese is over - and the one with the Russians is bound to begin before long.

"Sept. 30, 1945 [Sunday]

Dear Mother,
    Since I last wrote you mail has been catching up with me. Your letters are very interesting and I have to laugh how you and Dad are planning on my homecoming. From the way it looks now I don't think I will get home for Christmas but I don't think it will be very long now.
    All we hear over the radio and read in the papers is that we are going to go home soon, but it seems as though that's all talk and no facts.
    By the way, I forgot to tell you, I have a good goldbricking job now. I am manager of the Regimental Football Team, and it's a good deal.
    Well I guess football is in full swing back home. Ask Frankie what he thinks of Notre Dame's chances this year. You know Mother I am sorry I don't write much but there isn't anything to write about. It's the same from one day to another. All we want is to go home. Love to all.

Son John"

"Oct. 7, 1945 [Sunday]

Dear Mother,
    Today is Sunday and I am waiting to go to mass at 11 o'clock. For the first time in five days the sun is shining and boy does it look good to us.

Today is a big football game and I think I might go, our Division is playing the 71st Infantry Division and both teams are undefeated and it looks like a good game.

Well, we have a club in town now and they sell beer, wine, schnapps, so this gives a little to build up our morale. They also have dancing, so we bring in girls to dance with and on the whole we all have a good time. The movies they show are usually old ones or ones that we have already seen over here. When you see what I said about taking girls to dances I know what is in your mind so don't worry. The girls here aren't as bad as the papers write them up to be. Most of them can speak English and they help us a lot to learn German. There is one thing I got to say about the German girls and I think every soldier will say the same and that is that they are much cleaner than the French and have higher morals.

How is everything with Dad? Did he go on any fishing trips? I think flounders ought to be running now and I know how Dad likes to go fishing. Well Mother, I expect you have a new fall outfit by now. By the way, I didn't get the "News" paper yet. Do you know what could be holding it up? I would like very much to get it because there are many New York fellows in this outfit and we all like to know news about home. I will close now. Love to all.

Love,
Son John"

೭

"Oct. 16, 1945 [Tuesday]

Dear Mother,

Today was a very busy day in our company, for they are going on maneuvers for one week. I didn't have to go and I am glad of it, because the boys have to sleep out on the ground. You see the job I got now as football manager for our Regiment Football Team gets me out of a lot of details and work.

I don't know anything more about going home but what we hear there are still fellows here with 80 points and the movements are very slow. The fellows were just listening to the radio and are getting more disgusted every day. Today the radio said the waters of the Atlantic are very rough, and men are striking and they can't onload the boats. We were saying that when they need us over here they didn't care how rough the ocean was or how cramped up in the boats we were. We all hope they get these affairs straightened out so we can get home.

Everywhere you can see signs of winter coming on. It is getting colder day by day. The trees are starting to shed their leaves and all day we see the Germans bringing wood into their houses to keep them warm during the winter. The farmers over here aren't in a bad situation for they have enough to eat and enough of wood from the nearby forest to keep them alive. But the people in the cities have a critical situation for they have no coal and it is hard for them to get wood because the farmers are the only ones with wagons and they won't let the city people have them. The city people do get a little food in stores to keep them alive. You ought to see the way the farmers and the city people have split between themselves. Military Government is having a hard time but I think they will have everything under control. I had to laugh about you writing to Washington. Don't worry, Mother. I will go home when my turn comes. I don't think you can get me home any quicker. Well I will close now. By the way, I didn't get the paper yet. Tell Dad to see them. Maybe they haven't got my new address. Love to all.

Love,
Son John"

"Oct. 19, 1945 [Friday]

Dear Mother,
    I thought I would write you tonight because in the morning I am going to Munich to our football game and expect to stay overnight and come back Sunday night. From all the reports I think it will be a good game. So far this week I haven't received a letter from you yet but I expect to in the next few days.
    From what I hear I think I will be over here till March but you can't tell what they will do next. We have many high points here yet and from all the tie ups the point system seems to have slowed down some. Well, Mother, that's about all for now. Sorry I didn't write much more but everything is pretty quiet. Love to all.

Love,
Son John

P.S. I will write again Monday."

OCTOBER 24, 1945

The United Nations officially comes into existence as the Charter is ratified by member nations. Its first meeting will be on January 10, 1946, at the Methodist Central Hall in Westminster, London, England. On October 9, 1952, its permanent location in New York City will be completed. The first UN Secretary-General is elected, Norwegian Foreign Minister Tryqve Lie.

"Oct. 29, 1945 [Sunday]

Dear Mother,

Today is Sunday and it is a very beautiful day out. It all reminds us of home. The sun is shining brightly and there isn't a cloud in the sky. Everything is starting to change its color for autumn is here and you can see it in many ways such as the leaves falling from the trees and etc.

I haven't received any mail from you in about 2 weeks but being that I am not with my company I think that's the hold up. You see the football team is living in a separate house by ourselves and my company is about 30 miles from us so that means when they have a truck or jeep coming here they can send my mail.

Well yesterday we won our football game 7 to 6. It was a hard game and our Colonel said if we win 3 more games he will send us to our Division rest center for two weeks, so that will be a pretty good deal. I am enclosing a picture taken at a football game. You can see me standing next to a fellow I knew back in the 65th Division.

Mother, I was wondering if you ever heard how Walter Cubita or Pete Thomas is making out. If you write Richie Simmons again tell him to drop me a line for I would like to find out how he is making out in this redeployment.

This morning I went to 11 o'clock Mass which the American Chaplain said. He had the German choir sing the Mass. Boy that is something you ought to hear. The last time I heard them sing a Mass that was back in Linz, Austria. They have all our choirs back home beat by a mile and they can really sing. I will close now. Love to all.

Love,
Son John"

"Nov. 5, 1945 [Monday]

Dear Mother,

I just received three letters from you the other day and I was sorry to hear that it is taking such a long time for them to go home. Over the radio we heard that some of the air mail is going by boat because they haven't got the room for it.

Well first of all I will answer some of the questions you asked in your letters. I am in the 9th Infantry Division, 60th Infantry Regiment and our so-called name is "Go Devils". We are stationed in a town of Pfaffenhoffen which is about 20 miles north of Munich. See if you can pronounce that name. Our principal duty is guarding various things and doing drill such as marching and etc. Mother I don't want you to get your heart set on me being home for

Christmas because I don't think I will get home then. So send all the packages you can and don't feel bad about sending them. You will have your thoughts built up so high about me coming home for Christmas that when I don't come it will hurt you that much more. You know it's funny about that newspaper deal. If they say they sent it to me I don't see why I didn't get it. Maybe it got lost with all my movements but it should have caught up with me by now.

I was surprised to hear about Johnny Conniff being in the hospital. As soon as I get a chance to I will go and see him because I go to Munich practically every weekend. Mother, speaking about seeing people, where in Germany is John Lucas stationed? Maybe I could go to see him too.

How is Martin making out? Does he know when they are going to let him out of service? I would like to hear from him so tell him to drop me a few lines when he gets a chance.

Things are about the same with me. Saturday we went to Austria to play and we had a nice trip. The Colonel was saying he was going to try and get us a game in Berlin or in Italy and we would travel by plane. So all the fellows would like to go. Tonight we are going to have a party. The Colonel got us about 30 bottles of champagne, so we are all out for a good time. I will close now. Write again soon. Love to all.

Love,
Son John"

A sense is beginning to emerge that the trip back home may not be any time soon, and expectations among the remaining troops should be carefully managed. A hospital visit reveals the price of combat. The Division football team season continues.

"Nov. 11, 1945 [Sunday]

Dear Mother,

Well yesterday we had our first snowfall and it has been snowing a little today. Last night we were listening to the Army and Notre Dame game from New York and the announcer said that it was a nice afternoon with the sun shining. While over here it was 8 o'clock at night, snowing and very cold. From all the aspects I think we are going to have a very cold winter over here.

Saturday while we were on route to our football game we stopped in Munich at the 98th General Hospital.[341] So I went up and saw Johnny Conniff.

---

[341] The 98th General Hospital officially opened for the reception of patients on July 21, 1945, in the former "Krankenhaus Schwabing" on the northern outskirts of the city of Munich, Germany. The unit was activated in the United States, and had been set up in the United Kingdom for seven months prior to its arrival on the continent.

Boy was I surprised when I saw him. I could hardly recognize him, he has changed so. He has gotten a lot old and looks very bad. He told me if I wrote to not say anything on how he was. So Mother let's keep this a secret between you and me. I know how news travels home, so keep this a secret. He had a fractured skull and he hurt his back somehow. He said that he expects to get home shortly. If you see his people tell them I saw him and he is okay and getting along swell.

Yesterday we played a game in the snow, mud and rain. Boy were the fellows disgusted. Out of this day we lost the game 7 to 6, but we hope to win this week.

Nothing new has come up on redeployment except one fellow with 70 points left the other day for home. Most of the fellows with 60 or more points are starting to get mad because men with 60 points are eligible to go home this month but they haven't heard anything yet. Mother, there's one thing I say to myself and that is when they say I can go home, I will and won't bitch about it. Because there are many fellows over here with more points than I have and I don't think I am any better than they are to go home ahead of them. So Mother I will get home when my turn comes, so don't worry about it too much. Well goodbye for now. Love to all.

Love,
Son John

P.S. *I am enclosing a few pictures of Munich, Hitler's prize city."*

℘

"Nov. 22, 1945 [Thursday]

Dear Mother,

Today is Thanksgiving and all our thoughts turn toward home and as we listen to the songs of home over the radio. First of all I went to 11 o'clock mass this morning and gave thanks to God for having kept me alive and not maimed, as so many of the fellows I have known gave their lives and legs in this war. We went to dinner at 1 o'clock and boy what a meal we had. All from a pound and a half of turkey for each. To begin the meal we had a big glass of French wine, it was very good. I ate so much that I had to lay down after the dinner. Tonight I got a letter from you. It took it 21 days to get here. So it must have come by boat being that there is such bad flying weather.

I was glad to hear that Frankie's kids had a good time at the Halloween party. I had to laugh about Duke hiding the gates from the neighborhood kids. Did they ring the doorbell?

Well next week we are to go to Vienna to play a game. I think we will have a good time and it will be something to see. Well there's one thing, as long as I stay over here I will get around and see all that there is to see. Take a look on the map where Vienna is. You will see that I will be practically in Poland.

Tonight we are having a dance so we are getting dressed up for it. You said in your letter about us having trouble with the people here. I don't think they will have much trouble with them except in the cities or large populated parts. Well I will close now. Love to all.

Love,
Son John"

NOVEMBER 30, 1945 - NUREMBERG, GERMANY

The Nuremberg war crimes trials commence, the first systematic effort on the part of the international community to punish perpetrators of crimes against humanity. There are eight judges, and twenty-four accused political and military leaders of the Third Reich: Hess and Goering prominent among them. The Allied prosecutor is Colonel William Donovan, head of the OSS, precursor of today's CIA, and a man with an intense dislike of George S. Patton.

LOVE, SON JOHN | 340

TWENTY-EIGHT - "CHRISTMAS ABROAD"

DECEMBER 8, 1945 - KAFERTAL, GERMANY

General Patton is mortally injured in a suspicious motor vehicle accident. Patton's chief of staff, Major General Hobart Gay, had invited him on a pheasant hunting trip near Speyer to lift his spirits. Observing derelict cars along the side of the road, Patton remarked, "How awful war is. Think of the waste." Moments later his car collides with an American army truck at low speed. Gay and others are only slightly injured, but Patton hits his head on the glass partition in the back seat. He begins bleeding from a gash to the head, and complains that he is paralyzed and having trouble breathing. Taken to a hospital in Heidelberg, Patton is discovered to have a compression fracture and dislocation of the cervical third and fourth vertebrae, resulting in a broken neck and cervical spinal cord injury that renders him paralyzed from the neck down.

Patton spends most of the next 12 days in spinal traction to decrease the pressure on his spine. All nonmedical visitors, except for Patton's wife, who has flown from the U.S., are forbidden. Patton, who has been told he has no chance to ever again ride a horse or resume normal life, at one point comments, "This is a hell of a way to die."

౪

This next letter mentions Patton's accident, testimony to how quickly news travels through the ranks.

"Dec. 10, 1945 [Monday]

Dear Mother,
    This is just a short note to tell you that I am going to Switzerland Thursday. I also expect to celebrate Christmas there. Mother while I am in Switzerland I will try and call home. It costs $15 and I wonder if I could reverse the charge because we are only allowed to bring $40 into the country. I am going to get a watch for myself and maybe pick one up for you because they have beautiful women's watches there. They say you can really have a good time there. Will have all you want to drink and also I can buy a good steak with all that goes with it.
    I received about ten papers that Dad sent. I want to thank him for them and try and keep them coming. It took us two days to read them and I think I read everything that was printed in them.

I have been hearing a lot of new rumors going around. And if they come true I might get home earlier than I expected, but you can't believe in rumors. There is a big drive around now for fellows to re-enlist. I think it's better to sweat out your time here now than to wait and come back here for three years. What do you think about it? You know Mother if I had stayed in the company I could have gotten a rating[342] instead of my football job. But I don't think there is much sense to a rating now that the war is over and I had an easy job out of it, what I am doing now.

I was sorry to hear about Sonny[343] but maybe he will get lucky and get sent home. Because I heard of numerous cases where fellows got home on being sick. By the way, how many points does he have anyway? I was also sorry to hear about Mr. Bernabe selling his house. What do the people who bought it look like anyway? Are they up to the McGowan's standard of view or should I say caliber?

About that fellow from Milwaukee, Wisconsin, he is a buddy of mine.[344] You see he served before in Panama before coming over here and he had a number of points. In his letter he said that he landed in Virginia and he didn't get a chance to get up to see you people, but he expects to in the future. He went into business with his brother who got discharged a few months before him. They are in the real estate business and from what this fellow writes they are doing nicely. There is one funny thing about him. He could always find something good for us to drink when we were in combat. You see before coming into the army he used to own a big bar in his town and sold it before he got in. He always said to me he would like to get me and my old gang up to see him some time and he'd get us good and drunk and show us a good time.

The latest news around is that General Patton was in a motor accident. The roads are very icy here and there have been a lot of deaths. On the whole it has gotten very cold and the other night it was below zero. Well mother I better close now because if I continue I will probably fall asleep and make a lot of mistakes which you will tell me about in your next letter. Love to all.

*Love,
Son John"*

℘

---

[342] A "rating" signified a promotion in rank.

[343] Sonny Lucas, John's cousin.

[344] This could refer to "Riordan", whose post-war letter to John in 1947 is the last contained in this memoir.

DECEMBER 21, 1945

General George S. Patton dies in his sleep of pulmonary edema and congestive heart failure at about 1800 hours. Speculation as to whether the collision and Patton's injuries and death are the result of a mere accident or a deliberate assassination will continue for years, and indeed are still a topic of debate today, over seventy years later. In Private McGowan's opinion, expressed many years later, Patton's death was intentional, and just one more of the secrets of World War II that will never have the light of day shone upon it.

DECEMBER 24, 1945 -AMERICAN MILITARY CEMETERY, HAMM, LUXEMBOURG

Patton is buried at the Luxembourg American Cemetery and Memorial in the Hamm district of Luxembourg City, alongside wartime casualties of the Third Army, in accordance with his request to be buried with his men. His wife, Beatrice Patton, is present. Grief-stricken, she departs the next day, Christmas Day, to return home to the United States. Eight years later, upon her death, her children will sprinkle her ashes atop the grave of her husband, despite objections from the U.S. government and military.

℘

"*Dec. 28, 1945 [Friday]*

Dear Mother,
Christmas has come and gone already and we are looking forward to New Year's. Well Christmas Eve I arrived back from Switzerland where I had a swell time. We spent 7 days there and what a good time we had. I never knew what a nice country it is until I went there. It is really something to see. It's just like being back in the States. Most of the people talk English and at every night club play American jazz. It was the nearest thing to home yet and I hope if I get the chance again to go there. While I was there I bought myself a 20 jewel, self-winding watch for 17 dollars. I thought it a good buy. You see watches are very cheap there but they won't let us take in much money, only 46 dollars. And your money goes like water just like back home. You know when I was in Switzerland, I was thinking that Steven King's[345] people lived over there. I wonder if you could get their address so if I go again I could look them up.
I had a very nice Christmas back here in Germany. They made it as nice as they could. We had turkey and trimmings just like Thanksgiving. We

---

[345] Steven King, a cousin of John's. Not to be confused with the author, Steven King, of "*It*" and "*The Shining*" fame.

also had enough to drink if you wanted to drink. It seems the Russians sent us some of their strong stuff, "vodka", for a Merry Christmas and Happy New Year.

Well how did you and Dad spend your Christmas? I hope Dad didn't have to work. Did you get a tree this year and did you go to Midnight Mass as usual?

Today I received your package with the sardines and stuff, and also a few newspapers. We had a little snack after making sandwiches coming back from the movies.

At the present time I am back in the company and I don't know exactly what I am going to do now. I might go looking for another soft job or something.

By the way Mother I got a letter from Aunt Kitty and she told me about Sonny. She said that he might come back to the States. It's just like I told you in an early letter that if a fellow is really bad and able to be shipped home they send him home on a hospital ship.

I also want to thank you for your and Dad's Christmas card. I was sorry I couldn't have sent you a nicer one but that was all we had. I think I will close now for it is almost chow time. Love to all.

Love,
Son John"

TWENTY-NINE - "HOMEWARD BOUND"

As often happens, the first few dates in a New Year can carry the wrong year entirely. This letter, and several following, bear the year 1945, but clearly their context argues that they were written in the early months of 1946, when the war has been over for some time now and the men are waiting impatiently to be repatriated. Presents are being sent back home, or stocked up for the eventual reunion.

"Jan. 3, 1946 [Thursday]

Dear Mother,
    Well we all had a joyous New Year's Day and evening. We had a big dance New Year's Eve and it was quite a big affair. There was all that you wanted to drink and they got a good German band to play. I didn't get in till 4 in the morning. There is one thing I got to say and that is I had a better New Year than last year. I hope you all had a good time and didn't drink too much.
    We have been having a few snow storms but they didn't amount to much. Today is a beautiful day with the sun shining brightly.
    Mother I was wondering if you could send me a pair of shoes. Not an expensive pair but just something to wear around. I also want you to buy me a belt and a dark cap, size 6 and 7/8. You see we like to get dressed up a little now and then.
    There isn't much happening around except we are all recovering from New Year's doings. I was glad to hear that Dad liked that jacket. Well there is a little story behind it and that is a Colonel in the German Air Corps used it when he was bombing England during the Blitz.[346] I found out about it off of another German. Well Mother that's about all I can think of now so I will close. Give my love to all,

                                             Love,
                                             Son John"

---

[346] The "Blitz" was the incessant German bombing of major British cities during the war.

"Jan. 20, 1946 [Sunday]

Dear Mother,
    Well, I have been waiting for more than a week for mail from you but none has come. I wonder what the holdup could be. Maybe it's because of the storms they are having over the Atlantic.
    The biggest news around here is the new system of discharge. It gives us a little idea when we will get home. I am in the first bracket and I should be home on or by April 30. So that's something definite anyway. So Mother you can see about when I will get home. I know you think I should go home right away but we have to take our time going home. We all can't just leave here and go home. There's lots of Americans that gave their lives for what we are doing now cleaning house over here.
    You know I think it's better if I get home in the spring because the weather is much nicer and we can have a good ride across the Atlantic. Things here seem to be about the same except that we are getting rookies in from the states and all the fellows are taking it out on them. Speaking about rookies didn't you mention in one of your letters that Paulie the kid that lives across from Edlings was going into the Army? I was wondering if he went overseas yet and where, maybe I would run into him.
    Mother, do you know those fur hats I sent home? Well I was wondering if you use them. They are very warm and they keep your ears warm. Why don't you let Dad and Duke wear them? I bet Duke would get a kick out of wearing it.
    How is Dad getting along with that jacket I sent? Tell him to put that vest on too, that's supposed to go inside the jacket.
    Oh, I got a watch for you Mother. It's a 15 jewel shock proof. I hope you like it when I bring it home. I might be able to get Dad one too but I don't know. You see I have a friend there, that is I met this fellow and I made friends with him. He might be able to get one and send it home but I don't know. I will close now, love to all.

                                                Love,
                                                Son John"

"Feb. 10, 1946 [Sunday]

Dear Mother,
    You have probably been wondering why I haven't been writing. Well to tell you the truth Mother I have been waiting for a letter from you and answer it. Last night I got one that you wrote on the 21st of January. It seems it takes an awful long time for our mail to travel these days. I think its over a

week since I last had a letter from you and it is about the same since I last wrote.

Well all I am doing now is just sweating out the day when I will leave to go to Le Havre. I think it isn't very far off because this morning I had to sign papers telling how much time I had in the army and how many points I had.

From what you say in your letter it looks as though I will be getting home about the right time with all the big wedding events taking place. It brought me to wondering if maybe Robbie Mahon wouldn't get married too, but who knows? The weather here has been very changeable. One minute the sun is out and the next it is raining or snowing.

I was surprised to hear that Buddy Butler couldn't get into one of the schools back home. It got me wondering but I will probably find one in the 48 to go to. Well Mother that's about all for now as I have to go on guard duty. I hope your package arrives soon. Love to all.

Love,
Son John"

℘

"Feb. 14, 1946 [Thursday]

Dear Mother,
Enclosed you will find a few more pictures of Munich which I thought you would like to see. Munich was Hitler's prize city. He once wanted to move the capital from Berlin to Munich because he didn't like Berlin. Oh yes, Munich is the seat of Catholicism in Germany, and you can see many pictures of churches in the town. These pictures were taken before our bombers and artillery destroyed the city to a dump of rubble.

This is to let you know that I got the good news that I am going to ship home. Either tomorrow or the next day. The outfit we are going to is supposed to leave Le Havre about March 12 or 15 so I will be home for the first of April and maybe I will get home for my birthday. So Mother you can stop worrying about when I am going to leave for home. I will close now.

Love,
Son John"

℘

Again, a letter clearly written after the war's end is dated incorrectly, with the year as 1945 instead of 1946. The major topic of repatriation places it in its correct timeframe.

"Feb. 28, 1945 [Thursday]

Dear Mother,
    This is just a short letter to let you know that this morning they told us that we would sail or be ready to sail around the 15th of March so maybe I will get home for my birthday.[347]
    In case you are interested what outfit I am in, I am in the 66th Inf. Regt. so if you see in the paper our sailing date you can approximate when I will be home. Since I have moved into this outfit we have done a little traveling and also made a big deal with the Russians. You must have read in the paper how there were 2 thousand Russian traitors who fought with the Germans. Well these people were in our territory in a camp and the Russians wanted them back. They said when we were going to come for them they would commit mass suicide. So the commanding general over here picks us because he said we knew how to deal with these men and we were combat men and the only ones he could rely on. Well we went and we pulled all the Russians out of the camp and put them on the train with only two of them killing themselves. The Russians were very pleased and so were all of our generals. They all said we did a good job. You see Mother there are a lot of things like that over here that these new fellows couldn't handle so you can see they are going to have a rough time of things.[348]
    I am enclosing a few pictures of myself and of the town I am staying in. Well that's about all for now. Love to all.

                                       Love,
                                       Son John"

Sometime after this letter was posted, Private McGowan received the welcome news that he was being shipped stateside for processing and discharge. He left France on March 30, 1946, a few days after his twenty-first birthday, and arrived in New York, where he was discharged and returned home to 4030 Pratt Avenue in the Bronx. He had spent almost three years in uniform.

---

[347] March 27, 1946 would be Private McGowan's next birthday, when he would attain the ripe old age of 21, with almost three solid years in uniform.

[348] This is an item that definitely bears further investigation. Where was the camp? What were the particulars of the Russian traitors? What was their fate when returned to Russia? Who were the Allied commanders involved? At what level was the agreement made? What was the experience of the roundup like? A fascinating slice of WW II history, not one you would read much about in the standard history texts.

He took advantage of the G.I. Bill of Rights, and within months of his return had enrolled at Iona College in New Rochelle, New York, where he graduated with a Bachelor of Business Administration degree in June 1951. He carved out an extremely successful business career in sales, and held executive level positions with a number of high visibility firms. On his retirement at the age of 75, he could look back on an unbeaten string of successes, beginning with the experience he had as an infantryman slogging 835 miles through France, Germany and Austria.

His experiences in Europe served him well in later life, as he realized his early dreams to travel. In the years following the war, he became an international traveler, visiting diverse regions, some of them spots he had last seen as a young soldier.

Bridget Kenney McGowan, "Mom" died in 1947, just a year after John's return from war. Her husband Dennis McGowan, "The Duke", lived on until 1952, in his early 90's. John still has his grandfather's collection of Irish records. Eddy McGowan, John's father, died in 1963, finally succumbing to the ravages of the mustard gas that had seared his lungs in 1918 while he fought in the war that was supposed to end all wars. Anna Cecelia Lynch McGowan, whose voice has graced these pages so ably, survived her husband by two and a half decades. She died in 1988. In her obituary, she is memorialized as a resident not of New York City, or of the Bronx, but of her beloved Edenwald. She remained a passionate, gifted storyteller until her final days.

All are buried in the rolling hills of Gates of Heaven Cemetery, in Hawthorne, New York.

In 1965, John married Regina Field, of Queens, New York, a schoolteacher. They reside today in Garden City, a suburb of New York City in Nassau County. They are the parents of a son, John McGowan Jr. (Kirsten) and a daughter, Regina McGowan Trippe (Alan). They have four grandchildren. Among his many hobbies and interests, John is an active member of the Knights of Saint Patrick, an Irish-American fraternal organization that supports many causes, including the annual New York City Saint Patrick's Day Parade. Fiercely proud of his Irish heritage, he is a solid representative of that "Greatest Generation" who fought and gave their lives freely so that we today can enjoy the liberties and freedoms unique to the United States of America. He is still going strong in his nineties, with a mind as sharp as a tack, and a wit to match the ever-present Irish twinkle in his eye.

This letter, written a little short of two years after the war ended in Europe, is from a friend named "Riordan", living at 3010 West Wells Street, Milwaukee, Wisconsin.

"Milwaukee, Wisconsin

March 20, 1947 [Thursday]

Hello Mac,
    Vie Gates Soldaten! How's things in the Big town? Hope you are fine and dandy. Things are fair here. I am still on the railroad. Did you ever go back to school, Mac? You should before some "fraulein" - or "colleen" grabs you off. How about that "Frau Schnapps"? Wonder what the big Tech Sarge is doing these days?
    I am listening to the City College N.Y. and Wisconsin basketball game at the Garden. It sure is some game.
    Thanks for the Christmas card, Mac. I missed the boat. Well drop a line or two if you find time. Hope we can meet some time.
Your friend,
Riordan

P.S. How's the White Lightning? Never did taste anything stronger."

℘

And this letter, the last, dates five years after the war's end. Postmarked "COLGATE, OKLA FEB 9, 1950", it comes from the hand of Clarence B. Rushing. Unfortunately the first page of the letter is missing, but the gist comes through.

    "I had a little bad luck last Thursday nite. I was coming in home and as I was going around a curve I met another car coming at me on my side of the highway. I managed to cut her off the road and avoid a head on. But I sure wrecked my truck. I had a '49 Dodge pickup that I bought last October, hadn't rolled ten thousand miles on it. The thing looks like it got in the way of a Tiger tank now.[349]

---

[349] The Tiger tank here most likely refers to the Tiger II, a German heavy tank of the Second World War. The final official German designation was *Panzerkampfwagen Tiger Ausf. B*, often shortened to Tiger B. It is also known under the informal name *Königstiger* (the German name for the Bengal tiger), often translated literally as Royal Tiger, or somewhat incorrectly as King Tiger by Allied soldiers, especially by American forces. The Tiger II was the successor to the Tiger I, combining the latter's thick armor with the armor sloping used on the Panther medium tank. The tank

Do you ever see or hear from Webber? If you have his address send it to me. And how about you writing me a letter. Are you married? But of course you are. Any guy that was a whiz 'mit der fraulein' like you is sure to be hitched by now. If you have a wife I hope that she reads that, 'Yak, yak, yak!' I can't think of anything else to scribble. So answer soon and tell me all about yourself.

Your old A. H. Buddy,
Clarence Rushing

---

weighed almost 70 tons, and was protected by 3.9 to 7.3 inches of armor to the front. It was armed with the long barreled 8.8 cm KwK 43 L/71 anti-tank cannon. The chassis was also the basis for the *Jagdtiger* turretless tank destroyer. The Tiger II was issued to heavy tank battalions of the Army and the Waffen-SS. It was first used in combat by 503rd Heavy Panzer Battalion during the Allied Invasion of Normandy. On the Eastern Front, the first unit to be outfitted with Tiger IIs was the 501st Heavy Panzer Battalion, which by September 1, 1944 listed 25 Tiger IIs operational.

ACKNOWLEDGEMENTS

The idea for this book was first suggested to me several years ago by my cousin, John McGowan, Jr., son of the John McGowan whose signature, "Love, Son John", faithfully closed each letter written while he was away from home serving in the United States Army during World War Two. Plenty of Johns in the family, to be sure. It was my father's name, and appears frequently in all branches of a far flung clan. The suggestion was well received, of course. I have known John, Sr. my whole life. In fact, he is my older brother Frank's godfather, a connection I have always been a little envious of, truth be told. I, on the other hand, being the youngest of seven children my father sired, merited no relative for that cherished role. An old army buddy of my father's, whose name is mentioned in these pages, was called into service: Salem Ackary, or "Uncle Ack" as we all knew him. A wonderful gent to be certain; but not blood. I knew both of John's parents well, who we always referred to as "Uncle Eddie" and "Aunt Anna", respectful terms for relatives who were really cousins, but who were both held in higher esteem, and thus merited an honorific. I served as altar boy at Uncle Eddie's funeral, and frequently offered Aunt Anna a willing ear to listen to her tales of Old Ireland and the Lynches, spun from the fertile, amazing mind of this Newark, New Jersey native. John, Jr. told me his father had a trove of letters from his mother written during the war, and that there were apparently some "good stories" in them which might prove entertaining as a book.

I readily accepted the challenge, though life rapidly got in the way, and it was a year before I finally got into the task. The amount of letters was amazing, and often daunting, as each one had to be read, transcribed and placed into some semblance of order. At one point I considered "culling the herd", but by that point I had come to realize that each letter was precious, and my mission was to capture them all, and let their words ring loud and clear. I hope I have accomplished this, and given Anna Cecelia Lynch McGowan's wit, wisdom and guidance a new voice.

And so, a solid "thank you" to my cousin, John McGowan, Sr. ("Jack"), whose service to his country provided the platform for this book, and to his son, John McGowan, Jr., for being the initial intermediary. Thanks to John's wife Regina, for hosting many pleasant Sunday afternoons where John and I pored over not only letters, but also a trove of documents and photos many of which ultimately made their way into these pages.

Thanks to my wife, Joanie, herself a daughter of a World War Two combat veteran, for often being a companion on my trips to Garden City, and for tolerating my seizure of our dining room table and covering it with books and maps and photos as the work progressed. I also thank her for the enthusiastic reception she gave to early drafts, convincing me beyond a shadow of a doubt that this was a story that lived on it's own two feet.

Thanks to my friend and proofreader, Ken Foley, whose eagle eye caught the odd awkward phrase, misspelled word or grammatical misstep that can plague an author's work even after the most careful self-policing, proving that four eyes are always better than two. If there are any further incorrect items to be found, they are solely my doing.

The greatest thanks of all must go to Anna Cecelia Lynch McGowan, who I am happy to say I knew quite well in person, though half a century separated us in age, and it is now over three decades since she went to her reward. My deep immersion in her written words for an extended period of time gave me a far deeper appreciation of this woman than I ever had before. I hope her strength, character, faith and resilience shine through for all, as they did for me. She was truly a remarkable person in a remarkable time.

LOVE, SON JOHN | 358

Made in the USA
Middletown, DE
27 December 2022

20552159R00209